ETHICS AND LAW FOR SCHOOL PSYCHOLOGISTS

ETHICS AND LAW FOR SCHOOL PSYCHOLOGISTS

Fourth Edition

Susan Jacob

Timothy S. Hartshorne

John Wiley & Sons, Inc.

This book is printed on acid-free paper. ♾

For general information on our other products and services please contact our Customer Care Department within the U.S. at (800) 762-2974, outside the United States at (317) 572-3993 or fax (317) 572-4002.

Wiley also publishes its books in a variety of electronic formats. Some content that appears in print may not be available in electronic books.

For more information about Wiley products, visit our web site at www.wiley.com.

Library of Congress Cataloging-in-Publication Data:

Jacob, Susan, 1949–

Ethics and law for school psychologists / Susan Jacob, Timothy S. Hartshorne. — 4th ed.

p. cm.

Includes bibliographical references and index.

ISBN 0-471-20949-X (cloth : alk. paper)

1. School psychologists—Professional ethics—United States. 2. School psychologists—Legal status, laws, etc.—United States. I. Hartshorne, Timothy S. II. Title.

LB3013.6.J33 2003

174'.93717'130683—dc21 2002011155

Printed in the United States of America.

10 9 8 7 6 5 4

This book is dedicated to the memory of
Michael David Salem Hartshorne (1984–1992) and
Katherine Swift Hartshorne (1991–1992).
The brevity of their lives reminds us
just how precious are all children.

Preface

There are a number of excellent texts, journal articles, and book chapters on ethics in psychology, legal issues in school psychology, and special education law. However, our experience as school psychology trainers suggested a need for a single sourcebook on ethics and law specifically written to meet the unique needs of the psychologist in the school setting. Consequently, *Ethics and Law for School Psychologists* was written to provide up-to-date information on ethics, professional standards, and law pertinent to the delivery of school psychological services. Our goals for this fourth edition of the book remain unchanged. We hope that the book will continue to be useful as a basic textbook or supplementary text for school psychology students in training and as a resource for practitioners.

As noted in the preface to the first edition, one goal in writing the book was to bring together various ethical and legal guidelines pertinent to the delivery of school psychological services. We also introduce an ethical-legal, decision-making model. We concur with the suggestion that the educated practitioner is the best safeguard against ethical-legal problems (Diener & Crandall, 1978; Koocher & Keith-Spiegel, 1998). School psychologists with a broad knowledge base of ethics and law are likely to anticipate and prevent problems. Use of a decision-making model allows the practitioner to make informed, well-reasoned choices in resolving problems when they do occur (Eberlein, 1987; Tymchuk, 1986).

WHAT'S IN THE BOOK

Chapter 1 provides an introduction to ethical codes and professional standards, an ethical-legal, decision-making model, and the four broad ethical principles of respect for the dignity of persons (welfare of the client), responsible caring (professional competence and responsibility), integrity in professional relationships, and responsibility to community and society. We also describe ethics committees and sanctions for unethical conduct. Chapter 2 provides an introduction to education law that protects the rights of students and their parents in the school setting. We also address certification and licensure of school psychologists—mechanisms that help to ensure that psychologists meet specified qualifications before they are granted a legal sanction to practice. The chapter closes with a brief discussion of tort liability of schools and practitioners. In Chapter 3, we discuss privacy, informed consent, confidentiality, and record keeping—ethical-legal concerns that cut across all of the school psychologist's many roles.

Chapters 4 through 11 focus on ethical-legal issues associated with specific roles. Psychoeducational assessment is discussed in Chapter 4; Chapters 5 and 6 focus on the delivery of services to pupils with disabilities; and Chapter 7 addresses counseling and therapeutic interventions. Chapters 8 and 9 focus on indirect services. We discuss ethical-legal issues associated with consultative services to teachers and parents in Chapter 8 and address systems-level consultation in Chapter 9. A number of special consultation topics are covered in Chapter 9, including the ethical-legal issues associated with school testing programs; school entry and grade retention decisions; efforts to foster safe schools (discipline, school violence prevention, and the problem of harassment and discrimination); and schooling for pupils with other special needs (limited English proficiency, gifted and talented students, and students with communicable diseases). In Chapter 10, we discuss ethical and legal issues associated with research in the schools. Chapter 11 provides a brief overview of the ethical and legal considerations associated with school-based supervision of school psychologists in training.

WHAT'S NOT IN THE BOOK

We have chosen to focus on ethical-legal issues of interest to current and future school practitioners. Consistent with this focus, we did not include a discussion of issues associated with private practice. Interested readers are encouraged to consult Bersoff (1999), Koocher and Keith-Spiegel (1998), and Rosenberg (1995). We also did not address the legal rights of psychologists as employees in the public schools.

FOURTH EDITION REVISIONS

There have been a number of changes in ethical guidelines and law pertinent to the practice of school psychology since we completed work on the third edition early in the Fall of 1997. The National Association of School Psychologists revised its "Principles for Professional Ethics" and "Guidelines for the Provision of School Psychological Services" in 2000. The American Psychological Association adopted a revised "Ethical Principles of Psychologists and Code of Conduct" in 2002. On June 4, 1997, the Individuals with Disabilities Education Act Amendments or

IDEA (P.L. 105-17) became law. However, regulations implementing IDEA were not finalized until March 1999, after the publication of the third edition. The discussion of special education law in this edition incorporates the 1999 regulations as well as recent developments in case law.

In addition, several other changes were made in both the content and organization of the book. Diversity issues receive greater emphasis throughout the text, both in content and case examples. Discussion of ethical and legal issues in providing services to pupils and parents from diverse linguistic, racial, and cultural backgrounds now appears in several chapters, along with a discussion of services to sexual minority youth (see Chapters 7 and 8). A section addressing harassment and discrimination has been added to the chapter on systems-level consultation (Chapter 9). Other changes to the book include the addition of a brief chapter on ethical and legal issues in the supervision of school psychologists. We also developed an instructor's resource manual that will be available to trainers who adopt the textbook.

A number of the changes made in the fourth edition were suggested by readers. We welcome your suggestions for improving future editions of *Ethics and Law for School Psychologists*. Please contact: Susan Jacob, Professor of Psychology, 104 Sloan Hall, Central Michigan University, Mt. Pleasant, MI 48859. Email: jacob1s@cmich.edu.

TWO DISCLAIMERS

This text provides an overview and summary of constitutional, statutory, and case law pertinent to the practice of psychology in the schools. It does not provide a comprehensive or detailed legal analysis of litigation in education or psychology. The material included in the book, particularly the portions on law, is based on our review of the available literature. We are not attorneys. We often consulted the writings of attorneys and legal scholars for guidance in the interpretation of law rather than attempting to interpret it ourselves. However, original sources also were consulted when feasible, and citations have been provided so that interested readers can do the same.

Nothing in this text should be construed as legal advice. School psychology practitioners are encouraged to consult their school attorney through the appropriate administrative channels when legal questions arise. Our interpretations of ethical codes and standards should not be viewed as reflecting the official opinion of any specific professional association.

THE CAST OF CHARACTERS

Throughout the text, we have included a number of case incidents to illustrate specific principles. Some of the incidents are from case law; some were suggested by practitioners in the field; and others are fictitious. To make it easier for the reader to follow who's who in the vignettes, we have used the same six school psychologists throughout the book. Our cast of characters includes:

SAM FOSTER: Worked as a school psychologist for several years and then returned to school to pursue his Psy.D. degree. He is currently a doctoral intern in a suburban school district.

CARRIE JOHNSON: Provides school psychological services in a rural area. She faces the special challenges of coping with professional isolation and works in a community where resources are limited.

HANNAH COOK: Serves as a member of a school psychological services team in a medium-sized city. She is particularly interested in school-based consultative services.

CHARLIE MAXWELL: As a school psychologist in a large metropolitan district, he is a strong advocate of school efforts to prevent mental health problems.

WANDA ROSE: Provides services at the preschool and elementary level in a small town. Children, babies, parents, and teachers love Wanda Rose. She has been a school psychology practitioner for many years. Wanda needs an occasional push from her colleagues to keep current with changing practices, however.

PEARL MEADOWS: Is a school psychologist in a small university town. She works with a diverse student population, including pupils from farm families who live on the district's outskirts, Native American pupils from the neighboring Indian reservation, and children from many different cultures whose parents are part of the university community. Pearl also provides on-site supervision to school psychology interns.

SUSAN JACOB
TIMOTHY S. HARTSHORNE

Central Michigan University
Mt. Pleasant, Michigan

Acknowledgments

We would like to express our appreciation to the following school psychology trainers who reviewed the manuscript for the book and provided many valuable suggestions for improvement: Joel Erion, Edinboro University of Pennsylvania; and Kara McGoey, Kent State University.

We also would like to acknowledge the research assistance provided by Central Michigan University graduate students Carrie Cusmano, Suzanne Mikuski, Renee Thelen, Candy DuBord, and Andrea Syrek; and Vincent C. Dean, doctoral student at Michigan State University. A thank you also is due to our secretary, Tonia Bussear, who assisted with the typing of the manuscript. We also extend a special thanks to Tracey Belmont, editor at Wiley, for her assistance and support, and D & G Limited, LLC, for their patient and careful work.

A special thank you also is due to family members for their support during the completion of this and previous editions of the book: Andy Neal; and Nancy, Aaron, Seth, Jacob, Joshua, and Nathan Hartshorne.

Contents

Chapter 1

ETHICS IN SCHOOL PSYCHOLOGY: AN INTRODUCTION

In the late 1970s, the American Association for the Advancement of Science (AAAS) conducted a study of the ethical concerns of its affiliated societies (Chalk, Frankel, & Chafer, 1980). Haas, Malouf, and Mayerson (1986) summarized the AAAS findings as follows:

> Recent years have been marked by a rise in professional consciousness about ethical and legal responsibilities and by a concurrent rise in public consciousness about legal rights. The result, in part, is a level of concern (and confusion) about proper professional behavior that is unprecedented in all professions and is particularly evident in psychology. (p. 316)

Because the decisions made by school psychologists have an impact on human lives, and thereby on society, the practice of school psychology rests on the public's trust. School psychologists—both practitioners and trainers—have shared in the rising concerns about proper professional conduct.

QUALITY CONTROL IN SCHOOL PSYCHOLOGY

A number of sources of "quality control" are available in the provision of school psychological services. Ethical codes and professional standards for the delivery of psychological services are discussed in this chapter. Chapter 2 provides an introduction to law that protects the rights of students and their parents in the school setting. Educational law provides a second source of quality assurance. Chapter 2 also addresses the credentialing of school psychologists, a third mechanism of quality control. Credentialing helps to ensure that psychologists meet specified qualifications before they are granted a legal sanction to practice (Fagan & Wise, 2000). Training-program accreditation is an additional mechanism of quality control. Program accreditation helps to ensure the adequate preparation of school psychologists during their graduate coursework and field experiences. (For a discussion of training-program accreditation, see Fagan & Wise.)

This chapter focuses on the what and why of professional ethics, ethics training and competencies, and the ethical codes and professional standards of the National Association of School Psychologists (NASP) and the American Psychological Association (APA). Four broad ethical principles are introduced, along with an ethical-legal, decision-making model. We also describe ethics committees and sanctions for unethical conduct.

WHAT AND WHY OF PROFESSIONAL ETHICS

The term *ethics* generally refers to a system of principles of conduct that guide the behavior of an individual. Ethics derives from the Greek word *ethos,* meaning character or custom, and the phrase *ta ethika,* which Plato and Aristotle used to describe their studies of Greek values and ideals (Solomon, 1984). Accordingly, ethics is first

> of all a concern for individual character, including what we blandly call "being a good person," but it is also a concern for the overall character of an entire society, which is still appropriately called its "ethos." Ethics is participation in, and an understanding of, an ethos, the effort to understand the social rules which govern and limit our behavior. ...(p. 5)

A system of ethics develops within the context of a particular society or culture and is connected closely to social customs. Ethics is composed of a range of acceptable (or unacceptable) social and personal behaviors, from rules of etiquette to more basic rules of society.

The terms *ethics* and *morality* are often used interchangeably. However, according to philosophers, the term *morality* refers to a subset of ethical rules of special importance. Solomon suggests moral principles are "the most basic and inviolable rules of a society." Moral rules are thought to differ from other aspects of ethics in that they are more important, fundamental, universal, rational, and objective (pp. 6–7). W. D. Ross (1930), a 20th-century English philosopher, identified a number of moral duties of the ethical person: *nonmaleficence, fidelity, beneficence, justice*, and *autonomy*. These moral principles have provided a foundation for the ethical codes of psychologists and other professionals (Bersoff & Koeppl, 1993).

Our focus here is on *applied professional ethics,* the application of broad ethical principles and specific rules to the problems that arise in professional practice (Beauchamp & Childress, 1983). Applied ethics in school psychology is, thus, a combination of ethical principles and rules, ranging from more basic rules to rules of professional etiquette, that guide the conduct of the practitioner in his or her professional interactions with others.

Professionalism and Ethics

Professionalization has been described as "the process by which an occupation, usually on the basis of a claim to special competence and a concern for the quality of its work and benefits to society, obtains the exclusive right to perform a particular kind of work, to control training criteria and access to the profession, and to determine and evaluate the way the work is to be performed" (Chalk et al., 1980, p. 3). Professional associations or societies function to promote the profession by publicizing the services offered, safeguarding the rights of professionals, attaining benefits for its members, facilitating the exchange of and development of knowledge, and promoting standards to enhance the quality of professional work by its members (Chalk et al., 1980).

Codes of ethics appear to develop out of the self-interests of the profession and a genuine commitment to protect the interests of persons served. Most professional associations have recognized the need to balance self-interests against concern for the welfare of the consumer. Ethical codes are one mechanism to help ensure that members of a profession will deal justly with the public (Bersoff & Koeppl, 1993; Koocher & Keith-Spiegel, 1998).

However, the development of a code of ethics also serves to foster the profession's self-interests. A code of ethics is an indicator of the profession's willingness to accept responsibility for defining appropriate conduct and a commitment to self-regulation of members by the profession (Chalk et al., 1980). The adoption of a code of ethics often has been viewed as the hallmark of a profession's maturity. Ethical codes thus may serve to enhance the prestige of a profession and reduce the perceived need for external regulation and control.

The field of psychology has shown a long-standing commitment to activities that support and encourage appropriate professional conduct. As will be seen in this chapter, both NASP and APA have developed and adopted codes of ethics. These codes are drafted by committees within professional organizations and reflect the beliefs of association members about what constitutes appropriate professional conduct. They serve to protect the public by sensitizing professionals to the ethical aspects of service delivery, educating practitioners about the parameters of appropriate conduct, and helping professionals to monitor their own behavior. They also provide guidelines for adjudicating complaints (Koocher & Keith-Spiegel, 1998). By encouraging appropriate professional conduct, associations such as NASP and APA strive to ensure that each person served will receive the highest quality of professional service and, therefore, build and maintain public trust in psychologists and psychology.

Ethical Codes versus Ethical Conduct

Codes of ethics serve to protect the public. However, ethical conduct is not synonymous with simple conformity to a set of rules outlined in professional codes and standards (Hughes, 1986). As Kitchener (1986) and others (Bersoff, 1994; Hughes, 1986; Koocher & Keith-Spiegel, 1998) have noted, codes of ethics are imperfect guides to behavior for several reasons. First, ethical codes in psychology are composed of broad, abstract principles along with a number of more specific statements about appropriate professional conduct. They are at times vague and ambiguous (Bersoff, 1994; Hughes, 1986).

Second, competing ethical principles often apply in a particular situation (Bersoff & Koeppl, 1993; Haas & Malouf, 1989), and specific ethical guidelines may conflict with federal or state law (Kitchener, 1986; Koocher & Keith-Spiegel, 1998). In some situations, a primary or overriding consideration can be identified in choosing a course of action (Haas & Malouf, 1989). In other situations, however, no one principle involved clearly outweighs the other (Haas & Malouf, 1989). For example, the decision to allow a minor child the freedom to choose (or refuse) to participate in psychological services often involves a consideration of law, ethical principles (client autonomy and self-determination versus the welfare of the client), and the likely practical consequences of affording choices (e.g., enhanced treatment outcomes versus refusal of treatment).

A third reason ethical codes are imperfect is because they tend to be reactive. They frequently fail to address new and emerging ethical issues (Bersoff & Koeppl, 1993; Eberlein, 1987). Committees within professional associations often are formed to study the ways in which existing codes relate to emerging issues, and codes may be revised in response to new ethical concerns. Concern about the ethics of behavior modification techniques was a focus of the 1970s; while in the 1980s, psychologists scrutinized the ethics of computerized psychodiagnostic assessment. In the 1990s, changes in ethical codes reflected concerns about sexual harassment and fair treatment of individuals, regardless of their sexual orientation. In recent years, codes have emphasized the need for practitioner competence in the delivery of services to individuals from diverse linguistic and cultural backgrounds. Codes also have been scrutinized to ensure relevance to the use of electronic media.

Ethical codes thus provide guidance for the professional in his or her decision making. Ethical conduct, however, involves careful choices based on knowledge of codes and standards, ethical reasoning, and personal values. In many situations, more than one course of action is acceptable. In some situations, no course of action is completely satisfactory. In all situations, the responsibility for ethical conduct rests with the individual practitioner (Eberlein, 1987; Haas et al., 1986; Koocher & Keith-Spiegel, 1998).

ETHICS TRAINING AND COMPETENCIES

Prior to the late 1970s, many applied psychology graduate programs (clinical, school) required little formal coursework in professional ethics. Ethics was often taught in the context of supervised practica and internship experiences, a practice Handelsman labeled "ethics training by 'osmosis'" (1986a, p. 371). Handelsman (1986a, 1986b) and others have argued persuasively that a number of problems exist with this unsystematic approach to ethics training. Student learning is limited by the supervisor's awareness and knowledge of ethical issues (Dalton, 1984) and the range of issues that arise by chance in the course of supervision (Handelsman, 1986b). Results of a survey of practicing psychotherapists found that respondents gave only moderate ratings to their internship experience as a source of ethics education (Haas et al., 1986).

It is now generally recognized that ethical thinking and problem solving are skills that need to be explicitly taught as a part of graduate coursework (Haas et al., 1986; Handelsman, 1986a, 1986b; Tymchuk, 1985; Tymchuk et al., 1982). Both NASP and APA currently require formal coursework in ethics as a component of graduate training.

In the 1980s, psychology trainers began to ask, "What should be the goals of ethics education in psychology?" (Haas et al., 1986; Kitchener, 1986); "What are the desired cognitive, affective, and behavioral 'ethics competencies' for school psychologists?"; and "How should ethics be taught?" A number of goals for ethics training have been suggested in the literature. An emerging picture of desired competencies includes the following:

1. Competent practitioners are sensitive to "the ethical components of their work" and are aware that their actions "have real ethical consequences that can potentially harm as well as help others" (Kitchener, 1986, p. 307; also Rest, 1984; Welfel & Kitchener, 1992).
2. Competent psychologists have a sound working knowledge of the content of ethical codes, professional standards, and law pertinent to the delivery of services (Fine & Ulrich, 1988; Welfel & Lipsitz, 1984).
3. Competent practitioners are committed to a proactive rather than a reactive stance in ethical thinking and conduct (Tymchuk, 1986). They use their broad knowledge of ethical codes, professional standards, and law along with ethical reasoning skills to anticipate and prevent problems from arising.
4. Skilled practitioners are able to analyze the ethical dimensions of a situation and demonstrate a well-developed "ability to reason about

ethical issues" (Kitchener, 1986, p. 307). They have mastered and make use of a problem-solving model (Tymchuk, 1981, 1986).
5. Competent practitioners recognize that ethics develop within the context of a specific culture, and they are sensitive to the ways in which their own values and standards for behavior may be similar to or different from individuals from other cultural groups. They are aware of their personal values and feelings and the role of their feelings and values in ethical decision making (Corey, Corey, & Callanan, 1998; Kitchener, 1986).
6. Competent practitioners appreciate the complexity of ethical decisions and are tolerant of ambiguity and uncertainty. They acknowledge and accept that there may be more than one appropriate course of action (Kitchener, 1986).
7. Competent practitioners have the personal strength to act on decisions made and accept responsibility for their actions (Kitchener, 1986).

How should ethics be taught? A growing consensus indicates that ethics education needs to be taught as part of a planned, multilevel approach that includes formal coursework along with supervised discussion of ethical issues in practica and internship settings (Conoley & Sullivan, 2002; Fine & Ulrich, 1988; Meara, Schmidt, & Day, 1996). Formal coursework provides opportunities to introduce the student to broad ethical principles, professional codes, and a decision-making model in a systematic manner (Eberlein, 1987; Fine & Ulrich, 1988; Handelsman, 1986b; Tymchuk, 1986). Jacob-Timm (1998) and others (e.g., Tryon, 2000) recommend that students complete coursework in ethics early in their course of study so that they will be prepared to engage in the discussion of ethical issues throughout their training program. Tryon recommends that all graduate faculty engage students in discussions of ethical issues related to their speciality areas so that "students learn that ethical decision making is an active, ongoing activity that applies to almost everything psychologists do" (2000, p. 278). As Conoley and Sullivan note, however, "The actual formation of ethical practice occurs…during intense practice. Internship is, therefore, a prime time to develop ethical frameworks that will be useful throughout a professional career" (2002, p. 135). Internship supervisors consequently have a special obligation to model sound ethical decision making, and to monitor, assist, and support interns as they first encounter real-world ethical challenges (Conoley & Sullivan, 2002; Williams, Mennuti, & Burdsall, 2002).

Methods of ethics training include instruction in ethical problem solving, analysis of case incidents, and role playing difficult situations (Gawthrop & Uhlemann, 1992; Kitchener, 1986; Plante, 1995). These methods provide a means to enhance sensitivity to ethical issues and encourage the development of ethical reasoning skills.

Only a few empirical investigations of the effectiveness of formal ethics training have appeared in the literature (Welfel, 1992). Baldick (1980) found that psychology interns who received formal ethics training were better able to identify ethical issues than interns without prior coursework in ethics. Gawthrop and Uhlemann (1992) found that students who received specific instruction in ethical problem solving demonstrated higher quality decision making in response to a case vignette than students who did not receive the training. Several studies, however, have reported a gap between the knowledge of the appropriate course of action and a willingness to carry out that action (Bernard & Jara, 1986; Smith, McGuire, Abbott, & Blau, 1991; Tryon, 2000). Even when practitioners can identify what ought to be done, many would choose to do less than they believe they should (Bernard & Jara, 1986). Thus, at this time, additional research is needed to identify the types of ethics training that are most effective in developing ethical sensitivity and reasoning and in encouraging appropriate professional conduct (Nagle, 1987; Tymchuk, 1985; Welfel, 1992).

ETHICAL CODES AND PROFESSIONAL STANDARDS

Brown (1979) suggests that school psychology emerged as an identifiable profession in the 1950s. Two professional associations, APA and NASP, have shaped the development of the profession. Within APA, Division 16 is the Division of School Psychology.[1] Each organization has formulated its own ethical code, professional standards for the delivery of services, and standards for training programs.

APA and NASP Codes of Ethics

In joining APA or NASP, members agree to abide by the association's ethical principles. Additionally, psychologists who are members of the National School Psychologist Certification System and those who are members of state associations affiliated with NASP are bound to abide by NASP's code of ethics. We believe school psychology practitioners should be thoroughly familiar with NASP's "Principles for Professional Ethics" and "Guidelines for the Provision of School Psychological Services" (NASP, 2000a) and APA's "Ethical Principles of Psychologists and Code of Conduct" (APA, 2002), whether or not they are members of a professional association.

[1] For information about the history of APA's Division 16 and NASP and their policies and orientations, see Fagan and Wise, 2000, Chapter 2.

NASP's "Principles for Professional Ethics"

"Principles for Professional Ethics" (NASP-PPE) was first adopted by the National Association of School Psychologists in 1974 and revised in 1984, 1992, 1997, and 2000 (NASP, 2000a). (See Appendix A.) NASP's ethical principles were developed to provide guidelines specifically for school psychologists employed in the schools or in independent practice. NASP's code focuses on protecting the well-being of the student/client. It also prescribes conduct to protect the rights and welfare of parents, teachers, other consumers of school psychological services, trainees, and interns.

NASP's "Principles for Professional Ethics" provides guidelines in the following areas: professional competence; professional relationships with students, parents, the school, the community, other professionals, trainees, and interns; advocacy of the rights and welfare of the student/client; professional responsibilities in assessment and intervention; reporting data and sharing results; use of materials and technology; research, publication, and presentation; and professional responsibilities related to independent practice.

APA's "Ethical Principles of Psychologists and Code of Conduct"

The "Ethical Standards of Psychologists" was first adopted by the American Psychological Association in 1953. Nine revisions of APA's code of ethics were published between 1958 and 1992. The current version, "Ethical Principles of Psychologists and Code of Conduct" (EP), was adopted in 2002. (See Appendix B.) APA's EP differs from NASP's "Principles for Professional Ethics" in that it was developed for psychologists with training in diverse specialty areas (e.g., clinical, industrial-organizational, school) and who work in a number of different settings (private practice, industry, hospitals and clinics, public schools, university teaching, and research).

The "Ethical Principles of Psychologists and Code of Conduct" consists of the following sections: Introduction and Applicability, Preamble, General Principles, and Ethical Standards. The General Principles section includes five broadly worded *aspirational* goals to be considered by psychologists in ethical decision making: (A) Beneficence and Nonmaleficence, (B) Fidelity and Responsibility, (C) Integrity, (D) Justice, and (E) Respect for People's Rights and Dignity. The standards section sets forth *enforceable rules for conduct*. The standards are organized into six general sections on Resolving Ethical Issues, Competence, Human Relations, Privacy and Confidentiality, Advertising and Other Public Statements, and Record Keeping and Fees. These are followed by five sections on Education and Training, Research and Publication, Assessment, and Therapy (APA, 2002).

Professional Guidelines for Service Delivery

Both organizations have developed a set of guidelines for the delivery of school psychological services. NASP's "Guidelines for the Provision of School Psychological Services" was developed in 1978 and revised in 1984, 1992, 1997, and 2000. (See Appendix C.) APA's "Specialty Guidelines for the Delivery of Services by School Psychologists" was adopted in 1981. Professional guidelines for the delivery of school psychological services differ from ethical codes in both scope and intent. The guidelines represent a consensus among practitioners and trainers about the roles and duties of school psychologists, desirable conditions for the effective delivery of services, the components of a comprehensive psychological services delivery system, and the nature of competent practice. The guidelines can be used to inform practitioners, students, trainers, administrators, policy makers, and consumers about the nature and scope of appropriate and desirable practice. NASP and APA seek to ensure that members abide by their respective ethical codes and investigate and adjudicate code violations. In contrast, professional guidelines provide a model of excellence in the delivery of quality comprehensive school psychological services, and it is recognized that not all school psychologists or all school pschological service units will be able to meet every identified standard.

School psychologists also should be familiar with the *Standards for Educational and Psychological Testing (Standards)* developed by a committee of members from the American Educational Research Association, American Psychological Association, and the National Council on Measurement in Education (1999). As will be seen in Chapter 4, the *Standards* provide criteria for psychologists and educators to use "for the evaluation of tests, testing practices, and the effects of test use" (1999, p. 2).

We believe school practitioners also should be familiar with APA's "Guidelines for Providers of Psychological Services to Ethnic, Cultural, and Linguistically Diverse Populations" (1993a). In addition, APA's Division 16 developed and published "Providing Psychological Services to Racially, Ethnically, Culturally, and Linguistically Diverse Individuals in the Schools" (Rogers et al., 1999), a list of recommendations for competent practice in the delivery of school psychological services to culturally diverse clientele. APA's Division 44 (Committee on Lesbian, Gay, and Bisexual Concerns) published "Guidelines for Psychotherapy with Lesbian, Gay, and Bisexual Clients" (2000), which provides information and references that may be helpful for practitioners who work with sexual minority youth and sexual minority parents.

FOUR BROAD ETHICAL PRINCIPLES

This portion of the chapter provides an introduction to some of the ethical issues associated with the delivery of school psychological services. As noted earlier, codes of ethics are composed of broad principles along with more specific rule statements. A number of writers have identified general principles that provide the foundation for ethical choices in psychology (e.g., Bersoff & Koeppl, 1993; Fine & Ulrich, 1988; Kitchener, 1986; Prilleltensky, 1997). Our thinking about ethical principles was influenced by the content and organization of "A Canadian Code of Ethics for Psychologists" (Canadian Psychological Association [CPA], 2000; Eberlein, 1987; Sinclair, 1998). We have organized our introduction to ethical issues in terms of the following themes or broad principles: (a) Respect for the Dignity of Persons, (b) Responsible Caring (Professional Competence and Responsibility), (c) Integrity in Professional Relationships, and (d) Responsibility to Community and Society. An overriding principle underlying all ethical choices is a commitment to promoting the welfare of individuals and the welfare of society (CPA, 2000).

Respect for the Dignity of Persons

Psychologists "accept as fundamental the principle of respect for the dignity of persons" (CPA, 2000; also see EP Principle E). School psychologists "are committed to the application of their professional expertise for the purpose of promoting improvement in the quality of life for children, their families, and the school community. This objective is pursued in ways that protect the dignity and rights of those involved" (NASP-PPE, III, A, #1). Concern for protecting the rights and welfare of children is "the top priority in determining services" (NASP-PPE, IV, A, #3). However, practitioners also strive to protect the rights of parents, teachers, other recipients of services, and trainees and interns (NASP-PPE, IV, A, #1).

The general principle of respect for the dignity of persons encompasses respect for the client's right to *self-determination and autonomy, privacy and confidentiality,* and *fairness and nondiscrimination.*

Self-Determination and Autonomy

In providing services, practitioners respect the client's right to self-determination and autonomy. To the maximum extent feasible, school psychologists respect the client's right of choice to enter, or to participate, in services voluntarily (NASP-PPE, III, B, #3). Except for emergency situations, client decisions to participate in services are based on informed consent about the nature of services offered (EP 3.10; NASP-PPE, III, A, #3, B, #2, C, #2, #3, #4).

Respect for the client's right to self-determination and autonomy poses special problems when working with children. As will be seen in Chapter 3, school psychologists must seek the informed consent of parents to provide services to children who are minors. But what of the child's right to self-determination and autonomy—that is, to make choices about whether to participate in the services offered? "A Canadian Code of Ethics for Psychologists" (CPA, 2000) specifically addresses the issue of developmentally appropriate rights to self-determination and autonomy. This code attempts to balance the rights of self-determination and autonomy against concerns for the welfare of the child and advises the psychologist to, "Seek willing and adequately informed participation from any person of diminished capacity to give informed consent, and proceed without this assent only if the service or research activity is considered to be of direct benefit to that person" (2000, 1.35; also see EP 3.10).

Case 1–1

Sam Foster obtained permission from the school board to gather the data for his Psy.D. research project in the school district where he is an intern school psychologist. His study explores young children's feelings toward family members (mother, father, siblings) in the first year following divorce. Sam has located just enough families willing to participate in his study to ensure an adequate sample size. On the last day of data collection, he asks a 7-year-old study participant to express her feelings toward family members by giving messages to dolls that represent members of her family. She begins the task, but soon becomes visibly upset and asks to return to her classroom. Sam is uncertain whether to coax her to continue the data collection.

Sam Foster (Case 1–1) is ethically obligated to discontinue his data collection because participation in the research promises no direct benefit to the child. As will be seen in Chapter 10, he is further obligated to ensure that there are no harmful after-effects to the child from her brief but upsetting experience as a study participant.

Privacy and Confidentiality

Psychologists respect the privacy of pupil/clients and others; every effort is made to avoid undue invasion of privacy (EP Principle E; NASP-PPE, III,

B, #1). School psychology practitioners do not seek or store personal information that is not needed in the provision of services to the client (EP 4.04).

Practitioners also use appropriate safeguards to protect the *confidentiality* of client disclosures. They inform clients about the limits of confidentiality at the onset of offering services. In situations in which confidentiality is promised or implied, school psychologists ensure that the release of information is based on consent of the client. Only in unusual circumstances, such as when disclosure is necessary to protect the client or others from harm, is confidential information released without client consent (EP 4.01, 4.02, 405; also NASP-PPE, III, A, #9, #10, #11). (See Chapter 3 for an in-depth discussion of these issues.)

Fairness and Nondiscrimination

Respect for the dignity of persons also encompasses the obligation of professionals to ensure fairness and nondiscrimination in the provision of services. School psychologists "are aware of and respect cultural, individual, and role differences, including those based on age, gender, gender identity, race, ethnicity, national origin, religion, sexual orientation, disability, language, and socioeconomic status and consider these factors when working with members of such groups" (EP Principle E; also see NASP-PPE, III, A, #2). They "try to eliminate the effect on their work of biases based on those factors, and they do not knowingly participate in or condone activities of others based upon such prejudices" (EP Principle E; also see APA, 1993a; EP 3.01, 3.03; NASP-PPE, III, A, D, #3).

The practitioner's obligation to students from diverse cultural and experiential backgrounds goes beyond striving to be impartial and unprejudiced in the delivery of services. Practitioners have an ethical responsibility to actively pursue awareness and knowledge of how cultural and experiential factors may influence a student's development, behavior, and school learning and to pursue the skills needed to promote the mental health and education of diverse students. Ignoring or minimizing the importance of characteristics such as race, ethnicity, sexual orientation, or socioeconomic background may result in approaches that are ineffective and a disservice to children, parents, teachers, and other recipients of services (Hansen, Pepitone-Arreola-Rockwell, & Greene, 2000; Lopez & Rogers, 2001; Rogers et al., 1999).

Responsible Caring (Professional Competence and Responsibility)

A shared theme in ethical codes of the helping professions is that of *beneficence.* Beneficence, or *responsible caring,* means that psychologists engage in actions that are likely to benefit others, or at least do no harm (CPA, 2000; Kitchener, 1986; Welfel & Kitchener, 1992; also EP Principle A; NASP-PPE III, A, #1). To do this, psychologists must practice *within the boundaries of their competence* and *accept responsibility* for their actions.

Competence

School psychologists provide services "with populations and in areas only within the boundaries of their competence, based on their education, training, supervised experience, consultation, study or professional experience" (EP 2.01; also see NASP-PPE, II, A, #1). Practitioners must consider their competence to provide various types of services, to use techniques that are new to them, and to provide services in light of the client's characteristics such as age; disability; ethnic, racial, and language background; and sexual orientation.

Case 1–2

Carrie Johnson, a school psychologist in a rural district, received a referral to evaluate Melissa Gardner, a 4-year-old. Melissa receives special education and related services because she is hearing impaired; now her parents and teachers have begun to suspect she has learning and emotional problems as well. Carrie has no formal training or supervised experience working with hearing-impaired preschoolers, and she is uncertain how to proceed with the referral.

School practitioners have a responsibility to self-determine the boundaries of their competence. They are aware of their limitations and "enlist the assistance of other specialists in a supervisory, consultative or referral roles as appropriate in providing services" (NASP-PPE, II, A, #1). Carrie Johnson (Case 1–2) needs to seek assistance in evaluating Melissa to ensure a fair and valid assessment. Psychologists who step beyond their competence in assessing children place the pupil at risk for misdiagnosis, misclassification, miseducation, and possible psychological harm (see Chapter 4).

In the years ahead, the public school population will become increasingly diverse in terms of race, color, ethnicity, religion, and national origin (Aponte & Crouch, 2000). In addition, gay, lesbian, and bisexual youth are disclosing their sexual orientation at earlier ages than previous generations; some now "come out" during their high school years (D'Augelli, 1998). Consequently, it has become increasingly important for all practitioners to assess their competence to provide services to a diverse clientele and to seek the knowledge necessary to provide culturally sensitive services in the schools where they work. Where understanding of age, gender, gender identity, race, ethnicity, national origin, religion, sexual orientation, disability, language, or socioeconomic status is essential for effective implementation of services, psychologists have or obtain the training, experience, consultation, or supervision necessary to ensure the competence of their services, or they make appropriate referrals, except for emergency situations in which there is no more qualified professional available (EP 2.01). Because awareness of and respect for cultural, individual, and role differences is critical to ethical practice across the school psychologist's many roles, a list of suggested competencies for providing services to today's diverse school population and resources to enhance competence appears in Appendix D.

School psychologists are obligated to renew and update their skills to maintain an acceptable level of professional competence. They recognize the need for continued learning and pursue opportunities to engage in continuing professional development. They "remain current regarding developments in research, training, and professional practices that benefit children, families, and schools" (NASP-PPE, II, A, #4; also see EP 2.03).

Practitioners "refrain from any activity in which their personal problems or conflicts may interfere with professional effectiveness. Competent assistance is sought to alleviate conflicts in professional relationships" (NASP-PPE, II, A, #5; EP 2.06).

Responsibility

Consistent with the principle of responsible caring, psychologists accept responsibility for their actions and the consequences of their actions (EP Principle B; NASP-PPE, IV, C, #6). In all areas of service delivery, they strive to maximize benefit and avoid doing harm, and they work to offset any harmful consequences of decisions made.

Integrity in Professional Relationships

A psychologist-client relationship is a *fiduciary* relationship, that is, one based on trust. In order to built and maintain trust, practitioners must demonstrate integrity in professional relationships. The broad principle of integrity encompasses the moral obligations of fidelity, nonmaleficence, and beneficence. *Fidelity* refers to a continuing faithfulness to the truth and to one's professional duties (Bersoff & Koeppl, 1993). Practitioners are obligated to be open and honest in their interactions with others and to adhere to their professional promises (CPA, 2000; EP Principle B).

Case 1–3

Madeleine Fine, a new first-grade teacher, asks Hannah Cook, the school psychologist, for some ideas in handling Kevin, a child who has become a behavior problem in the classroom. After observing in the classroom, it is evident to Hannah that Madeleine needs some help working with Kevin and developing effective classroom management strategies. Hannah offers to meet with Madeleine once a week over a six-week period to work on classroom management skills, and Madeleine agrees. Shortly after their third consultation session, the building principal asks Hannah for her assessment of Madeleine's teaching competence. The principal indicates she plans to terminate Madeleine during her probationary period if there are problems with her teaching effectiveness. Hannah is not sure how to respond to the principal's request.

Consistent with the broad principle of integrity in professional relationships, school psychologists should inform students/clients of all relevant aspects of the potential professional relationship prior to beginning psychological services of any type (NASP-PPE, III, A, #5, B, #2, C, #1, E, #3). They strive to be accurate and straightforward about the nature and scope of their services. Case 1–3 illustrates the importance of openly defining the parameters of the services to be offered in the school setting. Madeleine has become Hannah's consultee in this consultant consultee relationship. Hannah is bound by the obligation and expectation that what is shared and learned in their professional interaction is confidential; she may not share information about her consultee with the principal without Madeleine's explicit consent to do so.

In defining their job roles to the school community, school psychologists are obligated to identify the services they provide and those that are outside the scope of their job roles (NASP-PPE, III, E, IV, B, #3; EP Principle C). It is the job role of the building principal, not the school psychologist, to gather information on teacher effectiveness. If Hannah violates the confidentiality of the consultative relationship and shares information about Madeleine's teaching with the school administration, her actions would most likely undermine teacher trust in school psychologists and diminish her ability to work with other teachers in need of consultative services. The ethical issues associated with the consultation role are discussed further in Chapters 8 and 9.

The general principle of integrity in professional relationships also suggests that psychologists must be honest and straightforward about the boundaries of their competencies. Competence levels, education, training, and experience are accurately represented to clients and others in a professional manner (NASP-PPE, II, A, #2, IV, F, #3; EP Principle C). School psychology interns and practicum students identify themselves as such prior to the initiation of services. Practitioners inform clients when the service they are offering is new to them so that the client can make an informed choice about whether to accept the service. Carrie Johnson (Case 1–2) is obligated to inform her supervisor and Melissa's parents that she has little expertise in the assessment of hearing-impaired preschoolers so that a course of action can be pursued that is in the best interests of the child.

Practitioners also respect and understand the areas of competence of other professionals in their work setting and community, and they work in full cooperation with other professional disciplines to meet the needs of students (NASP-PPE, III, E, #1, #2, #4; EP Principle B). They "encourage and support the use of all resources to best serve the interests of students and clients" (NASP-PPE, III, E, #2).

The principle of integrity in professional relationships also suggests that school psychologists must avoid conflicts of interest. When the practitioner's commitments, objectives, or personal loyalties might influence a professional relationship, the school psychologist informs all concerned persons of relevant issues in advance (NASP-PPE, III, A, #5; EP Principle C). When applicable, they notify their direct supervisor about conflicts that may influence professional relationships so that the reassignment of responsibilities can be considered (NASP-PPE, III, A, #5). If, nevertheless, unanticipated conflicts arise, they attempt to resolve such situations "in a manner which is mutually beneficial and protects the rights of all parties involved" (NASP-PPE, III, A, #4, #7; also see EP Principle B). As noted in NASP's code, "Personal and business relations with students/clients or their parents may cloud one's judgment. School psychologists are aware of these situations and avoid them whenever possible" (NASP-PPE, III, A, #7).

Furthermore, school psychologists "do not exploit clients through professional relationships nor condone these actions in their colleagues" (NASP-PPE, III, A, #6). They do not expose any individuals, including students, clients, employees, colleagues, and research participants to deliberate comments, gestures, or physical contacts of a sexual nature. School psychologists "do not engage in sexual relationships with their students, supervisees, trainees, or past or present clients" (NASP-PPE, III, A, #6; also EP 3.02, 3.08).

Psychologists also do not take credit for work that is not their own (NASP-PPE, IV, F, #7; EP Principle C). When publishing or making professional presentations, school psychologists acknowledge the sources of their ideas (NASP-PPE, IV, F, #7; also see EP 8.11). They acknowledge both published and unpublished material that influenced the development of the manuscript or presentation materials. Furthermore, psychologists take credit "only for work they have actually performed or to which they have contributed" (EP 8.12).

Responsibility to Community and Society

"Psychology functions as a discipline within the context of human society. Psychologists, both in their work and as private citizens, have responsibilities to the societies in which they live and work, such as the neighborhood or city, and to the welfare of all human beings in those societies" (CPA, 2000, Principle IV; also see EP Principle B). As Prilleltensky has suggested, "school psychologists have a moral responsibility to promote not only the well-being of their clients but also of the environments where their clients function and develop" (1991, p. 200).

Case 1–4

After several incidents of harassment of gay students, Charlie Maxwell, school psychologist, became increasingly convinced that the schools in his district were not a safe or supportive place for sexual minority youth. He began to read about the developmental needs and challenges of gay, lesbian and questioning youth; he spent time talking with gay teens about their experiences at school and then formed alliances with school and community leaders who shared his concerns. Although he will face much criticism, Charlie will advocate for district-wide changes to reduce harassment and improve the school climate for sexual minority youth.

Charlie's conduct (Case 1–4) is consistent with our ethical responsibility to speak up for the needs and rights of students even when it is difficult to so (NASP-PPE, I). School psychologists are obligated ethically to help ensure that gay, lesbian, and bisexual youth can attend school, learn, and develop their personal identity in an environment free from discrimination, harassment, violence, and abuse (NASP, 1999). Through advocacy and education of staff and students, Charlie will work to foster a school climate that promotes not only understanding and acceptance of, but also a respect for and valuing of individual differences.

In keeping with our responsibilities to the societies in which we live and work, school psychologists know and respect federal and state law and school policies (NASP-PPE, III, D, #5). According to Ballantine (1979), ethical behavior must conform with the law, not defy it. Both NASP and APA require practitioners to adhere to codes of ethics when ethical codes establish a higher standard than required by law. When ethical codes and law conflict, psychologists are obligated "to seek to resolve such conflict through positive, respected, and legal channels, including advocacy efforts involving public policy" (NASP-PPE, III, D, #5; also see EP 1.02).

Also consistent with the principle of responsibility to community and society, school psychologists monitor their own conduct to ensure that it conforms to high ethical standards, and they monitor the conduct of their professional colleagues. Self- and peer-monitoring for ethical compliance safeguards the welfare of others and fosters public trust in psychology. If concerns about unethical conduct by another psychologist cannot be resolved informally, practitioners take further action appropriate to the situation, such as notifying the practitioner's work-site supervisor of their concerns or filing a complaint with a professional ethics committee (NASP-PPE, III, A, #8; also EP 1.04, 1.05). (See "Unethical Conduct," later in this chapter.)

Finally, psychologists accept the obligation to contribute to the knowledge base of psychology and education in order to further improve services to children, families, and others and, in a more general sense, promote human welfare (CPA, 2000, Principle IV; EP Principle B).

Summary

In this section, four broad ethical principles were introduced. The first was respect for the dignity of persons. Consistent with this principle, we value client autonomy and safeguard the client's right to self-determination, respect client privacy and the confidentiality of disclosures, and are committed to fairness and nondiscrimination in interactions with the client and others. The second broad principle was responsible caring. We engage in actions that are likely to benefit others. To do so, we work within the boundaries of our professional competence and accept responsibility for our actions. The third principle was integrity in professional relationships. We are candid and honest about the nature and scope of the services we offer and work in cooperation with other professionals to meet the needs of children in the schools. The fourth principle was responsibility to community and society. We recognize that our profession exists within the context of society and work to ensure that the science of psychology is used to promote human welfare.

ETHICAL AND LEGAL DECISION MAKING

In the next portion of the chapter, we address the following questions: "What makes a situation ethically challenging?"; "When the needs and rights of multiple clients conflict, is our primary responsibility to the pupil, parent, teacher, or school system?"; "How do we evaluate whether a course of action is ethical?"; and "How can we make good choices when ethical-legal dilemmas arise?"

What Makes a Situation Ethically Challenging?

Jacob-Timm (1999) surveyed school psychology practitioners and asked them to describe ethically challenging situations they had encountered in their work. Most of the incidents described by practitioners concerned difficult situations rather than clear-cut violations of the specific rules for professional conduct outlined in professional codes of ethics. Ethical tugs were created by situations involving competing ethical principles, conflicts between ethics and law, dilemmas inherent in the dual roles of employee and pupil advocate, conflicting interests of multiple clients (e.g., pupil, parents, classmates), and poor educational practices resulting in potential harm to students (also see Humphreys, 2000). These findings support the view that, in addition to knowledge of the content of ethical codes, skill in using a systematic decision-making procedure is needed.

The Ethical Challenge of Multiple Clients

School psychologists frequently face the challenge of considering the needs and rights of multiple clients, including children, parents, teachers, and systems (Humphreys, 2000; Jacob-Timm, 1999; NASP-PPE, IV, A, #1). The Canadian Code of Ethics states that, "Although psychologists have a responsibility to respect the dignity of all persons with whom they come in contact in their role as psychologists, the nature of their contract with society demands that their greatest responsibility be to those persons in the most vulnerable position" (Principle I). Consistent with this view that ethical priority should be given to the most vulnerable persons, NASP's code of ethics states, "School psychologists consider children and other clients to be their primary responsibility, acting as advocates of their rights and welfare. If conflicts of interest between clients are present, the school psychologist supports conclusions that are in the best interest of the child" (NASP-PPE, IV, A, #2; also see EP Principle E).

How Do We Evaluate Whether a Course of Action Is Ethical or Unethical?

Ethics involves "making decisions of a moral nature about people and their interactions in society" (Kitchener, 1986, p. 306). Individuals may make choices of a moral nature primarily on an intuitive level or a critical-evaluative level (Hare, 1981; Kitchener, 1986). Choices made on the intuitive level are based on "people's immediate feeling responses to situations," along with personal beliefs about what they should or should not do (Kitchener, 1986, p. 309).

Psychologists, however, have special obligations when making ethical choices in the context of a professional relationship (Haas & Malouf, 1989). In the provision of psychological services, decision making on a critical-evaluative level is consistent with sound professional practice. The critical-evaluative level of ethical decision making involves following a systematic procedure. This procedure may involve the exploration of feelings and beliefs, but also includes consideration of general ethical principles and codes of ethics, and possibly consultation with colleagues. Psychologists need to be aware of their own feelings and values and how they may influence their decisions (Hansen & Goldberg, 1999; Newman, 1993). However, reliance on feelings and intuition alone in professional decision making may result in poor decisions or confusion (Corey et al., 1998; Kitchener, 1986).

How do we evaluate whether a course of action is ethical or unethical? Haas and Malouf (1989) suggest an act or decision is likely to be viewed as ethical if it has the following characteristics: (a) The decision is *principled,* based on generally accepted ethical principles; (b) the action is a *reasoned* outcome of a consideration of the principles; and (c) the decision is *universalizable,* that is, the psychologist would recommend the same course of action to others in a similar situation (pp. 2–3). The consequences of the course of action chosen must also be considered—namely, will the action chosen result in more good than harm? Evaluation of whether a course of action is ethical thus involves consideration of characteristics of the decision itself (i.e., based on accepted principles, universality), the process of decision making (i.e., reasoned), and the consequences of the decision.

Eight-Step Problem-Solving Model

Sinclair observed that "some ethical decision making is virtually automatic and the individual may not be aware of having made an ethical decision. In other situations, ethical decision making is not automatic but leads rapidly to an easy resolution," particularly if a clear-cut standard exists. However, "some ethical issues...require a time-consuming process of deliberation" (1998, p. 171).

Eberlein (1987) and others (Haas & Malouf, 1989; Kitchener, 1986; Tymchuk, 1986) suggest that mastery of an explicit decision-making model or procedure may help the practitioner make informed, well-reasoned choices when dilemmas arise in professional practice. Tymchuk (1986) has also noted that, in difficult situations, the course of action chosen may be challenged. Use of a systematic problem-solving strategy will allow the practitioner to describe *how* a decision was made. This may afford some protection when difficult decisions come under the scrutiny of others. Furthermore, practitioners may find a systematic decision-making model helpful in anticipating and preventing problems from occurring (Sinclair, 1998).

The following eight-step problem-solving model is adapted from Koocher and Keith-Spiegel (1998, pp. 12–15):

1. Describe the parameters of the situation.
2. Define the potential ethical-legal issues involved.
3. Consult ethical and legal guidelines and district policies that might apply to the resolution of each issue (Hansen & Goldberg, 1999). Consider the broad ethical principles as well as specific mandates involved (Hansen & Goldberg, 1999; Kitchener, 1986).
4. Evaluate the rights, responsibilities, and welfare of all affected parties (e.g., pupil, teachers, classmates, other school staff, parents, siblings). Hansen and Goldberg (1999) encourage consideration of the cultural characteristics of affected parties that may be salient to the decision.
5. Generate a list of alternative decisions possible for each issue.
6. Enumerate the consequences of making each decision. Evaluate the short-term, ongoing, and long-term consequences of each possible decision (Tymchuk, 1986). Consider the possible psychological, social, and economic costs to affected parties. Eberlein advises consideration of how each possible course of action would "affect the dignity of and the responsible caring for all of the people involved" (1987, p. 353). Consultation with colleagues may be helpful.
7. Present any evidence that the various consequences or benefits resulting from each decision will actually occur (i.e., a risk-benefit analysis).
8. Make the decision. Consistent with codes of ethics (APA, NASP), school psychologists accept responsibility for the decision made and monitor the consequences of the course of action chosen.

In recent years, a number of ethical decision-making models have appeared in the literature. Although many appear useful, it is important to recognize that, to date, it has not been established that the use of a decision-making model necessarily improves the quality of practitioner choices. Furthermore, researchers have yet to explore the relative effectiveness of various models (Cottone & Claus, 2000).

UNETHICAL CONDUCT

As noted previously, one of the functions of professional associations is to develop and promote standards to enhance the quality of work by its members (Chalk et al., 1980). By encouraging appropriate professional conduct, associations such as APA and NASP strive to ensure that each person served will receive the highest quality of service and, thus, build and maintain public trust in psychology and psychologists. Failure to do so is likely to result in increased external regulation of the profession.

Appropriate professional conduct is defined through the development and frequent revision of codes of ethics and professional standards. "But the presence of a set of ethical principles or rules of conduct is only part, albeit an important one, of the machinery needed to effect self-regulation. The impact of a profession's ethical principles or rules on its members' behavior may be negligible...without appropriate support activities to encourage proper professional conduct, or the means to detect and investigate possible violations, and to impose sanctions on violators" (Chalk et al., 1980, p. 2).

APA and NASP support a range of activities designed to educate and sensitize practitioners to the parameters of appropriate professional conduct. Both include ethics coursework as a required component in their standards for graduate training, and each organization disseminates information on professional conduct through publications and the support of symposia.

APA and NASP also each support a standing ethics committee. Ethics committees are made up of volunteer members of the professional association. Ethics committees respond to informal inquiries about ethical issues, investigate complaints about possible code of ethics violations by association members, and impose sanctions on violators.

Ethics Committees and Sanctions

APA has developed an extensive set of "Rules and Procedures" for investigation and adjudication of ethical complaints against association members (APA, 1996b). According to the "Rules and Procedures," the primary objectives of the Ethics Committee are "to maintain ethical conduct by psychologists at the highest professional level, to educate psychologists concerning ethical standards, [and] to endeavor to protect the public against harmful conduct by psychologists..." (1996b, p. 532). A number of possible sanctions for ethics violations are listed including the issue of an educative letter, reprimand or censure, expulsion, and stipulated resignation (APA, 1996a).

NASP's Ethical and Professional Standards Committee is charged with investigating and making recommendations to NASP's Executive Board when a complaint is filed concerning a NASP member or any psychologist who holds a National Certificate in School Psychology (NCSP) (NASP, 1997). In accordance with NASP's "Procedural Guidelines for the Adjudication of Ethical Complaints" (1997), NASP's Ethics and Professional Standards Committee addresses issues of ethical misconduct "in an investigatory, advisory, educative and/or remedial role" (II). The Committee is committed to resolving cases informally, if possible. It works to "bring about an adjustment through mediative efforts in the interest of correcting a general situation or settling the particular issues between the parties involved" (IV.C.). Nevertheless, NASP procedures allow for requesting that the respondent take corrective measures, censure or reprimand, requiring restitution or apology, imposition of a period of probation, and expulsion (V). Following a formal investigation and hearing, any actions taken by NASP's Executive Board concerning a psychologist who holds an NCSP certificate are reported to the national certification board (IX).

The legality of ethical complaint adjudication was tested in court in the case of *Marshall v. American Psychological Association* (1987). The plaintiff in this case claimed that APA had no legal right to expel him or to publicize his expulsion from the association following an investigation of ethical misconduct. The court upheld the authority of APA to expel the plaintiff, noting that he agreed to be bound by APA's ethical principles when he joined the association, that the principles were repeatedly published, and that he had detailed hearing rights to respond to any and all charges.

In recent years, there has been a tendency for respondents in ethical complaints to file lawsuits against members of the Ethics Committee. For this reason, many state associations no longer have adjudication procedures and take an exclusively educative approach, leaving adjudication up to the national association.

Complaints to Ethics Committees

APA's Ethics Committee periodically publishes an analysis of its actions in the *American Psychologist.* In 2000, there were approximately 402 inquiries (many involving nonmembers), 253 complaints against members, and 43 formal cases opened, the lowest level of activity since 1986. Complaints were filed against approximately 1 member per 1000. Based on categorization of the underlying behavior (rather than the basis for processing the case), categories with more than 10% of the complaints against members were sexual misconduct with adult clients (40%), child custody evaluations (16%), and nonsexual dual relationships (16%) (APA, 2001).

Between 1998 and 2001, NASP's Ethics and Professional Standards Committee received more than 125 inquires or complaints. Most were inquiries that led to informal clarification of issues rather than the filing of a formal complaint. Inquiries concerned confidentiality, unethical testing practices, how long to maintain test protocols, modification of psychological reports by supervisors without the permission of the report creator, testing without parent permission, working with students in a crisis situation without parent permission, obligations with regard to student advocacy, conflicts of interest, sexual relations between a school psychologist and student, slander, testifying in court, plagiarism, and failure to provide informed consent for research, among others. A number of the situations were serious and involved both legal and ethical issues, resulting in the recommendation that the psychologist seek legal assistance at the local level (M. Forcade, personal communication, September 10, 2001).

Reasons for Unethical Conduct

According to Koocher and Keith-Spiegel (1998), no one profile describes psychologists who become ethics violators. Ethics violations may occur because the psychologist is unaware of the parameters of appropriate conduct or not competent to provide the services being offered. This may occur because the psychologist is poorly trained, inexperienced, or fails to maintain up-to-date knowledge. Violations also may occur when a psychologist who usually works within the parameters of appropriate practice fails to think through a situation carefully. Some psychologists suffer from emotional problems or situational stressors that impair professional judgment and performance. Some practitioners lack sensitivity to the needs and rights of others; others may engage in unethical conduct because they are irresponsible or vengeful. Finally, a few psychologists (fortunately only a few) are self-serving and knowingly put their needs before those of their clients.

Peer Monitoring

Both APA and NASP require its members to monitor the ethical conduct of their professional colleagues (EP Principle B; NASP-PPE, III, A, #8). Both associations support attempts to resolve concerns informally before filing a complaint. NASP's code states that practitioners should "attempt to resolve suspected detrimental or unethical practices on an informal level" (NASP-PPE, III, A, #8; also see EP 1.04). They "make every effort to discuss the ethical principles with other professionals who may be in violation" (NASP-PPE, III, A, #8). Psychologists document specific instances of suspected violations as well as attempts to resolve such violations (NASP-PPE, III, A, #8).

If, however, an apparent ethical violation cannot be resolved informally, psychologists take further action appropriate to the situation, such as referral to a professional ethics committee, state licensing board, or appropriate institutional authorities (EP 1.05). If a decision is made to file an ethics complaint, "the appropriate professional organization is contacted for assistance, and procedures established for questioning ethical practice are followed" (NASP-PPE, III, A, #8). Practitioners "enter this process thoughtfully and with the concern for the well-being of all parties involved" (NASP-PPE, III, A, #8; also see EP 1.07).

Although most practitioners are aware of their obligation to report unethical practices if the situation cannot be resolved informally, many are reluctant to do so (Pope, Tabachnick, & Keith-Spiegel, 1987). Koocher and Keith-Spiegel (1998) provide a helpful list of hints for engaging in informal peer monitoring.

CONCLUDING COMMENTS

Students and practitioners often complain that codes of ethics are bothersome to read, a confusing and boring list of "shoulds" and "should-nots." Wonderly (1989) suggests, however, that codes of ethics in psychology are not so overwhelming if we remember their primary purpose, namely, to protect the public. Professionals do not have *rights* under a code of ethics, only *obligations.* We will be exploring those obligations in more detail in the chapters ahead.

STUDY AND DISCUSSION

Questions for Chapter 1

1. What are the sources of "quality control" in the provision of school psychological services?
2. What does the term *ethics* mean?
3. What does the term *applied professional ethics* mean?
4. Why do professional groups, such as school psychologists, develop a code of ethics?
5. Summarize the desired ethics competencies of school psychology practitioners.
6. Why are codes of ethics imperfect guides to behavior?
7. Summarize the broad ethical principles discussed in Chapter 1.

(Continued)

8. How do you evaluate whether a course of action is ethical?
9. What are some of the reasons for unethical conduct?
10. What are your responsibilities with regard to peer monitoring?

Discussion

You and a fellow student (a friend) are placed at the same school for your first practicum experience. You are aware that she is a problem drinker, but thus far, she has been able to conceal her problem from the program faculty. You discover that your fellow student drinks before coming to practicum, and you have observed some erratic behavior and poor judgment at the practicum site. What should you do? What will you do? Why? (adapted from Bernard & Jara, 1986). See also Betan and Stanton (1999).

VIGNETTES

Eberlein (1987) and others have suggested that mastery of an explicit, decision-making model or procedure may help the practitioner make well-reasoned ethical choices when difficult situations arise in professional practice. In this chapter, we introduced an eight-step problem-solving model adapted from Koocher and Keith-Spiegel (1998). The incidents that follow are included to provide an opportunity to practice the problem-solving model. At first, use of a decision-making model may seem quite cumbersome. However, it is important for practitioners to remember that ethical decision making "applies to almost everything psychologists do," and, over time, if practiced regularly, it is likely to become almost automatic (Tyron, 2000, p. 278).

In the situations described, assume the role of the school psychologist and then follow a decision-making model to determine the course of action most appropriate. Compare your decisions with those of colleagues or fellow students.

1. A few months after Carrie Johnson was hired as the school psychologist in a rural school district, the district superintendent of schools asked to meet with her. During this meeting, he said, "You'll be working closely with the principal at Pine Lake. Rumor has it he drinks a lot on the job. He's been caught twice and fined for driving while intoxicated. I think he's nuts, and we've got to get rid of him. Keep notes on what he says and does. I want a report later." How should Carrie handle this situation? (Vignette source unknown.)

2. After a series of devastating floods destroyed homes and schools in a nearby community, many Native American families moved into Carrie Johnson's school district. Carrie began receiving referrals from a number of teachers because the Native American children were having difficulty coping with the loss of their homes and adjusting to their new school and community. Carrie had no experience working with Native American children and their families, or with those who had suffered such losses. How should Carrie handle the referrals for assessment and counseling of the Native American pupils now attending her school?

3. As part of her effort to build a strong working relationship with school staff and community members, Hannah Cook joined the Parent-Teacher Association (PTA) and regularly attends their meetings. During a public meeting of the PTA, a parent openly complains about the treatment her daughter is receiving in a world history class at a school where Hannah is the psychologist. The parent contends that the history teacher lacks mental stability and consequently is causing her child much anguish. How should Hannah handle this situation? (Adapted from Bailey, 1980).

4. Michelle Phillips was born with Sanfilippo syndrome, a genetic disorder that results in progressive neurological deterioration and limited life expectancy. No effective treatment for the disorder exists. Wanda Rose, a school psychologist, has worked with the Phillips family since Michelle was diagnosed six years ago, and she has formed a warm working relationship with them. Michelle is now in the third and final phase of the disorder. She is severely mentally impaired, unable to communicate, and unable to sit or walk without support. She has difficulty swallowing and chokes frequently.

Mr. and Mrs. Phillips have made an appointment with Wanda. They believe Michelle is experiencing much pain and suffering. Although they want all comfort care to continue for their daughter, they do not want medical interventions that would prolong her life. They have brought along DNR orders (do not resuscitate, do not institute basic choking rescue) from Michelle's physician, and they would like Wanda's help in ensuring that the orders will be honored at school. How should Wanda respond to this situation? (See Rushton, Will, & Murray, 1994).

ACTIVITIES

To learn more about APA and NASP, visit their Web sites: http://www.apa.org and http://www.nasponline.org.

Chapter 2

LAW AND SCHOOL PSYCHOLOGY: AN INTRODUCTION

As noted in Chapter 1, codes of ethics are one source of quality control in the provision of school psychological services. This chapter explores two other mechanisms of quality control: public school law and the credentialing of school psychologists. The chapter begins with a brief introduction to the U.S. legal system and law pertinent to the delivery of school psychological services. The three basic sources of public school law are discussed: the U.S. Constitution, statutes and regulations, and case law.

We believe it is important for practitioners to be knowledgeable of law pertinent to school psychology so that they can help safeguard the rights of children and their parents in the school setting. Furthermore, many aspects of school psychological practice are regulated by law. Practitioners are ethically obligated to know and respect federal and state law and school policies. Failure to comply with law can result in legal action against the school and the practitioner and the possible loss of certification or licensure to practice.

THE U.S. CONSTITUTION

The U.S. Constitution is the supreme law of the land. All statutes enacted by the U.S. Congress, state and local governments, and even boards of education are subject to the provisions of the Constitution (Reutter, 1994).

The original Constitution outlined the duties and powers of the federal government. Concern that the Constitution provided the foundation for a federal government that was too powerful led to the passage of 10 amendments to the Constitution in 1791, the Bill of Rights. The Bill of Rights was created to provide a more distinct balance of power between the federal government and the states and to safeguard the rights of individual citizens. The remaining amendments, 11th through 26th, were adopted between 1795 and 1971.

No fundamental right to an education is guaranteed to citizens under the Constitution (see *San Antonio Independent School District v.*

Rodriguez, 1973). Nevertheless, the Constitution has been the foundation for many decisions affecting public school education, including the right to equal educational opportunity, student rights in the school setting, and church–state–school relationships. Portions of the Constitution most pertinent to education law are shown in Exhibit 2–1. The 10th, 14th, First, and Fourth Amendments are discussed in the following paragraphs.

The 10th Amendment

The Constitution does not specifically refer to education as a duty of the federal government. Under the 10th Amendment, the "powers not delegated to the United States by the Constitution, nor prohibited by it to the States, are reserved to the States, respectively, or to the people." Thus, under the 10th Amendment, state governments have assumed the duty to

Exhibit 2–1. The U.S. Constitution: Selected Amendments

Amendment 1

Freedom of Religion, Speech, and the Press; Rights of Assembly and Petition

Congress shall make no law respecting an establishment of religion, or prohibiting the free exercise thereof; or abridging the freedom of speech, or of the press; or the right of the people peaceably to assemble, and to petition the government for a redress of grievances.

Amendment 4

Search and Arrest Warrants

The right of the people to be secure in their persons, houses, papers, and effects, against unreasonable searches and seizures, shall not be violated, and no warrants shall issue, but upon probable cause, supported by oath or affirmation, and particularly describing the place to be searched, and the persons or things to be seized.

Amendment 9

Powers Retained by the People

The enumeration in the Constitution, of certain rights, shall not be construed to deny or disparage others retained by the people.

Amendment 10

Powers Retained by the States and the People

The powers not delegated to the United States by the Constitution, nor prohibited by it to the states, are reserved to the States respectively, or to the people.

Amendment 14

Civil Rights

No state shall make or enforce any law which shall abridge the privileges or immunities of citizens of the United States; nor shall any state deprive any person of life, liberty or property, without due process of law; nor deny to any person within its jurisdiction the equal protection of the law.

educate, the power to tax citizens of the state to finance education, and the power to compel school attendance.

Both federal and state governments have an interest in an "educated citizenry," as educated citizens are more capable of self-government and of making a positive contribution to community life (Hubsch, 1989). As noted previously, the duty to educate children and the power to do so have been left to the states. Most states delegate much of the authority for the management of public schools to local school boards. Public schools consequently are considered to be an arm of the government (Reutter, 1994). When school boards, principals, teachers, and school psychologists make decisions in their official roles, their actions are seen as actions by the state.

A public education is considered to be an *entitlement* given by the state to its citizens under state constitutional or statutory law. On the basis of state law, all children within a state have a legitimate claim of entitlement to a public education. This right to a public education given by state law is considered to be a *property right.*

The 14th Amendment

As previously noted, the Bill of Rights was passed to ensure a clearer balance of power between the federal government and the states and to safeguard the rights of individual citizens. The 14th Amendment was created to prevent state governments from trespassing on the rights of individual citizens: "No state shall make or enforce any law which shall abridge the privileges or immunities of citizens of the United States...without due process of law. ..."

As education is a duty left to the states, the courts have long held the position that "judicial interposition in the operation of the public school system requires care and restraint" (*Epperson v. State of Arkansas,* 1968). As the Supreme Court stated in *Epperson,*[1] "By and large, public education in our Nation is committed to the control of state and local authorities. Courts do not and cannot intervene in the resolution of conflicts which arise in the daily operation of school systems and which do not directly and sharply implicate basic constitutional values" (p. 104).

The 1950s, 1960s, and 1970s were decades of increasing federal court involvement in school-related issues, however, because of school actions that violated the constitutional rights of students and their parents. Two aspects of the 14th Amendment have been extremely important in decisions regarding schools: the *equal protection clause* and the requirement for *procedural due process.*

---

[1] This case concerned an Arkansas state law that prohibited the teaching of the Darwinian theory of evolution in the schools. The Court held the law to be an unconstitutional violation of First Amendment safeguards of freedom of speech and inquiry and belief.

Equal Protection Clause

The equal protection clause provides that no state shall "deny any person within its jurisdiction the equal protection of the laws." Beginning in the years of the Warren Court (1953–1969), this clause has been interpreted to mean that a state may not make a free public education available to some children but not to others within the state and that the state must provide equal educational opportunity to all citizens within its jurisdiction.

In the 1954 landmark Supreme Court ruling, *Brown v. Board of Education,* the Court made it clear that each state must provide equal educational opportunity to all children within its jurisdiction regardless of race. The Court ruled that the assignment of African-American children to separate and inferior public schools is a denial of equal protection under the 14th Amendment of the Constitution. In two important subsequent cases, *Pennsylvania Association for Retarded Children v. Commonwealth of Pennsylvania* (1971, 1972) and *Mills v. Board of Education* (1972), the courts ruled that exclusion of children with handicaps from public school education is a denial of equal protection.

In the years since *Brown,* the courts have sent an unwavering message to the states that they have a duty to provide equal educational opportunities to all children regardless of race, color, national origin, native language, sex, and disability under the 14th Amendment (see Chapter 6). The 14th Amendment equal protection clause also has protected school access rights of pregnant and married students.

Due Process

The 14th Amendment also provides that no state shall "deprive any person of life, liberty, or property, without due process of law." Courts have identified two aspects of due process: substantive and procedural. Substantive due process applies to the content of a law. A state may not pass a law that deprives citizens of life, liberty, or property if the law is not related to a legitimate governmental purpose; arbitrary and capricious laws that impact on citizens' rights will be ruled unconstitutional. In the public schools, substantive due process has been interpreted to mean that school rules restricting student rights must be reasonably related to the purpose of schooling. (See the discussion of *Tinker v. Des Moines Independent Community School District* [1969] later in this chapter.)

Procedural due process means that a state may not take away life, a liberty interest, or a property right without some sort of procedural fairness to safeguard citizens from unfair or wrongful infringement of rights by the government (Reschly & Bersoff, 1999). The requirement for procedural due process applies only to the infringement or deprivation of a liberty or property interest protected by the 14th Amendment; citizens are guaranteed procedural due process only if a substantive liberty or property interest is affected. The specific liberty and property interests protected under the umbrella of the 14th Amendment have been identified in court interpretations of the scope of substantive rights. In *Goss v. Lopez* (1975), the Supreme Court held that education is a property right protected by the 14th Amendment.

Procedural due process "is a flexible concept whose precise contours change relative to the nature and gravity of the interest infringed" (Bersoff & Prasse, 1978, p. 402). Notice (being told what action the state proposes to take and the reason for that action) and the opportunity to be heard are basic components of due process when state action may deprive a citizen of a liberty or property interest (Bersoff & Prasse, 1978).

Under the due process clause of the 14th Amendment, schools may not suspend or expel children from school (and therefore deprive them of their property interest) without some sort of fair, impartial due process procedures. The due process procedures required for school suspension or expulsion generally do not have to be complex or elaborate but must include notice and the opportunity to be heard (*Goss v. Lopez,* 1975). (The suspension or expulsion of students with disabilities for more than 10 days requires more formal procedures because of the protections afforded students with disabilities under statutory law. See Chapter 9.)

The due process clause of the 14th Amendment also protects individuals from arbitrary or unwarranted stigmatization by the state that may interfere with the ability to acquire property (*Wisconsin v. Constantineau*, 1971). More specifically, the courts have ruled that a school may not label a child as "mentally retarded" or "emotionally disturbed" without due process; that is, without some sort of fair decision-making procedure that includes parent notice of the proposed classification and the right to an impartial hearing to protest the classification (see Chapter 5).

As noted previously, the 14th Amendment also protects the basic personal freedoms of citizens outlined in the Bill of Rights from arbitrary infringement by the state. The First and Fourth Amendments are an important source of fundamental rights.

The First and Fourth Amendments

In 1969, the Supreme Court decided an important case concerning student rights in the public schools, *Tinker v. Des Moines Independent Community School District* (1969). This case involved three students who were suspended from school for violating a school policy prohibiting pupils from wearing black armbands in protest of the war in Vietnam. In *Tinker,* the Court recognized the need to balance the school's interest in maintaining discipline in order to foster learning, and fundamental personal freedoms guaranteed citizens in the Bill of Rights. In the Court's view, the school's policy of banning armbands was seen as an unreasonable violation of the students' constitutional right to freedom of expression because there was no evidence that the silent wearing of armbands interfered with or disrupted the functioning of the school.

Thus, although children in the school setting are not afforded the full range of personal freedoms guaranteed citizens by the Bill of Rights, they do maintain certain fundamental rights in the school setting. In *Tinker,* the Court stated that "students in school as well as out of school are 'persons' under our Constitution . . . possessed of fundamental rights which the State must respect" (p. 511).

Freedom of Speech and Assembly

The First Amendment prohibits the government from interfering with the rights of free speech and assembly and freedom of religious choice. In *Tinker* and subsequent cases, the courts generally have acknowledged the right of students to free speech and assembly, as long as the exercise of those rights does not significantly interfere with or disrupt the functioning of the school. Freedom of speech and assembly can be restricted when their exercise "materially and substantially" interferes with schooling. The right to free speech does not protect the use of "obscene" language, gestures, or materials (see Fischer & Sorenson, 1996).

Privacy Rights

No "right to privacy" is mentioned expressly in the Constitution. A number of different privacy rights have been carved out of the First Amendment concept of "liberty," Fifth Amendment protections against self-incrimination, Ninth Amendment reservation of rights to the people, and the Fourth Amendment prohibition against unreasonable search and seizure (Hummel, Talbutt, & Alexander, 1985).

In a case that received considerable attention from legal scholars, a federal district court ruled that parents of school children have a right to be free from the invasion of family privacy by the school (*Merriken v. Cressman,* 1973; see Chapter 10). This right to privacy was recognized only for the parents or family unit; the courts generally have not recognized an independent student right to privacy in the schools. However, federal education law (e.g., the Family Educational Rights and Privacy Act discussed later in this chapter) now provides some guidance regarding protection of the privacy rights of pupils and their parents.

Under the Constitution, the courts generally have held that students have a Fourth Amendment right to be free from unreasonable search and seizure in the schools. The courts have ruled that students have a legitimate expectation of privacy rights with regard to their person and possessions, but they have allowed a more lenient standard of "reasonable suspicion" as opposed to "probable cause" for conducting searches in school. (Privacy is discussed further in Chapter 3.)

Freedom of Religion

The First Amendment also ensures the basic right to free exercise of religious choice, and, under the 14th Amendment, both Congress and the states are prohibited from passing laws "respecting an establishment of religion." As Reutter (1994) notes, the First Amendment is the source of two types of church–school–state cases: those involving the use of public funds for parochial schools and those involving school policies or classroom procedures objected to on religious grounds.

In general, court interpretations of the First Amendment suggest that the state is not allowed to provide funds directly to parochial schools. However, under the "child benefit theory," the state may provide some educational services for pupils attending parochial schools as long as those services directly aid the pupil and are not used for the purpose of religious instruction, and no impermissible entanglement of church and state exists.

In *Wolman v. Walter* (1977), the Supreme Court was asked to rule on the constitutionality of an Ohio statute that provided public school aid to children attending church-related schools. The Court upheld those portions of the law allowing the use of public school funds for secular textbooks (those approved for use in the public schools); standardized testing services; and speech, hearing, and psychological diagnostic services provided by public school personnel on the premises of the nonpublic school. The Court also upheld the provision of therapeutic services (guidance services and remedial instruction) but only if performed by public school personnel in public schools or centers located off the premises of the nonpublic school. The Court reasoned that teaching or counseling services posed a risk of fostering ideological views, an impermissible church–state entanglement, whereas diagnostic services did not.

Similarly, in *Aguilar v. Felton* (1985), the Supreme Court was asked to rule on the constitutionality of the City of New York's program of providing remedial instruction and guidance services to pupils in parochial schools. The program was funded by Title I of the Elementary and Secondary Education Act of 1965 and carried out by public school teachers, guidance counselors, psychologists, and social workers on the premises of the nonpublic schools. The City of New York monitored the religious content of the Title I instruction, and teachers and other professionals were directed to avoid involvement with religious activities conducted by the private schools. The Supreme Court held that New York City's program of providing Title I instruction and guidance services on the premises of parochial schools violated the Establishment Clause of the First Amendment.

In 1997, however, the Supreme Court overturned its *Aguilar v. Felton* ruling. In writing the majority opinion in *Agostini v. Felton* (1997), Justice O'Connor stated that case law decisions since 1985 dictate that *Aguilar v. Felton* is no longer good law. The Court held that the City of New York public schools may now provide Title I instruction and services on the premises of parochial schools. The provision of remedial instruction on the premises of a parochial school is no longer viewed as an impermissible church-state entanglement.

In 2002, the Supreme Court decided *Zelman v. Simmons-Harris*, a case concerning whether the First Amendment prohibition against Congress establishing a religion prevents a state from providing tuition monies to parents and allowing them to use that aid to enroll their children in a private school of their own choosing, without regard to whether the school is religiously affiliated. In a narrow 5–4 ruling, the Court held that such school voucher plans are constitutionally permissible, so long as the money that flows to the parochial schools results from the true private choice of parents.

STATUTES AND REGULATIONS

A second source of law within the U.S. legal system is statutory law. The U.S. government is composed of three parallel systems of government at the federal, state, and local levels, a form of government known as "federalism" (Turnbull & Turnbull, 2000). At the federal level, the Constitution is the basic law of the land. Congress is empowered to enact federal laws as long as they do not violate the U.S. Constitution. Similarly, each state has its own constitution and legislative body for enacting laws at the state level. State laws may not violate either the state or federal constitutions.

Many countries have a nationalized school system operated by the central government (Hubsch, 1989). Under the 10th Amendment of the Constitution, Congress is forbidden from creating a nationalized school system. However, the U.S. Congress has the power to shape educational policy and practices by offering monies to states contingent on compliance with federal mandates. Congress has passed two types of legislation that have had a dramatic impact on the public schools, *antidiscrimination legislation* and *federal education legislation*. Key federal statutes affecting the schools are highlighted in the paragraphs that follow.

Federal Education Legislation

Some federal education legislation is grant legislation; that is, funds are provided to states on the condition that schools comply with certain educational policies and practices. The No Child Left Behind Act of 2001 and the Individuals with Disabilities Education Act are important examples of this type of legislation. Other federal education legislation stipulates that no federal funds will be made available to schools unless they adhere to specific educational policies and practices outlined in the law; the Family Educational Rights and Privacy Act of 1974 (FERPA) is an example of this type of legislation.

No Child Left Behind Act of 2001

As noted previously, education generally has been regarded as a responsibility of state and local governments. The Elementary and Secondary Education Act of 1965 (ESEA) (Pub. L. No. 89–750) was one of the first major federal programs to aid education. With the passage of ESEA, Congress accepted the proposition that although "education is primarily a state function…the Federal Government has a secondary obligation to see that there is a basic floor under those essential services for all adults and children in the United States" (Taft, 1965, p. 1450). ESEA was initially a permissive law that gave the schools much latitude in how funds would be spent. A major thrust of early amendments of the law was to target funds more specifically for economically disadvantaged school children.

The No Child Left Behind Act of 2001 (Pub. L. No. 107–110) includes the most recent set of amendments to ESEA. Like its precursors, the Act provides financial assistance for schools with high concentrations of children from disadvantaged homes. Its purpose is, "To close the achievement gap with accountability, flexibility, and choice, so that no child is left behind." Resources are targeted for high-poverty school districts, and monies are provided to meet the educational needs of children with limited English proficiency; children of migrant workers; Native American children; children who are homeless, neglected, delinquent, or at risk of dropping out; and young children and their parents who are in need of family literacy services. Unlike previous amendments of ESEA, the No Child Left Behind Act of 2001 requires statewide reading and mathematics tests each year in grades 3–8, beginning in 2005–2006. Each state must attain academic proficiency for all students within 12 years, and districts must document progress toward that goal each year. Districts must make public school choice available to pupils in schools that fail to demonstrate progress for two consecutive years and offer supplemental tutoring after a third year of failure to demonstrate progress. The Act also requires a "highly qualified teacher" in each classroom by the end of 2005–2006.

Individuals with Disabilities Education Act

Prior to 1990, the Education of the Handicapped Act (EHA),[2] referred to a series of federal statutes concerning the education of children with handicapping conditions (e.g., Pub. L. No. 94–142). In 1990, President G. H. Bush signed into law the Education of the Handicapped Act Amendments of 1990 (Pub. L. No. 101–476), which changed the name of EHA to the Individuals with Disabilities Education Act (IDEA). In 1997, President Clinton signed into law the Individuals with Disabilities Education Act Amendments of 1997 (Pub. L. No. 105–117). This Act reauthorized IDEA and introduced a number of changes to improve the law.

IDEA-Part B allocates funds to states that provide a free and appropriate education to all children with disabilities as defined by the law. In order to receive funds, each state must have developed a plan to ensure that every child with disabilities receives special education and related services in conformance with an individualized education program. Children must be assessed on the basis of nondiscriminatory testing and evaluation procedures and provided an individualized education program in the least restrictive (most normal) setting feasible. Individualized education planning decisions are made by a multidisciplinary team that includes the pupils' parents, and a number of safeguards are required in the law to ensure parent participation in decision making (see Chapters 4 and 5).

IDEA-Part C provides funds to states that offer early intervention programs for infants and toddlers with known or suspected disabilities in conformance with an individualized family service plan (see Chapter 5).

Family Educational Rights and Privacy Act of 1974

This law (a part of Pub. L. No. 93–380) commonly is called FERPA or the Buckley Amendment. FERPA is a 1974 amendment to the Elementary and Secondary Education Act of 1965. Under FERPA, no federal funds will be made available to schools unless they adhere to the pupil record-keeping procedures outlined in the law. FERPA record-keeping guidelines are designed to ensure confidentiality of records and parent access to school records concerning their children. In accordance with FERPA, parents have access to all official school records of their children, the right to challenge the accuracy of those records, and the right to a hearing regarding the accuracy of them. Pupil records are to be available only to those in the school setting with a legitimate educational interest, and parent consent must be obtained before records are released to agencies outside of the school (see Chapter 3).

---

[2] Also EAHCA.

The Protection of Pupil Rights Act

The Protection of Pupil Rights Act was a 1978 amendment to the Elementary and Secondary Education Act of 1965. It was amended in 1994 and 2001 (Pub. L. No. 107–110 § 1061). The Act requires schools to obtain written parental consent before a pupil can be required to submit to a survey, analysis, or evaluation that reveals certain types of personal information (e. g., political affiliation, potentially embarrassing psychological problems, sexual or criminal behavior, religious practices, family income) if the survey, analysis, or evaluation is funded by the U.S. Department of Education. It also requires school districts that receive any federal funds to develop policies ensuring parents the opportunity to review the content of surveys prior to their distribution if the survey requests certain types of private information from students. Such policies must allow parents to have their child opt-out of survey participation (see Chapter 3.)

Federal Antidiscrimination Legislation

Congress also has passed antidiscrimination or civil rights legislation that has had an impact on public school policies and practices. These statutes prohibit state and school authorities from discriminating against individuals on the basis of race, color, or national origin;[3] sex;[4] or handicapping condition[5] in any program or activity receiving any federal funding. A state department of education may choose not to pursue monies available under federal grant statutes (e.g., funds for infants and toddlers with disabilities). School districts must comply with antidiscrimination legislation if they receive *any* federal funds for any purpose, however.

Federal antidiscrimination laws also protect students from harassment and hate crimes based on race, color, national origin, sex, or disability, and make schools responsible for taking reasonable steps to remedy harassment based on those factors. Federal statutory law does not currently protect public school students from discrimination or harassment based on sexual orientation. However, harassment on the basis of sexual orientation may violate state laws or the U.S. Constitution (*Nabozny v. Podlesny*, 1996) (see Chapter 9).

---

[3] Title VI of the Civil Rights Act of 1964.

[4] Title IX of the Education Amendments of 1972.

[5] Title II of the Americans with Disabilities Act of 1990.

The Rehabilitation Act of 1973

Section 504 of The Rehabilitation Act of 1973 (Pub. L. No. 93–112) specifically prohibits discrimination against any otherwise qualified individual solely on the basis of a handicapping condition in any program or activity receiving federal financial assistance. Section 504 is discussed in Chapter 6.

Americans with Disabilities Act of 1990

The Americans with Disabilities Act of 1990 (ADA) (Pub. L. No. 101–336) is considered to be the most significant federal law ensuring the civil rights of all individuals with disabilities. ADA guarantees equal opportunity to individuals with disabilities in employment, public accommodation, transportation, state and local government services, and telecommunications. Title II, Subtitle A, is the portion of the law most pertinent to public schools (see Chapter 6).

Civil Rights Act of 1871

School personnel also should be familiar with Section 1983 of the Civil Rights Act of 1871. This statute was passed following the Civil War as a reaction to the mistreatment of African Americans, and it originally was known as the Ku Klux Klan Act. Under Section 1983, any person whose constitutional rights (or rights under federal law) have been violated by a government (school) official may sue for damages in federal court, and the official may be held liable for damages (see the section on "Civil Lawsuits Against Schools and School Psychologists," in this chapter).

Rules and Regulations

When federal legislation is enacted, an executive agency is charged with the responsibility of developing rules and regulations implementing the law. For example, rules and regulations implementing IDEA and FERPA are issued by the Department of Education. For all intents and purposes, *rules and regulations have the same impact as actual legislation*. School psychologists need to be familiar with both the statute itself and the rules and regulations implementing the law.

Federal statutes are compiled and published in the *United States Code* (USC). Rules and regulations implementing a law first appear in a daily publication called the *Federal Register* (FR) and subsequently are published in the *Code of Federal Regulations* (C.F.R.), which is updated each year. These government publications typically can be found in state or university libraries. The U.S. Department of Education Web site also has links to statutes and regulations pertinent to education (http://www.ed.gov/). Citations for important federal statutes are provided in the "Table of Federal Legislation" at the back of this book.

State Education Laws

As Hubsch (1989) notes, the majority of public school *statutory* law is enacted at the state level. School psychologists must become familiar with the laws pertinent to the delivery of school psychological services in the state where they are employed, in addition to federal statutes and regulations. Copies of state laws affecting education typically can be purchased from a state's department of education, downloaded from their Web site, or located in a college library law collection.

CASE LAW

A third source of law is case law. Case law, or common law, is law that emerges from court decisions (Reutter, 1994). The common-law system can be traced back to medieval England. At that time, it was widely accepted that there were "laws of nature" to guide solutions to problems if those laws could be discovered. Legal scholars studied past court decisions for the purpose of discovering these "natural laws." The rules and principles that judges customarily followed in making decisions were identified and, at times, articulated in case decisions, and judges tended to base new decisions on these earlier "legal precedents." Common law is, thus, discovered law rather than enacted law (Reutter, 1994, p. 1). Many aspects of public school law today are based on common law rather than enacted law (Reutter, 1994). For example, the courts generally have upheld a teacher's right to use corporal punishment to discipline students where no state laws or school board policies prohibit its use. The court's acceptance of the use of corporal punishment in the schools has a long history in case law (see Chapter 9).

There are 51 court systems in the United States; the federal court system and a court system within each state (Fischer & Sorenson, 1996). The federal court system has three tiers or layers; most state court systems also have three tiers or layers. As Turnbull and Turnbull observed, "Why a case may be tried in one court, appealed or reviewed by another, and finally disposed of by yet another is a matter of great complexity" (2000, p. 6). The following is a brief discussion of the state and federal court systems.

State court systems vary in organization and complexity. Cases filed in the lowest court may be appealed to an intermediate-level court, if a state has them. Decisions then may be appealed to the supreme court of the state, the "court of last resort" (Reutter, 1994). The U.S. Supreme Court may review cases from a state court if a question of federal law is involved.

Within the federal system, at the lowest level are the trial courts, called district courts. Nearly 100 federal district courts exist. At the intermediate level are 11 numbered federal circuits or geographical areas and the District of Columbia. Each court at this level is called a Circuit Court of Appeals. The highest court in the federal system is the U.S. Supreme Court. A person who loses a case in a federal court of appeals or the highest state court may submit a written petition requesting the Supreme Court to review the case. The Court agrees to review a case by granting a *writ of certiorari* (an order calling up a case from a lower court for review). However, the Supreme Court selects only those cases it considers most important to review, and consequently, only a small percentage of the requests for review are granted.

The federal court system decides both civil and criminal cases. Criminal cases involve crimes prosecuted by the government, not private citizens (e.g., murder, theft, and assault). Civil cases are lawsuits brought by private parties. Federal courts rule only on cases that involve federal constitutional or statutory law or cases that involve parties from two different states. The U.S. Supreme Court has the final authority in interpreting the U.S. Constitution and federal statutes. State courts also decide both civil and criminal cases. State courts rule on cases involving state constitutional and statutory law, but also may rule on cases involving the federal constitution and statutory laws.

The role of the courts is to resolve disputes involving citizens, organizations, and the government. Courts also decide the guilt or innocence of those accused of crimes. In education, most disputes are decided in civil court. Courts decide conflicts by applying law to a given set of facts and interpreting the meaning of the law in that context. It is the function of courts to say what the Constitution or statute means in a given case, set forth the findings of fact that the interpretation is based on, and enter an order commanding the parties in the case to take certain action (or, if the case is on appeal, the judge may enter an order for another court to take action) (Turnbull & Turnbull, 2000). If there is no *codified* law (no Constitutional or statutory provision) found controlling in a case, the court is likely to rely on common law (legal precedents) in rendering a decision (Hubsch, 1989).

In reading about court rulings, remember that decisions of the U.S. Supreme Court are binding throughout the country. The decisions of the lower federal courts are binding only within their jurisdictions, and the decisions of state courts are binding only within the state (Fischer & Sorenson, 1996).

SUMMARY

We have explored the three basic sources of public school law within the American legal system, namely the Constitution, statutes and regulations, and case law. It is evident from the material presented that the federal courts and legislature have had a powerful impact on public schools, particularly since *Brown,* in 1954. But, as Hubsch (1989) points out, the role that the federal government can play in fostering quality public education in our nation's schools is limited. Court decisions spanning almost 50 years have sent a clear message that our schools must provide equal educational opportunities for all children. Equal educational opportunity for all children is not the same as a quality education for all, however (Hubsch, 1989). By providing grants and resources, the federal government can encourage quality educational programs, but the bulk of the responsibility for ensuring a quality education for all children must be carried at the state and local levels. Individual teachers, principals, and school psychologists must accept and share in this responsibility.

CREDENTIALING OF SCHOOL PSYCHOLOGISTS

As part of the obligation to protect the health and welfare of their citizens, state governments enact laws to regulate the provision of psychological services. State credentialing of professionals, such as school psychologists, protects the consumer by requiring individuals to hold specified qualifications before they are granted a legal sanction to practice within the state. Generally two types of legislation regulate school psychologists. Title acts limit who may use the title *school psychologist.* These laws, or regulations, typically are referred to as *certification* acts. In contrast, a *licensing* act restricts the offering of certain types of services to a group of professionals holding a specific title (Pryzwansky, 1999).

Credentialing for School-Based Practice

Certification laws typically regulate public school professionals. In most states, the state department of education (SDE) certifies school psychologists for practice in the school setting. An SDE certificate is the credential most commonly held by school psychology practitioners (Fagan & Wise, 2000).

The credentialing of school psychologists for school-based practice is a state matter. Although commonalities in credentialing standards exist across states, equivalence of requirements between states is the exception rather than the rule. Furthermore, different states may use differing titles or designations (e.g., school psychologist, school diagnostician), and some states have more than one level of certification, depending on the level of graduate preparation and years of experience.

Fagan and Wise (2000) identified two models of certification: *transcript review* and *program approval*. *Transcript review* requires submission of transcripts and other supporting materials to a state certifying agency. The agency then determines whether the applicant successfully has completed the prescribed set of courses and field experiences outlined in the state's certification standards. The *program approval* process means that applicants who have the recommendation from an approved state training program will be certified by the state agency. The procedure used may be different for applicants from instate training programs and those from out-of-state.

Because certification and licensure are controlled at the state level, students and practitioners need to contact the state in which they wish to practice for up-to-date information about credentialing. The *Credentialing Requirements for School Psychologists* may be a helpful resource (Curtis, Hunley, & Prus, 1998).

Credentialing for Independent Practice

Licensure acts typically regulate the private practice of psychology. Licenses usually are issued by a state psychology board (Pryzwansky, 1999). Currently only about 11 states license school psychologists for independent practice at the subdoctoral level (Prus & Mittelmeier, 1995). Information on licensing boards is available at http://www.asppb.org/. (Also see Curtis, Hunley, and Prus, 1998).

Nonpractice Credentials

In addition to state credentials to practice, nonpractice credentials also recognize the quality of professional preparation (Fagan & Wise, 2000). The National School Psychology Certification System allows school psychologists who complete training consistent with NASP standards, achieve a passing score on the National School Psychology Examination, and meet continuing education requirements, to be identified as a Nationally Certified School Psychologist (NCSP). Currently, more than 10,500 school psychologists hold the NCSP credential (NASP, 2001). It is important to recognize that the NCSP title alone does not authorize a school psychologist to render services (Fagan & Wise, 2000); practitioners must hold a valid certificate or license in the state where they want to practice. However, 18 states use the NCSP as part of their standards for certification (NASP, 2001).[6]

CIVIL LAWSUITS AGAINST SCHOOLS AND SCHOOL PSYCHOLOGISTS

In the last portion of this chapter, we discuss civil lawsuits against schools and school psychologists. Civil liability, simply stated, "means that one can be sued for acting wrongly toward another or for failing to act when there was a recognized duty to do so" (Hopkins & Anderson, 1985, p. 21). Civil liability rests within the basic framework of the law of tort. A tort is a civil (not criminal) wrong that does not involve contracts. It is a complex area of law.

In general, the court considers four questions in tort cases: (1) Did injury occur? Injury means a wrong or damage done to the student's person, rights, reputation, or property. (2) Did the school owe a duty in law to the student? (3) Was there a breach of duty—that is, did the school fail to do what it should have done? A tort can arise when an improper act, or failure to act, causes injury to the student. (4) Is there a promixate cause (causal) relationship between the injury and the breach of duty? (Evans, 1997; Turnbull & Turnbull, 2000).

Lawsuits Against Schools under State Laws

The most common tort committed by school personnel is negligence (Evans, 1997). Negligence suits often are precipitated by a physical injury to a student (e.g., injury resulting from student-on-student violence, student suicide). When a student suffers harm, and his or her parents seek vindication in court, the parents are most likely to file a negligence lawsuit in state court (Schill, 1993). Such lawsuits generally allege that the school had a duty (under state common or statutory law) to protect students from foreseeable harm, had knowledge of a specific danger, negligently failed to take reasonable precautions to protect the student, and thus caused the injury by allowing the incident to occur (Schill, 1993; Wood & Chestnutt, 1995).

---

[6] Additional information about the National Certified School Psychologist system can be obtained from NASP, 4340 East West Highway, Suite 402, Bethesda, MD 20814.

As noted previously, public schools are an arm of state government. Historically, under common law, a school district could not be held liable for torts committed by the district, officials, or other employees (Reutter, 1994). In some states, the immunity of school districts was based on the old English doctrine of *sovereign immunity*: "the King (state) can do no wrong; you can't sue the King." In other states, immunity of school districts was based on the fact that state law provides no funds for the payment of damages; funds for education could not be diverted to pay legal claims (Reutter, 1994).

Currently, the doctrine of immunity of school districts has been modified by legislation or case law in most states. However, the exceptions to the doctrine of immunity vary from state to state, making it extremely difficult to make generalizations about the kinds of tort actions that will be successful against school districts in various states. Immunity usually exists to the extent that the school's or school board's liability insurance does not cover the particular injury suffered (Schill, 1993, p. 1). This means that, in many states, state legislation or case law permits lawsuits against school districts but allows recovery only up to the limits of the school's liability insurance (see Reutter, 1994).

School psychology practitioners must remember that they are state actors and district employees. They have a legal duty to take steps to protect pupils in their schools from reasonably foreseeable risk of harm (Reutter, 1994). This obligation extends to all students, not just their own clients. Furthermore, school employment contracts often contain a provision, whereby any act or failure to act that jeopardizes pupil health, safety, or welfare can result in the suspension or termination of employment. Schools are not likely to be held liable when spontaneous, unforeseeable acts by students result in injury (Wood & Chestnutt, 1995).

As noted previously, whether a state will allow recovery of damages in lawsuits against school districts is a complicated matter. Whether individual school employees can be sued is also a complicated matter, determined by state legislation and case law. Michigan courts, for example, typically have held teachers and other individual school employees immune from liability during performance of duties within the scope of their employment. They may, however, be disciplined by their district for inappropriate actions.

Many of the negligence suits filed against school districts by parents are precipitated by a physical injury to a student (Evans, 1997). In the 1970s and 1980s, however, a number of "instructional malpractice" suits were decided. These suits were filed by students or their parents when a student graduated from high school but was unable to read or write well enough to secure employment, or when the student did not achieve academically what his or her parents expected. The plaintiffs in these cases claimed poor instruction (instructional malpractice) was the cause of the injury (student failure to learn). Such claims generally failed for several reasons. First, the courts prefer not to intervene in the administration of the public schools except in unusual circumstances involving clear violations of constitutional rights or federal law. Second, the courts have held that the award of monetary damages for instructional malpractice suits would be overly burdensome to the public education system in terms of both time and money (*Peter W. v. San Francisco Unified School District,* 1976). In addition, as noted in *Donohue v. Copiague Union Free School District* (1979), it would be difficult, if not impossible, to prove a causal link between a school's instructional practices and student failure.

Lawsuits under Federal Law (504, ADA, IDEA, Section 1983)

Federal antidiscrimination laws such as Section 504, ADA, and Title IX of the Education Amendments of 1972 allow parents to sue a school district for violation of their child's rights under those laws. In successful suits, parents have been able to secure a court order commanding the school to take steps to comply with the law, and they have at times been awarded monetary damages (see Chapters 6 and 9).

IDEA also allows parents of special education students to file a lawsuit when they believe their child's rights under the law have been violated. Except for unusual circumstances, parents are required to exhaust administrative remedies (e.g., due process hearings) available to them before they pursue a court action under IDEA. If parents prevail in a court action under IDEA, they may recover their attorney fees (see Chapter 5). Parents typically have not been able to recover monetary damages under IDEA (see Turnbull & Turnbull, 2000).

In addition to claims filed under Section 504, ADA, and IDEA, an increasing number of lawsuits are filed against schools and school personnel under Section 1983 of the Civil Rights Act of 1871. In accordance with Section 1983, any person whose constitutional rights (or rights under federal law) have been violated by a government official may sue for damages in federal court, and the official may be held liable for the actual damages. A pupil whose civil rights have been violated under Section 1983 may sue in federal court the school board, principal, teacher, and/or school psychologist responsible.

A number of student lawsuits concerning school disciplinary actions (e.g., illegal search and seizure, unreasonable corporal punishment) have been filed under Section 1983. School officials may have qualified immunity from Section 1983 lawsuits. The standard for qualified immunity applicable to government (school) officials is as follows: "[G]overnment officials performing discretionary functions are shielded from liability for civil damages unless their conduct violated clearly established statutory or constitutional rights of which a reasonable person would have known" (*Harlow v. Fitzgerald,* 1982, p. 2738). Hummel et al. (1985) suggest that school personnel generally will not be held liable in Section 1983 lawsuits as long as they are "acting clearly within the scope of their authority for the betterment of those they serve" (p. 78; for example, see *Landstrom v. Illinois Department of Children and Family Services,* 1990). However, if they are acting outside of their authority and violate a pupil's civil rights, then school personnel may be held personally liable (Hummel et al., 1985).

Paul D. Coverdell Teacher Protection Act of 2001

The most recent set of amendments to ESEA, the No Child Left Behind Act of 2001, includes the Paul D. Coverdell Teacher Protection Act (Pub. L. No. 107-110 §§ 2361–2368). The purpose of the Act is to provide a limitation on liability for teachers, principals, or other school professionals when they undertake reasonable actions to maintain order, discipline, and an appropriate educational environment. As a condition for accepting ESEA monies, the Act states that no punitive damages may be awarded against a school professional for harm caused by an act or omission if the school professional was acting on behalf of the school; within the scope of his or her authority; in furtherance of efforts to maintain order or control in the school; and if the actions were carried out in conformity with federal, state, and local laws, unless clear and convincing evidence shows that the harm was proximately caused by willful or criminal misconduct on the part of the school professional, or a conscious, flagrant indifference to the rights or safety of the individual harmed.

Professional Malpractice

Professional malpractice suits are filed against individual practitioners under state statutory and common law. Professional malpractice occurs when harm to a client is in the context of a psychologist-client professional relationship and when it is determined that the harm was caused by departure from acceptable professional standards of care. The APA Insurance Trust reports that the likelihood of a psychologist being sued for malpractice is small; less than one half of 1% (Bennett, Bryant, VandenBos, & Greenwood, 1990). As noted perviously, whether an individual school psychologist is immune from liability during performance of duties within the scope of his or her school-based employment varies from state to state. Psychologists in independent practice, however, can be held liable for malpractice in all states.

When a professional-client relationship exists, and the psychologist is acting in a professional capacity, he or she is expected to provide "due care," or a level of care that is "standard" in the profession. To succeed in a malpractice claim, the plaintiff must prove: (a) a professional relationship was formed between the psychologist and plaintiff so that the psychologist owed a legal duty of care to the plaintiff; (b) the duty of care was breached, that is, a standard of care exists and the practitioner breached that standard; (c) the client suffered harm or injury; and (d) the practitioner's breach of duty to practice within the standard of care was the proximate cause of the client's injury—that is, the injury was a reasonably foreseeable consequence of the breach (Bennett et al. 1990; also Bernstein & Hartsell, 1998).

How does the court determine the standard of care? As Bennett et al. (1990) note, in most cases, the courts look to the profession itself to identify the customary standard of care used by others in the same field. Expert testimony may be used to establish the customary standard of care. In addition, codes of ethics and professional standards may be presented as evidence of the parameters of accepted practice. Sometimes the client's condition is a key factor in determining the expected standard of care (e.g., acceptable and reasonable actions in handling a suicidal adolescent). If the psychologist is not qualified to work with a particular type of problem situation, he or she is obligated to refer the client to someone with appropriate training (Bennett et al., 1990).

According to Woody (1988), the key words related to defining the appropriate standard of care are ordinary, reasonable, and prudent. Ordinary pertains to what is accepted or customary practice. Reasonable relates to the appropriate and adequate use of professional knowledge and judgment. Prudent means the exercise of caution, not in the sense of being traditional or conservative, but rather maintaining adequate safeguards. It is important to recognize that the courts do not expect psychologists to be all-knowing and perform without error (Knapp, 1980). They do not decide malpractice from the application of standard techniques. Plante (1999) and Bernstein and Hartsell (1998) provide advice for psychologists on how to avoid malpractice suits.

Professional Liability Insurance

To protect themselves, and perhaps ease their fear of litigation, some school psychologists purchase professional liability insurance. Prior to purchasing a policy, school psychologists should investigate what type of coverage, if any, is provided by their employers, and whether any professional liability insurance is provided by their membership in a professional union, such as the National Education Association or American Federation of Teachers. Both the National Association of School Psychologists (http://www.nasponline.org) and the American Psychological Association (http://www.apa.org) have information about professional liability insurance on their Web sites. Internship students are well-advised to consider purchasing liability insurance (often available at a student rate) because they may not be covered by their school district's policies.

In choosing an insurance policy, several points should be kept in mind. First, be sure to study the policy carefully to know what is and is not covered. Some professional liability policies cover school psychologists only when their services are performed as those of an educational institution employee. In other words, they do not cover independent practice. Such policies are generally much less expensive than those that do cover private work. Second, policies may be either claims made or occurrence based. Under the former, the practitioner is covered only if insured when the alleged malpractice took place *and* when the claim was filed. Under the latter, an occurrence-base policy, the practitioner is covered as long he or she was insured when the alleged malpractice took place, regardless of when the claim was filed. Third, many policies reserve the right to select legal counsel and to settle the case. This may be discouraging to practitioners who want their day in court. The psychologist may still hire his or her own attorney to work with the one supplied by the insurance carrier, but that is an additional expense.

CONCLUDING COMMENTS

This chapter has provided a brief overview of public school law pertinent to school psychology. Legal aspects of the delivery of psychological services in the schools will be dealt with in more detail in the chapters ahead. School psychologists are ethically and professionally obligated to be familiar with law and to keep abreast of changes in law affecting practices. We concur with Reschly and Bersoff's view that understanding of law is important "as means to protect precious rights, as well as a method to resolve disagreements over rights and responsibilities. The better understanding of legal influences is one way to enhance opportunities for implementing the best professional practices" (1999, p. 1077).

STUDY AND DISCUSSION

Questions for Chapter 2

1. What are the three sources of public school law within the U.S. legal system?
2. Why was the Bill of Rights passed? What is the significance of the 10th Amendment with regard to public education? Do citizens have a right to a public education under the U.S. Constitution?

(Continued)

3. Identify the two aspects of the 14th Amendment that have been extremely important in court decisions regarding public schools.
4. What was the significance of the Supreme Court decision in *Tinker v. Des Moines Independent School District?*
5. If public education is a duty of the states, how does the U.S. Congress have the power to shape educational policy and practices? Cite two examples of federal education legislation and two examples of federal antidiscrimination legislation.
6. What is case law, and why is it important?
7. What is civil liability?
8. What is professional malpractice? What aspects of the situation do courts evaluate to determine whether malpractice occurred? How is appropriate standard of care generally determined?

ACTIVITIES

1. The majority of public school statutory law is enacted at the state level. School psychologists must become familiar with the laws pertinent to the delivery of school psychological services in the state where they are employed. Obtain a copy of the rules governing special education and school psychological services in the state where you live. Copies of state laws affecting education typically can be purchased from a state's department of education, downloaded from their Web site, or located in a college library law collection.

2. During the course of their career, many school psychologists will be asked to provide testimony in a legal proceeding, such as a special education due process hearing. Read about school psychologists' involvement in special education due process hearings (Havey, 1999) and the legal and ethical issues associated with being an expert witness in the courtroom (Elias, 1999).

3. Visit the U.S. Department of Education (DOE) Web site at http://www.ed.gov/. Can you locate information about the No Child Left Behind Act of 2001? IDEA?

Chapter 3

PRIVACY, INFORMED CONSENT, CONFIDENTIALITY, AND RECORD KEEPING

This chapter explores four important ethical-legal concepts in the delivery of psychological services in the schools: *privacy, informed consent, confidentiality*, and *privileged communication*. School record keeping also is discussed. Privacy, informed consent, confidentiality, and record keeping are discussed together in this chapter because they are ethical-legal concerns that cut across all of the school psychologist's many roles. The chapter closes with a discussion of parent access to test protocols and the use of technology in communication and record keeping.

PRIVACY

The term *privacy* meshes complicated concepts from case law, statutory law, and professional ethics. We will first briefly explore privacy as a legal concept and then discuss respect for privacy as an ethical mandate.

Privacy and Law

As will be seen in this portion of the chapter, the privacy rights of pupils and their parents have been addressed in case and statutory law. However, there are many areas in which the legal boundaries of pupil privacy are not clearly delineated. Furthermore, some tension between the school's perceived need for personal information about pupils, and the right of students and parents to be free from unnecessary intrusions on their privacy, is likely inevitable, even as additional privacy guidelines become available.

Case Law

As noted in Chapter 2, "right to privacy" is not mentioned expressly in the Constitution (Reschly & Bersoff, 1999). However, a number of privacy rights have been carved out of the First Amendment concept of liberty, the Fifth Amendment protections against self-incrimination, Ninth Amendment reservation of rights to the people, and Fourth Amendment prohibition against unreasonable search and seizure (Hummel, Talbutt, & Alexander, 1985).

Court decisions regarding the rights of students have recognized the need to balance the interest of the state (school) in fulfilling its duty to maintain order, ensure pupil safety, and educate children, and the personal freedoms and rights generally afforded citizens. Thus, in the school setting, students do not have the full range of privacy rights afforded adult citizens. Two court cases that addressed the issue of privacy rights are *Merriken v. Cressman* (1973) and *New Jersey v. T.L.O.* (1985); a third case, *Sterling v. Borough of Minersville* (2000), also may have implications for the privacy rights of students.

In *Merriken v. Cressman* (1973), a case decided in federal district court, a school district planned to administer a questionnaire to students as part of a program designed to identify drug abusers. The questionnaire inquired about the nature of the parent-child relationship and parenting practices and was to be administered without parent consent. The court ruled that parents of schoolchildren have a right to be free from invasion of family privacy by the school. However, this right to privacy was recognized for the parents only; the court did not address the issue of an independent student's right to privacy in the schools. (This case is discussed further in Chapter 10.)

In *New Jersey v. T.L.O.* (1985), the Supreme Court held that students have the Fourth Amendment right to be free from unreasonable search and seizure in the schools. The case concerned whether school officials had the right to search a student's purse. The Court engaged in a two-part inquiry to determine the legality of the search, namely, "Was the search justified at its inception?" and "Was the search, as actually conducted, reasonably related in scope to the circumstances which justified the search in the first place?" While holding that students have a legitimate expectation of privacy rights with regard to their person and possessions in school, the Court in *T.L.O.* upheld the standard of *reasonable suspicion* as opposed to *probable cause* for conducting individual searches, thus giving more latitude in the case of students than provided adults by the Fourth Amendment. School officials must, however, have reasonable grounds to suspect that a search will produce evidence that the student violated school rules or committed a crime; the search must be justified at its inception by more than a rumor or hunch.

The Court also noted that a search must not be "excessively intrusive in light of the age and gender of the pupil and the nature of the infraction" (*T.L.O.*, 1985, p. 342). The more personal the search (i.e., the closer the search comes to the body), the more serious the reasons the school must have for conducting the search. Thus, a search of a student's body for a weapon would more likely be viewed as legally permissible than an intrusive search for missing money. In our opinion, strip searches should be avoided if at all possible because they may result in emotional distress, anger, and alienation (Hyman & Perone, 1998). (See Ferraraccio [1999] for a review of recent court cases addressing the scope of constitutionally valid school searches.)

A recent case decided in federal appeals court may have implications for the privacy rights of students with regard to sexual orientation. In *Sterling v. Borough of Minersville* (2000), the court determined that police may have violated a gay teen's constitutional right to privacy when they threatened to tell his family that he was gay. The boy committed suicide after the threat was made. In the majority opinion, the judge stated that disclosure of an individual's sexual orientation by government officials is a violation of the individual's constitutional right to privacy unless there is a "genuine, legitimate, and compelling" government interest in making the disclosure (*Sterling*, 2000, p. 196). This case has been interpreted to suggest that principals, teachers, psychologists, and other school personnel should not divulge information about a student's sexual orientation without his or her permission (Bradley, 2001).

Statutory Law

The Individuals with Disabilities Education Act (IDEA), the Protection of Pupil Rights Act (PPRA), and the Family Educational Rights and Privacy Act of 1974 (FERPA) provide some statutory protection for the privacy rights of pupils and their parents. IDEA requires informed consent prior to the evaluation of a pupil for special education eligibility and protects the privacy of pupil records (see Chapter 5). The requirements of FERPA are discussed in "Record Keeping in the Schools" later in this chapter.

The Protection of Pupil Rights (PPRA) Act, enacted in 1978, provides protection from school actions that intrude on pupil or family privacy. It was amended in 1994 (Pub. L. No. 103–227) and 2001 (Pub. L. No. 107–110 § 1061). The Act has two major provisions regarding the collection of sensitive information from students. First, in accordance with PPRA, no student may be required to submit without prior consent to a survey, analysis, or evaluation funded by the Department of Education (DOE) that reveals information concerning: (1) political affiliations or beliefs of the student or the student's parent; (2) mental and psychological problems potentially embarrassing to the student or his or her family; (3) sex behavior and attitudes; (4) illegal, antisocial, self-incriminating, and demeaning behavior; (5) critical appraisals of other individuals with whom respondents have close family relationships; (6) legally recognized privileged and analogous relationships; (7) religious practices, affiliations, or beliefs of the student or student's parent; or (8) income, other than required by law to determine eligibility for participation in a program or for receiving financial assistance under a program. *Prior consent* is defined as the prior consent of the student, if the student is an adult or emancipated minor; or prior written consent of the parent or guardian, if the student is an unemancipated minor (20 U.S.C. § 1232h). These privacy protections of PPRA apply only to schools that receive and use federal funds in connection with the use or administration of surveys, analyses, or evaluations concerning one or more areas listed in the statute (*Altman v. Bedford Central School District*, 1999).

A second provision of the Protection of Pupil Privacy Act requires local school districts that receive any federal funds to develop policies, in consultation with parents, to notify parents when the school intends to administer a survey containing one or more of the eight items listed in the preceeding paragraph. The parent of a student must be given the opportunity to inspect the survey, upon request, prior to its distribution. Parents must be given the opportunity to have their student "opt out" of the information-gathering activity.

If an adult or emancipated student, or the parent of a minor child, feels that they have been affected by a violation of PPRA, they may file a complaint in writing with the U.S. Department of Education (DOE). DOE investigates complaints and may terminate federal funds if a school refuses to comply with the Act within a specified time period.

Privacy as an Ethical Issue

Privacy is also an ethical issue. Siegel has defined privacy as "the freedom of individuals to choose for themselves the time and the circumstances under which and the extent to which their beliefs, behaviors, and opinions are to be shared or withheld from others" (1979, p. 251).

Consistent with the general principle of respect for the dignity of persons and the valuing of autonomy, *psychologists respect the client's right to self-determine the circumstances under which they disclose private information.* Furthermore, every effort is made to minimize intrusions on privacy (EP Principle E, 4.04 also NASP-PPE, III B, #1). Psychologists do not seek or store personal information about pupils, parents, teachers, or others that is not needed in the provision of services.

INFORMED CONSENT FOR PSYCHOLOGICAL SERVICES

Ethical codes and law are consistent in respecting the individual's right to self-determine whether to share private thoughts, behaviors, and beliefs with others. In ethics and law, the requirement for informed consent grew out of deep-rooted notions of the importance of individual privacy. As Bersoff notes, "It is now universally agreed, though not always honored in practice, *that human beings must give their informed consent prior to any significant intrusion of their person or privacy*" (italic added, 1983, p. 150).

In the school setting, IDEA and PPRA suggest parent consent (or the consent of an adult student) is needed for school actions that may result in a significant intrusion on personal or family privacy beyond what might be expected in the course of ordinary classroom and school activities (Corrao & Melton, 1988; also see Bersoff, 1983; DeMers & Bersoff, 1985). *Ethical codes, professional standards, and law show agreement that, with the exception of urgent situations, informed consent should be obtained prior to the provision of school psychological services.*

The Meaning of Informed Consent

Case law and statutory regulations concur that the three key elements of informed consent are that it must be *knowing, competent,* and *voluntary* (Dekraai, Sales, & Hall, 1998). *Knowing* means that the individual giving consent must have a clear understanding of what it is they are consenting to. The person seeking consent must make a good faith effort to disclose enough information to the person from whom consent is sought that the person can make an *informed choice* (Dekraai et al., 1998).

In seeking consent for the provision of psychological services, the practitioner is obligated to provide information about the nature and scope of services offered, assessment-treatment goals and procedures, the expected duration of services, any foreseeable risks or discomforts for the student or client (including any risks of psychological or physical harm), the cost of the services to the parent or student (if any), the benefits that reasonably can be expected, the possible consequences and risks of not receiving treatment or services, and information about alternative treatments or services that may be beneficial. The extent to which confidentiality of information will be maintained also should be discussed as part of the informed consent procedures. This information must be provided in language (or by other mode of communication) understandable to the person giving consent (Weithorn, 1983).

The individual giving consent must also be *legally competent* to give consent. As Bersoff and Hofer (1990) have observed, the law presumes that every adult is competent to consent, unless they have been judged incompetent following a full hearing conducted by an impartial factfinder. However, in the legal system, children generally are presumed to be incompetent and not capable of making legally binding decisions (Bersoff,

1983). Consequently, in the school setting, informed consent typically is sought from the parent or guardian of a minor child, or from the student if an adult. Parent consent may be bypassed in emergency situations (e.g., a student may be suicidal).

The third element of informed consent is that it must be voluntary. Consent must be "obtained in the absence of coercion, duress, misrepresentation, or undue inducement. In short, the person giving consent must do so freely" (Bersoff & Hofer, 1990, p. 951).

Specific ethical and legal requirements for informed consent vary across different situations within the school setting. Informed consent for release of school records is discussed in this chapter. Consent for psychoeducational assessment is addressed in Chapter 4, counseling and therapeutic intervention in Chapter 7, and participation in research in Chapter 10.

The Consent of Minors for Psychological Services

In the next portion of the chapter, we explore children's competence to consent to psychological services from legal, ethical, and cognitive-developmental perspectives.

Consent of Minors as a Legal Issue

As noted above, legally, in the school setting, informed consent for psychological services rests with the parent of a minor child. Legislators and the courts generally have presumed that minors are not developmentally competent to consent to (or refuse) psychological assessment or treatment on their own. The courts have viewed parents as typically acting in their children's best interests and have reasoned that allowing minors a right to consent to (or refuse) services or treatment independent of parental wishes might be disruptive to the parent-child relationship and interfere with effective treatment programs (*Parham v. J.R.*, 1979).

Parham (1979) was an important case regarding the competence of minors to participate in decisions affecting their own welfare. In *Parham,* the Supreme Court upheld a Georgia statute allowing parents to commit a minor child to a mental institution for treatment (with the approval of a physician) in the absence of a formal or quasi-formal hearing to safeguard the child from arbitrary commitment. Although the Court recognized that children have an interest in being free from misdiagnosis and unnecessary confinement, the Court viewed minors as incompetent to make decisions concerning their own need for treatment.

It should be noted, however, that minors are granted access to psychological or medical treatment without parental consent in emergency situations, and most states allow minors access to treatment independent of parent notice or consent for certain health-related conditions (e.g., venereal disease, alcohol, or drug abuse) (see Dekraai et al., 1998). School districts are well-advised to adopt written policies stating that students may be seen by the school psychologist or other school mental health professional without parent notice or consent to evaluate whether the pupil is in danger (e.g., child abuse) or a danger to self or others.

Consent of Minors as an Ethical Issue

Although minors are not generally seen as legally competent to consent autonomously to (or refuse) psychological services in the schools, practitioners are ethically obligated to respect the dignity, autonomy, and self-determination of their clients. As discussed in the paragraphs that follow, we find the notion of developmentally appropriate rights to self-determination and autonomy suggested in "A Canadian Code of Ethics" (CPA, 2000) more satisfactory than an absolute stance that children always (or never) be afforded the choice to accept or refuse psychological services. The term *assent,* rather than *consent*, typically is used to refer to a minor's affirmative agreement to participate in psychological services.

Minors and Capacity to Consent: A Research Perspective

What standards are used to determine whether a client is competent to provide consent to psychological treatment? In law and professional practice, the following tests or standards of competency to consent have been applied in psychological treatment situations involving adult clients: (1) the simple expression of a preference relative to alternative treatment choices; (2) the choice is seen as one a "reasonable" person might make; (3) a logical or rational decision-making process was followed; and (4) the person giving consent demonstrates understanding (factual or abstract) of the situation, choice made, and probable consequences (adapted from Weithorn, 1983, pp. 244–245). Evidence of a preference is probably the most lenient standard; evidence of understanding, the most stringent (Weithorn, 1983).

Findings from cognitive-development research suggest that many children have a greater capacity to make competent choices about psychological treatment than recognized in law. Research suggests that a pupil's capacity to effectively participate in treatment decisions depends on a number of factors including cognitive and personal-social development and functioning, motivation to participate, prior experiences with decision making, and the complexity of the situation and choices under consideration (Melton, Koocher, & Saks, 1983).

Preschoolers have limited language and reasoning abilities. However, they may be able to express preferences when choices are presented in concrete, here-and-now terms (Ferguson, 1978). Although children in middle childhood (ages 6–11) have not attained adult reasoning capabilities, research suggests they typically are able to make sensible treatment choices (Weithorn, 1983), and parents and professionals have judged the participation of children this age in treatment decisions to be effective (Taylor, Adelman, & Kaser-Boyd, 1985).

The years between ages 11 and 14 are seen as transitional ones with much individual variation in cognitive development and the ability to make truly voluntary choices. Pupils in this age range, like younger children, may defer to authority in decisions, or they may make choices based on anti-authority feelings. Minors age 14 and older typically have reasoning capabilities similar to adults, and many are capable of participating in treatment decisions as effectively as adults (Grisso & Vierling, 1978; also Abramovitch, Freedman, Henry, & Van Brunschot, 1995). Cooper (1984) proposes the use of a written therapist-child agreement as a strategy for involving minors ages 9 and older in treatment decisions.

Research findings not only suggest that minors have greater capacity to make treatment decisions than generally recognized in law, but that a child's participation in intervention decisions may lead to enhanced motivation for treatment, an increased sense of personal responsibility for self-care, greater treatment compliance, and reduced rates of early treatment termination (Holmes & Urie, 1975; Kaser-Boyd, Adelman, & Taylor, 1985; Weithorn, 1983). For these reasons, Weithorn (1983) suggests practitioners permit and encourage student/client involvement in decision making within the parameters of the law and the child's capacity to participate. However, psychologists must guard against overwhelming children with choices they do not wish to make for themselves. Furthermore, when children are given a choice whether to participate, it is important to recognize that they may have little knowledge of, or perhaps misconceptions about, the services offered. The practitioner should ensure that the pupil understands what participation means before soliciting assent so that the child can make an informed choice. For example, a psychologist might ask a pupil to attend a counseling group session before making a choice about participation.

In sum, the decision to allow a minor child the opportunity to choose (or refuse) psychological services and participate in treatment decisions involves a consideration of law, ethical issues (e.g., self-determination versus welfare of the client), the child's competence to make choices, and the likely consequences of affording choices (e.g., enhanced treatment outcomes versus choice to refuse treatment). As suggested in the Canadian code of ethics, it may be ethical to proceed without the child's explicit assent if the service is considered to be of direct benefit to the child (CPA,

2000). We concur with Corrao and Melton (1988) that it is disrespectful to solicit assent from the child if refusal will not be honored.

It also is important to distinguish between the right to consent to (or refuse) services and *the right to be informed about the services offered* (Fleming & Fleming, 1987). Practitioners have an ethical obligation to inform clients of the scope and nature of psychological services whether or not they are given a choice about participating (NASP-PPE, III, B, #2).

Informed Consent versus Notice

Informed consent differs from *notice*. The term means that the school supplies information about impending actions. Consent requires "affirmative permission before actions can be taken" (Bersoff & Hofer, 1990, p. 950).

Case 3–1

Wanda Rose was concerned about the children in her elementary school experiencing adjustment difficulties related to parent separation and divorce. She decided to form counseling groups for children experiencing parent separation and those from single-parent homes. She asked teachers to identify pupils who might benefit from the group counseling and then sent letters home with the children, notifying parents that their child would be seen for group counseling sessions. She asked parents to contact her if further information about the counseling was desired.

Wanda's letter to parents (Case 3–1) is not sufficient; it does not meet the requirement of informed consent for services. If parents do not receive the letter, they have no opportunity to deny consent (J. H. Correll in Canter, 1989). Wanda also has failed to fulfill her ethical obligation to seek direct parent contact prior to the provision of nonemergency counseling services (NASP-PPE, III, C, #2; also see Chapter 7).

In seeking informed consent from the parents, Wanda is obligated to describe the nature, scope, and goals of the counseling sessions, their expected duration, any foreseeable risks or discomforts for the pupil (e.g., loss of pupil and family privacy), any cost to parent or student (e.g., loss of classroom instructional time), any benefits that can reasonably be expected (e.g., the possibility of enhanced adjustment to parent separation), alternative services available, and the likely consequences of not receiving services. After consideration of the ethical issues involved and the possible consequences of her decision, Wanda also must decide whether to offer each child the opportunity to make an informed choice about participating (or not participating) in the counseling groups.

Blanket Consent

Practitioners also should be aware that blanket consent procedures (i.e., the psychologist requests parental consent to provide services "as needed") do not meet the requirements for informed consent. Blanket consent is not permissible because parents are not fully informed of the specific nature of the services to be provided (J. H. Correll in Canter, 1989).

CONFIDENTIALITY

Confidentiality is primarily a matter of professional ethics. Confidentiality has been described as "an ethical decision not to reveal what is learned in the professional relationship" (Hummel et al., 1985, p. 54). Siegel describes confidentiality as "an explicit promise or contract to reveal nothing about an individual except under conditions agreed to by the source or subject" (1979, p. 251). Although primarily a matter of professional ethics, in some states psychologists can be held civilly liable under state law for impermissible breach of client confidentiality (Dekraai et al., 1998).

School psychologists ethically are obligated to "respect the confidentiality of information obtained during their professional work. Information is revealed only with the informed consent of the client, or the client's parent or legal guardian, except in those situations in which failure to release information would result in clear danger to the client or others" (NASP-PPE, III, A, #9; also EP 4.05).

The interpretation of the principle of confidentiality as it relates to the delivery of psychological services in the school setting is a complicated matter. However, one clear guideline emerges from the literature on confidentiality in the school setting. With the exception of urgent situations, school psychologists define the parameters of confidentiality at the onset of offering services (Davis & Sandoval, 1982; also EP Principle E, 4.02; NASP-PPE, III, A, #11). The parameters of the promise of confidentiality will vary depending on the nature of the services offered. In the paragraphs that follow, we discuss confidentiality and its limits in providing direct services to the student, services that involve collaboration with the teacher or parent, and consultative services to the teacher.

Confidentiality and Direct Services to the Student

For our purposes, the provision of "direct services to the student" means that the practitioner works with the student directly (e.g., individual counseling). Consistent with the principle of integrity in professional relationships, the initial interview with the student "should include a direct and candid discussion of the limits that may exist with respect to any confidences communicated in the relationship" (Koocher & Keith-Spiegel, 1998, p. 117; also EP 4.02; NASP-PPE, III, A, #11).[1]

Much has been written about the importance of confidentiality for building and maintaining the trust essential to a helping relationship (Dekraai et al., 1998; Siegel, 1979; Watson & Levine, 1989). However, as Taylor and Adelman (1989) have observed, the promise of confidentiality can also limit the psychologist's ability to help when the client is a minor child. Furthermore, for a troubled student, candor about the limits of confidentiality may be more important in fostering trust in adult helpers than a promise of absolute confidentiality that is later broken (Pitcher & Poland, 1992). Consequently, school psychologists must weigh a number of factors in deciding the boundaries of a promise of confidentiality (e.g., age and maturity of the student/client, self-referral or referral by others, reason for referral). Whatever the parameters, the circumstances under which the psychologist might share confidences with others must be clear.

In the provision of direct services to the student, in three situations the school psychologist is obligated to share confidential student/client disclosures with others (Hummel et al., 1985). First, when the student requests it. Second, as noted previously, confidential information may be disclosed when there is a situation involving danger to the student or others. Situations involving danger are discussed later in this chapter under "Duty to Protect." Third, it may be necessary for the psychologist to disclose confidential information when there is a legal obligation to testify in a court of law. This is discussed in "Privileged Communication."

Taylor and Adelman (1989) provide suggestions regarding how to create an atmosphere of safety and trust in which the pupil knows and understands the exceptions to the promise of confidentiality, yet is motivated to disclose personal thoughts, feelings, and important information. Findings from a study by Muehleman, Pickens, and Robinson (1985) suggest that discussion of the limits of confidentiality with clients does not limit self-disclosure if self-disclosure is encouraged verbally.

As Poland (1989) has noted, the ideal situation is for mental health professionals to discuss the limits of confidentiality at the onset of services. However, students at times are referred for assessment of whether they are a threat to self or others, or self-refer because they are in immediate need of assistance. In such situations, Poland suggests gathering the most

---

[1] It is generally not necessary to discuss confidentiality with preschool-age student/clients. Preschool children lack cognitive awareness that their own thoughts and feelings differ from those of the people around them, and consequently, discussions of confidentiality have little meaning for this age group.

complete information possible about the student's thoughts and plans first and then dealing with the issue of the limits of confidentiality (also EP 4.02). If students offer to disclose personal matters "on the condition that the counselor promises not to tell anyone," the practitioner should not enter into such an agreement, as the student is likely to feel betrayed if the promise cannot be kept.

If it becomes apparent in working with a student that confidentiality must be broken, only information "essential to the understanding and resolution" of the student's difficulties is disclosed (Davis & Sandoval, 1982, p. 548; also NASP-PPE, III, A, #10). Furthermore, information is shared only with persons clearly concerned with the situation (EP 4.05). The decision to divulge information also should be discussed with the student. Taylor and Adelman (1989) suggest three steps: (1) explaining to the pupil the reason for disclosure; (2) exploring with the pupil the likely repercussions in and outside the student-psychologist relationship; and (3) discussing with the pupil how to proceed in a manner that will minimize negative consequences and maximize potential benefits.

In their work with troubled youth, Pitcher and Poland (1992) have found that, if handled with sensitivity, most students come to understand that a decision to disclose confidential information to others is based on the need to help the student or protect others.

Duty to Protect

Psychologists who work with clients in schools or mental health care settings should be familiar with the "Tarasoff" case, summarized here as Case 3–2.

Case 3–2

Prosenjit Poddar, a foreign student from India attending Berkeley, was in psychotherapy with a psychologist at the university's health center. The psychologist recognized that Poddar was quite dangerous, based in part on his pathological attachment to Tatiana Tarasoff, his ex-girlfriend, toward whom he made some threats. After consultation with his supervisor, the psychologist notified the campus police that Poddar was dangerous and should be committed. The police visited Poddar, who denied he had any intentions of harming Tarasoff. Poddar subsequently refused to return for therapy and two months later killed Tarasoff. Tarasoff's parents brought suit against the Regents, the student health center staff members involved, and the campus police. Ultimately, the California Supreme Court ruled twice on the case.

Case 3–2 *(Continued)*

The 1974 ruling (Tarasoff I) *held that the therapists had a duty to warn Tarasoff. The court held that "public policy favoring protection of the confidential character of patient-psychotherapist relationships must yield in instances in which disclosure is essential to avert danger to others; the protective privilege ends where the public peril begins"* (Tarasoff v. Regents of California, *1974, p. 566). The second ruling in 1976* (Tarasoff II), *held that a therapist has a "duty to exercise reasonable care to protect the foreseeable victim" from harm* (Tarasoff v. Regents of California, *1976, p. 345).*

The *Tarasoff I* court decision triggered a lengthy debate between APA psychologists, who asserted that confidentiality is absolute and can be broken under no circumstances, and those who insisted that limits to confidentiality be built into APA's ethical code. The 1981 revision of APA's "Ethical Principles of Psychologists" included the statement that psychologists reveal confidential information to others "only with the consent of the person or the person's legal representative, *except in those unusual circumstances where not to do so would result in clear danger to the person or others*" [italic added]. The current code states that "Psychologists disclose confidential information without the consent of the individual only as mandated by law, or where permitted by law for a valid purpose, such as to … protect the client/patient, psychologist, or others from harm …" (EP 4.05; also NASP-PPE, III, A, #9). Psychologists refer to this obligation to breach confidentiality to ensure the safety of the client or others as the duty to warn (*Tarasoff I*) or, more generally, a duty to protect (*Tarasoff II*). Following the *Tarasoff* decisions, some, but not all, states enacted laws requiring psychologists to make reasonable efforts to warn potential victims of violent clients, and in some states, appropriate law enforcement agencies must be notified as well.

Although direct service to the student is in many ways analogous to the therapist-client relationship in nonschool settings, some important differences exist. Schools have a strong obligation to protect and safeguard the welfare of students under their supervision. Furthermore, most students are minors. Consequently, in the school setting, student confidences may need to be disclosed to others in situations involving dangerous students, potential student suicide or other self-injurious behavior, student substance abuse, and suspected child abuse. The ethical-legal responsibilities of the school psychologist in situations involving a duty to protect are discussed in Chapter 7.

Collaboration and Confidentiality

As noted earlier, school psychologists may provide direct services to the student. However, they typically work in collaboration with teachers, parents, and others to assist the student, a situation that complicates the translation of the principle of confidentiality into appropriate action. In collaboration, the individuals involved carry joint responsibility for assisting the student (Hansen, Himes, & Meier, 1990). Thus, if the psychologist is working in collaboration with the teacher and/or parent in assisting the student, information will most likely be shared by those involved in the collaborative effort.

At the onset of offering services, the psychologist needs a clear prior agreement about confidentiality and its limits among those involved in the collaborative effort. The student is informed of those who will receive information regarding the services and the type of information they will receive (NASP-PPE, III, A, #11, B, #2). In interactions with the parent, practitioners discuss confidentiality and its limits (NASP-PPE, III, A, #11), and parent and student rights regarding "creation, modification, storage, and disposal of confidential materials that will result from the provision of school psychological services" (NASP-PPE, III, C, #6). Teachers and other staff involved in the collaborative effort also need a clear understanding of the parameters of confidentiality.

If information received in a confidential situation subsequently is disclosed in order to assist the teacher or parent in meeting the needs of a student, it is recommended that *only generalizations,* not specific confidences, are shared (Davis & Sandoval, 1982; also NASP-PPE, III, A, #10). Furthermore, generalizations are shared with others involved in the collaborative effort only if those generalizations "are essential to the understanding and resolution" of the student's difficulties (Davis & Sandoval, 1982, p. 548). Similarly, Zingaro (1983) suggests that the psychologist share insights about pupils with others in terms of what they can do to help the child.

In sum, information obtained in a professional relationship and subsequently shared with others is discussed only for professional purposes and only with persons clearly concerned with the situation (EP 4.04). Disclosure of information is "limited to the minimum that is necessary to achieve the purpose [of the disclosure]" (EP 4.04). This is often called the "need-to-know" principle.

Case 3–3

Carrie Johnson is exhausted. She just completed another parent conference with Mrs. Farwell. Mrs. Farwell's daughter, Amy, age 3, was diagnosed as having a rare genetic disorder characterized by mild-to-moderate mental retardation. After the diagnosis was made more than a year ago, Mr. Farwell soon focused his attention on how to best help his daughter, but Mrs. Farwell has not yet been able to accept her daughter's diagnosis. She has spent thousands of dollars during the past year shopping for a different diagnosis and seeking miracle cures. She continues to refuse Carrie's referrals for family counseling and involvement with a support group for parents of children with disabilities. Although she finally acquiesced to Amy's special education placement, she continues to insist that Amy will "grow out of it" and doesn't seem to hear Carrie's careful explanations of Amy's abilities, limitations, and needs. Today, Carrie learned that Mr. and Mrs. Farwell have separated and that Amy's older siblings are showing many adjustment problems at home and in school. She enters the teacher's lounge for a cup of coffee and is greeted by Amy's teacher who asks, "How's it going with the Farwells?" What, if anything, should Carrie disclose?

In Case 3–3, Carrie may wish to discuss the parent conference with Amy's teacher in a private setting, but she must take care not to disclose specific information conveyed during her conference with Mrs. Farwell. For example, Amy's teacher, in working with Mrs. Farwell, may need to know about her difficulty in accepting Amy's disabilities. She does not need to know about Mrs. Farwell's specific disclosures (e.g., the details of her search for a miracle cure).

As Davis and Sandoval (1982) note, sometimes social pressures to "gossip" exist, particularly in the teacher's lounge or lunchroom, in order to be accepted as part of the school staff. Resisting the temptation to "join in" when teachers and other staff share their frustrations about pupils, parents, and school life may be particularly difficult for Carrie because of her professional isolation in a rural area. However, in order to safeguard confidential disclosures and maintain teacher trust in her as a professional, Carrie must avoid discussing her knowledge of pupils, parents, or school staff in casual conversations with others.

Confidentiality and Consultation

Maintaining confidentiality can be particularly problematic for practitioners when the teacher is the primary recipient of services. In consultation with the teacher, the parameters of confidentiality should be discussed at the onset of the delivery of services, and, consistent with the notion of integrity in professional relationships, the psychologist should have a clear prior agreement about those parameters with others in the school setting (e.g., principal).

In general, in consultation with the teacher, the guarantees of client confidentiality apply to the consultant-consultee relationship. All that is said between the psychologist and teacher must be kept confidential by the psychologist, particularly when the psychologist is confronted by requests for information about the teacher from administrators (Davis & Sandoval, 1982). As noted in Chapter 1, violation of confidentiality in consultation with teachers is likely to result in a loss of trust in the psychologist and impair his or her ability to work with the consultee and other staff (also see Chapter 8).

PRIVILEGED COMMUNICATION

School psychologists must be familiar with the term *privileged communication.* Privileged communication is a legal term that refers to "the right of a person in a 'special relationship' to prevent the disclosure in legal proceedings of information given in confidence in the special relationship" (Fischer & Sorenson, 1996, p. 18).

Under English law, the courts first began to recognize a duty for witnesses to testify in judicial proceedings more than 400 years ago. The rule that witnesses can be compelled to testify is based on the principle that the administration of justice benefits all members of society, and the determination of justice requires full access to relevant information (Shah, 1969). It is now well established that courts should have broad access to evidence to ensure fair and just decisions (Knapp & VandeCreek, 1985).

However, the need for information in the determination of justice at times conflicts with the need to safeguard the trust and privacy essential to special relationships, such as the relationship between attorney and client, and husband and wife. Historically, privileged communication applied only to the attorney-client relationship. Most jurisdictions now also recognize the communications between marital partners and clergy-penitent as having privileged communication status (Knapp & VandeCreek, 1985).

Many states have enacted legislation to expand privilege to include other special relationships such as between physician and patient and psychologist and client. Thus, privilege status for psychologists, where it exists, "is granted by statutes, protects the client from having his/her communications revealed in a judicial setting without explicit permission, and is vested in the client by legislative authority" (Siegel, 1979, p. 251).

Privileged communication refers to the right of the *client* (the parent or guardian of a minor child) to prevent disclosure of confidential information in a legal proceeding. The client may voluntarily waive privilege, and then the psychologist must provide the relevant testimony. As Knapp and VandeCreek (1985) note, the waiver belongs to the client, and the psychologist has no independent right to invoke privilege against the client's wishes.

Practitioners need to consult state laws to determine whether their states grant privileged communication to school psychologists. Several key questions need to be asked:

1. Does the state in which you are employed have a specific law granting privileged communication to school psychologists?
2. Does the law grant privilege in civil cases, criminal cases, or both?
3. Does the law list exceptions such as child abuse matters?
4. Does the law state that the court may waive the privilege when it deems the professional's testimony necessary for fairness and justice? (adapted from Hummel et al., 1985, p. 57).

In the absence of state legislation specifically granting privilege to psychologists, practitioners probably can be required to testify in court (Hummel et al., 1985). Refusal to testify may result in the psychologist being held in contempt of court.

In 1996, in *Jaffee v. Redmond*, the Supreme Court ruled that communications between a licensed psychotherapist (a master's level social worker) and her client are privileged and do not have to be disclosed in federal court cases. Most lawsuits are tried in state courts. However, the *Jaffee* decision may give impetus to the passage of strengthened state privileged communication statutes for mental health professionals (Remley, Herlihy, & Herlihy, 1997; also see Shuman & Foote, 1999).

Even in states that grant privileged communication status to school psychologists, the court may not view all disclosures to the psychologist as privileged, and, as noted previously, many states allow the judge to waive privilege during a court proceeding to ensure justice. Psychologist-client privilege typically is waived in legal proceedings involving child abuse, danger to the client or others, court-ordered psychological examination of a client, and malpractice suits filed by a client against the psychologist.

In states where school psychologists are not specifically granted privileged communication status, the practitioner may ask that privilege be extended to them during a legal procedure. As Herlihy and Sheeley (1987) note, judges are reluctant to extend privilege to relationships not covered by existing law. However, school psychologists are most likely to be successful in being granted privilege status if they can demonstrate that their relationship with the client meets the following four requirements identified by Wigmore (1961):

1. The communication must have originated in the confidence that it would not be disclosed.
2. Confidentiality must be essential to full and satisfactory maintenance of the psychologist-client relationship.
3. The relationship must be one that, in the opinion of the community, should be deliberately and carefully fostered.
4. The injury to that relationship, caused by disclosure, would be greater than the benefit gained to the process of litigation.

Additional strategies for coping with subpoenas or compelled testimony regarding client records are outlined in Herlihy and Sheeley (1987) and the APA's Committee on Legal Issues (1996).

The issue of whether communication between the school psychologist and client has privileged communication status can raise difficult legal questions. School psychologists are urged to consult their school attorney when questions arise.

RECORD KEEPING IN THE SCHOOLS

In 1925, the National Education Association recommended that schools maintain health, guidance, and psychological records on each student so that information would be available about the "whole child" along with the academic record (Schimmel & Fischer, 1977). Although these records were to be made available to governmental agents, employers, and other nonschool personnel, they were to be closed to parents and students.

In 1969, the Russell Sage Foundation convened a conference on the ethical and legal aspects of school record keeping, and many abuses of school records began to be identified:

1. Public elementary and secondary school officials released student records to law enforcement agencies, creditors, prospective employers, and so on, without obtaining permission from parents or students.
2. Parents and students typically had little knowledge or information concerning the contents of student records or how those records were used. Parent and student access to records usually was limited to attendance and achievement records.
3. The secrecy with which the records were maintained made it difficult for parents or students to ascertain the accuracy of information contained in them. Because procedures for challenging the veracity of the information did not exist, an unverified allegation of misconduct could become part of a student's permanent record and

be passed on, unbeknownst to the student or parents, to potential employers, law enforcement agencies, and other educational institutions.

4. Few provisions existed for protecting school records from examination by unauthorized persons.
5. Formal procedures for regulating access to records by nonschool personnel did not exist in most schools (Russell Sage Foundation, 1970).

Family Educational Rights and Privacy Act

In 1974, the Family Educational Rights and Privacy Act (FERPA) was passed, sponsored by Senator James Buckley (sometimes referred to as the Buckley Amendment). This legislation specifically addresses the privacy of student records and access to those records. The Individuals with Disabilities Education Act outlines similar requirements for parent access to records.

Although FERPA was passed more than 25 years ago, it still generates considerable confusion among teachers, school officials, and school psychologists. In the text that follows, FERPA is discussed under the following headings: (a) Educational Records Defined, (b) Right to Inspect and Review Records, (c) Right to Confidentiality of Records, (d) Right to Request Amendment of Records, and (e) Complaints. Practitioners also need to be familiar with their state's laws regarding confidentiality and disclosure of student records.

Educational Records Defined

Under FERPA, educational records are defined as any records maintained by the schools (or their agent) that are directly related to the student (34 C.F.R. § 99.3). However, a number of different types of records are maintained by schools, which are explicitly excluded from the definition of educational records under FERPA. For example, FERPA excludes records maintained by a school-based law enforcement unit for the purpose of law enforcement and records of employees who are not also students. In the case of an eligible student (one who is 18 or attending a post-secondary institution), education record does not apply to the records of a physician, psychiatrist, psychologist, or related professional, working in a treatment capacity with the student, unless that treatment is in the form of remedial education or is a part of the instructional program.

The Act also defines another category of record, called *directory information.* Directory information "means information contained in an education record of a student that would not generally be considered harmful or an invasion of privacy if disclosed" (34 C.F.R. § 99.3). This category includes name, address, telephone number, electronic mail address, activities and sports participation, and degrees and awards received. As long as the school informs parents or eligible students about what kind of directory information they maintain and gives them an opportunity to object to the release of this information, the school may freely release such information (34 C.F.R. § 99.3).

The definition of education record under FERPA also does not include *sole possession records*, which are described as follows:

> Records that are kept in the sole possession of the maker, are used only as a personal memory aid, and are not accessible or revealed to any other person except a temporary substitute for the maker of the record ... (34 C.F.R. § 99.3)

In its comments regarding "sole possession record" or "private notes," the Department of Education stated that, "The main purpose of this exception to the definition of 'educational records' is to allow school officials to keep personal notes private. For example, a teacher or a counselor who observes a student and takes a note to remind himself or herself of the student's behavior has created a sole possession record, so long as he or she does not share the note with anyone else" (65 FR 41856).

A number of attorneys and psychologists have interpreted FERPA to suggest it is permissible for school psychologists to keep private or personal notes about their contacts with pupils (Martin, 1979; Slenkovich, 1988a, March). School psychologists who keep private notes need to be aware of several cautions. First, any information about the child that is shared with other persons (except for a school psychologist's substitute) is no longer private and becomes part of the student's education record whether or not it is kept separately from the student's cumulative folder (Martin, 1979, also see *Parents Against Abuse in Schools v. Williamsport Area School District,* 1991). Second, a psychologist's personal notes can be subpoenaed (Slenkovich, 1988a, March). In a court of law, the problem reverts to one of privilege. Third, as discussed under "Parent Access to Test Protocols," raw test data and test protocols are not considered to fall within the category of private notes. Practitioners are well-advised to work with their districts to develop policies that provide clear guidance to parents and staff regarding what types of notes are considered "sole maker" records (NASP's *Guidelines for the Delivery of School Psychological Services*, 2000, Unit Guideline 4).

Right to Inspect and Review Records

FERPA was developed to ensure appropriate access to school records by parents or eligible students. *Parent* is defined as a parent of a student and includes "a natural parent, a guardian, or an individual acting as a parent in the absence of a parent or guardian" (34 C.F.R. § 99.3). Parental separation, divorce, and custody do not affect the right to inspect records, unless a court order or legally binding document specifically revokes parental right to access records (34 C.F.R. § 99.4). In the absence of notification to the contrary, school personnel may assume that a noncustodial parent has access to the records of his or her child (see *Fay v. South Colonie Central School District,* 1986).

An *eligible student* is a student who is 18 years of age or older, or enrolled in a post-secondary school. When a student reaches the age of 18, the rights of the parent transfer to the student (34 C.F.R. § 99.5). However, parents maintain the right to inspect and review the files of a student age 18 or older as long as the student is a dependent as defined by federal tax law (34 C.F.R. § 99.32).

Under FERPA, schools must provide annual notice to parents and eligible students of their right to inspect, review, and request amendments of the student's education records (34 C.F.R. § 99.7). On request, the school must provide parents with a written copy of its procedures and policies for review and amendment of records and a list of the types and the location of all education records (34 C.F.R. § 99.6).

When parents or eligible students make a request to inspect records, the school must comply with the request for access to records "within a reasonable period of time, but in no case more than 45 days after it has received the request." The school must respond to "reasonable requests for explanations and interpretations of the records." The school also must "give the parent or eligible student a copy of the records if failure to do so would effectively prevent the parent or student from exercising the right to inspect and review the records." The school may charge a fee for copies unless the fee effectively prevents parents or eligible students from exercising their right to inspect records. The school may not destroy any records if there is an outstanding request to review them (34 C.F.R. § 99.10–99.11).

School psychologists occasionally receive reports from physicians or psychologists outside the school setting that include sensitive information about a student or the student's family (e.g., comments about a marital problem, parent drug or alcohol abuse). This may pose a dilemma for the practitioner who feels the report should not become part of the student's education record, yet it also includes some information about the student that is helpful in meeting educational needs. A strategy for handling this dilemma is to return the report to the sender with a request that the sender delete any private information not needed in the school setting.

Right to Confidentiality of Records

FERPA was designed in part to protect the privacy of students and their parents. The school may not disclose personally identifiable information from student education records without informed consent of the parent or eligible student, except for disclosures specifically authorized by the Act. When records are disclosed to specific persons or agencies at the request of the parent or an eligible student, the school must obtain the signed written consent of the parent or eligible student. The written consent must specify the records to be disclosed, state the purpose of the disclosure, and identify the party to whom the disclosure may be made (34 C.F.R. § 99.30).

Certain disclosures of education records specifically are authorized by FERPA and do not require the special permission of the parent or eligible student. The Act specifies that school personnel who have "legitimate educational interests" may have access to pupil records. Additionally, access is granted to officials of other schools upon notification by parents of a transfer of schools.

Certain governmental representatives also may have access for audit or regulation enforcement purposes, and other officials in health or safety emergencies, or when required by state laws. Also, organizations conducting appropriate research studies on behalf of the school may have access, as long as personally identifiable information concerning students or their families is destroyed when no longer needed. If a school initiates a legal action against a parent or student, or a parent or eligible student initiates a legal action against the school, information may be disclosed to the court without a court order or subpoena if the records are relevant to the legal action. In addition, schools may be required to release education records in compliance with a valid subpoena or judicial order. However, under FERPA, the school must notify parents before records are released in response to a subpoena or judicial order because the parents may be entitled to a hearing regarding the release (Johnson, 1993).

The school must maintain a record of disclosures, that is, a listing of the persons other than school officials who have been granted access to the student's records.

Right to Request Amendment of Records

A parent or eligible student has essentially three bases for requesting an amendment to records: (1) if the information is inaccurate, (2) if the information is misleading, or (3) if the information violates the privacy or other rights of the student. The school then may agree and so amend the record or disagree, and so advise the parent or student, and inform the parent or student of their right to a hearing on the matter.

The hearing is to be conducted by an individual who has no direct interest in the outcome, but it may be an official of the school. The parent or student may present any evidence they choose and be represented by any individual they choose. The school then makes a decision about whether to amend the record and must present written findings related to its decision. If it agrees with the parent or student, the record is then amended. If it disagrees, the parent or student may then place in the file a statement commenting on the record (34 C.F.R. § 99.20).

Complaints

Persons may file complaints about violations of FERPA with the U.S. Department of Education (DOE). Complaints are investigated by DOE, and DOE may terminate federal funds to schools that do not comply with FERPA within a specified time period. Prior to 2002, some federal courts allowed parents to pursue Section 1983 lawsuits against school districts because of alleged FERPA violations. In 2002, however, the Supreme Court ruled that FERPA does not confer a personal right to enforcement under Section 1983 (*Gonzaga University v. John Doe*, 2002).

Summary

Schools must have a written policy consistent with FERPA regarding parent access to education records and confidentiality of records and provide annual notice to parents and eligible students of their right to inspect records. School psychologists should be familiar with and abide by district policies and procedures.

School Health Records: Special Privacy Protections

Student health records may include sensitive medical information about the pupil (e.g., diagnosis of hepatitis, HIV, or AIDS). State law and district policies may be more protective of the privacy of student health records than education records. This generally means that access to pupil health records may be limited to parents and specific school personnel rather than all staff with an educational interest in the child. In addition, in some states, penalties exist for unauthorized disclosure of certain types of pupil health status information by school personnel. In Michigan, for example, the passing of information about a person with a serious communicable disease by school personnel is a felony punishable by a prison term of up to three years and a $5,000 fine, or both (Public Act 488, Section 5131 [10]).

Practitioners need to be familiar with state law and district policies regarding school health records. A national task force on confidential student health information recently recommended that school health records be recognized as distinct from other education records and stored separately … and that schools extend to pupil health records the same protections granted medical records by law ("Task Force Releases New Privacy Guide," 2001). The U.S. Department of Health and Human Services has ruled that pupil health records protected by FERPA are not subject to the requirements of the Health Insurance Portability and Accountability Act of 1996, the federal law that protects the privacy and security of patient information (*Federal Register*, Thursday, December 28, 2000, p. 82383).

Parental Access to Test Protocols

Two questions often arise with regard to school psychological records: "Do parents have the right to inspect and review their child's test protocols?" and "Is it ever ethically and legally permissible to make copies of test protocols?"

Right to Inspect and Review Protocols

The U.S. Department of Education Office of Special Education Programs (OSEP) and Office for Civil Rights (OCR) have responded to numerous inquiries from school personnel, parents, and attorneys regarding parent access to test protocols. Their responses to letters of inquiry and reports subsequent to complaints are published in the *Education of Individuals with Disabilities Law Report* (I.D.E.L.R.). Reschly and Bersoff (1999) reviewed 115 interpretations of the issue of parent access to test protocols that appeared in the I.D.E.L.R. and concluded that it is "unequivocal" that test protocols and answer sheets are part of the child's education records under FERPA. Parents have a legal right to inspect and review their child's test protocols. Protocols cannot be considered as private notes. (Also see *John K. and Mary K. v. Board of Education for School District #65, Cook County*, 1987.)

Thus, under FERPA, parents and eligible students have the right to inspect and review all educational records that contain personally identifiable information, including test protocols. The right to access also includes the right to "reasonable requests for explanations and interpretations of records." In addition, in accordance with FERPA, the school is required to make copies of education records *if failure to do so would prevent the parent or student from exercising their right to inspect the records*. The parent access requirements of FERPA thus *appear* to conflict with the school psychologist's ethical obligation to maintain test security, purchase agreements with test publishers, and the obligation to observe copyright laws.

However, a careful reading of codes of ethics reveals that less conflict exists between the legal right of parents to inspect test protocols and ethical standards than practitioners might imagine. APA's code states, "Psychologists make reasonable efforts to maintain the integrity and security of test materials and other assessment techniques consistent with law, contractual obligations, and in a manner that permits adherence to this Ethics Code" (EP 9.11; also 9.04). NASP's code requires practitioners to maintain test security (NASP-PPE-IV, E, #10), but also comply with all laws and regulations, including those regarding the release of test information. Similarly, purchase agreements with test publishing companies recognize that practitioners may be required legally to review a test and test answers with a parent of a child who has taken a test (see, for example, "Maintenance of Test Security," at http://www.psychcorp.com).

When school psychologists must balance the obligation to protect test security against the parent's legal right to inspect test protocols, we believe the parent's right to inspect records is of paramount importance (also see M. B. Canter, Bennett, Jones, & Nagy, 1994). However, practitioners may be able to avoid parent requests to inspect test protocols by establishing a good collaborative relationship early in the assessment process, by explaining the conflict between their professional obligation to maintain test security and the parents' right to review records, and by communicating assessment findings in a manner that satisfies the parents' need for information about their child. Providing handouts for parents that describe what a test measures with fictitious sample items may be helpful (see, for example, Sattler, 2001, pp. 222, 337, 457, 509–510). Reschly and Bersoff (1999) caution against using "slick" strategies such as hiding or destroying protocols in order to avoid sharing raw test data with parents. Such actions could result in the school being found in noncompliance with federal law.

If, nevertheless, parents do request to see their child's test protocols, FERPA requirements are met if the school allows the parent to examine and discuss the protocols under school supervision (Irvin, January 9, 1979).

APA's Division 16 Ethics Committee recommends this inspection might include "a discussion of sample test items and responses to them." This should be done under the supervision of the school psychologist or other appropriately trained person, and the parent should not be allowed to copy down questions and answers (Martin, 1985, reprinted in Sattler, 1988, p. 772). Psychologists have no obligation under FERPA to disclose "nonidentifying information" to parents. Thus, it is appropriate to deny parent requests to inspect test materials (e.g., manuals and stimulus materials) that are not part of the child's individual performance record (Hehir, October 25, 1993).

Many states have adopted freedom of information laws to ensure that citizens have access to information regarding the activities of government and to safeguard against abuse of power by officials. Parents and others occasionally request access to test questions and answers under such laws. Tests used in academic settings typically are exempt from disclosure under freedom of information acts unless a court determines that public interest in disclosure outweighs public interest in nondisclosure. Practitioners need to consult their state laws on this matter, however.

Making Copies of Test Protocols

As A. Canter observed, "One of the more controversial issues regarding release of school psychologists's records concerns the actual copying of test protocols—for parents, other professionals or attorneys" (2001a, p. 30). Copying test protocols raises legal questions with regard to violation of copyright law. Test publishers warn users that any reproduction of a test protocol without permission is a violation of copyright law ("Copyright Notice," at http://www.psychcorp.com) (also see discussion in A. Canter, 2001a). Reschly and Bersoff (1999) counter, however, that providing a single copy of a used protocol probably would fall under the fair use provisions of copyright law.

Practitioners ethically are obligated to maintain test security and integrity and ensure that test data is not misused by unqualified persons (EP 9.11; NASP-PPE, IV, C, #5, E, #1). Ethically, it is permissible to provide a test protocol to another professional who is qualified to interpret it (e.g., a psychologist in independent practice), as long as consent to release the record to a nonschool professional has been obtained from the parents. The protocol should be released directly to the psychologist; not given to the parent (see A. Canter, 2001a). Providing a protocol to another psychologist may allow the parent to obtain a second opinion on their child's educational needs without additional testing.

However, a copy of a student's test protocols should not be released to the parent unless required by law (M. B. Canter et al., 1994). Many years ago, the Bureau for the Education of the Handicapped (BEH) suggested that if the school provides an opportunity for the parent to inspect protocols under school supervision, the school is not legally required to provide copies of protocols except under the following unusual circumstances:

> An agency must give test protocols to parents if (a) the parent cannot come to school during a 45-day period after a request has been made to review the records if the reasons for not coming during this period are serious illness, extended travel, or related reasons, and if parents request copies of their child's protocol, or (b) if the parents or agency request a due process hearing in which the test questions will be introduced by either party as evidence at the hearing. (BEH policy letter by Irvin, dated January 9, 1979)

We concur with A. Canter (2001a) that it is important for school districts to have policies on parent access to test protocols that are consistent with state and federal law and communicated to parents and school staff. (See A. Canter, 2001a, for additional information.)

Storage and Disposal of Psychological Records

Psychologists ethically are obligated to maintain records to document their professional work. They "create, and to the extent the records are under their control, maintain, disseminate, store, retain, and dispose of records and data relating to their professional services and scientific work in order to (1) facilitate provision of services later by them or by other professionals . . . (3) meet institutional requirements, (4) ensure accuracy of billing and payments, and (5) ensure compliance with law" (EP 6.01). Because school psychological records may be used in special education due process hearing or other legal proceedings, practitioners have a responsibility to ensure "the kind of detail and quality that would be consistent with reasonable scrutiny in an adjudicative forum" (Nagy, 2000).

As noted in Chapter 1, school psychologists do not seek or store personal information about pupils, parents, teachers, or others that is not needed in the provision of services (EP Principle E, 4.04; NASP-PPE, III, B, #1). They also are obligated to ensure that records are stored in a manner that protects confidentiality (EP 4.01; NASP-PPE, IV, D, #5). They take special precautions to ensure that electronically stored information is safe from unauthorized access and that important information is not lost in the event of equipment failure (see "Technology in Communication and Recording Keeping" later in this chapter).

Under FERPA and IDEA, schools must establish policies regarding the storage, retrieval, and disposal of educational records. Under IDEA, parents of pupils with disabilities must be provided a summary of the school's record-keeping policies (34 C.F.R. § 300.561). Schools also must notify parents when personally identifiable information is no longer needed for providing educational services and, upon parent request, obsolete records must be destroyed (34 C.F.R. § 300.573). However, Turnbull and Turnbull (2000) recommend that schools advise parents that their child's records may be needed for purposes such as securing Social Security benefits.

How long should psychological records be maintained? We are not aware of any federal guidance with regard to how long school psychological records should be maintained, except that the school may not destroy any records if an outstanding request to review them exists. Attorneys advise psychologists in independent practice to keep records on minor clients from 5 to 10 years after the minor has reached the age of majority in the state where the psychologist practices (Bernstein & Hartsell, 1998; also see APA, 1993b). This advice is to ensure that records are maintained beyond the state statute of limitations for filing a lawsuit against the psychologist.

Practitioners should consult their state education laws and district policies for guidance with regard to what information to store, how to store it, and for how long and procedures for the periodic review of files and destruction of obsolete information. As Canter suggests (2001b), it may be desirable to specify different timelines for storage of different types of psychological records in the district's policies. She recommends that reports and summaries of psychological services be maintained "at least five years beyond the student's graduation or last day of enrollment, or until the date required by state law" (p. 19). If permitted under state law, test protocols and other raw data might be maintained for a shorter period. However, in our opinion, it is advisable to retain a student's test protocols until there is a pattern of relatively stable findings across multiple re-evaluations, at which time protocols and other raw data from early evaluations might be destroyed. Parents should be notified in advance of the district's intent to destroy such records (Canter, 2001b). Furthermore, when obsolete confidential information is purged from files, psychologists are obligated to ensure that it is shredded or otherwise destroyed (NASP-PPE, III, A, #9, IV, D, #5). (For additional information, see Canter, 2001b.)

Technology in Communication and Record Keeping

Computers and other technological devices can provide school personnel with quick access to pupil information. However, computerized record keeping may result in unauthorized access to student files and violations of the confidentiality of pupil records, particularly if a networked computer-information system is used. Confidentiality of student information can be protected by requiring passwords to gain access to sensitive files or by substituting child codes for names in computerized record keeping (see EP 6.02). Psychologists also should ensure that no one can recover confidential information from old or failed computers (or other hardware) after their disposal (McMinn, Buchanan, Ellens, & Ryan, 1999; also see Pfohl & Pfohl, 2002).

School psychologists need to ensure that "student/client records are not transmitted electronically without a guarantee of privacy. In line with this principle, a receiving fax machine must be in a secure location and operated by employees cleared to work with confidential files, and e-mail messages must be encrypted or else stripped of all information that identifies the student/client" (NASP-PPE, IV, E, #6). McMinn et al. (1999) also caution practitioners to consider whether messages left for the psychologist on answering machines and in voice mail boxes are secure from unauthorized access.

Computerized storage makes it possible to keep on file large amounts of information about individuals that may or may not be needed in the provision of services. As Zachary and Pope (1984) have suggested, the indiscriminate gathering and storage of nonessential personal information is an unnecessary invasion of privacy (also EP 4.04).

CONCLUDING COMMENTS

In light of the ethical and legal issues of privacy, confidentiality, and school record keeping, Eades' (1986) recommendation is helpful: School psychologists need to ensure that the statements they make orally or in writing are necessary, permitted, and required as a part of their employment and their professional responsibility to their client.

STUDY AND DISCUSSION

Questions for Chapter 3

1. What is "privacy?"
2. Do school children have a legal right to privacy in the public schools?
3. The chapter states that "Codes of ethics, professional standards, and law show growing agreement that informed consent should be obtained prior to the provision of school psychological services." What does *informed consent* mean?

(Continued)

4. Under what circumstances is it ethically permissible to provide psychological services to a child without his or her explicit assent for services?
5. Research suggests that involving children in treatment decisions may result in better treatment outcomes. What factors affect a child's capacity to participate effectively in treatment decisions?
6. What does *confidentiality* mean? Identify three situations in which the school psychologist is obligated to share student disclosures with others.
7. What is the *need-to-know* principle?
8. What is *privileged communication?* Who has the right to waive privilege in a legal proceeding?
9. Briefly discuss school responsibilities under FERPA with regard to (a) ensuring parent access to pupils records, (b) safeguarding the privacy of pupil's records, and (c) affording parents opportunities to ensure the accuracy of records.

Discussion

In this chapter, we recommend that school psychology practitioners encourage a child's participation in treatment decisions to the maximum extent appropriate to the child and the situation. This statement reflects our belief that children are individuals who should be given choices when feasible. This valuing of autonomy, choice, and independence has its foundation in Anglo-European culture and American psychology. In contrast, in many other cultures, children are seen as an extension of the parent; they are expected to obey authority, and they are not offered choices to make on their own (Lynch & Hanson, 1998). Discuss how contrasting beliefs about allowing a child to participate in decisions might effect psychologist-parent communication and collaboration when working with families from culturally diverse backgrounds (see Lynch & Hanson, 1998).

VIGNETTES

1. Todd, a student with a history of behavior problems, made an appointment with Sam Foster. Now that he has turned 18, he would like to see all of the psychological reports that have been written about him over the years. He also would like to restrict his parents' right of access to his school records. How should Sam respond? What are the ethical-legal issues involved? (Adapted from Davis & Mickelson, 1994)

2. Pearl Meadows opens her door to a man who states that he is the father of Jeff Blume, a child Pearl recently evaluated. The man asks politely to see the test results, including protocols, Pearl obtained. He also wants to know what comments, if any, Jeff may have made about his parents, as they are divorced, and Mr. Blume plans to go to court seeking custody of Jeff. What, if anything, should Pearl share with this man?

3. During a school vacation day, Sam Foster returned to campus to meet with his faculty advisor about completion of his Psy.D. degree. Because he was concerned about upcoming deadlines for psychological reports of students he has been evaluating in the district where he is an intern, Sam took several pupil folders with him to campus, completed the psychological reports using a computer in the campus computer lab, and then e-mailed the reports back to his secretary at work. What are the ethical problems associated with this situation?

4. As a result of Hannah Cook's assessment and other information gathered by the school's multidisciplinary team, the school recommended that John Malamo be classified as educable mentally impaired in the team meeting with his parents. Mr. Malamo is furious with Hannah and the school. He has made an appointment with Hannah to review the results of the psychological evaluation in more detail. When he appears for his appointment, Mr. Malamo demands copies of all information in John's psychological file, including the WISC-III test protocol, so that he can seek an independent opinion about John's needs from a psychologist in private practice. How should Hannah handle this situation?

Chapter 4

ETHICAL AND LEGAL ISSUES IN PSYCHOEDUCATIONAL ASSESSMENT

> Psychological testing and assessment techniques, in common with most tools, can be used for a diversity of purposes, some destructive and some constructive, and their use cannot be separated from the training, competence, and ethical values of the clinician-user. (Matarazzo, 1986, p. 18)

Surveys of school psychologists consistently have found that practitioners spend the greatest proportion of their professional time in assessment activities (Curtis, Hunley, Walker, & Baker, 1999). Based on a sample selected from the membership roster of the National Association of School Psychologists, Reschly and Wilson (1995) found that practitioners devote an average of 22 hours per week to assessment. This chapter focuses on ethical and legal issues associated with the school psychological assessment of individual pupils. School testing programs are discussed in Chapter 9.

TESTING VERSUS ASSESSMENT

In their work with teachers, parents, and children (and in their own thinking), it is important for school psychologists to distinguish between *testing* and *assessment.* Testing and assessment are not synonymous, interchangeable terms (Matarazzo, 1986, p. 18). A test is a tool that may be used to gather information as part of the assessment process.

Assessment is a broader term. Mowder has defined the assessment process as "the planning, collection, and evaluation of information pertinent to a psychoeducational concern" (1983, p. 145). Psychoeducational assessment is conducted by a psychologist trained to gather a variety of different types of information (review of school history and health records, observations, interviews, and test results) from a number of different sources (pupil, teacher, parents, and specialists) and to interpret or give meaning to that information in light of the unique characteristics of the pupil and his or her situation.

Practitioners also need to be familiar with the distinction between the medical and ecological models of school psychological assessment. In past years, practitioners often were trained to accept a medical model. The medical model views learning and behavior problems as a result of within-child disorders or disabilities (Ysseldyke & Christenson, 1988). In contrast, the ecological model encourages an assessment approach that takes into account the multiple factors that affect learning and behavior, including classroom variables, teacher and instructional variables, characteristics of the referred student, and support available from the home for school achievement. The ecological perspective has gained acceptance in recent years because it is viewed as potentially more beneficial to the child. In order to reverse a student's pattern of poor progress, systematic assessment of factors in the child's learning environment is needed (Ysseldyke & Christenson, 1988). Messick (1984) has suggested that, ethically, a child should not be exposed to the risk of misdiagnosis unless deficiencies in instruction first have been ruled out.

The psychologist has certain pre-assessment responsibilities to parent and pupil. After discussing these, we address ethical-legal concerns associated with assessment planning, selection of technically adequate tests and evaluation procedures, data collection and interpretation, report writing, and sharing findings. Nonbiased assessment and projective personality assessment then are discussed. The final portions of the chapter focus on the professional issues of competence and autonomy in conducting psychoeducational evaluations and the use of computers in assessment.

A number of ethical codes, professional standards, and legal documents provide guidelines for psychological assessment in schools. NASP's *Principles for Professional Ethics* (NASP-PPE) (2000) and APA's Ethical Principles of Psychologists and Code of Conduct (EP) (2002) each include ethical principles for psychological assessment. The *Standards for Educational and Psychological Testing* or *Standards* (American Educational Research Association, American Psychological Association, and National Council on Measurement in Education, 1999) provide criteria for psychologists and educators to use in "the evaluation of tests, testing practices, and the effects of test use" (p. 2). The *Standards* have no official legal status. However, the *Standards* have been referred to in federal regulations concerning acceptable testing practices, and they have been cited in Supreme Court cases as an authoritative source on issues concerning the technical adequacy of testing practices (Adler, 1993).

The Individuals with Disabilities Education Act (IDEA) and Section 504 of The Rehabilitation Act of 1973 each outline legal requirements for evaluation procedures used in the identification of children with disabilities. The regulations implementing IDEA-Part B that pertain to tests and evaluation procedures are shown in Exhibit 4–1.

Exhibit 4–1. Excerpt from the Regulations Implementing the Individuals with Disabilities Education Act

§300.531 Initial evaluation.

Each public agency shall conduct a full and individual initial evaluation, in accordance with §§300.532 and 300.533, before the initial provision of special education and related services to a child with a disability under Part B of the Act.

(Authority: 20 U.S.C. 1414(a)(1))

§300.532 Evaluation procedures.

Each public agency shall ensure, at a minimum, that the following requirements are met:

(a)

(1) Tests and other evaluation materials used to assess a child under Part B of the Act—

(i) Are selected and administered so as not to be discriminatory on a racial or cultural basis; and

(ii) Are provided and administered in the child's native language or other mode of communication, unless it is clearly not feasible to do so; and

(2) Materials and procedures used to assess a child with limited English proficiency are selected and administered to ensure that they measure the extent to which the child has a disability and needs special education, rather than measuring the child's English language skills.

(b) A variety of assessment tools and strategies are used to gather relevant functional and developmental information about the child, including information provided by the parent, and information related to enabling the child to be involved in and progress in the general curriculum (or for a preschool child, to participate in appropriate activities), that may assist in determining—

(1) Whether the child is a child with a disability under §300.7; and

(2) The content of the child's IEP.

(c)

(1) Any standardized tests that are given to a child—

(i) Have been validated for the specific purpose for which they are used; and

(ii) Are administered by trained and knowledgeable personnel in accordance with any instructions provided by the producer of the tests.

(2) If an assessment is not conducted under standard conditions, a description of the extent to which it varied from standard conditions (e.g., the qualifications of the person administering the test, or the method of test administration) must be included in the evaluation report.

(d) Tests and other evaluation materials include those tailored to assess specific areas of educational need and not merely those that are designed to provide a single general intelligence quotient.

(e) Tests are selected and administered so as best to ensure that if a test is administered to a child with impaired sensory, manual, or speaking skills, the test results accurately reflect the child's aptitude or achievement level or whatever other factors the test purports to measure, rather than reflecting the child's impaired sensory, manual, or speaking skills (unless those skills are the factors that the test purports to measure).

(f) No single procedure is used as the sole criterion for determining whether a child is a child with a disability and for determining an appropriate educational program for the child.

Exhibit 4–1. *(Continued)*

(g) The child is assessed in all areas related to the suspected disability, including, if appropriate, health, vision, hearing, social and emotional status, general intelligence, academic performance, communicative status, and motor abilities.

(h) In evaluating each child with a disability under §§ 300.531-300.536, the evaluation is sufficiently comprehensive to identify all of the child's special education and related services needs, whether or not commonly linked to the disability category in which the child has been classified.

(i) The public agency uses technically sound instruments that may assess the relative contribution of cognitive and behavioral factors, in addition to physical or developmental factors.

(j) The public agency uses assessment tools and strategies that provide relevant information that directly assists persons in determining the educational needs of the child.

(Authority: 20 U.S.C. 1412(a)(6)(B), 1414(b)(2) and (3))

PRE-ASSESSMENT RESPONSIBILITIES

When a school psychologist receives a referral for psychoeducational assessment, he or she is obligated to obtain informed consent prior to beginning the assessment procedures, and to ensure that the pupil is fully informed about the scope and nature of the assessment.

Parental Involvement and Consent

Codes of ethics and special education law contain provisions to ensure parental involvement when a pupil is referred for psychoeducational evaluation (NASP-PPE, III, C, #2; IDEA). Practitioners are ethically obligated to ensure that there is direct parent contact before beginning pupil assessment procedures (NASP-PPE, III, C, #2). This initial contact with the parents hopefully sets the stage for effective home–school collaboration.

Standards for professional practice require the informed consent of the parent (or student if of the age of majority) prior to initiating an individual psychological testing or assessment procedure (EP 9.03; *Standards*, p. 85). Under IDEA, written consent of the parent is needed for the initial pre-special education placement evaluation. Parent consent also is required for subsequent reevaluations, unless the school can demonstrate that it has taken reasonable measures to obtain consent and that the child's parent failed to respond (34 C.F.R. § 300.505).

Professional standards and regulations implementing IDEA are highly similar with regard to the necessary components of the informed consent agreement for psychoeducational assessment. According to the *Standards*

(Standard 8.4) and consistent with IDEA, the parent granting permission for the diagnostic evaluation should be made aware of the reasons for the assessment, the type of tests and evaluation procedures to be used, for what the assessment results will be used, and who will have access to the results. This information must be presented to the parent in his or her native language or other mode of communication. Many pupil services teams have developed materials for parents describing the evaluation procedures and assessment instruments used by multidisciplinary team members. Bersoff (1983) notes that a simple listing of the test names does not meet the intent of the law; an explanation of the nature and purpose of assessment instruments should be provided.

Psychologists also may wish to explain their professional commitment to maintaining test security during a preassessment meeting with parents. This will allow parents to know in advance that the psychologist has an ethical obligation to limit the disclosure of test items in reporting findings.

Most parents cooperate with school attempts to secure approval for psychoeducational assessment. However, a school has several means of overcoming parent refusal to consent (Bersoff, 1983). Under IDEA, the school may use mediation and other due process procedures (e.g., a hearing by an impartial hearing officer) to pursue evaluation of a child without parental consent (34 C.F.R. § 300.505). In unusual circumstances, state child neglect laws may provide another means to override parental refusal (Bersoff, 1983).

School psychologists should be aware that this requirement for parent consent prior to initiating an individual psychoeducational assessment does not extend to educational testing that is done as part of regular school activities (Standard 8.4; also IDEA 34 C.F.R. § 300.505). Parental permission for testing done as part of school-based research is discussed in Chapter 10.

Responsibilities to the Pupil

In addition to prior parental consent to initiate a psychoeducational evaluation, school psychologists also have a number of obligations to the student. As noted in Chapter 3, children are not seen as *legally* competent to make autonomous decisions about whether to participate in a psychological assessment; minors have no *legal* right "to consent, assent, or object to proposed psychoeducational evaluations" (Bersoff, 1983, p. 153). In our opinion, it is ethically permissible to assess a minor child without his or her explicit assent if the assessment promises to benefit his or her welfare (e.g., the planning of an individualized instructional program to enhance student learning). We concur with Corrao and Melton (1988) that it is disrespectful to solicit the assent of the child if refusal will not be honored. Consistent with good testing practices, practitioners need to make full use of their professional skills to gain the active cooperation of the pupil (NASP-PPE, III, B, #3).

Every student/client has the right to be fully informed about the scope and nature of the assessment process whether they are given a choice to assent to (or refuse) services. Practitioners are obligated ethically to explain the assessment process to the pupil in a manner that is understood by the student. This explanation includes the uses to be made of assessment information, who will receive information, and possible implications of results (NASP-PPE, III, B, #2). Even preschoolers and children who are developmentally disabled should receive an explanation in a language they can understand as to why they are being seen by the school psychologist (Standard 8.4).

ASSESSMENT PLANNING

Each phase of the assessment process—assessment planning, information gathering, and interpretation of findings—requires professional judgment and decision making. School psychologists are obligated to make decisions that promote the welfare of the student in each phase of the assessment process and accept responsibility for decisions made (NASP-PPE, I; III, A, #1). The following case description illustrates how psychological test results can have a powerful impact on the lives of children:

Case 4–1

Joseph McNulty was the unwanted child of a woman who was raped. He was placed in Willowbrook State Hospital in 1966 at the age of 4, after being diagnosed as "an imbecile" on the basis of an IQ score of 32. Subsequent re-evaluations suggested that Joseph had some hearing problems, but those findings were "initially ignored or simply not seen." Joseph grew up among severely retarded children and adults, and during his stay at Willowbrook, he was given high doses of drugs including Valium, Thorazine, and Haldol. In 1976, at the age of 14, an audiologist observed that Joseph showed a greater interest in learning than other severely retarded youth and confirmed that Joseph was hearing-impaired. After years of intensive therapy, Joseph's IQ tested in the normal range in 1980. In his late 20s, Joseph was not yet able to live independently, and he continued to need therapy and training. In 1988, he won a $1.5 million damage suit against the State of New York for medical malpractice (adapted from Bauder, 1989, p. B–1).

Five Ethical-Legal Concerns

Psychologists have long recognized that the use of an IQ score in isolation is not sound practice in the diagnosis of mental retardation. However, prior to the passage of Pub. L. No. 94–142 in 1975 (now IDEA), IQ test scores were frequently the sole basis for labeling children as mentally retarded (Matarazzo, 1986). The 1960s and 1970s were years of increasing court and federal government involvement in the regulation of psychological testing as a result of this type of misuse of tests.

Five broad ethical-legal concerns emerge from an analysis of our codes of ethics, professional standards, and federal laws that address psychological assessment: Psychologists must strive to ensure that psychoeducational evaluations are *multifaceted, comprehensive, fair, valid,* and *useful.* Each of these concerns will be addressed briefly, and then the selection of technically adequate assessment instruments will be discussed.

Multifaceted

Psychoeducational assessment of a child with learning or behavior problems must be based on a variety of different types of information from different sources. Practitioners "use multiple assessment methods such as observations, background information, and information from other professionals, to reach comprehensive conclusions" (NASP-PPE, IV, C, #3). No important decisions (e.g., special education classification) should be made on the basis of a single test score (34 C.F.R. § 300.532; Standard 13.7).

Comprehensive

Children with suspected disabilities must be assessed "in all areas related to the suspected disability, including, if appropriate, health, vision, hearing, social and emotional status, general intelligence, academic performance, communicative status, and motor abilities" (34 C.F.R. § 300.532). As was apparent in Case 4–1, failure to have a child evaluated for possible sensory impairments can result in misdiagnosis with tragic consequences for the child.

Fair

In the selection of assessment tools, the psychologist strives to choose the most appropriate instruments and procedures in light of the child's age, gender, native language, disabilities, and socioeconomic and ethnic background (NASP-PPE, IV, C, #1; also EP 9.02). Regulations implementing

IDEA-Part B outline requirements for the assessment of children with limited English proficiency, pupils with disabilities, and those from culturally different backgrounds.

Limited English Proficiency. Regulations implementing IDEA-Part B require that tests and other evaluation materials used in the evaluation of children with suspected disabilities are "provided and administered in the child's native language or other mode of communication, unless it is clearly not feasible to do so" (34 C.F.R. § 300.352; also EP 9.02; *Standards* pp. 91–100). Furthermore, "Materials and procedures used to assess a child with limited English proficiency are selected and administered to ensure that they measure the extent to which the child has a disability and needs special education, rather than measuring the child's English language skills" (34 C.F.R. § 300.352). *Native language* is defined as "the language normally used by the child in the home or learning environment" (34 C.F.R. § 300.19).

According to Dana (2000) and Paredes Scribner (2002), competent assessment of children from culturally and linguistically diverse backgrounds requires the practitioner to gather information about the family's degree of acculturation and to assess the child's language proficiency *prior* to selecting assessment tools. For children who come from homes where English is not the primary language, it is important to assess both the child's native and English language proficiency. This assessment should include evaluation of spoken and written language skills in each language, using both formal and informal measures, in order to obtain a full picture of functional language usage (Lopez, 1997). Language proficiency information is needed to guide selection and interpretation of measures of aptitude, achievement, and adaptive behavior, and in planning instruction and interventions (see Jitendra & Rohena-Diaz, 1996; Paredes Scribner, 2002). Even if a child from a culturally different background demonstrates some proficiency in spoken or written English, it is important to remember that commonly used tests (e.g., Wechsler Intelligence Test for Children-III, Wechsler, 1991) tap the language, symbols, and knowledge children encounter in the dominant U.S. culture and schools. Consequently, practitioners must also consider the degree of acculturation of the child and his or her family in selecting and interpreting assessment tools (see "Nonbiased Assessment" later in this chapter).

The National Association of School Psychologists maintains a directory of bilingual school psychologists who may be available to assist in the assessment of a child with limited English proficiency. When a bilingual psychologist is not available, and the services of an interpreter are used during psychological assessment, the psychologist is obligated ethically to obtain consent for the use of an interpreter, ensure that the interpreter is adequately trained to assist in the assessment (including training in maintaining confidentiality), and report any limitations regarding the results obtained (EP 9.03; also *Standards* pp. 95–96). In addition, the practitioner is obligated to ensure that he or she has the necessary skills to work effectively with an interpreter (APA, 1993; also Lopez, 2002).

When assessing the cognitive abilities, adaptive behavior, or achievement of a child whose native language is not English, the examiner should select tests or portions of tests that do not require knowledge of English (34 C.F.R. § 300.352). Practitioners are advised not to translate (or have an interpreter translate) items from a test developed for English-speaking examinees into the child's native language because translation of an item is likely to change item difficulty (Figueroa, 1990; Rogers et al., 1999; *Standards*, 1999, p. 92, 95). An "on-the-spot" translation of a test or subtest thus results in scores of unknown validity. In accordance with the *Standards*, when a test is translated, it must be restandardized in the new language. The test publisher is obligated to describe the methods used in establishing the adequacy of the translation and the evidence for reliability and validity of the translated test's scores. As many dialects and differences in word usage exist among groups with the same official language (e.g., Spanish), the test producer should identify the intended target linguistic groups for the test (e.g., Cubans, Puerto Ricans, Mexicans) and provide evidence of score validity for each linguistic group (Standard 9.7).

Children with Disabilities. IDEA-Part B also mandates careful selection of assessment procedures for children with sensory, motor, or speech impairments. Children with deafness or blindness or no written language must be evaluated using "the mode of communication that is normally used by the individual (such as sign language, braille, or oral communication)" (34 C.F.R. § 300.19). Furthermore, tests "are selected and administered so as best to ensure that if a test is administered to a child with impaired sensory, manual, or speaking skills, the test results accurately reflect that child's aptitude or achievement level, or whatever other factors the test purports to measure, rather than reflecting the child's impaired sensory, manual, or speaking skills (unless those are the factors which the test purports to measure)" (34 C.F.R. § 300.532; also see *Standards*, 1999).

Ethnic Minority Children. Codes of ethics, professional standards, and special education law also mandate *nonbiased* assessment of children from minority cultural, ethnic, and racial backgrounds. As the issue of bias is complex, it is discussed separately later in the chapter.

Valid

School psychologists are obligated to select tests and other evaluation procedures that meet high professional standards and that have been validated for the purpose for which they are used (NASP-PPE, IV, C, #2; also EP 9.02; *Standards* pp. 9–24; 34 C.F.R. § 300.532).

Useful

Evaluation procedures must be selected to provide a profile of the child's strengths and difficulties to aid in instructional planning. Regulations implementing IDEA state that, "Tests and other evaluation materials include those tailored to assess specific areas of educational need and not merely those that are designed to provide a single general intelligence quotient" (34 C.F.R. § 300.532). The assessment is planned to ensure that the information gathered will result in maximum feasible assistance to the child (NASP-PPE, IV, C, #2, #7).

Selecting Technically Adequate Instruments

School psychology practitioners select assessment techniques that are consistent with responsible, evidence-based practice (NASP-PPE, IV, C, #4; also EP 9.02). As previously mentioned, the *Standards* were developed to guide selection of instruments for a variety of different measurement applications (psychodiagnosis, applicant selection for jobs and colleges, program evaluation, research) in diverse settings. Consequently, absolute psychometric standards of technical adequacy based on specific statistical procedures are not prescribed. Evaluating the adequacy of assessment practices ultimately rests with the test user and involves professional judgment based on knowledge of behavior science, psychometrics, and assessment standards for the field; the degree to which the test developer has met the intent of the *Standards*; and knowledge of alternatives (*Standards,* 1999, p. 4).

When assessment results play an important role in decision making for the individual pupil, the school psychologist is obligated to choose the best available assessment procedures. Considerable agreement exists in the school psychology literature that a variety of different types of information are appropriate within the framework of a *successive-levels model* of psychoeducational assessment. Consistent with this model, primary emphasis is given to scores and information from the most reliable and valid sources (e.g., composite scores on technically adequate measures) in interpretation and decision making. However, findings from less reliable and valid sources (scores on various subtest groups, individual subtest scores, performance on individual items, observations, and impressions) may also play a role in generating hypotheses about the student's profile of abilities, skills, and needs. These hypotheses then may be confirmed or abandoned by collecting additional information that verifies (i.e., cross-validates) or disconfirms the hypothesis (Kaufman, 1994).

According to the *Standards*, evaluating the technical adequacy of assessment instruments and procedures involves careful consideration of the evidence for test *reliability*, *validity*, and the *adequacy of the standardization norms*. Each of these areas is addressed next.

Test Reliability

Test reliability refers to the consistency of test scores when a testing procedure is repeated on a group of individuals. Two types of reliability information should be reported in the manuals for tests to be used in psychoeducational decision making: test stability and internal consistency reliability. *Test stability* or *test-retest reliability* studies provide information about the consistency of scores from one testing session to another. This information typically is obtained by administering the same test to the same group of examinees on two occasions and correlating the resultant test scores (Sattler, 2001).

Internal consistency reliability is based on scores obtained during one administration of the test. The reliability coefficient obtained in this manner provides information about the extent to which items on the test are intercorrelated. According to the *Standards*, coefficients of internal consistency should not be substituted for estimates of stability unless evidence supports that interpretation in a particular context (p. 28).

How reliable must a test be? There is no simple answer to this question. Shorter, less time-consuming, and less reliable measures may be adequate when tests are selected to provide information about groups rather than individuals (as in program evaluation and research) or when the results are used for decisions that are tentative and reversible (as when teacher-made tests are used to group children for reading instruction). A review of the literature suggests that some consensus exists in the field of school psychology about desirable levels of reliability for tests used in the schools. Reliability coefficients of .60 to .65 are seen as adequate for measures of group performance, coefficients of .80 to .85 are acceptable for screening instruments, and correlations of .90 or above are desirable for instruments that play a key role in making educational decisions about individual pupils (Hammill, Brown, & Bryant, 1989; Sattler, 2001).

Test producers have primary responsibility to obtain and report reliability information (*Standards*, p. 30). Unlike some types of validity information (e.g., predictive validity) that require a longitudinal design, reliability data can be gathered during test development and standardization and should be included in the supporting manuals when the test is marketed. The *Standards* recommend that reliability estimates be provided for each total score, subscore, or combination of scores that the test reports (Standard 2.1). Both internal consistency and test stability estimates should be reported for each age or grade level and population for which the test is intended, along with a description of the research procedures and sample used in the reliability studies (Standard 2.4, 2.12). The test user is responsible for evaluating this information to ensure that the test selected is reliable for its intended use.

Validity

Validity is the single most important consideration in evaluating tests and assessment procedures (*Standards*, p. 9). Validity refers to the degree to which a test or assessment procedure measures what it purports to measure. However, "no test is valid for all purposes or valid in the abstract;" tests are valid (or not valid) for a specific purpose (Sattler, 2001, p. 115). IDEA requires that assessment instruments used in the identification of children with suspected disabilities "have been validated for the specific purpose for which they are used" (34 C.F.R. § 300.532).

As noted in the *Standards*, "Validity is a unitary concept. It is the degree to which all the accumulated evidence supports the intended interpretation of test scores for the proposed purpose" (1999, p. 11). However, test producers gather and report validity information in a number of different ways. A distinction is often made among content-related, criterion-related, and construct-related validity.

Content-related validity refers to the degree to which the sample of items, tasks, or questions on a test are representative of the domain that the test is supposed to measure (Sattler, 2001). Test authors are obligated to specify adequately the universe of content that a test is intended to represent and provide evidence that the test content agrees with specifications of what the test should measure (Standard 1.6).

Criterion-related validity refers to evidence that test scores are related systematically to one or more criterion or outcome (Sattler, 2001). Criterion-related validity typically is reported as a correlation between scores on the test and scores on some type of outcome of interest called the "criterion" measure. As suggested in the *Standards*, the key issue is "How accurately do test scores predict criterion performance?" (p. 14).

Two types of criterion-related evidence may be provided. Concurrent validity studies involve obtaining information from the predictor and criterion measures at the same point in time. Predictive validity studies involve administering the criterion measure after a specified time interval in order to evaluate how well a test correlates with future performance.

What levels of criterion-related validity are acceptable for tests used in psychoeducational assessment? Again, no simple answer exists. Estimates of criterion-related validity are affected by a number of factors including the extent to which the predictor and criterion tests measure the same traits and abilities, the reliability of the predictor and criterion measures, the heterogeneity or spread of scores on either measure, and the time interval between the administration of the two measures (see Gregory, 2000). According to the *Standards,* criterion-related validity studies should be described by the test producer in enough detail to evaluate the adequacy of the research design and findings. This description should include the types of test-takers, research procedures including the time interval between tests, and statistical analysis including any correction for attenuation of range of scores (Standard 1.15,1.18). The psychometric characteristics of the criterion measure also should be described in detail (Standard 1.16).

Construct validity is "a term used to indicate that the test scores are to be interpreted as indicating the test taker's standing on the psychological construct measured by the test" (*Standards*, p. 174). This type of validity focuses on the test score as a measure of a construct (i.e., psychological characteristic or trait) such as intelligence, scholastic ability, reading comprehension, anxiety, or sociability. No single study can establish the construct validity of a test or other measure (Messick, 1995). Evidence for construct validity may be based on studies of test content (item analysis, factor analysis) and an accumulation of evidence based on a multitrait–multimethod construct validation paradigm. This model of construct validation suggests that evidence should be provided showing that the test correlates well with other measures of the same construct (convergent evidence) but does not correlate highly with measures of theoretically unrelated constructs (discriminant evidence) (Campbell & Fiske, 1959).

How do you decide whether a test instrument is valid? Both the quality and quantity of the supporting evidence are important in evaluating the validity of a test for the child being evaluated (*Standards,* p. 17). Although the test manual and supportive materials are the starting points for test review, practitioners are obligated ethically to keep abreast of the recent research related to the validity of tests used in psychoeducational diagnosis.

Adequacy of Test Norms

Norm-referenced tests allow us to interpret a child's test performance in comparison with a reference group of children of the same age, in the same grade, or perhaps with the same type of disability. In selecting norm-referenced instruments, the school psychologist has a responsibility to evaluate the adequacy and appropriateness of the test norms for the intended use of the test. Test norms must be (a) based on a sample representative of the intended target population for the test, (b) recent, and (c) appropriate for the child being evaluated.

Test producers have a responsibility to identify the intended target population for a test and to describe fully the extent to which the norm group is characteristic of that specific population. Norming studies should be described in the test manual or supportive materials in sufficient detail for the user to evaluate their adequacy and appropriateness for intended test use (Standard 4.6). Test users have a responsibility to evaluate the extent to which the children they test are represented within the published norms.

INFORMATION GATHERING

Ethical-legal concerns that arise during information gathering include ensuring that assessment procedures are administered by qualified examiners under appropriate conditions, and that family and pupil privacy are respected.

Invasion of Privacy

The school psychologist seeks to gather the information needed to develop a picture of the pupil that is comprehensive enough to be useful in decision making and in planning appropriate interventions. However, in responsible psychological assessment, the practitioner also remains sensitive to pupil and family privacy (Matarazzo, 1986). School psychologists are obligated ethically to respect the privacy of others (EP Principle E). They do not seek or store personal information about the student/client, parents, teachers, or others that is not needed in the provision of services (EP 4.04).

Assessment Conditions

School psychologists must ensure that the assessment conditions are in the best interests of the pupil being evaluated. The testing environment should be of "reasonable comfort and with minimal distractions" (Standard 5.4); otherwise, findings may not be accurate and valid. Testing done by computers should be monitored to ensure that results are not adversely affected by a lack of computer test-taking skills or by problems with the equipment (*Standards,* p. 62).

In accordance with professional standards and law, tests and other assessment procedures must be "administered by trained personnel in accordance with the instructions provided by the producer of the tests" (34 C.F.R. § 300.352). Practitioners are obligated to "follow carefully the standardized procedures for administration and scoring specified by the test developer, unless the situation or a test taker's disability dictates that an exception should be made" (Standard 5.1). Modifications are based on carefully considered professional judgment. Furthermore, "If an assessment is not conducted under standard conditions, a description of the extent to which it varied from standard conditions ... must be included in the evaluation report" (34 C.F.R. § 300.352; also EP 9.06; NASP-PPE, IV, D, #3; Standard 5.2).

Psychological and educational tests should be administered only by individuals qualified to do so (EP 9.07). "School psychologists do not condone the use of psychological or educational assessment techniques ... by unqualified persons in any way" (NASP-PPE, IV, C, #5).

Test Security

The development of valid assessment instruments requires extensive research and considerable expense. Disclosure of the underlying principles or specific content of a test is likely to decrease its validity for future examinees. Disclosure of test content also may infringe on the intellectual property and/or copyright interests of the test producer (APA, 1996c). APA's code states that psychologists are obligated to "make reasonable efforts to maintain the integrity and security of test materials and other assessment techniques consistent with law, contractual obligations, and in a manner that permits adherence to this Ethics Code" (EP 9.11; also NASP-PPE, IV, E, #1; Standards 11.7, 11.8).

ASSESSMENT INTERPRETATION

School psychologists combine observations, background information, multidisciplinary results, and other pertinent data in order to reach comprehensive conclusions and present the most valid picture possible of the student (NASP-PPE, IV, C, #3). As noted previously, in reporting assessment results, psychologists indicate any reservations that exist concerning validity or reliability due to assessment circumstances or norm appropriateness (EP 9.06; NASP-PPE, IV, D, #3).

Psychologists also are obligated to ensure that assessment results are useful. Psychologists use assessment tools and strategies "that provide relevant information that directly assists persons in determining the educational needs of the child" (34 C.F.R. § 300.532). Assessment findings should be linked to appropriate intervention strategies. Criterion-referenced testing and curriculum-based assessment are assessment strategies that have gained popularity because they facilitate the linking of data gathered to appropriate instructional interventions (see Shinn, 2002).

Psychological assessment often results in the assignment of a formal diagnostic label. Legally and ethically, practitioners are obligated to ensure that when labels are assigned they are based on valid assessment procedures and sound professional judgment. Furthermore, when labels are used, "The least stigmatizing labels, consistent with accurate representation, should always be assigned" (Standard 8.8).

Report Writing and Sharing Findings

School psychologists typically share their assessment findings in written reports and orally in meetings with the parties involved. Ethically, the practitioner must ensure that they "adequately interpret information so that the recipient can better help the child or other clients" (NASP-PPE, IV, D, #1).

Report Writing

The written psychological report documents the assessment process and outcomes and outlines recommendations to assist the child. It potentially serves a number of different purposes. It may be used in making special education decisions and identifying instructional needs. It may serve as a history of psychological performance for subsequent evaluations of pupil progress or deterioration. It also may be used as a communication tool in referrals to professionals outside the school setting (neurologist, clinical psychologist) and as documentation in a legal proceeding such as hearings and court procedures (Sattler, 2001).

Along with these potential multiple purposes, the writer of a psychological report must take into account the fact that it may be read by professionals and nonprofessionals (Harvey, 1997). IDEA requires that parents be given a copy of their child's evaluation report (34 C.F.R. § 300.534). In accordance with NASP's code of ethics, school psychologists take responsibility for preparing information that is written in terms that are "readily understood by the intended recipient" (NASP-PPE, IV, D, #2). Furthermore, as noted previously, reports should emphasize recommendations and interpretations rather than a simple passing along of test scores (NASP-PPE, IV, D, #1, #3). Unedited computer-generated reports and preprinted check-off or fill-in-the-blank reports are seldom useful (NASP-PPE, IV, D, #3).

School psychologists also are obligated to ensure the accuracy of their reports by reviewing them and signing them only when correct

(NASP-PPE, IV, D, #4). Reports prepared by interns and practicum students should be cosigned by the supervising school psychologist (NASP-PPE, IV, D, #4). Alterations of reports previously released should be done only by the original author of the report (NASP-PPE, IV, D, #3).

Practitioners ensure the confidentiality of assessment findings as outlined in Chapter 3, and they ensure that assessment findings are not misused by unqualified persons (NASP-PPE, III, A, #9).

Sharing Findings with the Parent and Pupil

School psychologists "secure continuing parental involvement by a frank and prompt reporting to the parent of findings and progress" (NASP-PPE, III, C, #2; also EP 9.10; Standard 5.10). School psychologists are obligated to confer with parents in language understandable to the parent and "strive to propose a set of options that takes into account the values and capabilities of each parent" (NASP-PPE, III, C, #1). Discussion includes recommendations for assisting the student and alternatives associated with each set of plans. These suggestions "show respect for the ethnic/cultural values of the family" (NASP-PPE, III, C, #5). (Also see Chapter 8.)

School psychologists also discuss the outcomes of the assessment with the student. Recommendations for program changes or additional services are discussed with the student, along with any alternatives that may be available (NASP-PPE, III, B, #4). Ethical codes and professional standards clearly indicate that the student should be afforded opportunities to share in decision making.

NONBIASED ASSESSMENT

In Chapter 1, we suggested that psychologists have an ethical obligation to help ensure that the science of psychology is used to promote human welfare in the schools, neighborhoods, and communities in which they work and in the larger society. Unfortunately, American history is replete with examples of the ways in which the "science" of psychology has been used to oppress ethnic, racial, and linguistic minorities in the United States and justify discriminatory practices in society and in our schools. For example, following the introduction of the Stanford-Binet Intelligence Scales in 1916 and the development of group ability tests, IQ tests were used to characterize Negroes as a genetically inferior race and justify discriminatory treatment in society, to characterize non-Anglo immigrants as intellectually inferior and therefore undesirable, and in support of laws allowing sterilization of women of below normal IQ without their consent (Gould, 1996). In schools, IQ and other mental ability tests have been used to track and segregate ethnic, racial, and linguistic minority pupils in inferior, dead-end classes; to deny them access to the college preparatory curriculum; to misclassify them as retarded; and to justify their placement in poorly equipped special education classes taught by inadequately trained staff (see Exhibit 5–2). School psychology practitioners need to be knowledgeable of the history of the misuse of tests in the United States so that they can understand the roots of current controversies regarding the use of IQ tests with children from diverse backgrounds, as well as the concerns of parents of ethnic, racial, and linguistic minority children referred for psychological testing (see Appendix D).

Today, nonbiased assessment is both an ethical and a legal mandate. IDEA requires that, "Tests and other evaluation materials used to assess a child are selected and administered so as not to be discriminatory on a racial or cultural basis" (34 C.F.R. § 300.530). Our codes of ethics and professional standards include multiple statements with regard to valid and fair assessment of clients from culturally diverse backgrounds. APA's *Ethical Principles of Psychologists* addresses these issues in General Principles D (Justice) and E (Respect for People's Rights and Dignity), Standards 2.01 (Competence), 2.05 (Delegation of Work to Others), 3.01 (Unfair Discrimination), 9.02 (Use of Assessments); and 9.06 (Interpreting Assessment Results) (also APA, 1993). NASP's *Principles for Professional Ethics* also includes multiple statements with regard to valid and fair assessment of diverse students (III, A, #2; C, #3, IV, C, #1; #2). In addition, the *Standards* (1999) includes extensive discussion of fairness in testing.

Although the ethical, professional, and legal mandate for nonbiased assessment is clear, it is not easy to translate the "nondiscrimination principle" into practice. As Reschly and Bersoff note, "widely varying" interpretations of the meaning of nondiscriminatory assessment have appeared in the professional literature and court interpretations (1999, p. 1085).

Culture and Acculturation

Although little consensus exists regarding the meaning of nonbiased assessment, there appears to be growing agreement in the professional literature that competent assessment of children from culturally different backgrounds requires the practitioners to seek knowledge of the child's culture and how that background may influence development, behavior, and school learning and gather information about the pupil's degree of acculturation (APA, 1993; Dana, 2000; Rogers et al., 1999, Sattler, 2001; *Standards*, 1999, p. 91).

With regard to the pupil's degree of acculturation, Dana views *cultural orientation* on a continuum ranging from traditional (retention of original culture) to nontraditional (assimilation into the majority Anglo-American culture) (2000, p. 60). Information about cultural orientation can be gathered through interviews with the pupil and his or her family, and a number of acculturation measures also are available (see Aponte & Johnson, 2000, p. 24). Information about acculturation should inform test selection, examiner interactional style, assessment interpretation, and intervention planning. The closer a pupil's cultural orientation falls toward the "traditional" end of the continuum, the greater the need for caution in use and interpretation of IQ measures that draw upon knowledge of language, symbols, and information specific to the dominant U.S. culture. For some groups, such as African-American children, information about *cultural identity* may assist in providing effective services (see Dana, 2000).

Test Bias

For the purposes of the following discussion, bias in assessment will be discussed in terms of *test bias, bias in clinical application,* and *fairness of consequences. Test bias* here refers to the psychometric adequacy of the instrument; that is, evidence that a test or procedure is not equally valid when used with children from differing ethnic or racial backgrounds (Coles, 1981; Messick, 1965, 1980; Reynolds, Lowe, & Saenz, 1999). In selecting tests for minority group children, the practitioner needs to ask, "Is this test a valid measure of what it purports to measure for examinees from this ethnic group?"

Test bias may be defined and evaluated in terms of *content validity, criterion-related validity,* and *construct validity.* "An item or subscale of a test is considered to be biased in content when it is demonstrated to be relatively more difficult for members of one group than another when the general ability level of the groups being compared is held constant and no reasonable theoretical rationale exists to explain group differences on the item (or subscale) in question" (Reynolds et al., 1999, p. 564). The question of content bias is resolved by research that shows equal (or unequal) item difficulties for various groups (Flaugher, 1978). Biased items usually can be identified and eliminated during the test development phase. Reynolds et al. (1999) reviewed available studies and found little evidence of any consistent content bias in well-prepared, standardized tests when such tests are used with English-speaking examinees. When content bias was found, it accounted for a relatively small proportion of the variance (2–5%) in the group score differences associated with minority group membership.

Test bias may also be defined in terms of differential concurrent or predictive (criterion-related) validity. "A test is considered biased with respect to predictive validity if the inference drawn from the test score is not made with the smallest feasible random error or if there is constant error in an inference or prediction as a function of membership in a particular group" (Reynolds et al., 1999, p. 577). A test may be shown to be nonbiased in criterion-related validity if it predicts the criterion-measure performance equally well for children from different ethnic backgrounds. Based on a review of the school psychology literature, Brown, Reynolds, and Whitaker (1999) concluded that "empirical evidence overwhelmingly supports the conclusion that well-developed, currently-used mental tests are of equivalent predictive validity for American-born, English-speaking individuals regardless of their subgroup membership" (p. 231). Less is known about bias in adaptive behavior and personality assessment instruments.

Test bias may also be defined in terms of construct validity. "Bias exists in regard to construct validity when a test is shown to measure different hypothetical traits (psychological constructs) for different groups; that is, differing interpretations of a common performance are shown to be appropriate as a function of ethnicity, gender, or another variable of interest" (Reynolds et al., 1999, p. 573). Studies that show a test has the same factor structure for children from different ethnic backgrounds provide evidence that the test is measuring the same construct for different groups; that it is nonbiased with respect to construct validity. Reynolds et al. (1999) reported "no consistent evidence of bias in construct validity" was found with any of the well-constructed and well-standardized tests they investigated (p. 577).

The *Standards* recommends that test developers research and report results of differential concurrent and predictive validity studies for various groups, particularly if test results may be used in making classification decisions (*Standards*, p. 79, Standard 7.1). The practitioner is obligated to evaluate the research on test bias when selecting instruments for ethnic minority children and to choose the fairest and most appropriate instruments available.

Bias in Clinical Application

Bias in clinical application refers to fairness in administration, interpretation, and decision making. The use of biased tests may lead to unfair decisions. However, poor decisions can be made on the basis of fair tests because of atmosphere bias and bias in interpretation and/or decision making. *Atmosphere bias* refers to factors in the testing situation that may inhibit performance of children from ethnic minority backgrounds (Flaugher, 1978). As noted previously, practitioners are obligated to seek knowledge of the child's background so that they can build and maintain rapport during testing in a culturally sensitive manner (see Appendix D).

Atmosphere bias may occur because of limited test-taking skills (e.g., lack of responsiveness to speed pressures), wariness of the examiner (e.g., race of the examiner effects, reluctance to verbalize), and differences in cognitive style and test achievement motivation that hinder optimal performance. Sattler (2001) suggests that atmosphere bias can be minimized by a competent, well-trained examiner who is sensitive to the child's personal, linguistic, and cultural background. (See Frisby [1999a,1999b] for a comprehensive review of the empirical literature on culture/ethnicity of the examinee, test session behaviors, and test performance.)

As Ortiz (2002) observed, "Although psychometric data are often viewed as objective, they have no inherent meaning and derive significance only from interpretation" (2002, p. 1323). To minimize bias in data collection and interpretation, he suggests the process of assessment ". . . begin with the hypothesis that the examinee's difficulties are not intrinsic in nature, but rather that they are more likely attributable to external or environmental problems" (p. 1323). Examiners must use their knowledge of students' unique experiences and backgrounds to evaluate and interpret all information gathered. The hypothesis of normality is not rejected unless the data strongly suggest the contrary.

Fairness in Consequences

A third area of concern is *fairness of the consequences* of test use. This involves an appraisal of the outcomes or consequences of test use for a particular group (Messick, 1980). If testing and assessment practices result in children from a particular ethnic group being placed in inferior educational programs, then the outcomes or consequences of testing are biased and unfair, no matter how adequate the tests and decision-making procedures (Reschly, 1997; also *Standards*, p. 80).

Closing Comments on Nonbiased Assessment

In these closing comments on nonbiased assessment, we refer the reader back to Messick's (1984) statement that, consistent with responsible, ethical practice, no child should be seen for psychological evaluation unless deficiencies in instruction have first been ruled out. A service delivery model that emphasizes early (prereferral) intervention may help safeguard ethnic, racial, and linguistic minority children from unnecessary testing and the risk of misdiagnosis or misclassification. By working with teachers and parents to pinpoint learning and behavior problems before they become severe and by intervening early, many problems can be remedied without formal psychological assessment. If, however, such efforts to remediate problems are unsuccessful, and a psychological assessment is needed, "best practice" recommendations to avoid assessment bias are summarized as follows: The practitioner should (a) be knowledgeable of the child's culture and able to establish and maintain rapport in a culturally sensitive manner; (b) consider the influence of culture and the degree of acculturation in selecting assessment methods; (c) gather developmental, health, family, and school history information; (d) observe the child in the classroom and other settings as appropriate to the problem; (e) consider teacher characteristics, instructional variables, classroom factors, and support available from the home in understanding the child's difficulties and possible interventions; (f) use a variety of formal and less formal assessment strategies, including interviews, behavioral assessments, evaluation of classroom work samples, curriculum-based assessment, testing-the-limits, and test-teach-test; and (g) interpret findings in light of the child's background, to ensure a valid and useful picture of the child's abilities and educational needs (Figueroa, 1990; Ortiz, 2002, also see APA, 1993). Practitioners also assume responsibility for monitoring the outcomes of assessment for culturally diverse pupils in their schools to ensure that the consequences of testing are fair and in the best interests of children.

PERSONALITY ASSESSMENT

Three ethical-legal concerns associated with the use of personality tests in the schools, in particular projective techniques, have been identified in the literature. First, there has been a long-standing concern among psychologists that the use of personality tests may result in unwarranted invasion of privacy (Messick, 1965). Personality tests have been a special focus of concern because, unlike achievement or ability tests, questions on personality tests are often indirect, and the test-taker may unknowingly reveal aspects of the self, including emotional problems, that he or she is not prepared to unveil (Messick, 1965).

Two strategies to safeguard privacy in the use of personality tests have been suggested. First, consistent with ethical codes and legal requirements (e.g., IDEA), explicit informed consent should be obtained before administering such tests, and second, the psychologist must consider carefully whether the use of such tests is justified in assisting the pupil; that is, weigh the risk of intrusion on pupil and family privacy against the likelihood that such techniques will result in information helpful in promoting pupil welfare.

A second ethical-legal issue specific to the use of projective personality tests in the schools focuses on whether such tests meet professional and legal standards for demonstrated test validity. A number of writers have argued that evidence for the technical adequacy of many projective techniques is lacking or does not support their use with children and that projective test results appear to lack educational relevance (Batsche & Peterson, 1983; but also see Knoff, 1983).

There can be no absolute answer about whether or not to use projectives with school children. Concerns about the validity and usefulness of personality tests, like other assessment tools, are appropriately addressed by considering test properties in relation to the purposes of the assessment (Messick, 1965; *Standards,* 1999). Practitioners must strive to select tests that have demonstrated validity for the purpose used and ensure that findings are cross-validated within the framework of a multimethod model.

A third concern about the use of projectives is that school psychologists may not be adequately trained in their use. Consistent with the broad ethical principle of responsible caring, school psychologists must evaluate their own competence to use particular assessment strategies. Practitioners who use personality tests need to have knowledge of the test's conceptual model of personality development and deviation, skills in the administration and interpretation of the particular assessment tool, and competent judgment about when to use that test or strategy. Projective tests should be used only by psychologists with verifiable training in their use.

PROFESSIONAL COMPETENCE AND AUTONOMY

In order to ensure valid results, psychologists must offer assessment services only within the boundaries of their competence, and they must insist on professional autonomy in the selection of assessment methods.

Competence

School psychologists are obligated ethically to recognize and define the boundaries of their competence and to offer assessment services only within those boundaries (EP 2.01; NASP-PPE, II, A, #1, #2; Standard 11.3). Psychologists who step beyond their competence in assessing children place students at risk for misdiagnosis, misclassification, miseducation, and possible psychological harm. This question of competence is likely to arise when practitioners are asked to assess children whose characteristics (e.g., age, native language, or cultural background) or suspected problems are outside the scope of their training or supervised experience as illustrated in Case 4-2. In such situations, practitioners need to "enlist the assistance of other specialists in supervisory, consultative or referral roles as appropriate in providing services" (NASP-PPE, II, A, #1).

Case 4–2

Hannah Cook accepted a position as a school psychologist with an Intermediate School District in Michigan after working for several years as a school psychologist in another state. Her graduate coursework and prior work experiences focused only on school-aged children; she had no formal training in preschool child development and assessment. In her new job in Michigan, she began receiving referrals for the evaluation of infants with suspected developmental delays. She read the Bayley Scales manual and began conducting assessments of the referred babies (adapted from Koocher & Keith-Spiegel, 1998).

As noted previously, it has become increasingly important for practitioners to assess their competence to provide services to a diverse clientele and to acquire the knowledge and skills needed to conduct a valid psychoeducational assessment with pupils they typically serve in their work setting (see EP 2.01). Practitioners are well-advised to develop a directory of colleagues with expertise in evaluating children from special backgrounds or with low-incidence disabilities. Seeking assistance through supervision, consultation, and referral are appropriate strategies for psychologists faced with a difficult or unusual case. However, practitioners who plan to shift or expand their services to a new age group or special pupil population are obligated to seek formal training or professional supervision before offering such services. Hannah was obligated to clarify the scope of her expertise before accepting the position in Michigan and make arrangements for training (coursework and/or supervised experience) before accepting referrals for infant assessments.

Professional Autonomy

IDEA-Part B requires the consideration of certain types of pupil information in the evaluation of children with suspected disabilities. For example, intellectual ability, achievement, adaptive behavior, and developmental history all must be considered in the evaluation of children who may qualify for services as mentally impaired. State education laws and local district policy may specify additional *types* of information to be considered in evaluation of children with suspected disabilities. School psychologists need to be knowledgeable of these requirements.

However, in order to serve the best interests of the student, school psychologists must insist on professional autonomy in the selection of specific assessment instruments and procedures.

Case 4–3

A Director of Special Education felt clearer guidelines were needed to determine whether or not children qualified as learning disabled under IDEA-Part B. He developed a district policy that required all children with suspected learning disabilities to be evaluated using the Woodcock-Johnson III Tests of Cognitive Abilities (COG) and the Woodcock-Johnson Tests of Achievement (ACH) (Woodcock, McGrew, & Mather, 2001), and that comparisons of scores on the COG and ACH be used to identify children with aptitude-achievement discrepancies suggestive of a learning disability.

As illustrated by Case 4–3, in some school districts, administrators have attempted to dictate the specific tests that the psychologist must use. Practitioners must speak out against district-mandated assessment batteries because they are inconsistent with professional standards and may result in unsound assessment choices for the pupil being evaluated (EP 9.02; NASP-PPE, IV, C#1, #2; *Standards*, p. 20). Such policies also violate the intent of special education laws that require tests be selected in light of the unique characteristics of the individual child (Reschly, 2000).

COMPUTERS IN PSYCHOEDUCATIONAL ASSESSMENT

Software programs are now available for the administration, scoring, and interpretation of a variety of psychological tests. A special challenge of this assessment technology has been to interpret our ethical codes, professional standards, and special education laws as they relate to computer-assisted assessment (Jacob & Brantley, 1987a). APA's *Guidelines for Computer-Based Tests and Interpretations* (GCBTI) (1986) were formulated to interpret the APA's EP and the *Standards* as they relate to computer-based testing and test interpretation. Jacob and Brantley (1987b) also developed a list of informal suggestions for best practices for computer use in school psychology.

Case 4–4

The school board of a suburban high school was concerned about an increase in drug abuse and suicide attempts among high school students. They decided to ask a member of their school psychological services team to become involved in the identification of troubled adolescents and set up a counseling program in cooperation with the local mental health clinic. Sam Foster, the school psychologist assigned to this new job role, felt inadequately trained in the diagnosis of adolescent emotional problems. He decided to purchase a computer-administered suicide risk and depression personality scale he saw advertised in a professional newsletter. Computer administration of the scale required only 20 minutes. Results were computer-scored and printed out in narrative form. Sam had a number of high school students take the computer-administered test, and he then included paragraphs from the narrative printout in his reports. (Adapted from Jacob & Brantley, 1989.)

Case 4–4 illustrates a number of important ethical-legal considerations associated with computer-assisted assessment. First, and perhaps most important, it is the psychologist's responsibility to ensure that all assessment procedures, including those that are computer-assisted, yield valid results prior to using the results in decision making (GCBTI, p. 8; NASP-PPE, IV, E, #3, #4). Some software programs have not been developed according to accepted standards for psychodiagnostic assessment tools and lack adequate documentation of their validity. Selection of psychodiagnostic software should be limited to those programs that have been reviewed by experts in the field and found to meet high standards for professional practice (NASP-PPE, IV, C, #2).

It also is important to note that Sam is not personally qualified to evaluate the validity of the computer-generated results for the individual students tested because of his lack of training in diagnosis of adolescent emotional problems. He is attempting to use a computer program to extend his competence beyond its current boundaries. This blind acceptance of computer-generated findings places the students at high risk for misdiagnosis and possible psychological harm. Computer-generated test interpretations should be considered as a tool to be used in conjunction with the clinical judgment of well-trained professionals (NASP-PPE, IV, E, #4, #5).

CONCLUDING COMMENTS

In recent years, some school psychologists have modified their job role so that more time is devoted to consultation and intervention activities, and less time is devoted to assessment. Although current job roles may place more emphasis on consultation and intervention, the school psychologist will continue to be one of the members of the pupil services team most knowledgeable in assessment. Consequently, school psychologists must continue to accept responsibility for ensuring that tests and assessment procedures are used only in ways that protect the rights and promote the well-being of students.

STUDY AND DISCUSSION

Questions for Chapter 4

1. What is the difference between *testing* and *assessment?*
2. Identify the school psychologist's ethical-legal obligations to the parent prior to beginning an assessment and during interpretation of findings.
3. Describe five ethical-legal concerns a psychologist should consider in planning and conducting psychoeducational assessments.
4. What is *test bias, bias in clinical application,* and *fairness of consequences?*
5. Identify the ethical-legal problems associated with district-mandated assessment batteries.
6. Identify the ethical concerns associated with the use of projective personality tests with school children.
7. Identify the ethical-legal issues associated with the selection and use of computer-assisted test interpretation programs.

VIGNETTES

1. Wanda Rose's school district has a backlog of referrals for children suspected of qualifying for special education services. In order to increase the number of evaluations she could complete, Wanda carefully trained a teacher's aide in the administration of the Wechsler Intelligence Scale for Children-Third Edition (Wechsler, 1991) and several achievement tests.

She used the results of the tests administered by the teacher's aide to determine whether or not the referred pupils qualified for special education services. What are the ethical-legal issues involved in this vignette?

2. Each May, the elementary schools in Carrie Johnson's district invite children who will enter kindergarten in the fall and their parents to a kindergarten round-up. During the round-up, hearing, vision, and speech screenings are conducted, and Carrie administers the Vocabulary and Picture Completion subtests from the Wechsler Preschool and Primary Scale of Intelligence-III (Wechsler, 2002) to identify children who might need further evaluation of their learning needs. When a new resort-hotel complex was built in the area, the hotel management recruited several families from Dominica for their job openings. Carrie was delighted when a Dominican child came to her screening table. Relying on the French she had learned in college, Carrie spoke to the child in French and attempted an on-the-spot translation of the WPPSI-III subtests from English to French. What are the ethical issues in this situation?

3. Hannah Cook, school psychologist, and Bob Smoke, the reading consultant at the junior high school, were interested in decreasing the amount of time needed to complete individual assessment of reading achievement so that more time could be devoted to consultation activities. They contacted the high school computer sciences teacher and worked together to create a computer-administered version of a popular, well-standardized paper and pencil test of reading comprehension. Students referred for assessment of reading achievement were then routinely given the computer-administered version of the test in a testing carrel in the school library. The computer program computed raw scores, and the raw scores then were transformed to standard scores by the reading consultant using tables from the test manual. The test scores were used by the psychologist and reading consultant for both placement and program planning purposes. What are the ethical-legal issues involved in this vignette? (Adapted from Jacob & Brantley, 1989.)

4. During his internship in a suburban school district, Sam Foster received a disproportionately high number of referrals for special education evaluation of children who lived in federally funded low-income scatter-site housing in his district. Most of these children were African-American or Hispanic, but attending predominately white elementary schools. Sam is concerned about potential over-identification of minority children for special education in his district. What are some strategies he might use to prevent this problem?

ACTIVITIES

A 7-year-old child has been referred for psychoeducational assessment because of her slow academic progress. Her teacher suspects that she may qualify for special education services as educable mentally impaired. Role play your initial meeting with the child's parents during which you seek informed consent for assessment. Role play your meeting with the child during which you describe the scope and nature of the assessment process.

Chapter 5

ETHICAL-LEGAL ISSUES IN THE EDUCATION OF PUPILS WITH DISABILITIES UNDER IDEA

> Education law is one thing; educational action is quite another. Between the two events, the passing of a law and the behavior of the school, must occur a chain of intermediate events: The interpretation of the law in terms of practice; the study of the feasibility of the interpretation; the successive adjustments, reorganizations, retrainings, and redesign of administrative procedures; the self-monitoring and reporting—the reality testing. (Page, 1980, p. 423)

This chapter provides a summary of law pertinent to providing services to children with disabilities. It focuses on the Individuals with Disabilities Education Act (IDEA). Special education services for children with disabilities ages 3 through 21 are discussed first in some detail (IDEA-Part B). This is followed by a summary of the federal legislation that provides funds for early intervention services for infants and toddlers with disabilities (IDEA-Part C).

EDUCATION OF CHILDREN WITH DISABILITIES: A HISTORICAL PERSPECTIVE

It is important for school psychology practitioners to have some knowledge of the history of IDEA in order to appreciate fully the meaning of current law. In the text that follows, we have summarized case law and early legislation that foreshadowed the most important special education law, the Education of All Handicapped Children Act of 1975 (Pub. L. No. 94–142), renamed the Individuals with Disabilities Education Act in 1990.

Right-to-Education Case Law

As discussed in Chapter 2, no fundamental right to an education is mentioned in the U.S. Constitution. Public education is an entitlement granted to citizens of a state under state law. However, on the basis of state laws, all children within a state have a legitimate claim to an education at public expense. In legal terms, education is a property right protected by the 14th Amendment of the Constitution, which provides that no state shall "deny any person within its jurisdiction the equal protection of the laws."

For many years, children with disabilities, particularly those with severe or multiple impairments, were routinely excluded from a public education. School districts typically had policies that required a child to meet certain admissions standards (e.g., toilet trained, ambulatory, mental age of at least 5 years) before they were allowed to enter school. One of the responsibilities of many school psychologists prior to 1975 was to assess pupils to certify that they were not eligible or unable to profit from public school education and, therefore, excused from school attendance. Children who were behavior problems in the classroom or simply too difficult to teach were often expelled from school.

Few options existed for the parents of children who did not qualify to attend public school. Institutionalization was the recommended treatment for children with disabilities prior to the 1960s. Well-to-do families often placed their children in private schools. Others kept their children at home.

In the 1960s, following successful court challenges to racial discrimination in the public schools (e.g., *Brown v. Board of Education*, 1954), parents of children with disabilities began to file lawsuits against public school districts, alleging that the equal protection clause of the 14th Amendment prohibits states from denying school access to children because of their disabilities. Two landmark court cases, *Pennsylvania Association for Retarded Children v. Commonwealth of Pennsylvania (P.A.R.C.)* (1971, 1972) and *Mills v. Board of Education of District of Columbia* (*Mills*) (1972), marked a turning point in the education of children with disabilities and gave impetus to the development of federal legislation ensuring a free and appropriate education for all children with disabilities.

P.A.R.C.

In *P.A.R.C.*, parents of children with mental retardation brought suit against the state of Pennsylvania in federal court because their children were denied access to public education. In a consent decree (where parties involved in a lawsuit consent to a court-approved agreement), parents won access to public school programs for children with mental retardation, and the court ordered comprehensive changes in policy and practices regarding the education of children with mental retardation within the state. The consent decree in *P.A.R.C.* marked the beginning of a redefinition of education in this country, broadened beyond the "three Rs" to include training of children with disabilities toward self-sufficiency (Martin, 1979). The consent decree in *P.A.R.C.* stated:

> Expert testimony in this action indicates that all mentally retarded persons are capable of benefitting from a program of education and training; that the greatest number of retarded persons, given such education and training, are capable of achieving self-sufficiency, and the remaining few, with such education and training, are capable of achieving some degree of self-care; that the earlier such education and training begins, the more thoroughly and the more efficiently a mentally retarded person can benefit at any point in his life and development from a program of education and training. (p. 1259)

P.A.R.C. is a particularly important case as it foreshadowed and shaped subsequent federal laws regarding schools' responsibilities in educating children with disabilities. The state of Pennsylvania was required to locate and identify all school-age persons excluded from the public schools, to place all children in a "free program of education and training appropriate to the child's capacity," to provide home-bound instruction if appropriate, and to allow tuition grants for children who needed alternative school placements. *P.A.R.C.* also required parent notice before children were assigned to special education classes and an opportunity for an impartial hearing if parents were unsatisfied with the placement recommendation for their children.

Mills

Mills was a lawsuit filed on behalf of seven children with behavioral, emotional, and learning impairments in the District of Columbia.[1] The court order in *Mills* reiterated many of the requirements of *P.A.R.C.*, and a number of additional school responsibilities in educating children with disabilities were identified. The decision required the schools to "provide each handicapped child of school age a free and suitable publicly supported education regardless of the degree of the child's mental, physical or emotional disability or impairment" (p. 878). The decision also required the schools to prepare a proposal outlining a suitable educational program for each child with a disability, and the court set limits on the use of disciplinary suspensions and expulsions of children with disabilities.

Following the successful resolution of *P.A.R.C.* and *Mills*, 36 right-to-education cases were soon filed in 27 jurisdictions (Martin, 1979). These cases signaled to Congress that a need existed for federal laws to ensure educational opportunities for all children with disabilities.

---

[1] The suit was initially resolved by a consent decree in 1972. However, the District of Columbia Board of Education failed to comply with the consent decree, and the suit ultimately resulted in a contempt of court judgment against the school board.

Early Legislation

Congress's attempts to address the needs of pupils with disabilities took two routes: the passage of antidiscrimination legislation and the amendment of federal education laws (Martin, 1979). One of the first bills that attempted to ensure equal educational opportunity for children with handicaps in the public schools was an amendment to Title VI of the Civil Rights Act of 1964. The bill later became Section 504 of The Rehabilitation Act of 1973, civil rights legislation that prohibits discrimination against pupils with handicaps in school systems receiving federal financial assistance. School responsibilities under 504 to pupils with handicaps are discussed in Chapter 6.

In addition to antidiscrimination legislation, Congress attempted to meet the needs of pupils with disabilities by amending federal education laws. In 1966, Congress amended the Elementary and Secondary Education Act of 1965 (Pub. L. No. 89–750) to provide grants to states to assist them in developing and improving programs to educate children with disabilities. In 1970, Congress repealed the 1966 law but established a similar grant program to encourage states to develop special education resources and personnel (Pub. L. No. 91–230) (Turnbull & Turnbull, 2000). Four years later, Congress passed the Education Amendments of 1974 (Pub. L. No. 93–380), which increased aid to states for special education and served to put the schools on notice that federal financial assistance for special education would be contingent on the development of state plans with "a goal of...full educational opportunities to all handicapped children." Congress intended that this interim legislation would encourage states to begin a period of comprehensive planning and program development to meet the needs of pupils with disabilities. The Education Amendments of 1974 is primarily of historical interest now, except for Section 513, The Family Rights and Privacy Act, discussed in Chapter 3 (Martin, 1979).

INDIVIDUALS WITH DISABILITIES EDUCATION ACT

The most important federal statute concerning the education of children with disabilities is The Education of All Handicapped Children Act of 1975 (Pub. L. No. 94–142). This legislation was introduced as a Senate bill in 1972. A Senate subcommittee on the handicapped held extensive hearings on the proposed legislation. The witnesses (numbering more than 100) included teachers, parents, education associations, parent organizations, and legislators, among others (Martin, 1979). Their testimony made it increasingly evident that more clear-cut federal incentives were needed to assure educational opportunities for children with disabilities. As of 1975, it was estimated that there were more than eight million children with handicaps in the United States. More than half were not receiving an appropriate education, and one million were excluded from public education entirely (Pub. L. No. 94–142, § 601 [b]).

In 1975, Congress passed the Education of All Handicapped Children Act (EHA) (Pub. L. No. 94–142), and President Ford signed it into law. The purpose of the law was

> to assure that all handicapped children have available to them...a free appropriate education which emphasizes special education and related services designed to meet their unique needs, to assure that the rights of handicapped children and their parents or guardians are protected, to assist States and localities to provide for the education of all handicapped children, and to assess and assure the effectiveness of efforts to educate handicapped children. (Pub. L. No. 94–142, § 601 [c])

In 1990, President G. H. Bush signed into law the Education of the Handicapped Act Amendments of 1990 (Pub. L. No. 101–476), which changed the name of the Education of All Handicapped Children Act to Individuals with Disabilities Education Act (IDEA).[2] Throughout the law, the term *handicap* was replaced by *disability*. On June 4, 1997, President Clinton signed into law the Individuals with Disabilities Education Act Amendments of 1997 (Pub. L. No. 105–17), which reauthorized IDEA and introduced changes to improve the law.

IDEA provides funds to state (SEA) and local (LEA) educational agencies that provide a free and appropriate education to children with disabilities in conformance with the requirements of the law. The 1997 amendments restructured the law into four parts: Part A, General Provisions; Part B, Assistance for Education of All Children with Disabilities; Part C, Infants and Toddlers with Disabilities; and Part D, National Activities to Improve Education of Children with Disabilities. IDEA-Part B refers to special education legislation that provides funds for services to children with disabilities ages 3 through 21. IDEA-Part C provides funds for early intervention services for infants and toddlers. IDEA-Part C is discussed later in this chapter. Unlike early special education law that focused on access to schools, "IDEA 1997" is an outcome-oriented law that focuses on providing special education that allows students with disabilities to make meaningful educational progress (Yell, Drasgow, & Ford, 2000).

It is important to recognize that IDEA is not a fully funded federal statute; it funds only a modest portion of the extra expenses schools incur in providing special education to students with disabilities. The level of funding provided to states by the law has never exceeded 14 percent of the additional

---

[2] Pub. L. No. 94–142 was amended in 1978 (Pub. L. No. 98–773), 1983 (Pub. L. No. 98–199), twice in 1986 (Pub. L. No. 99–457 and Pub. L. No. 99–372), 1988 (Pub. L. No. 100–630), 1990 (Pub. L. No. 101–476), and 1991 (Pub. L. No. 102–119).

costs for special education services borne by state governments and school districts (Reschly & Bersoff, 1999). Parts of IDEA are funded permanently and can be changed only if Congress repeals or amends that portion of the law. Other parts are funded for a specified time period. Part A, the general provisions of the law, does not contain funding and does not require periodic reauthorization. Part B, the portion that provides funds to states for children with disabilities ages 3 through 21, is funded permanently. Part C, Infant and Toddler Programs, and Part D, National Activities to Improve Education of Children with Disabilities, are funded for a limited time period (usually 4 or 5 years) and must be reauthorized when the specified period ends.

Reauthorizations of IDEA funds are often accompanied by amendments to the statute. In the years since 1975, some of these amendments have been minor; others have resulted in significant changes in the law (Yell et al., 2000). IDEA was due for reauthorization in 2002. Rules and regulations implementing IDEA are developed by the U.S. Department of Education (DOE) and are revised following changes in the law. The Part B and Part C regulations cited in this chapter were issued in March 1999, and codified at Title 34 of the *Code of Federal Regulations* (C.F.R.) Parts 300 and 303, respectively.

The major provisions of IDEA-Part B are discussed under the following headings: "State Plans and Single Agency Responsibility," "The Zero Reject Principle," "Children Eligible for Services," "Pupil Evaluation Procedures," "Individualized Education Program," "Least Restrictive Environment," "The Meaning of Appropriate Education," "The Scope of Required Related Services," "Procedural Safeguards," and "Right to Private Action."

State Plans and Single Agency Responsibility

Each state must develop a plan to provide special education and related services to pupils with disabilities and identify the state agency responsible for carrying out the plan.

State Plans

In order to receive funds, IDEA-Part B requires each state educational agency (SEA) (usually the state department of education) to have submitted to the U.S. Secretary of Education a plan that describes state policies and procedures to ensure a free appropriate public education for all children with disabilities residing within the state between the ages of 3 and 21, inclusive. The SEA is not required to provide special education and related services to children in the 3–5– and 18–21-year age groups if the provision thereof is in conflict with state law or practice. IDEA 1997 specifies that ensurances for a free appropriate public education must extend to children with disabilities who have been suspended for more than 10 days or expelled from school. However, states are not required to provide special education and related services to youth ages 18 through 21 who are incarcerated in adult correctional facilities if they were not identified as disabled or did not have an individualized education program (IEP) prior to their incarceration (34 C.F.R. § 300.311).

Federal funds are provided to each state that develops an acceptable state plan. DOE may require revisions in state plans following changes in law or findings of compliance problems (34 C.F.R. § 300.112). To ensure responsiveness to the needs of children with disabilities and their parents, the SEA must provide opportunities for public comment prior to a revision of its plan. Each state also must maintain an advisory panel for the purpose of providing policy guidance with respect to special education and related services for children within the state (34 C.F.R. § 300.650).

The Office of Special Education Programs (OSEP) within DOE monitors compliance with IDEA at the level of the state and only indirectly (e.g., through the review of the state plan). States are responsible for monitoring local school districts to ensure compliance with IDEA regulations and the state's plan (see Reschly & Bersoff, 1999). OSEP responds to written inquiries regarding interpretation of IDEA, but it does not attempt to enforce compliance at the level of the individual school district (Zirkel & Kincaid, 1993).

Single Agency Responsibility

In legislating IDEA-Part B, Congress sought to ensure that a single state agency was responsible for carrying out the requirements of the law (Turnbull & Turnbull, 2000). The single agency responsibility aspect of the law has several implications. First, under IDEA-Part B, the SEA is the agency responsible for monitoring all educational programs for children with disabilities ages 3 through 21 within the state and ensuring that they meet appropriate education standards. IDEA-Part B allows the SEA to delegate the responsibility to provide special education and related services to intermediate school districts (or other regional units) and local educational agencies (LEAs). An LEA is usually the board of education of a public school district, the educational administrative unit of a public institution (e.g., school for the deaf, blind), or a charter school that is established as an LEA under state law. The SEA must ensure that policies and programs administered by intermediate and local education agencies (LEAs) are in conformance with IDEA-Part B requirements. If an LEA is unable or unwilling to provide appropriate services under IDEA-Part B, the SEA must ensure that special education and related services are provided to students with disabilities residing in those areas (Turnbull & Turnbull, 2000). If a charter school is a part of an LEA, the LEA is required to serve children with disabilities who attend the charter school and provide funds to charter schools in the same manner in which funds are provided to other schools (34 C.F.R. § 300.312).

Second, consistent with the idea of single agency responsibility, the SEA also must ensure IDEA-Part B rights and protections to children with disabilities who are enrolled in programs administered by other state agencies. As illustrated by the Joseph McNulty case (Case 4–1), prior to 1975, many state residential facilities provided custodial care but little training or education for children with disabilities. With the exception of children unilaterally placed in schools or facilities by their parents, the SEA is responsible for ensuring an appropriate education for all children with disabilities in the state, including those residing in mental health facilities, homes for the developmentally disabled, and hospitals. IDEA 1997, however, allows an SEA to delegate its responsibility for providing special education to youth in adult prisons to another agency (e.g., the prison system) (34 C.F.R. § 300.600).

Third, the SEA must ensure that special education and related services are available to children with disabilities enrolled in private schools or facilities. Congress identified two types of private school placements: A child with a disability may be placed in a private school or facility by the SEA or LEA as a means of providing special education and related services; or children may attend private schools or facilities by parental choice.

Private School Placement by the SEA or LEA

Some children with disabilities are placed in a private school or facility as a means of providing the child appropriate special education and related services. Children placed in a private school or facility by the SEA or LEA must be provided special education and related services in conformance with an individualized education program (IEP) developed by an IEP team as described in the law. Publically placed private school students are entitled to the same benefits and services as those attending public schools. The child must retain all IDEA rights in the private school setting, and the SEA or LEA must monitor the services provided to ensure compliance with IDEA requirements (34 C.F. R. § 300.402). When the placement is made by the SEA or LEA, the placement must be at no cost to the parents, including the program, nonmedical care, and room and board if placement is in a residential facility (34 C.F.R. § 300.341, 300.401–402).

Unilateral Placement by Parents

If an LEA makes available a free appropriate public education for a child with a disability, but the parents choose to place their child in a private school, the child does not have an individual right to receive some or all of the special education and related services the child would receive if enrolled in a public school (34 C.F.R. § 300.454). A school system must provide parentally placed private school children Part B programs and services in accordance with a service plan (34 C.F.R. § 300.452). Amounts expended for the provision of services by the LEA must be equal to a proportionate amount of available federal funds, excluding funds expended for child find activities.

Decisions about the services that will be provided to private school children are made in consultation with representatives of the private school children with disabilities. However, the LEA makes the final decision with respect to the services to be provided to eligible children. Based on this consultation; the funding available; and the number, location, and needs of private school children with disabilities, the LEA decides which children will receive services, what services will be provided, how and where the services will be provided, and how the services will be evaluated. If a child enrolled in a private school will receive special education or related services from an LEA, the LEA initiates and conducts meetings to develop, review, and revise a services plan for the child and ensures that a representative of the private school attends or otherwise participates (e.g., telephone calls) in each meeting (34 C.F.R. § 300.454).

Thus, parentally placed private school children with disabilities may receive a different amount of service than children with disabilities in public school. School systems are given broad discretion with regard to which private children with disabilities will receive services and what services will be provided. Services to private school children may be provided on-site at the child's private school, including a religious school, to the extent consistent with law. LEA's may not use federal funds to benefit private schools, but they may provide instruction at the site of a private school and property, equipment, and supplies to benefit private school children with disabilities as long as the LEA maintains control over the equipment and supplies (34 C.F.R. §§ 300.459–462). LEA's may count the cost of transporting children to participate in services as part of their required expenditure on private school children.

Parents have, at times, recovered private school tuition costs from the SEA or LEA through administrative hearings or lawsuits in which they demonstrated that the SEA or LEA failed to offer their child an appropriate education program in the public schools, leaving them no option but to place him or her at their own expense (see *School Committee of the Town of Burlington, Massachusetts v. Department of Education of Massachusetts*, 1985). IDEA 1997 specifically addresses this issue. If the parents of a child with a disability who previously received special education under the authority of a public agency enroll the child in a private school without the consent or referral of the agency, a court or hearing officer may require the agency to reimburse the parents for the cost of enrollment if it is found that the agency failed to make a free appropriate public education available to the child in a timely manner prior to that enrollment (34 C.F.R. § 300.403).

However, IDEA 1997 also states that the cost of reimbursement may be reduced or denied if

1. At the most recent IEP the parents attended prior to removal of the child from the public school, the parents did not inform the IEP team that they were rejecting the placement proposed by the public agency, including stating their concerns and their intent to enroll their child in a private school at public expense;
2. The parents did not give written notice of their concerns and their intent to enroll their child in a private school at public expense to the public agency at least 10 business days prior to the removal of the child from the public school;
3. The public agency notified the parents of its intent to evaluate the child (and the reasons for the evaluation) prior to the parents' removal of the child from the public school, but the parents did not make the child available for such evaluation; or
4. A judicial finding is made that the actions taken by the parents were unreasonable.

The cost of reimbursement may not be reduced or denied for failure of the parent to provide notice of his or her intent if the parent is illiterate and cannot write in English; compliance would likely result in physical or serious emotional harm to the child; the school prevented the parent from providing notice; or the parents had not been informed of the notice requirement (34 C.F.R. § 300.403).

The Zero Reject Principle

The "zero reject principle" requires states to locate and evaluate pupils with disabilities and provide them with full educational opportunity, regardless of the severity of the disability.

Child Find

Consistent with the court decisions in *P.A.R.C.* and *Mills,* Congress recognized that in order to ensure services to all children with disabilities (i.e., the zero reject principle), it was necessary for the SEA to actively seek to locate all children with disabilities within the state. This aspect of the law is called the *child find* requirement. IDEA requires the SEA to implement policies and procedures to ensure that all children with disabilities (including those who attend private schools) are identified, located, and evaluated (34 C.F.R. § 300.125). The SEA also must ensure that accurate child counts are made to Washington each year (34 C.F.R. § 300.750).

Severity of the Disability

The zero reject principle also encompasses the notion that the SEA must provide full educational opportunity to all children with disabilities, regardless of the severity of their disability. A 1989 court case raised the question of whether some children are so severely impaired that they do not qualify for services under IDEA. *Timothy W. v. Rochester, New Hampshire School District* concerned a child who was profoundly retarded, deaf, blind, spastic, and subject to convulsions. The school alleged that Timothy was so impaired he was "not 'capable of benefitting' from an education, and therefore was not entitled to one" (1989, p. 956). In a surprise ruling, the district court agreed with the school. On appeal, however, this decision was reversed. In a lengthy opinion the court stated, "The language of the Act [IDEA] in its entirety makes clear that a 'zero-reject' policy is at the core of the Act ..." (p. 960). As the court noted in *Timothy W.*, there is no requirement under IDEA that a child be able to demonstrate that he or she will benefit from special education in order to be eligible for services.

Children Eligible for Services

The funds available under IDEA-Part B are earmarked to provide special education and related services only for children with disabilities as defined by the law. Under IDEA-Part B, a *child with a disability* means a child evaluated in accordance with the procedures in the law as having

> mental retardation, hearing impairments (including deafness), speech or language impairments, visual impairments (including blindness), serious emotional disturbance (hereafter referred to as "emotional disturbance"), orthopedic impairments, autism, traumatic brain injury, other health impairments, or specific learning disabilities; and ... who, by reason thereof, needs special education and related services (Pub. L. No. 105–17, § 602, 111 Stat. 43 [1997]).

It is important to note that eligible children under IDEA-Part B must have a disability as outlined in one of the 13 disability categories (see Exhibit 5–1), and they must need special education and related services because of that disability. Identification of a pupil as needing special education is thus "a two-pronged determination: (a) A disability in obtaining an education must be documented, and (b) a need for special education must be established" (Reschly, 2000, p. 87). Also, a child is not eligible for special education and related services if "the determinant factor for such determination is lack of instruction in reading or math or limited English proficiency" (34 C.F.R. § 300.534).

Exhibit 5–1. Disability Categories under IDEA-Part B

Definitions of disability terms. The terms used in this definition are defined as follows:

(1) (i) Autism means a developmental disability significantly affecting verbal and nonverbal communication and social interaction, generally evident before age 3, that adversely affects a child's educational performance. Other characteristics often associated with autism are engagement in repetitive activities and stereotyped movements, resistance to environmental change or change in daily routines, and unusual responses to sensory experiences. The term does not apply if a child's educational performance is adversely affected primarily because the child has an emotional disturbance, as defined in paragraph (b)(4) of this section.

(ii) A child who manifests the characteristics of "autism" after age 3 could be diagnosed as having "autism" if the criteria in paragraph (c)(1)(i) of this section are satisfied.

(2) Deaf-blindness means concomitant hearing and visual impairments, the combination of which causes such severe communication and other developmental and educational needs that they cannot be accommodated in special education programs solely for children with deafness or children with blindness.

(3) Deafness means a hearing impairment that is so severe that the child is impaired in processing linguistic information through hearing, with or without amplification, that adversely affects a child's educational performance.

(4) Emotional disturbance. See text.

(5) Hearing impairment means an impairment in hearing, whether permanent or fluctuating, that adversely affects a child's educational performance but that is not included under the definition of deafness in this section.

(6) Mental retardation. See text.

(7) Multiple disabilities means concomitant impairments (such as mental retardation-blindness, mental retardation-orthopedic impairment, etc.), the combination of which causes such severe educational needs that they cannot be accommodated in special education programs solely for one of the impairments. The term does not include deaf-blindness.

(8) Orthopedic impairment means a severe orthopedic impairment that adversely affects a child's educational performance. The term includes impairments caused by congenital anomaly (e.g., clubfoot, absence of some member, etc.), impairments caused by disease (e.g., poliomyelitis, bone tuberculosis, etc.), and impairments from other causes (e.g., cerebral palsy, amputations, and fractures or burns that cause contractures).

(9) Other health impairment. See text.

(10) Specific learning disability. See text.

Exhibit 5–1. *(Continued)*

(11) Speech or language impairment means a communication disorder, such as stuttering, impaired articulation, a language impairment, or a voice impairment, that adversely affects a child's educational performance.

(12) Traumatic brain injury means an acquired injury to the brain caused by an external physical force, resulting in total or partial functional disability or psychosocial impairment, or both, that adversely affects a child's educational performance. The term applies to open or closed head injuries resulting in impairments in one or more areas, such as cognition; language; memory; attention; reasoning; abstract thinking; judgment; problem-solving; sensory, perceptual, and motor abilities; psychosocial behavior; physical functions; information processing; and speech. The term does not apply to brain injuries that are congenital or degenerative, or to brain injuries induced by birth trauma.

(13) Visual impairment including blindness means an impairment in vision that, even with correction, adversely affects a child's educational performance. The term includes both partial sight and blindness.

Source: 34 C.F.R. § 300.7.

IDEA-Part B allows states to use a broader definition of disability for children ages 3 through 9. States may use the term *child with a disability* for a 3–9-year-old who is experiencing developmental delay (as defined by the state) in one or more of the following areas: physical, cognitive, communication, social or emotional, or adaptive development; and who, for that reason, needs special education and related services (34 C.F.R. § 300.7).

IDEA-Part B definitions that concern sensory, motor, and speech impairments typically pose few problems. The definitions of *mental retardation, specific learning disability, emotional disturbance,* and *other health impairment* frequently have been a source of confusion and disagreement, and they are discussed in the text that follows.

The present discussion focuses on the federal definitions of disability categories under IDEA-Part B. School psychologists also must be knowledgeable of the broader definition of handicapped under Section 504 of The Rehabilitation Act of 1973 (see Chapter 6) and their state code eligibility requirements. Different states used different names for special education categories (e.g., mental retardation, mental handicap, mental impairment), and state classification criteria vary as well (Reschly & Bersoff, 1999). It is important to note that IDEA does not require states to label pupils, and some states have adopted a noncategorical system for the delivery of special education services (34 C.F.R. § 300.125). However, states must provide data to DOE each year regarding the number of children with disabilities by disability category (34 C.F.R. § 300.751), and federal funds are available only for those children who are eligible under the IDEA-Part B definition of a disability.

Mental Retardation

> "Mental retardation" means significantly subaverage general intellectual functioning, existing concurrently with deficits in adaptive behavior and manifested during the developmental period, that adversely affects a child's educational performance. (34 C.F.R. § 300.7)

Prior to the passage of Pub. L. No. 94–142, many children were labeled mentally retarded on the basis of a single IQ score (see Case 4–1). The use of an IQ score as the sole criterion for diagnosing mental retardation in the schools resulted in the overidentification of children as mentally retarded, particularly pupils from ethnic minority backgrounds and those with limited English proficiency. In the 1950s and 1960s, the American Association of Mental Deficiency argued persuasively for a change in the definition of mentally retarded. They recommended that a diagnosis of mental retardation be based on the finding of deficits in both intellectual functioning and adaptive behavior. This view gained wide acceptance and was incorporated into the IDEA-Part B definition of mental retardation.

Under IDEA-Part B, eligibility for special education is determined by a team of qualified professionals and the parents of the child. The team must consider three types of assessment information in determining whether a child has mental retardation: general intellectual functioning, adaptive behavior, and school performance. To be eligible for special education under the mental retardation category, the child must show subaverage performance on a measure of general intellectual functioning. Most states recommend the use of IQ tests for this measure. However, this evaluation can be accomplished by testing "or by means other than testing" as long as the procedures are valid and nondiscriminatory (Heumann, 1993, p. 539). Subaverage is usually further defined in state guidelines as performance at least two standard deviations below the population mean for the child's age group (i.e., a score below 70 on the Wechsler Scales, below 68 on the Stanford-Binet).

The child also must demonstrate concurrent deficits in adaptive behavior and school performance. Measures of adaptive behavior focus on the child's effectiveness in meeting age-appropriate standards of personal independence and social responsibility. They typically are based on observations of behavior and competencies provided by an informant (usually a parent or teacher) (Sattler, 2002). Deficits in school performance are most often assessed by standardized achievement tests. Michigan, for example, requires reading and arithmetic standardized test scores in the lowest six percentiles for a child to qualify as mentally impaired.

State regulations often further classify pupils with mental retardation into one of three subgroups based on intellectual functioning and adaptive behavior. Educable mentally retarded children typically achieve IQ scores 2 to 3 standard deviations below the mean; trainable mentally retarded achieve scores 3 to 4.5 standard deviations below the mean; and severely mentally retarded achieve IQs 4.5 or more standard deviations below the mean.

The IDEA-Part B definition of mental retardation has generated debate among experts in the fields of school psychology and special education. Many believe the IDEA definition of mental retardation continues to overidentify children as mentally retarded.

Specific Learning Disability

> "Specific learning disability" means a disorder in one or more of the basic psychological processes involved in understanding or in using language, spoken or written, that may manifest itself in an imperfect ability to listen, think, speak, read, write, spell, or to do mathematical calculations, including conditions such as perceptual disabilities, brain injury, minimal brain dysfunction, dyslexia, and developmental aphasia. The term does not include learning problems that are primarily the result of visual, hearing, or motor disabilities, of mental retardation, of emotional disturbance, or of environmental, cultural, or economic disadvantage. (34 C.F.R. § 300.7)
>
> A team may determine that a child has a specific learning disability if—
>
> (1) The child does not achieve commensurate with his or her age and ability levels in one or more of the areas listed...if provided with learning experiences appropriate for the child's age and ability levels; and
>
> (2) The team finds that a child has a severe discrepancy between achievement and intellectual ability in one or more of the following areas:
>
> (i) Oral expression.
> (ii) Listening comprehension.
> (iii) Written expression.
> (iv) Basic reading skill.
> (v) Reading comprehension.
> (vi) Mathematics calculation.
> (vii) Mathematics reasoning. (34 C.F.R. § 300.541)

The team may not identify a child as having a specific learning disability if the severe discrepancy between ability and achievement is primarily the result of a visual, hearing, or motor impairment; mental retardation; emotional disturbance; or environmental, cultural, or economic disadvantage (34 C.F.R. § 300.541).

The rules and regulations further require an observation of the child's academic performance in the regular classroom (or an age-appropriate setting if not in school) by a team member other than the child's teacher (34

C.F.R. § 300.542). The team report and documentation for a child suspected of having a specific learning disability (LD) must include a statement of (a) whether the child has a specific learning disability; (b) the basis for making the determination; (c) the relevant behavior noted during the observation of the child; (d) the relationship of that behavior to the child's academic functioning; (e) the educationally relevant medical findings, if any; (f) whether there is a severe discrepancy between achievement and ability that is not correctable without special education and related services; and (g) the determination of the team concerning the effects of environmental, cultural, or economic disadvantage. Each team member is required to certify in writing whether the report reflects his or her conclusion. If it does not reflect his or her conclusion, the team member must submit a separate statement presenting his or her conclusions (34 C.F.R. § 300.543).

Probably the two most problematic aspects of the IDEA LD definition are determining whether a *severe discrepancy* exists between achievement and ability and ruling out environmental, cultural, and economic disadvantage as the primary determinants of the discrepancy. Many approaches to establishing a severe discrepancy between achievement and ability have been suggested (Cone & Wilson, 1981). States may recommend the use of specific formulas to help determine whether one exists. However, formulas should be used for guidance only. In *Riley v. Ambach* (1982), the court enjoined the New York commissioner of education from using a standard statewide formula for determining a learning disability. The court held that rigid quantitative approaches to the identification of learning-disabled children were too inflexible and not sufficiently individualized.

Some consensus now exists among measurement specialists that guidelines for evaluating whether a severe achievement-ability discrepancy exists ought to include consideration of at least two types of information. First, the school psychologist needs to evaluate the likelihood that the observed difference in achievement and ability scores is due to measurement error. (For a discussion of methods for determining this, see Cone & Wilson, 1981.) Second, in addition to establishing that the achievement-aptitude discrepancy is most likely not due to measurement error, measurement specialists suggest that the evaluation team consider whether the magnitude of the discrepancy is unusual or uncommon for the child's age (Flanagan, Andrews, & Genshaft, 1997). Achievement-IQ discrepancies of 15 points or more occur with as many as 20–40 percent of the general population (McDermott & Watkins, 1985). Test developers have recognized the importance of standardizing ability and achievement measures on the same population so that the prevalence of various achievement-ability discrepancies can be calculated and reported by age group. This information has become increasingly available in test manuals. Regression analysis procedures also can be used to estimate the prevalence of achievement-ability discrepancies (Evans, 1996).

When the existence of a significant discrepancy between achievement and ability has been established, IDEA requires the team to consider whether the discrepancy is primarily the result of environmental, cultural, or economic disadvantage. This portion of the definition also poses problems for team members. Based on her review of comments in the *Congressional Record* and Department of Education policy statements, Slenkovich concluded that the intent of this part of the definition is to ensure that services are targeted for children whose learning problems are primarily the result of a disorder within the child (1986, November). Congress did not intend IDEA-Part B funds for children whose learning problems stem from a disadvantaged homelife, poor teaching, immaturity, or a lack of motivation to learn.

Slenkovich also identified two common misunderstandings in the area of LD eligibility. First, a spelling disability alone does not qualify a child as LD; the child must qualify in one of the seven categories indicated. Spelling could, however, be included as a component of the category of written expression (1986, November).

Second, to qualify for special education and related services within the category of LD, the child must have a disability that adversely affects educational performance. High-ability children may demonstrate a significant and unusual discrepancy between ability and achievement in one or more of the seven categories. However, if they are achieving at or near grade level in that area, they do not qualify as LD under IDEA-Part B (Slenkovich, 1988b, March; also *J. D. by J. D. v. Pawlet School District*, 2000).

The 1980s witnessed a steady increase in the number of children identified as LD. Chalfant (1989) believed that this increase raises serious questions about the concept of LD and identification practices. Furthermore, evidence suggests that team members often fail to adhere to the eligibility criteria outlined in the law. Mentally or emotionally impaired pupils are at times qualified as learning disabled because LD is seen as a relatively stigma-free classification (Turnbull & Turnbull, 2000). Team members also sometimes classify children who are simply slow learners as LD to provide a child with more individualized instruction than is available in regular education. These practices are inconsistent with the federal regulations implementing IDEA-Part B.

Emotional Disturbance

Emotional disturbance is defined as follows:

> (i) The term means a condition exhibiting one or more of the following characteristics over a long period of time and to a marked degree that adversely affects a child's educational performance:

(A) An inability to learn that cannot be explained by intellectual, sensory, or health factors.

(B) An inability to build or maintain satisfactory interpersonal relationships with peers and teachers.

(C) Inappropriate types of behavior or feelings under normal circumstances.

(D) A general pervasive mood of unhappiness or depression.

(E) A tendency to develop physical symptoms or fears associated with personal or school problems.

(ii) The term includes schizophrenia. The term does not apply to children who are socially maladjusted, unless it is determined that they have an emotional disturbance. (34 C.F.R. § 300.7)

The IDEA-Part B definition of emotional disturbance (ED) has been controversial since it was adopted in 1975. It is a modification of a definition of the emotionally disturbed schoolchild first outlined by Bower in 1957 (Bower, 1982). Bower's definition grew out of a California study in the late 1950s of children identified by school personnel as emotionally disturbed. This study found that emotionally disturbed children differed from their classmates on a number of characteristics: They were poor learners; they had few, if any, satisfactory interpersonal relationships; they behaved oddly or inappropriately; they were depressed or unhappy; and they developed illnesses or phobias. These characteristics also were found among nondisturbed children; however, the disturbed children displayed the characteristics to a marked degree over a period of time (Bower, 1982).

Bower did not differentiate between emotionally disturbed and socially maladjusted (SM) children in his definition. He believed that emotionally disturbed and socially maladjusted children were not separate entities. Federal policy makers, however, feared that a definition of emotionally disturbed based on Bower's original description would result in a category of special education eligibility that was too broad and costly for schools. They consequently added a clause excluding children who are socially maladjusted unless they also are emotionally disturbed.

The ED definition, particularly the exclusionary clause, has generated diagnostic disagreements and confusion. Slenkovich has advocated a rather narrow, legally correct interpretation of emotionally disturbed. She advises the team to consider the IDEA requirements point by point when making eligibility decisions for the emotional disturbance classification (1988, February).

Under IDEA-Part B, the term emotional disturbance means that the child suffers from an emotional "condition exhibiting one or more … characteristics over a long period of time and to a marked degree." Bower found that one or more of the emotionally disturbed characteristics were found among almost all nondisturbed students in the California study to some extent at different times. The crucial differentiation was based on the observation that in children with emotional disturbance, "the characteristics existed to *a marked degree over a long period of time*" (Bower, 1982, p. 57). Slenkovich suggested that, consistent with the psychiatric diagnosis of schizophrenia, six months might be seen as the minimum period of time (1988, February).

Consistent with Bower's original definition, the disturbance also must be present to a marked degree; it must be overt and observable. The definition of emotionally disturbed "avoids presumptions about the child's intrapsychic condition, psychiatric nosology, or clinical designation. It does not presume to go beyond what is observable in the school setting....It accepts as given that emotional disturbance is disturbing to others" (Bower, 1982, p. 57). As Slenkovich suggests, school personnel can perceive that the child is experiencing a problem (1988, February).

Also consistent with Bower's original definition, the emotional disturbance must adversely affect educational performance. If a student is performing within his or her expected range for age and ability, then he or she does not qualify as ED under IDEA-Part B (Slenkovich, 1988, February).

The child with emotional disturbance under IDEA-Part B must exhibit one or more of five characteristics:

1. *An inability to learn* because of the emotional disturbance. Emotional difficulties interfere with the school performance of many children. However, in order to qualify as ED using this part of the definition, the child must be so disturbed he or she cannot learn.
2. *An inability to build or maintain satisfactory interpersonal relationships with peers and teachers.* Children who are simply unpopular or associate with an undesirable peer group do not manifest this characteristic. The child must be so disturbed that he or she cannot enter into or maintain relationships with peers and teachers.
3. *Inappropriate types of behavior or feelings under normal circumstances,* appears to mean odd, bizarre, unusual behavior; not simply behavior that is disturbing to the class and teacher.
4. *A general or pervasive mood of unhappiness or depression.* The mood of unhappiness or depression must be observable.
5. *A tendency to develop physical symptoms or fears associated with personal or school problems.* Again, the fears or symptoms must be marked and occur over a long period of time (adapted from Slenkovich, 1988, February, pp. 153–164).

The ED definition also expressly includes children diagnosed as schizophrenic. Children diagnosed as autistic are eligible under a separate disability category.

The last element of the ED definition excludes children who are socially maladjusted unless they also are emotionally disturbed. This portion of the definition has generated much discussion because the federal regulations do not define socially maladjusted, and differentiating between emotionally impaired and socially maladjusted children is problematic. The two categories are not mutually exclusive; some children are emotionally disturbed *and* socially maladjusted (Clarizio, 1987; McConaughy & Skiba, 1993).

Bower (1982), as noted previously, believed that attempts to differentiate between emotionally disturbed and socially maladjusted children are artificial and that such distinctions miss the more important point that both groups of children are in need of special help (see also Short & Shapiro, 1993). Some have called for a broader interpretation of emotional disturbance to include socially maladjusted (Council for Children with Behavior Disorders Executive Committee, 1987); others have challenged regular education to develop better programs for socially maladjusted students who are not emotionally disturbed (Clarizio, 1987). As will be seen in Chapter 6, some pupils not eligible for special education and related services under the emotional disturbance category of IDEA-Part B may qualify as handicapped under Section 504.

Thus, aspects of the ED definition are vague, subjective, and controversial. Confusion also arises from the fact that nonschool mental health professionals typically are trained to use a system for classifying childhood disorders that differs from IDEA. The system of classification that is most frequently used outside the schools is the *Diagnostic and Statistical Manual of Mental Disorders* (*DSM-IV-TR*) (American Psychiatric Association, 2000). As Slenkovich has observed, psychologists and psychiatrists in nonschool settings often assume (and state in reports to schools) that a child diagnosed as suffering from an emotional problem under *DSM-IV-TR* automatically qualifies for special education and related services as emotionally disturbed (1988, February). However, in order to qualify for special education as ED under IDEA-Part B, a child must be found eligible under the IDEA-Part B definition.

Other Health Impairment

> Other health impairment means having limited strength, vitality or alertness, including a heightened alertness to environmental stimuli, that results in limited alertness with respect to the educational environment, that—
>
> (i) Is due to chronic or acute health problems such as asthma, attention deficit disorder or attention deficit hyperactivity disorder, diabetes, epilepsy, a heart condition, hemophilia, lead poisoning, leukemia, nephritis, rheumatic fever, and sickle cell anemia; and
>
> (ii) Adversely affects a child's educational performance. (34 C.F.R. § 300.7)

Beginning in the 1980s, the courts and the Office of Special Education Programs (OSEP) began to address questions regarding whether students with Acquired Immune Deficiency Syndrome (AIDS), alcohol and chemical dependency, and Attention Deficit Disorder/Attention Deficit Hyperactivity Disorder (ADD/ADHD) qualify as having an other health impairment under Part B. Court rulings have determined that students with AIDS qualify under the other health impairment classification only if their physical condition is such that it adversely affects educational performance (*Doe v. Belleville,* 1987). However, as will be seen in Chapter 6, pupils with AIDS are protected by Section 504 of The Rehabilitation Act of 1973.

OSEP also has addressed the question of whether chemically dependent pupils (alcohol- or drug-addicted) qualify as having an other health impairment under IDEA. According to OSEP, chemical dependency does not, in and of itself, qualify a child for special education and related services within the other health impairment classification (quoted in Slenkovich, 1987, June). However, students with drug or alcohol dependency may be protected by Section 504 (see Chapter 6).

A third question was whether students with ADD/ADHD qualify for special education and related services under the other health impairment classification of IDEA-Part B. Unlike its precursors, IDEA 1997 specifically includes ADD/ADHD among the disabling conditions listed under "other health impairment." To be eligible within this category, the child must have limited strength, vitality, or alertness due to the ADD/ADHD, and the condition must adversely impact the child's education performance and result in the need for special education and related services. Thus, some pupils with ADD/ADHD qualify within the IDEA definition of other health impairment. Other students do not qualify under the other health impairment classification but may be eligible for accommodations in regular education under Section 504 if the ADD/ADHD *substantially limits* (rather than *adversely affects*) their educational performance (see Chapter 6) ("ADD/ADHD Students," 1999).

Pupil Evaluation Procedures

This portion of the chapter describes a series of lawsuits concerning the misclassification of racial and ethnic minority pupils as "mentally retarded," and the safeguards Congress subsequently included in IDEA to protect against misclassification.

The Problem of Misclassification

As noted previously, right-to-education court cases signaled to Congress that federal legislation was needed to ensure educational opportunities for all children with disabilities. A second type of court case was important in shaping the nondiscriminatory testing, classification, and placement procedures required by IDEA-Part B. These cases concerned the misclassification of racial and ethnic minority group children as "mentally retarded" and their placement in special classes for the educable mentally retarded. They raised questions regarding school violations of the due process and equal protection guarantees of the 14th Amendment (Bersoff, 1979).

Due Process. The due process clause of the 14th Amendment protects individuals from arbitrary or unwarranted stigmatization by the state that may interfere with the ability to acquire property (*Wisconsin v. Constantineau*, 1971). Under the protections of the 14th Amendment, the state (school) may not assign a negative label such as mentally retarded without due process; that is, without some sort of fair and impartial decision-making procedures (Bersoff & Ysseldyke, 1977). In the *P.A.R.C.* ruling, a number of procedural safeguards against misclassification were required. For example, parents were given the right to an impartial hearing if they were dissatisfied with their child's special education classification or placement.

Equal Protection. With the landmark *Brown v. Board of Education* decision in 1954, the Supreme Court ruled that school segregation by race was a denial of the right to equal protection (equal educational opportunity) under the 14th Amendment. Following this decision, the courts began to scrutinize school practices that suggested within-school segregation; that is, where minority group children were segregated and treated differently within the schools. A number of suits against the public schools were filed in which minority group children were overrepresented in lower education tracks and special education classes. These lower tracks and special education classes were seen as educationally inferior and a denial of equal education opportunities. The claimants in these cases maintained that many children were misclassified and inappropriately placed based on racially and culturally discriminatory classification and placement procedures (see Exhibit 5–2).

Exhibit 5–2. Cases Concerning Misclassification of Ethnic Minority Children

Hobson v. Hansen (1967, 1969)

The first significant legal challenge to the use of aptitude tests for assigning minority group children to low-ability classes was *Hobson v. Hansen*. In this case, African American and poor children were disproportionately assigned to the lower tracks in the Washington, D.C., public schools on the basis of scores on group-administered aptitude tests. Federal Judge Wright noted that the tracking system was rigid, it segregated students by race, and that the lower tracks were educationally inferior. He further stated that because the aptitude tests were "standardized primarily on and are relevant to a white middle-class group of students, they produce inaccurate and misleading test scores when given to lower class and Negro students" (*Hobson*, 1967, p. 514). He ruled that the tracking system was a violation of equal protection laws and ordered the system abolished.

Diana v. State Board of Education (1970)

Diana was a class action suit filed in California on behalf of nine Mexican American children placed in classes for the educable mentally retarded (EMR) on the basis of Stanford-Binet (LM) or WISC IQ scores. Diana, one of the plaintiffs, came from a Spanish-speaking family and was placed in an EMR classroom based on an IQ score of 30. When she was later retested in Spanish and English by a bilingual psychologist, she scored 49 points higher on the same test and no longer qualified for special class placement (Bersoff & Ysseldyke, 1977). The consent decree in *Diana* required children be assessed in their primary language or with sections of tests that do not depend on knowledge of English (Reschly, 1979).

Guadalupe Organization, Inc. v. Tempe Elementary School District (1972)

Guadalupe was a class action suit filed on behalf of Yaqui Indian and Mexican American pupils. The consent decree in *Guadalupe* also required assessment in the child's primary language or the use of nonverbal measures if the child's primary language was not English. *Guadalupe*, however, went further than *Diana* in requiring a multifaceted evaluation that included assessment of adaptive behavior and an interview with the parents in the child's home (Reschly, 1979). *Guadalupe* also required due process procedures, including informed consent for evaluation and placement.

Larry P. v. Riles (1984)

Larry P. was a class action suit filed on behalf of African American pupils placed in classes for the educable mentally retarded (EMR) in the San Francisco School District. The plaintiffs claimed that many African American children were misclassified as mentally retarded, and that IQ tests were the primary basis for classification as EMR. The court asked the schools to demonstrate that their methods of classification (i.e., use of IQ test scores) were "rational" or valid for the purpose of classifying African American children as mentally retarded and in need of special education. The school district was unable to convince the court that IQ tests were valid for the purpose of placing African American children in EMR classes, and in 1972 the court temporarily enjoined the schools from any further placement of African American children in EMR classes on the basis of IQ test results.

In the second phase of *Larry P.*, the trial on the substantive issues, the plaintiffs requested that the court consider their claims under both the 14th Amendment and the new federal statute, Pub. L. No. 94-142. More than 10,000 pages of testimony were

Exhibit 5–2. (*Continued*)

presented during this phase. In his lengthy opinion, Judge Peckham characterized the EMR classes as "inferior" and "dead-end." Based on his analysis of the expert testimony, he found IQ tests to be racially and culturally discriminatory. He ruled that the school failed to show that IQ tests were valid for the purpose of selecting African American children for EMR classes, and, in his view, IQ scores weighed so heavily in decision making that they "contaminated" and biased the assessment process. He permanently enjoined the state from using any standardized intelligence tests to identify African American children for EMR classes without prior permission of the court (Bersoff, 1982; Reschly, 1979). In 1986, Judge Peckham banned the use of IQ tests to assign African American children to any special education program except for the state-supported gifted and talented program.

In 1988, a group of parents filed a suit claiming that the state's ban on IQ tests discriminated against African American children by denying them an opportunity to take the tests helpful in determining special education needs. In 1992, Judge Peckham issued an order allowing African American children to be given IQ tests with parent consent (*Crawford v. Honig*, 1994). The California State Department of Education continued to prohibit the use of IQ tests with African American children, however. The California Association of School Psychologists made an unsuccessful attempt to challenge the state's ban on IQ testing in 1994 (*California Association of School Psychologists v. Superintendent of Public Instruction*, 1994).

P.A.S.E. v. Hannon (1980)

This case was filed on behalf of African American children in the Chicago public schools. As Bersoff notes, "the facts, issues, claims and witnesses" were similar to *Larry P.*, but the outcome was different (1982, p. 81). Judge Grady carefully listened to the same expert witnesses who testified in San Francisco. He decided that the issue of racial and cultural bias could best be answered by examining the test questions himself. He proceeded to read aloud every question on the WISC, WISC-R, and Stanford-Binet (LM) and every acceptable response. As a result of his analysis, he found only eight items on the WISC or WISC-R to be biased and one item on the Stanford-Binet. He concluded that the use of IQ tests within the context of a multifaceted assessment process as outlined in IDEA was not likely to result in racially or culturally discriminatory classification decisions and found in favor of the school system (Bersoff, 1982).

The first three court cases summarized in Exhibit 5–2, along with *P.A.R.C.* and *Mills*, were extremely influential in shaping the IDEA-Part B requirements for nondiscriminatory testing and classification and the procedural or due process safeguards against misclassification. *Larry P. v. Riles* and *P.A.S.E. v. Hannon* addressed the question of whether IQ tests are valid for the purpose of classifying and placing minority group children in special classes. The court in *P.A.S.E.* ruled that the use of IQ tests within the context of the assessment process outlined in IDEA-Part B was not likely to result in racially or culturally discriminatory placement decisions. As an additional safeguard against misclassification of ethnic minority children, IDEA 1997 requires each state to gather and examine data to determine whether a significant disproportionality of race is occurring in the state in relation to the identification of children as disabled and the children's placement. If it is determined that a significant disproportionality exists, the state must provide for the review and, if appropriate, revision of policies and practices (34 C.F.R. § 300.755).

Protection in Evaluation Procedures

The early court cases concerning the misclassification of pupils as mentally impaired prompted Congress to include a number of standards with regard to both the content and the process of assessment, classification, and special education placement in IDEA-Part B. IDEA-Part B requires each SEA or LEA to establish and implement procedures to ensure a full and individual initial evaluation of each child's education needs before any action is taken with respect to the initial classification and placement in special education (34 C.F.R. § 300.320). Informed parental consent for assessment and the nondiscriminatory testing and assessment procedures required by IDEA-Part B were discussed in Chapter 4. Since the mid-1980s, many schools have introduced building-based (prereferral) problem-solving teams to assist teachers in planning interventions for pupils with learning or behavior problems. Such programs are seen as an additional safeguard against inappropriate referral, unnecessary testing, and misclassification (see Chalfant & Pysh, 1989).

Student Evaluations and Eligibility Determination

In conducting an evaluation, IDEA-Part B requires the LEA to (a) use a variety of assessment tools and strategies to gather relevant functional and developmental information, including information provided by the parent, that may assist in determining whether the child has a disability and the content of the child's individualized education program, including information related to enabling the child to be involved in and progress in the general curriculum or, for preschool children, to participate in appropriate activities; (b) not use any single procedure as the sole criterion for determining whether a child has a disability or determining an appropriate educational program for the child; and (c) use technically sound instruments that may assess the relative contribution of cognitive and behavioral factors, in addition to physical or developmental factors. In addition, assessment tools must be validated for the purpose used and fair, and the child must be assessed in all areas related to the suspected disability (see Chapter 4). The assessment strategies must provide relevant information that directly assists in determining the education needs of the child (34 C.F.R. § 300.532).

After completion of the administration of tests and other evaluation materials, the determination of whether the child has a disability is made by a team that includes qualified professionals and the parent. School personnel may develop *tentative* alternative proposals for meeting a child's educational needs, but actual eligibility and placement decisions must be made at a meeting with the parents (see *Spielberg v. Henrico County Public Schools*, 1988). The group making the eligibility determination must include individuals with the knowledge and skills necessary to (a) interpret the evaluation data, (b) make an informed determination as to whether the child is a child with a disability, and (c) determine whether the child needs special education and related services. The composition of this team will vary depending upon the nature of the child's suspected disability. Some or all of the persons who serve on this eligibility determination team may also serve on the IEP team. The parent is given a copy of the evaluation report (34 C.F. R. §§ 300.530-300.534).

Under IDEA-Part B, parents have the right to obtain an independent educational evaluation (IEE) of their child, and those findings must be considered by the school "in any decision made with respect to the provision of FAPE [a free appropriate public education] to the child." An IEE is an evaluation conducted by a qualified examiner who is not employed by the district responsible for the education of the child in question. The school, on request, must provide parents with information about where an independent educational evaluation may be obtained, and the district's criteria for an IEE (34 C.F.R. § 300.502).

Depending on the circumstances, an IEE may be conducted at parent or school expense. If the parent disagrees with the evaluation done by the school, the district is required, with no unnecessary delay, to either ensure that an IEE is conducted at district expense or initiate a due process hearing if it believes its evaluation was appropriate. If the hearing officer determines that the evaluation was appropriate, parents may proceed with an IEE, but at their own expense.

When a child is seen for re-evaluation, professionals qualified to make eligibility determinations and the IEP team review existing evaluation data on the child and, on the basis of that review (along with input from the parents), identify what additional data are needed to determine (a) whether the child continues to have a particular category of disability, (b) the present levels of performance and education needs of the child, (c) whether the child continues to need special education services, and (d) what services are needed for the child to meet education goals and participate, as appropriate, in the general curriculum. If, as part of a re-evaluation, it is determined that no additional data are needed to determine whether a child continues to have a disability, then the school ensures that the child's parents are notified of that determination and the reasons for it, along with their right to request an assessment of the child, and the LEA is not required to conduct an assessment unless requested by the child's parents. However, an LEA is required to evaluate a child with a disability before determining that the child no longer qualifies as disabled under Part B (34 C.F.R. § 300.533). (Also see the discussion of "Least Restrictive Environment," later in this chapter).

Placements

In determining the educational placement of a child with a disability, including preschool children, the LEA is required to ensure that the placement decision is made by a group of persons, including the parents, and other persons knowledgeable of the child, the meaning of the evaluation data, and the placement options. Placement must be determined at least annually based on the child's IEP, in the least restrictive environment, and be as close as possible to the child's home, and unless a child with a disability requires some other arrangement, the child is educated in the school he or she would attend if not disabled. In selecting the least restrictive environment, consideration is given to any potential harmful effect on the child or services that he or she needs, and a child is not removed from education in an age-appropriate regular classroom solely because of needed modifications in the general curriculum (34 C.F.R. § 300.552).

Individualized Education Program

As previously noted, in the *P.A.R.C.* consent decree, the court required that instructional programs for each child with disabilities be "appropriate for his learning capabilities," and the *Mills* ruling required that a disabled child's education be "suited to his needs." This policy of providing an appropriate education for children with disabilities is achieved in IDEA-Part B by the individualized education program (IEP). Congress viewed the IEP as a means of preventing functional exclusion of children with disabilities from opportunities to learn, and the yearly review of the IEP was seen as a safeguard against misclassification and as a way to encourage continued parent involvement (Turnbull & Turnbull, 2000). Children placed in private schools by the SEA or LEA must receive special education and related services in conformance with an IEP; in contrast, schools districts are given broad latitude in developing a service plan that determines which parentally placed private school children with disabilities will receive special education and related services and the types of services to be provided (Borreca et al., 1999).

The Meeting

The SEA or LEA is responsible for initiating and conducting a meeting for the purpose of developing the child's IEP. The IEP meeting must be held within 30 calendar days after the determination that the child needs special education and related services (34 C.F.R. § 300.343). Schools are not required to hold the IEP meeting within 30 days of the *referral* for evaluation; the 30-day countdown to the IEP starts the day that the group making the eligibility determination finds that the child qualifies for and needs special education.

The Team

The IEP team is composed of (a) the parents of the child; (b) at least one regular education teacher of the child (if the child is, or may be, participating in a regular education environment); (c) at least one special education teacher, or if appropriate, at least one special education provider of the child; (d) a representative of the LEA who is qualified to provide, or supervise the provision of, specially designed instruction to meet the needs of children with disabilities, who is knowledgeable about the general curriculum, and who is knowledgeable about the availability of resources of the LEA; (e) an individual who can interpret the instructional implications of evaluation results (who may already be a member of the team in another capacity); (f) at the discretion of the parent or the LEA, other individuals who have knowledge or special expertise regarding the child, including related services personnel as appropriate; and (g) if appropriate, the child (34 C.F.R. § 300.344).

If private school placement is under consideration by the IEP team, the LEA must ensure that a representative of the private school attends the meeting or in some way participates in the meeting to develop the initial IEP (e.g., telephone conference call). After a child with a disability enters a private school or facility, any meetings to review and revise the child's IEP may be initiated and conducted by the private school or facility at the discretion of the LEA, as long as the LEA and parents are involved in any decisions about the IEP (34 C.F.R. § 300.349).

If the purpose of the IEP meeting is to consider transition services for the student (services to promote movement from school to postschool activities), the school must invite the student to attend. If the student is not able to attend, the school must take steps to ensure that the student's preferences and interests are considered. Schools also must ensure that representatives of agencies responsible for providing or paying for transition services attend the meeting or in some way participate in the planning of any transition services (34 C.F.R. § 300.344).

Prior to 1975, parents often were not included in special education placement decisions, and school policies of closed records made it difficult for parents to gain access to information about how such decisions were made. IDEA 1997 clarified that each SEA or LEA must ensure that the parents of a child with a disability are members of any group that makes decisions on the identification, evaluation, and educational placement of their child (34 C.F. R. § 300.501). In order to ensure parent participation and shared decision making in the development of the IEP, IDEA-Part B requires the school to provide adequate prior notice of team meetings, and the meeting must be scheduled at a mutually agreed upon time and place. Notice must include the purpose, time, place, and location of the meeting and who will be in attendance. A *meeting* does not include informal or unscheduled conversations among school personnel or conversations on issues such as teaching methodology, lesson plans, or coordination of services if those issues are not addressed in the IEP. A meeting also does not include preparatory activities that school personnel engage in to develop a proposal (or a response to a parent proposal) that will be discussed at a later meeting.

Schools must make reasonable efforts to ensure that parents understand, and are able to participate, in any group discussions relating to the educational placement of their child, including providing interpreters for parents who are deaf or whose native language is other than English. If neither parent can attend, the school must attempt to ensure parent participation using other means such as conference telephone calls (34 C.F.R.§ 300.501). The IEP meeting may be conducted without parent participation only if the school is unable to convince the parents to attend. The school must document its efforts to arrange a mutually agreed upon meeting. This documentation might include records of telephone calls and the results of those calls, copies of correspondence to parents and responses, or records of home visits or visits to the parent's place of employment (34 C.F.R. § 300.501, also 34 C.F.R. § 300.345).

Development of the IEP

IDEA-Part B outlines a number of factors the IEP team is obligated to consider in developing each child's IEP. The team must consider the strengths of the child and the concerns of the parents for enhancing the education of their child, and the results of the initial evaluation or most recent evaluation of the child. In addition, the team should consider the following special factors: (a) in the case of a child whose behavior impedes his or her learning or that of others, the team should consider strategies, including positive behavioral interventions, and supports to address that behavior; (b) in the case of a child with limited English proficiency, the team should consider the language needs of the child as such needs relate to his or her IEP; (c) in the case of a child who is blind or visually impaired, the team should consider providing instruction in Braille and the use of Braille, unless the IEP team determines after evaluation of reading and writing skills, needs, and media, that use of Braille is not appropriate for the child; (d) in the case of the child who is deaf or hard of hearing, the team should consider the child's full range of needs, including language and communication needs, opportunities for direct communications with peers and professional personnel in the child's language and communication mode, opportunities for direct instruction in the child's language and communication mode, and academic level; and (e) whether the child requires assistive technology devices and services (34 C.F.R. § 300.346).

Content of the IEP

IDEA-Part B requires a written IEP for each child that includes the following:

1. A statement of the child's present levels of educational performance, including how the child's disability affects the child's involvement and progress in the general curriculum; or for preschool children, as appropriate, how the disability affects the child's participation in appropriate activities.
2. A statement of measurable annual goals, including benchmarks or short-term objectives, related to meeting the child's needs that result from the child's disability, to enable the child to be involved in and progress in the general curriculum, and meeting each of the child's other educational needs that result from the child's disability.
3. A statement of the special education and related services and supplementary aids and services to be provided to the child, or on behalf of the child, and a statement of the program modifications or supports for school personnel that will be provided for the child to advance appropriately toward attaining the annual goals, to be involved and progress in the general curriculum, and to participate in extracurricular and other nonacademic activities, and to be educated and participate with other children with disabilities and nondisabled children.
4. An explanation of the extent, if any, to which the child will not participate with nondisabled children in the regular class and in nonacademic activities.

5. A statement of any individual modifications in the administration of state or districtwide assessments of student achievement that are needed in order for the child to participate in such assessments and, if the IEP team determines that the child will not participate in a particular state or districtwide assessment of student achievement (or part of such assessment), a statement of why that assessment is not appropriate for the child; and how the child will be assessed.
6. The projected date for the beginning of the services and modifications, and the anticipated frequency, location, and duration of those services and modifications.
7. A statement of how the child's progress toward his or her annual goals will be measured and how the child's parents will be informed regularly (through such means as periodic report cards), at least as often as parents are informed of their nondisabled children's progress, of their child's progress toward the annual goals and the extent to which that progress is sufficient to enable the child to achieve the goals by the end of the year.
8. Beginning at age 14 (or younger, if determined appropriate by the IEP team) and updated annually, a statement of the transition service needs of the child that focuses on the child's courses of study (such as participation in a vocational education program); beginning at age 16 (or younger, if determined appropriate by the IEP team), a statement of needed transition services for the child including, when appropriate, a statement of the interagency responsibilities or any needed linkages.
9. In a state that transfers rights at the age of majority, beginning at least one year before the child reaches the age of majority under state law, the IEP must include a statement that the child has been informed of his or her rights that will transfer to the child on reaching the age of majority (34 C.F.R. § 300.347).

As noted previously, in the case of a child whose behavior impedes his or her learning or that of others, the team should consider strategies, including positive behavioral interventions and supports, to address that behavior (34 C.F.R. § 300.346). When problem behaviors are evident, the IEP team must conduct an assessment to determine the function the behavior serves and develop a plan to teach appropriate replacement behaviors (Yell et al., 2000). As Yell et al. (2000) suggest, the IEPs of students with disabilities who evidence problem behaviors should address those behaviors in the present levels of performance, goals and objectives, and special education services section of the IEP. (Also see Chapter 7.)

The IEP team also must identify any individual modifications in the administration of state or districtwide assessments of student achievement that are needed in order for the child to participate in such assessments. An assessment accommodation "is an alteration in the way a test is administered or in the way the student takes a test" (Council for Exceptional Children [CEC], 2000, p. 15) and may involve changes in the duration of or place of testing, changes in the scheduling of when testing occurs, alterations in the way items are presented, or alterations in how a students responds to an assessment. Such accommodations should be based on individual student need and are likely to be the same as or similar to the kinds of accommodations made for the student in the classroom (see CEC, 2000; also *Standards*).

Parents are given a copy of the IEP at no cost to the parent (34 C.F.R. § 300.345).

Special Education. The IEP must include a statement of the specific special education and related services to be provided to the child. The term *special education* is defined as specially designed instruction, at no cost to the parents, to meet the unique needs of a child with a disability, including instruction in the classroom, in the home, in hospitals and institutions, and in other settings (34 C.F.R. § 300.26). Special education includes instruction in physical education, vocational education, and travel training (i.e., instruction in the skills necessary to move effectively and safely from place to place), if designed to meet the unique needs of a child with a disability. Speech pathology instruction is included as special education; however, speech pathology also can be a related service (34 C.F.R. § 300.26) .

IDEA-Part B requires schools to provide a statement of needed transition services for pupils with disabilities beginning at age 16 (or younger if appropriate) as part of the IEP. *Transition services* are defined as a coordinated set of activities for a student with a disability that (a) are designed within an outcome-oriented process, that promote movement from school to post-school activities, including post-secondary education, vocational training, integrated employment (including supported employment), continuing and adult education, adult services, independent living or community participation; (b) are based upon the individual student's needs, taking into account the student's preferences and interests; and (c) include instruction, related services, community experiences, the development of employment and other post school adult living objectives, and, when appropriate, acquisition of daily living skills and functional vocational evaluation (34 C.F.R. § 300.29).

Related Services. *Related services* means transportation and such developmental, corrective, and other supportive services as may be required to assist a child with a disability to benefit from special education and includes speech-language pathology and audiology, psychological services, physical and occupational therapy, recreation (including therapeutic recreation services), social work services, counseling services (including rehabilitation counseling), orientation and mobility services, medical services for diagnostic or evaluation purposes, and early identification and assessment of disabilities in children. The term also includes school health services, social work services in schools, and parent counseling and training (34 C.F.R. §§ 300.24, 300.26).

Under IDEA-Part B, a related service cannot "stand alone—it must be attached to a special education program, and it must be a necessary service for the child to benefit from special instruction" (Slenkovich, 1988c, March, p. 168). If the child is not eligible for special education under IDEA-Part B, there can be no related services, and the child (lacking a disability) is not covered under the Act.

Supplementary Aids and Services. *Supplementary aids and services* means aids, services, and other supports that are provided in regular education classes or other education-related settings to enable children with disabilities to be educated with children who are not disabled to the maximum extent appropriate (34 C.F.R. § 300.28).

Implementation of the IEP

The IEP must be made accessible to each of the child's teachers and service providers, and each must be informed of his or her responsibilities under the IEP and of the specific accommodations, modifications, and supports that must be provided under the IEP (34 C.F.R. § 300.342). The school is accountable for providing the special education instruction and related services outlined in the IEP. The description of services to be provided is an "enforceable promise" (Slenkovich, 1988c, March, p. 168). Recommendations for nonspecial education services the school is not required to provide (e.g., for family therapy) should be made separate from the IEP (Slenkovich, 1987, December).

As noted previously, the IEP must include a statement of annual goals and benchmarks or short-term instructional objectives. Neither the school nor the teacher may be held accountable if a child does not achieve the IEP goals; they must, however, make a good faith effort toward helping the child achieve his or her goals (34 C.F.R. § 300.350).

If the school and parents agree on the child's classification, placement, and proposed program plan, the IEP is implemented as soon as possible following the meeting (34 C.F.R. § 300.343). If the parents and school do not agree, either party may request mediation or a due process hearing. Unless parents and the school agree otherwise, the student remains in his or her present placement during any due process proceeding. This is the *stay put* rule (34 C.F.R. § 300.514). It also should be noted that individual members of the IEP team may express a dissenting opinion in writing if they do not agree with the child's classification, placement, or proposed program plan.

Each child's IEP must be reviewed and revised at least annually, and each child must be seen for re-evaluation at least once every three years, or more often if warranted. However, if the IEP team determines that no additional assessment data are needed as part of a re-evaluation, the LEA is not required to conduct additional assessments unless requested by the child's parents. During the annual review of the IEP, the team must determine whether the annual goals for the child are being achieved and revise the IEP as appropriate to address (a) any lack of expected progress toward annual goals and progress in the general curriculum, (b) the results of any re-evaluations conducted, (c) information about the child provided by the parents, or (d) the child's anticipated needs. The regular education teacher is required to participate in the IEP review as appropriate (34 C.F.R. § 300.343). The LEA also must convene an IEP meeting if an agency fails to provide the transition services described in a child's IEP.

Least Restrictive Environment

As noted earlier in the chapter, prior to 1975, children with moderate or severe impairments were often routinely excluded from school. Children with mild disabilities frequently were segregated in special classes with few opportunities to interact with their nonhandicapped peers. In some cases, these classes were located in a separate corridor of the school. At times, the less capable teachers were assigned to teach children with disabilities, and typically the classroom facilities and equipment were less adequate than for nondisabled children (Turnbull & Turnbull, 2000). Few special class children ever returned to the mainstream.

The "least restrictive alternative" doctrine evolved from court decisions during the 1960s (e.g., *Wyatt v. Stickney,* 1971). Turnbull and Turnbull (2000) summarized this constitutionally based doctrine as follows: "[E]ven if the legislative purpose of a government action is appropriate…the purpose may not be pursued by means that broadly stifle personal liberties if it can be achieved by less oppressive restrictive means" (p. 243). The doctrine of least restrictive alternative was at the foundation of the deinstitutionalization movement in the field of mental health in the late 1960s and early 1970s. The doctrine recognizes that it may be necessary to restrict personal freedoms when treating a mentally ill individual, but the state should deprive the patient of his or her liberties only to the extent necessary to provide treatment (Turnbull & Turnbull, 2000).

This principle also was applied to the education of the disabled in IDEA-Part B with the requirement that special education and related services be provided in a setting that is the least restrictive environment (LRE) appropriate for the child. Congress recognized that integration of children with disabilities into the educational mainstream was not likely to occur without a legal mandate. Many educators and nondisabled pupils and their parents held negative stereotypes and attitudes toward special education students (Martin, 1979). Consequently, IDEA-Part B requires the SEA or LEA to ensure that:

> To the maximum extent appropriate, children with disabilities, including children in public or private institutions or other care facilities, are educated with children who are nondisabled, and special classes, separate schooling or other removal of children with disabilities from the regular educational environment occurs only when the nature or severity of the disability is such that education in regular classes with the use of supplementary aids and services cannot be achieved satisfactorily. (Pub. L. No. 105–17, § 612, 111 Stat. 61 [1997])

Congress intended that the SEA or LEA make available a continuum of alternative placements to meet the needs of children with disabilities, including instruction in regular classes with supplementary services, special classes, special schools, home instruction, and instruction in hospitals and institutions (34 C.F.R. § 300.551). Congress also intended that decisions about the extent to which pupils with disabilities can be educated with nondisabled children be made on the basis of the child's individual needs and capabilities.

A number of court decisions have addressed the school's responsibility to ensure that children with disabilities are educated in the least restrictive, appropriate environment (e.g., *Daniel R. R. v. Texas Board of Education, El Paso Independent School District,* 1989; *Greer v. Rome City School District,* 1991; *Sacramento City Unified School District, Board of Education v. Rachel H.,* 1994). In *Greer v. Rome City School District,* the judge noted that "Congress created a statutory preference for educating handicapped children with nonhandicapped children" (1991, p. 695). In *Board of Education, Sacramento City Unified School District v. Holland,* the court stated that the Act's preference for inclusion of children with disabilities in the regular educational environment "rises to the level of a rebuttable presumption" (1992, pp. 877–878). This means that placement decision making must begin with the assumption that the child can be educated in the regular classroom:

> [B]efore the school district may conclude that a handicapped child should be educated outside the regular classroom, it must consider whether

> supplemental aids and services would permit satisfactory education in the regular classroom. The school district must consider the whole range of supplemental aids and services, including resource rooms and itinerant instruction, for which it is obligated under the Act...Only when the handicapped child's education may not be achieved satisfactorily, even with one or more of these supplemental aids and services, may the school board consider placing the child outside of the regular classroom. (*Greer,* 1991, p. 696)

In *Board of Education, Sacramento City Unified School District v. Holland* (1992) and, on appeal, *Sacramento City School District v. Rachel H.* (1994), [the *Holland* case], the courts established a four-part test for determining compliance with IDEA's mainstreaming requirement. These rulings concerned Rachel, an elementary school child with moderate mental impairment (IQ 44), whose parents requested full-time placement in a regular classroom with supplemental services. The school district, however, believed that Rachel was too severely disabled to benefit from full-time regular class and recommended special education placement for all academic instruction. The Hollands appealed the school's placement decision to a state hearing officer who ordered the district to place Rachel in a regular classroom with supportive services. The school district appealed this determination to the district (1992) and circuit court (1994), and to the Supreme Court (*certiorari denied,* 1994). The courts affirmed the hearing officer's decision that Rachel should be educated in the regular classroom.

In *Holland,* the courts considered the following factors in determining the least restrictive appropriate environment: (a) the educational benefits available in a regular classroom, supplemented with appropriate aids and services, as compared with the educational benefits of a special education classroom; (b) the nonacademic benefits of interaction with children who are not disabled; (c) the effect of the child's presence on the teacher and other children in the classroom; and (d) the cost of educating the child in a regular classroom (*Holland,* 1994, p. 1404).

In evaluating the educational benefit of inclusion in the regular classroom, the *Holland* rulings (1992, 1994) considered the learning opportunities available in alternative settings and the child's likely progress toward IEP goals if placed in the regular education classroom. In evaluating nonacademic benefits, the court considered whether the child was likely to interact with and learn from other children in the inclusive placement. As noted in an earlier case, the presumption of inclusion in the regular classroom is not rebutted unless the school shows the child's disabilities are so severe that he or she will receive little or no educational benefit from inclusion (*Devries v. Fairfax County School Board,* 1989).

With regard to the effect of the child's presence on the teacher and other children, the court in *Holland* considered two aspects of disruptive behavior: (a) whether there was detriment because the child was disruptive, distracting or unruly, and (b) whether the child would take up so much of the teacher's time that the other students would suffer from lack of attention (1994, p. 1401). *Holland* thus suggested an IEP team may consider the impact of the child's behavior on the setting where services are provided in determining an appropriate placement. However, the education of the other children must be impaired significantly by the inclusion of the child with a disability to justify exclusion on this basis. The child may be excluded from the regular education environment only if "after taking all reasonable steps to reduce the burden to the teacher, the other children in the class will still be deprived of their share of the teacher's attention" (*Holland,* 1992, p. 879; see also *Daniel R. R. v. Texas Board of Education, El Paso Independent School District,* 1989). According to Turnbull and Turnbull (2000), IDEA 1997 codified the *Holland* decision. It requires implementation of a positive behavior intervention plan to remedy problem behaviors but also allows a more restrictive placement when, despite such efforts, the student's behavior has a detrimental impact on other students and the teacher.

Schools also may consider the cost of providing an inclusive education. However, the cost must be *significantly* more expensive than alternative placements to justify an exclusion from the regular classroom on the basis of cost (*Holland,* 1994).

Some state-level administrators and parents have misinterpreted the LRE requirement of the law to mean that children with disabilities cannot be placed in separate special schools or centers. However, as Turnbull and Turnbull (2000) note, the courts have recognized that appropriate sometimes means more, rather than less, separation from normal or regular education. The LRE favors integration but allows separation when separation is needed to achieve a satisfactory educational program for the child. In *A. W. v. Northwest R-1 School District,* the judge noted that the mainstreaming requirement is "inapplicable" where it cannot be achieved satisfactorily (1987, p. 163).

A school placement that allows a child to remain with his or her family is considered to be less restrictive than a residential placement. IDEA also indicates a preference for a neighborhood school. Part B regulations state that unless "the IEP of a child with a disability requires some other arrangement, the child is educated in the school which he or she would attend if not nondisabled" (34 C.F.R. § 300.552). However, although the law indicates a preference for neighborhood schooling, proximity of the school is only one factor the IEP team must consider in making placement decisions. The court in *Flour Bluff Independent School District v. Katherine M.* (1996) noted, "Distance remains a consideration in determining the least restrictive environment...The child may have to travel farther, however, to obtain better services" (p. 675).

The SEA or LEA also must ensure that a child with a disability has opportunities to participate with nondisabled children in nonacademic and extracurricular activities (e.g., meals, recess, clubs, and interest groups) to the maximum extent appropriate to the needs of the child (34 C.F.R. § 300.553). However, in several cases (e.g., *Rettig v. Kent City School District,* 1986), the courts ruled that IDEA-Part B does not require schools to provide nonacademic and extracurricular activities to children with disabilities without regard for the child's ability to benefit from the experience.

We share in the belief that schools have a responsibility to educate disabled and nondisabled students together so that all children will be prepared to live in an integrated society. However, the trend toward inclusion raises important questions about balancing a pupil's right to an education in the least restrictive setting (LRE) with his or her right to an individualized and appropriate education (FAPE) (Turnbull & Turnbull, 2000). School psychologists, along with other team members, have an ethical and legal responsibility to ensure that decisions about inclusion are made based on a consideration of the needs of the individual child and that appropriate supports are made available to the child and his or her teachers to ensure that efforts at inclusion will benefit the child both academically and socially. Unfortunately, little research-based information is available to assist psychologists in identifying children for whom inclusion is likely to be effective (Bradley-Johnson, Johnson, & Jacob-Timm, 1995). Psychologists also must accept responsibility to ensure the academic and social progress of each special-needs child is monitored when inclusionary models are implemented, so that problems can be remedied quickly. (See Cases 8–2 and 8–3 for a discussion of the competing principles that may arise in making a decision whether to integrate a child with disabilities into the regular classroom.)

The Meaning of Appropriate Education

IDEA-Part B thus requires that children with disabilities be provided a free and appropriate education in the least restrictive environment. Since the passage of Pub. L. No. 94–142, a number of court cases have provided further interpretation of *appropriate education.* In their decision making about what is appropriate, the courts have considered several different factors, including whether IDEA-Part B procedures were followed in developing the IEP and whether the IEP is consistent with the intent of the law (Turnbull & Turnbull, 2000).

Board of Education of the Hendrick Hudson Central School District v. Rowley (1982) was the first case to reach the Supreme Court in which the Court attempted to define appropriate education (see Exhibit 5–3). The

Supreme Court's interpretation of appropriate education in *Rowley* has shaped all subsequent court decisions concerning the meaning of appropriate under IDEA-Part B. *Rowley* suggests that IDEA ensures only an education program reasonably designed to benefit the student, not the best possible or most perfect education. The *Rowley* decision set forth a two-prong test of appropriate, namely, "Were IDEA procedures followed?" and "Is the program reasonably designed to benefit the child?"

Since *Rowley*, in a number of court cases parents have challenged whether their child's special education program was reasonably calculated to enable their child to receive educational benefits (e.g., *Cordrey v. Euckert*, 1990; *Cypress-Fairbanks Independent School District v. Michael F.*, 1997; *Florence County School District Four v. Carter*, 1993). Consistent with the majority opinion in *Rowley*, these decisions suggest that the determination of whether a program is reasonably designed to confer benefits must be made on the basis of the individual child's potential (*Carter*, 1993; *Cordrey*, 1990). Furthermore, the program must be likely to provide meaningful benefit, that is, more than *de minimus* or trivial benefit, in relation to the child's potential (*Cordrey*, 1990, *Hall v. Vance County Board of Education*, 1985).

The courts also have ruled that when two or more appropriate placements are available, IEP team members may consider costs to the school in determining a child's education placement (e.g., *Clevenger v. Oak Ridge School Board*, 1984).

Exhibit 5–3. Board of Education of the Hendrick Hudson Central School District v. Rowley (1982)

The case involved Amy, a deaf child with minimal residual hearing, who understood about 50 percent of spoken language by lipreading. During her kindergarten year, the school provided an FM hearing aid to amplify speech. Her IEP for first grade included continued use of the hearing aid, instruction from a tutor for the deaf one hour each day, and speech therapy three hours each week.

Amy's parents also requested that the school provide an interpreter for the deaf in the classroom in order for her to make optimal school progress. The school and a hearing officer agreed that an interpreter was too costly and not needed because "Amy was achieving educationally, academically, and socially without such assistance" (p. 3040). A district court, however, found in favor of the parents and noted that without the interpreter Amy was not afforded the opportunity to achieve her full potential.

Based on a review of the history of IDEA, the Supreme Court concluded that Congress only intended to provide an education program "reasonably calculated to enable the child to receive educational benefits" (p. 3051) or a "basic floor of opportunity" (p. 3047) It was noted that there is no requirement under IDEA that the school provide services that maximize the potential of a child with disabilities; the "furnishing of every special service necessary to maximize each handicapped child's potential is, we think, further than Congress intended to go" (p. 3047). The Court found in favor of the school.

Extended School Year

IDEA requires extended school year services (ESY) for a child with a disability if such services are necessary to ensure an appropriate public education for the child. ESY are services provided beyond the normal school year, in accordance with the child's IEP and at no cost to the child's parents (34 C.F.R. § 300.309). The following standard for determining whether a child with disabilities is entitled to an extended school year (ESY) has gained acceptance:

> If a child will experience severe or substantial regression during the summer months in the absence of a summer program, the handicapped child may be entitled to year-round services. The issue is whether the benefits accrued to the child during the regular school year will be significantly jeopardized if he is not provided an educational program during the summer months. (*Alamo Heights Independent School District v. State Board of Education,* 1986, p. 261)

According to *Cordrey v. Euckert* (1990) and *Reusch v. Fountain* (1994), "this standard is satisfied when it is shown that the student will suffer a significant regression of skills or knowledge without a summer program, followed by an insufficient recoupment of the same during the next school year" (*Reusch v. Fountain*, 1994, p. 1434). The courts have ruled that parents do not need empirical data demonstrating regression during summer and slow recoupment to establish that their child is entitled to ESY services (*Cordrey v. Euckert,* 1990; *Johnson v. Independent School District No. 4 of Bixby, Tulsa County, Oklahoma,* 1990). The court in *Cordrey* noted that it is unfair to require that a child demonstrate regression in the absence of summer programming in order to be entitled to such programming in subsequent summers and suggested that decisions about whether a child is entitled to ESY can be based on predictive factors (i.e., the child is likely to show significant regression and slow recoupment of skills). Furthermore, decisions about whether a child is likely to show regression and slow recoupment may be based on "expert opinion, based on professional individual assessment" when empirical data are not available (*Cordrey,* 1990, p. 1472). Thus, rulings suggest schools may not require definitive empirical evidence of prior regression and slow recoupment in determining whether a child is entitled to ESY.

Extended School Day/Shortened School Day

The Supreme Court decision in *Rowley* defined an appropriate education as a program that is sufficient to confer educational benefit or a "basic floor of opportunity." *Garland Independent School District v.*

Wilks (1987) raised the question of whether a disabled child might require an extended school-day program (more than six hours) in order for the child's special education program to confer benefit. In *Garland,* the court awarded the mother of a disabled child reimbursement for the after-school tutor she paid to help her son because the school's regular day program for the child was seen as inadequate to confer academic benefit. The courts also have favored extended school-day programs as an alternative to placement in a residential facility (*Kerkam v. Superintendent., D.C. Public Schools,* 1991; *Roland M. v. Concord School Committee,* 1990).

In addition to recognition of extended school-day programs, the courts have acknowledged that some children may need a shortened school day in order to confer academic benefit (for example, see *Christopher M. v. Corpus Christi Independent School District,* 1991).

Assistive Technology

IDEA requires schools to ensure that assistive technology devices and services are made available to a child with a disability if the child requires the devices and services in order to receive an appropriate public education. Assistive technology device means any item, piece of equipment, or product system, whether acquired commercially off the shelf, modified, or customized, that is used to increase, maintain, or improve the functional capabilities of a child with a disability (34 C.F.R. § 300.5). Schools are not obligated, however, to provide eyeglasses, hearing aides, or braces. *Assistive technology service* means any service that directly assists a child with a disability in the selection, acquisition, or use of an assistive technology device. Assistive technology services include evaluation of the needs of a child with a disability; providing for the acquisition of an assistive technology device; selection, designing, fitting, customizing such devices; coordinating and using devices with other therapies or interventions; and training the child and the professionals involved in the use of the device (34 C.F.R. § 300.6). (For additional information, see McGivern & McKevitt, 2002).

Summary

Schools are required to provide an extended school year, extended school day, and assistive technology devices and services if they are necessary to provide a disabled child with an appropriate education reasonably designed to confer benefit. However, consistent with *Rowley,* IDEA does not require that the school provide such services in order to maximize the potential of a child with disabilities.

The Scope of Required Related Services

As noted earlier in the chapter, a child must be found eligible for special education before he or she qualifies to receive related services, and the related service must be necessary to assist the child with disabilities to benefit from special education. The related services provision includes school health and counseling services, but medical services are provided only for diagnostic and evaluation purposes to determine a child's medically related disability (34 C.F.R. § 300.24). This is the *medical exclusion.*

Whether certain services fall within the parameters of school health or counseling services (and are thus provided under IDEA-Part B) has been the focus of a number of court cases. *Irving Independent School District v. Tatro* (1994) (Exhibit 5–4) was a key case in determining the scope of school health services required under IDEA-Part B. In this case, the Supreme Court ruled that the school must provide clean intermittent catheterization (CIC) for a disabled child as a related service needed for her to benefit from special education. In the Court's opinion, CIC is not a medical service because it can be performed by a trained layperson and requires only several minutes every three or four hours.)

Thus, in accordance with *Tatro,* schools are not responsible for providing school health services that must be performed by a physician rather than a nurse or trained layperson. But what if a child requires *full-time* nursing care? Until recently, courts ruled that full-time nursing care was beyond the scope of the services that must be provided by the schools (e.g., *Detsel v. Board of Education of the Auburn Enlarged City School District*, 1997). In 1999, however, the Supreme Court decided *Cedar*

Exhibit 5–4. Irving Independent School District v. Tatro (1984)

Amber Tatro was born with spina bifida and suffered from orthopedic and speech impairments and a neurogenic bladder. Because she was unable to empty her bladder voluntarily, she required clean intermittent catheterization (CIC) every three or four hours. This procedure involves insertion of a catheter into the urethra to drain the bladder and can be performed in a few minutes by a trained layperson.

Amber first received special education services at age 3, and her IEP provided early child development classes, occupational therapy, and physical therapy. There was no provision for CIC as requested by Amber's parents, however. The school held that CIC was a medical service and, under IDEA, the school is required to provide medical services only for the purpose of diagnosis to determine the child's medically related disability.

Irving v. Tatro ultimately reached the Supreme Court, and the Court decided in favor of the parents. The Court reasoned that Amber could not attend class (and, therefore, could not benefit from special education) without CIC as a related supportive service, and held that CIC is not a medical service because it can be performed by a trained layperson or school nurse (i.e., a physician is not required). The Court also noted that the service is not overly burdensome to the school.

Rapids Community School District v. Garret F., a case concerning a ventilator-dependent student who required continuous, one-on-one nursing services to remain in school. Contrary to previous lower court rulings, the Supreme Court held that the school must provide full-time nursing services if such services are necessary for a child with a disability to benefit from special education. The Court reiterated *Tatro* in stating that schools are not responsible for services that must be performed by a physician but made clear that the nursing services a child needs to benefit from special education must be provided without regard to cost to the school.

Another question that arises under the related services provision of IDEA-Part B is, "When is the school responsible for the cost of psychotherapy as a related service?" Counseling services identified as related services in the regulations include "services provided by qualified social workers, psychologists, guidance counselors, and other qualified personnel" (34 C.F.R. § 300.24). Psychological services include, "Planning and managing a program of psychological services, including psychological counseling for children and parents" (34 C.F.R. § 300.24). Schools are required to provide these services at no cost to the parent when they are included in the child's IEP.

However, more difficult questions have arisen with regard to psychotherapy provided by a physician (i.e., psychiatric treatment) and that provided in a residential facility. Court rulings on these issues have been inconsistent (Turnbull & Turnbull, 2000). In *Darlene L. v. Illinois State Board of Education* (1983), the court ruled that "states may properly consider psychiatric services as medical services and therefore not related services which the state must provide as part of a free appropriate education" (p. 1345). The court in this case saw the cost of psychiatric treatment as overly burdensome to the schools.

In another case, however, the court ruled that psychotherapy provided by a psychiatrist does not automatically mean that the service is a medical service. In *Max M. v. Thompson* (1984), the court held, "The simple fact that a service *could be* or *actually is* rendered by a physician rather than a non-physician does not dictate its removal from the list of required services under EAHCA *[IDEA]*" (p. 1444). The court went on to say that the limit to psychiatric services is cost: "[A] school board can be held liable for no more than the cost of the service as provided by the minimum level health care personnel recognized as competent to perform the related service" (p. 1444). Thus, this ruling suggests that in states where a psychologist or social worker is recognized as competent to provide psychotherapy, the school is responsible only for the amount it would cost for a psychologist or social worker to perform the service.

Whether the school is responsible for the cost of psychotherapy when a pupil is placed in a residential facility also has been addressed by the courts. The key issue in these cases appears to be whether the psychotherapy provided in the facility is seen as necessary for educational reasons, that is, to assist the child in benefitting from special education (Weirda, 1987). In *In the Matter of the "A" Family* (1979), the court ruled that the school must pay for psychotherapy provided at a residential facility for a seriously emotionally disturbed child who was placed there as a way of meeting his education needs. In contrast, in *McKenzie v. Jefferson* (1983), a child was hospitalized in a treatment facility for serious mental illness. The court in this case held that the placement was not made in support of a special education program. The primary purpose of the placement was for "much needed *medical* treatment" (p. 411). Psychiatric treatment costs were not seen as a related service in this case.

Coordination of IDEA, Medicaid, and Private Health Insurance

When a child with disabilities has multiple health-related needs, the cost of school nursing services can be extraordinarily high. IDEA monies, however, typically fund only a small portion of the extra expenses involved in educating a child with disabilities. Consequently, since 1990, the U.S. Department of Health and Human Services (HHS) has signaled greater willingness to allow Medicaid coverage for health-related services for children receiving special education (see the 1991 "HHS Policy Clarification" prepared by HHS in cooperation with OSEP and DOE). In its 1991 policy clarification statement, HHS stated that school districts can bill the Medicaid program for medically necessary health-related services provided at school, home, or in a residential facility if the child is eligible under the state's Medicaid plan. Medicaid now covers a broad range of medical services (e.g., physician's services, prescription drugs, therapeutic interventions such as occupational therapy, psychological services), and states have considerable flexibility in defining Medicaid eligibility groups. Under IDEA 1997, the state's governor must ensure that the state has interagency agreements regarding Medicaid. Medicaid precedes the financial responsibility of the LEA and SEA, but the SEA remains the payor of last resort (34 C.F.R. § 300.142).

In addition, under IDEA, it is permissible for schools to ask parents to use their own private health insurance to cover the costs of health services provided at school. However, because related services must be provided at no cost to the parent, the school must pay copays or other deductibles (34 C.F.R. § 300.142).

Procedural Safeguards

A number of Part B procedural safeguards to ensure the rights of children with disabilities and their parents were foreshadowed in the *P.A.R.C.* and

Mills decisions. Under IDEA-Part B, the SEA must ensure that each LEA establishes and implements procedures to safeguard the parent's right to confidentiality of records and right to examine records; right to participate in meetings with respect to the identification, evaluation, and placement of their child; right to consent to pupil evaluation; right to written prior notice before changes are made in identification, evaluation, placement, and special services; right to present findings from an independent evaluation; right to resolution of complaints by mediation; right to resolution of complaints by an impartial hearing officer; and right to bring civil action in court. Notice and consent, transfer of parental rights at age of majority, surrogate parents, and mediation and due process hearings are discussed.

Consent and Notice

Depending on the proposed school action or refusal to act, IDEA my require consent or written notice, and procedural safeguards notice.

Consent. Under IDEA-Part B, parental written consent (permission) must be obtained before conducting a preplacement evaluation and before the initial placement of a child in special education. If the parent refuses consent, the LEA may request mediation or a hearing to override a parent's refusal to consent. Parent consent also is required for subsequent re-evaluations of a child, unless the school can demonstrate that it has taken reasonable measures to obtain consent, and the child's parent failed to respond (34 C.F.R. § 300.505).

Notice. IDEA divides information sent to parents into two different types of notice: prior written notice and procedural safeguards notice. Prior written notice is required a reasonable time before the proposed school action whenever the SEA or LEA proposes to change the identification, evaluation, education placement, or program of the child or refuses to change the identification, evaluation, placement, or program. Notice must be provided in a mode of communication understandable to the parent (unless it is clearly not feasible to do so) and must include a description of the proposed action (or refusal to act); an explanation of why the school proposes or refuses to take action; a description of any other options considered and why those were rejected; a description of each evaluation procedure, test, record, or report used as the basis for the school's action; a statement that the parents have protection under procedural safeguards and, if the notice is not an initial referral for evaluation, the means by which a copy of a description of the procedural safeguards can be obtained; and sources for parents to contact to obtain assistance in understanding these provisions (e.g., nonprofit group that could assist the parents) (34 C.F.R. § 300.503).

A procedural safeguards notice includes information on protections available to the parents of a child with a disability. This information must be provided at the time of initial referral for evaluation, with each notification of an IEP meeting, on re-evaluation of the child, and following registration of a complaint. It must include a full explanation of the procedural safeguards written in an understandable manner. The content of the notice must include information pertaining to independent educational evaluation, prior written notice, parent consent, access to educational records, opportunity to present complaints, the child's placement during pendency of due process proceedings, procedures for students who are subject to placement in an interim alternative educational setting, requirements for unilateral placement by parents of children in private schools at public expense, mediation, due process hearings, state-level appeals, civil action, and attorney fees (34 C.F.R. §§ 300.503–300.504).

Transfer of Parent Rights at Age of Majority

Under IDEA, a state may require that when an individual with a disability reaches the age of majority or a child with a disability is incarcerated in an adult correctional facility, all rights accorded to parents transfer to the individual with a disability. The school or other agency must notify the individual and parents of the transfer of rights. For youth who have reached the age of majority and who have not been determined to be incompetent, but who are determined not to have the ability to provide informed consent with respect to their education program, the state will establish procedures for the appointment of the parent of the youth (or other appropriate person if the parent is not available) to represent the educational interest of the youth as long as he or she is eligible for special education under IDEA (34 C.F.R. § 300.517).

Surrogate Parents

Under IDEA-Part B, the school must ensure that the rights of a child with disabilities are protected when no parent can be identified (e.g., the child is a ward of the state under state laws). The school must assign a surrogate parent for the child, and this surrogate may not be an employee of the school or have interests that conflict with the interests of the child (34 C.F.R. § 300.515).

Mediation and Due Process Hearings

The school and parents may attempt to resolve disputes regarding the identification, evaluation, educational placement or program of a child through a mediation process and/or due process hearings. IDEA requires parents to provide notice to the LEA of a complaint. The notice must include (a) the name and address of the child and the name of the school he or she is attending; (b) a description of the nature of the problem regarding the child's current or proposed identification, evaluation, placement, or program and the facts relating to the problem; and (c) a proposed resolution of the problem to the extent known and available to the parents at that time. The SEA must develop a model form to assist parents in filing a complaint in compliance with the requirements of the law (34 C.F.R. § 300.507).

Mediation. Any SEA or LEA that receives IDEA funds must ensure that procedures are established and implemented to allow parties to resolve disputes regarding the identification, evaluation, educational placement, or program of a child through a mediation process. At minimum, this process must be available whenever a due process hearing is requested. The procedures must ensure that the mediation process (a) is voluntary on the part of the parties; (b) is not used to deny or delay a parent's right to a due process hearing, or to deny any other parental rights; and (c) is conducted by a qualified and impartial mediator who is trained in effective mediation techniques. The SEA or LEA may establish procedures to require a parent who chooses not to use the mediation process to meet, at a time and location convenient to the parent, with a disinterested party who is under contract with an appropriate alternate dispute resolution agency to explain and discuss the benefits of the mediation process. The SEA is responsible for maintaining a list of qualified mediators and bears the costs of the mediation process. The mediator must be selected at random from the list of qualified individuals (e.g., rotation), or both parties must agree with the selection of the individual who will mediate. The mediator must not be an employee of the school, and no individual with a personal or professional conflict of interest may serve as mediator. An agreement reached by the parties is recorded in a written mediation agreement. Discussions that occur during mediation are confidential and may not be used as evidence in any subsequent due process hearing or civil proceeding (34 C.F. R. § 300.506).

Due Process Hearings. IDEA-Part B also grants parents and the school a right to an impartial due process hearing on any matter regarding the identification, evaluation, educational placement, or program of a child. Under IDEA-Part B, the due process hearing must be conducted by the SEA or other school agency responsible for the child. Each SEA or LEA must maintain a list of hearing officers and their qualifications. The hearing officer may not be an employee of the school, and no person with a personal or professional interest in the outcome may serve as the hearing officer. The school must inform the parents of any free or low-cost legal and other relevant services available (34 C.F.R. § 300.507–300.509). The school also must inform parents that they may be able to recover attorney fees if they prevail in a hearing or judicial proceeding (34 C.F.R. §§ 300.504, 300.513).

IDEA-Part B further specifies a number of hearing rights. The hearing must be held at a time and place reasonably convenient to the parents. Each party has a right to be accompanied and advised by legal counsel and other experts, to present evidence and confront, cross-examine, and compel the attendance of witnesses (34 C.F.R. § 300.509). No evidence may be introduced by any party unless it was disclosed at least five business days before the hearing; each party must disclose to all other parties all evaluations completed by that date and the recommendations based on those evaluations if the findings from such evaluations will be used at the hearing. The parents are afforded the right to have their child present and to have the hearing open to the public (34 C.F.R. § 300.509).

The hearing must be held and a final decision reached within 45 days after the request for a hearing. Each party has a right to a written record of the hearing (or an electronic verbatim recording if the parent so chooses) and to a copy of the written findings of fact and the decision. The decision of the hearing officer is final unless a party initiates an appeal or begins a court action (34 C.F.R. § 300.511).

If the parent or the school is not satisfied with the decision of the hearing officer, an appeal may be filed to the SEA for an impartial review of the hearing and the decision of the hearing officer (34 C.F.R.§ 300.510).

Right to Private Action

IDEA grants the parent and the school the right to civil action if they are not satisfied with the SEA decision. This means that parents may initiate a court action against the school on behalf of a child with a disability if they believe the school has violated the provisions of IDEA with respect to their child. Except for very unusual circumstances, parents are required to exhaust administrative remedies (e.g., due process hearings) available to them before they pursue a court action (34 C.F.R. § 300.12).

Recovery of Attorney Fees

In 1986, Congress enacted the Handicapped Children's Protection Act of 1986 (Pub. L. No. 99–372), an amendment to IDEA that provides, "In any action or proceeding brought under this subsection, the court in its discretion, may award reasonable attorneys' fees as part of the costs to the parents or guardian of a handicapped child or youth who is the prevailing party" (20 U.S.C. 1415[a][4][B]). In *Hensley v. Eckerhart* (1983), the Supreme Court found that "plaintiffs may be considered 'prevailing parties' for the purposes of recovery of attorney fees if they succeed on any significant issue in litigation which achieves some of the benefit the parties sought in bringing the suit" (1983, p. 433). IDEA prohibits recovery of attorney's fees for an IEP meeting unless the meeting is convened as a result of an administrative proceeding or judicial action; for mediation that is conducted prior to filing a complaint; or if the parent declines a written settlement offer, and the court later awards the parent a lesser amount. In addition, an attorney's fees may be reduced if the parent unreasonably protracted the resolution of the dispute; the fees unreasonably exceeded the prevailing rate in the community; the time spent on legal services was excessive in light of the nature of the proceedings, or the attorney representing the parent did not provide required information to the school district (34 C.F. R. § 300.513).

Abrogation of State Sovereign Immunity

Under IDEA, states and their departments of education can be sued by private citizens if they violate the law. This provision in IDEA waives the traditional immunity from private lawsuits that states enjoy under the 11th Amendment to the Constitution.

INFANTS AND TODDLERS WITH DISABILITIES

Pub. L. No. 99–457, The Education for the Handicapped Act Amendments of 1986 (now IDEA-Part C), provides grants to states to develop and implement a statewide, comprehensive system of early intervention services for infants and toddlers with disabilities and their families. The purpose of IDEA-Part C is (a) to enhance the development of infants and toddlers with disabilities and to minimize their potential for developmental delay; (b) to reduce the education costs to our society, including our nation's schools, by minimizing the need for special education and related services after infants and toddlers with disabilities reach school age; (c) to minimize the likelihood of institutionalization of individuals with disabilities and maximize the potential for their independent living in society; (d) to enhance the capacity of families to meet the special needs of their infants and toddlers with disabilities; and (e) to enhance the capacity of state and local agencies and service providers to identify, evaluate, and meet the needs of historically underrepresented populations, particularly minority, low-income, inner-city, and rural populations (Pub. L. No. 105–17; § 631, 111 Stat. 106 [1997]).

A number of similarities and differences exist between legislation providing a free and appropriate education for children with disabilities in the 3–21-year age group (IDEA-Part B) and the legislation providing grants for early intervention services for infants and toddlers (IDEA-Part C). Part C is described under the following sections: "Statewide System," "Child Find," "Eligible Children," "Evaluation and Assessment," "Individualized Family Service Plan," "Early Intervention Services," and "Procedural Safeguards."

Statewide System

Prior to 1986, services for infants and toddlers with disabilities typically were provided by a number of different agencies in each state (social services, public health, education), often resulting in service gaps or unnecessary duplication (Gallagher, 1989). IDEA-Part C was designed to encourage states to develop and implement a statewide, comprehensive, coordinated, multidisciplinary, interagency program of early intervention services for infants and toddlers with disabilities and their families (34 C.F.R. § 303.1). The law requires each state to identify a lead agency responsible for administration, supervision, coordination, and monitoring of programs and activities in the state. Different states have chosen different lead agencies, including state departments of health, education, and social welfare (Gallagher, 1989). In order to receive funds, each state must have submitted an application to Washington that outlines state policies and procedures for the delivery of services consistent with the requirements of Part C. Part C also requires the development of an interagency coordinating council to advise and assist the lead agency, identify and coordinate financial resources, and promote interagency agreements (34 C.F.R. § 303.141–142).

Child Find

IDEA-Part C requires each state to establish a public awareness program and a comprehensive child find system to ensure that eligible children are identified and referred for evaluation in a timely manner. Each state also must develop a central directory of public and private early intervention services, resources, demonstration projects, and experts in the state that is accessible to parents of infants and toddlers with disabilities and the general public (34 C.F.R. § 303.301; § § 303.320–321).

Eligible Children

IDEA-Part C defines *infant or toddler with a disability* to mean a child under 3 years who needs early intervention services because he or she (a) is experiencing developmental delays, as measured by appropriate diagnostic instruments and procedures, in one or more of the areas of cognitive, physical, communication, social or emotional, or adaptive development; or (b) has a diagnosed physical or mental condition that has a high probability of resulting in developmental delay. The term also may include, at a state's discretion, at-risk infants and toddlers. The term *at-risk infant or toddler* means a child under 3 years who would be at risk of experiencing a substantial delay if early intervention services were not provided. The factors that put the child at risk may be biological or environmental (34 C.F.R. § 303.16).

Evaluation and Assessment

IDEA-Part C requires a multidisciplinary assessment of the unique strengths and needs of each child and the identification of services appropriate to meet such needs. The evaluation must be based on nondiscriminatory procedures, be conducted by personnel trained to utilize appropriate methods and procedures, be based on informed clinical opinion, and include a review of pertinent records related to the child's current health status and medical history. The evaluation must include an assessment of the unique needs of the child in each of the following five developmental areas: cognitive, physical (including hearing and vision), communication, social or emotional, and adaptive. The evaluation includes the identification of services appropriate to meet the needs of the child in each of these areas (34 C.F.R. § 303.322–323).

IDEA-Part C also requires a family-directed assessment of the resources, priorities, and concerns of the family, and the identification of the supports and services necessary to enhance the family's capacity to meet the developmental needs of the infant or toddler. Any assessment that is conducted must be voluntary on the part of the family. If an assessment of the family is carried out, the assessment must be conducted by personnel trained to utilize appropriate methods and procedures, be based on information provided by the family through a personal interview, and incorporate the family's description of its resources, priorities, and concerns related to enhancing the child's development (34 C.F. R. § 300.322).

With the exception of unusual circumstances, the evaluation and initial assessment of each child (including the family assessment) must be completed within 45 days after the lead agency receives the referral (34 C.F. R. § 303.321).

Individualized Family Service Plan

IDEA-Part C requires a written individualized family service plan (IFSP) rather than an IEP for each infant or toddler. The IFSP is developed at a meeting that includes the parents of the child; other family members, as requested by the parent, if feasible to do so; an advocate or person outside of the family, if the parent requests that the person participate; the service coordinator; a person directly involved in conducting the evaluations and assessment; and, as appropriate, persons who will be providing services to the child or family. If one of these persons is unable to attend, arrangements are made for his or her involvement via telephone conference calls or other means. Agencies must provide adequate prior written notice regarding meetings, and IFSP meetings must be conducted in settings and at times that are convenient to families and in the native language of the family or other mode of communication used by the family, unless it is clearly not feasible to do so. For the child who has been referred for evaluation for the first time and found eligible, the meeting to develop the IFSP must be conducted within 45 days of the referral (34 C.F.R. § 303.342). With the consent of the parent, services may be provided prior to the completion of the assessment (34 C.F.R. § 303.345).

The IFSP includes the following: (a) a statement of the infant's or toddler's present levels of physical, cognitive, communication, social or emotional, and adaptive development, based on professionally acceptable objective criteria; (b) with the concurrence of the family, a statement of the family's resources, priorities, and concerns relating to enhancing the development of the infant or toddler; (c) a statement of the major outcomes expected to be achieved for the infant or toddler and the family and the criteria, procedures, and timelines used to determine the degree to which progress toward achieving the outcomes is being made and whether modifications of the outcomes or services are necessary; (d) a statement of the specific early intervention services necessary to meet the unique needs of the infant or toddler and the family, including the frequency, intensity, and method of delivering services; a statement of the natural environments in which early intervention services will appropriately be provided, including a justification of the extent, if any, to which services will not be provided in a natural environment; the location of services; and payment arrangements, if any; (e) as appropriate, medical and other services that the child needs but are not provided under IDEA-Part C, and how those services might be obtained through public or private sources; (f) the projected dates for the initiation of services and the anticipated duration of those services; (g) the identification of the service coordinator from the profession most immediately relevant to the child's or family's needs (or who is otherwise qualified to carry out all applicable responsibilities) who will be responsible for the implementation of the plan and coordination with other agencies and persons; and (h) the steps to be taken to support the transition of the toddler with a disability to preschool or other appropriate services (34 C.F. R. § 300.344).

The content of the IFSP must be explained fully to the parents and informed written consent from the parents must be obtained prior to the provision of the early intervention services described in the plan. If the parents do not provide consent for a particular service, then the early intervention services to which consent is obtained are provided (34 C.F.R. § 300.342). An annual meeting is conducted to evaluate the IFSP, and the family is provided with a review of the plan every 6 months, or more often if needed.

Early Intervention Services

Under Part C, early intervention services include both special instruction and related services; an infant or toddler can receive a related service under Part C without receiving special instruction. (This differs from the requirement under Part B that children with disabilities ages 3–21 only receive related services in order to benefit from special education.)

The term *early intervention services* means services that are (a) designed to meet the developmental needs of the child and the needs of the family related to enhancing the child's development; (b) are selected in collaboration with the parents; (c) are provided under public supervision by qualified personnel in conformity with an individualized family service plan; and (d) are provided at no cost, unless federal or state law provides for a system of payments by families. Types of services include family training, counseling, and home visits; special instruction; speech-language pathology and audiology services; occupational therapy; physical therapy; psychological services; service coordination services; medical services only for diagnostic or evaluative purposes; early identification, screening, and assessment services; health services necessary to enable the infant or toddler to benefit from the other early intervention services; nursing services, nutrition services, social work services; vision services; assistive technology devices and services; and transportation and related costs that are necessary to enable the infant or toddler and his or her family to receive other early intervention (34 C.F.R. §§ 300.12–300.13).

Procedural Safeguards

The procedural safeguards under Part C are similar to those under Part B. Parents are afforded the right to confidentiality of personally identifiable information; the right to examine records; the right to consent to or decline any early intervention service without jeopardizing the right to other services; the right to written prior notice before changes are made in identification, evaluation, placement, or provision of services; the right to use mediation; the right to timely administrative resolution of complaints; and the right to bring civil action in state or federal court (34 C.F.R. §§ 303.400–303.406).

CONCLUDING COMMENTS

Pub. L. No. 94–142 was enacted almost 30 years ago. Amendments, court interpretations, changing rules and regulations, and policy statements have further shaped special education law. Education law will continue to change. School psychologists must keep abreast of these changes to ensure that the educational rights of pupils are safeguarded.

STUDY AND DISCUSSION

Questions for Chapter 5

1. Why did Congress require single agency responsibility for children with disabilities?
2. What is the *zero reject principle*?
3. What is the purpose of the IEP meeting? Who attends? Briefly describe the content of the IEP.
4. Briefly describe what is meant by *least restrictive appropriate environment* in special education law. Does this aspect of the law mean that all children with disabilities must be integrated into the regular classroom? What are the guiding principles for determining a child's educational placement?
5. How is *appropriate education* defined in *Rowley*?
6. What is the *medical exclusion*?
7. What are some of the ways that Part C and Part B differ?

ACTIVITIES

1. Compare the 13 disability categories under IDEA-Part B with the categories and eligibility criteria that appear in the special education guidelines of your state.

2. Does your local school district distribute a special education handbook or pamphlet to parents outlining their rights and the school responsibilities under special education law? Obtain and review copies of informational materials given to parents and review forms used by school districts for referral for special education evaluation, parent consent for evaluation under special education law, and team meeting decisions.

Chapter 6

SECTION 504 AND THE AMERICANS WITH DISABILITIES ACT

This chapter begins with a summary of those portions of Section 504 of The Rehabilitation Act of 1973 most pertinent to school psychological practice. Special attention is given to the similarities and differences between Section 504 and Individuals with Disabilities Education Act (IDEA) regarding school responsibilities to pupils with special needs.[1] The second portion of the chapter provides a brief overview of the Americans with Disabilities Act (1990).

SECTION 504 AND PUPILS WITH HANDICAPPING CONDITIONS

Section 504 of The Rehabilitation Act of 1973 is civil rights legislation that prohibits discrimination against pupils with handicaps in school systems receiving federal financial assistance. Although it was passed many years ago, Section 504 has often been ignored or misunderstood by the public schools (Martin, 1992). Since the late 1980s, however, Office of Civil Rights (OCR) enforcement activities, court decisions, and parent advocacy efforts have heightened awareness of Section 504, and the law has begun to impact schools and school psychology.

Historical Framework

One way in which Congress attempted to ensure a free and appropriate education for all children with disabilities was through federal grant legislation such as IDEA. A second way in which the federal government

---

[1] Portions of this chapter appeared previously in Jacob-Timm and Hartshorne (1994). Consistent with the language of the law, individuals with "handicapping conditions" is used in this chapter to refer to individuals who qualify for protection under The Rehabilitation Act of 1973; pupils with "disabilities" is used to refer to students who are eligible for special education under IDEA.

attempted to address the problem of discrimination against pupils with handicapping conditions was through antidiscrimination laws. One of the first bills that attempted to ensure equal educational opportunity for children with handicaps in the public schools was an amendment to Title VI of the Civil Rights Act of 1964. The bill was introduced in the House of Representatives by Congressman Vanek and in the Senate by Senator Humphrey and later became part of The Rehabilitation Act of 1973 (Pub. L. No. 93–112) (Martin, 1979). Section 504 of The Rehabilitation Act of 1973 states that "No otherwise qualified handicapped individual in the United States ... shall, solely by reason of his handicap, be excluded from the participation in, or be denied the benefits of, or be subjected to discrimination under any program or activity receiving Federal financial assistance ..." (29 U.S.C. § 794).

Both Vanek and Humphrey saw Section 504 as requiring all states to provide educational services to all children. However, The Rehabilitation Act of 1973 is concerned primarily with discrimination in employment settings, and many interpreted Section 504 as a prohibition against employment discrimination in the schools. The 1974 amendments to The Rehabilitation Act of 1973 (Pub. L. No. 93–516) clarified the intent of the law by specifically prohibiting discrimination against physically or mentally handicapped pupils in federally supported school systems (Martin, 1979).[2]

There was still no immediate impact on school policies regarding children with handicaps, however. Advocates for the rights of handicapped pupils staged wheelchair sit-ins to encourage the quick development of regulations implementing the law, while school officials quietly protested this legislation as too costly for the public schools (Martin, 1979). The Department of Health, Education, and Welfare (HEW), caught in the middle, was slow to develop and approve regulations implementing Section 504. As Martin (1979) noted, HEW did not require compliance with Section 504 until the 1978–1979 school year, a full five years after the law was passed.

Rules and regulations implementing Section 504 appear at 34 *Code of Federal Regulations* (C.F.R.), Part 104. The Office for Civil Rights (OCR), an agency within the U.S. Department of Education, is charged with investigating Section 504 complaints pertaining to department programs or activities. Although an OCR investigation may be triggered by a complaint regarding possible discriminatory treatment of an individual student with handicaps, OCR may choose to expand its investigation to encompass school policies and practices regarding all students within the district who have a particular type of handicapping condition (e.g., mental retardation, attention deficit disorder).

---

[2] The Rehabilitation Act of 1973 was further amended by Pub. L. No. 98–221 in 1983, by Pub. L. No. 99–506 in 1986, and by Pub. L. No. 101–336 in 1990.

Following the passage of Pub. L. No. 94–142 in 1975, public school districts typically concentrated on fulfilling their obligation to provide special education and related services to pupils with disabilities in conformance with the requirements of IDEA-Part B. Many school administrators were unaware that the broad definition of handicapped under 504 includes a number of students who do not qualify as disabled under IDEA. They falsely believed that compliance with IDEA meant that the school was in full compliance with Section 504 (Martin, 1992). In the late 1980s, a number of lawsuits and complaints to OCR were filed on behalf of pupils in regular education programs because schools failed to make accommodations for their handicapping conditions under 504 (e.g., *Elizabeth S. v. Thomas K. Gilhool,* 1987; Lake Washington [WA] School District No. 414, 1985; Rialto [CA] Unified School District, 1989).[3]

Advocacy efforts on the part of children with Attention Deficit Disorder (ADD) and Attention Deficit Hyperactivity Disorder (ADHD) also were an important trigger for increased attention to Section 504 requirements. When Congress considered the 1990 amendments of Part B, there was discussion of including ADD/ADHD as a separate eligibility category within the law. An invitation to public comment on special education for children with ADD/ADHD under Part B resulted in more than 2,000 written comments (Hakola, 1992). Parents of children with ADD/ADHD testified to Congress that many schools were unwilling to make even simple modifications of educational programming because their children did not qualify for special education under Part B (Martin, 1992). On September 16, 1991, the U.S. Department of Education (DOE) issued a memorandum (jointly by the assistant secretaries of the Office of Special Education and Rehabilitative Services, Office of Civil Rights, and Office of Elementary and Secondary Education) to clarify DOE policy regarding appropriate education for children with ADD/ADHD.

The 1991 memorandum addressed eligibility for services under IDEA-Part B and suggested that some pupils with ADD/ADHD may qualify within the IDEA definitions of *other health impairment, specific learning disability,* or *emotional disturbance.* The IDEA 1997 definition of other health impairment now specifically identifies ADD/ADHD as an example of a health condition that may result in a need for special education. The 1991 memorandum also discussed school obligations under Section 504 to children with ADD/ADHD found not to require special education and related services under IDEA. The memorandum

---

[3] References to court cases are italicized; references to OCR opinions and administrative hearings are not.

thus provided an explicit DOE interpretation of school responsibilities to children who have handicaps that impair their functioning in school, but who do not qualify for special education and related services under IDEA.

In sum, a series of events including advocacy efforts, the 1991 DOE memorandum, OCR activities, and case law made it increasingly clear that many schools in compliance with IDEA have not met their obligations to other special needs students under Section 504. Section 504 and IDEA are different in several important respects including purpose, funding, eligibility, and school responsibilities to students. Schools and school psychologists must now be knowledgeable of 504 as well as IDEA.

Purpose and Funding

As previously noted, Section 504 of The Rehabilitation Act of 1973 was designed to eliminate discrimination on the basis of handicap in any program or activity receiving federal financial assistance. Subpart D applies to preschool, elementary, and secondary education programs and activities and requires schools to make special accommodations for students with handicaps to ensure that they are afforded educational opportunity equal to their nonhandicapped peers.

Section 504 specifically prohibits schools from discriminating on the basis of handicap in providing any aid, benefit, or service, either directly or through contractual arrangements. Schools may not deny pupils with handicaps an opportunity to participate in or benefit from any of the services or benefits it affords others. This means that schools must provide aids, benefits, or services that are equal to and as effective as those provided to nonhandicapped pupils. Schools are not required to produce the identical result or level of achievement for handicapped and nonhandicapped pupils, but they *must afford students with handicaps equal opportunity* to obtain the same result, to gain the same benefit, or to reach the same level of achievement, in the most integrated setting appropriate to the pupil's needs. Schools may not provide different or separate aid, benefits, or services to pupils with handicaps unless such action is necessary to provide them with services that are as effective as those provided to others. When separate programs or activities exist in order to meet the needs of students with handicaps, a school may not deny a qualified handicapped student the opportunity to participate in programs or activities that are not separate or different (34 C.F.R. § 104.4).

Case 6–1

Mrs. Drew, a middle school special education teacher, teaches an English class for students with cognitive impairments who cannot keep pace in regular education English. After observing that several of Mrs. Drew's students had problems with handwriting, Hannah Cook offered to take Mrs. Drew and her students to the school's computer lab to show them how to use a simple word processing program for English writing assignments. When Hannah contacted the teacher responsible for scheduling the school's computer lab, she was told that in accordance with school policy, special education classes were not allowed to use the computer lab because the students were too likely to damage the expensive equipment.

Case 6–1 is based on a real-life incident. The school's policy of barring special education classes from the school's computer lab was clearly in violation of Section 504. The policy was changed quickly after it was challenged by the special education teacher and school psychologist.

Unlike IDEA, Section 504 does not require states to develop a written plan to meet the requirements of the law. However under 504, each school district must designate at least one person to coordinate its efforts to comply with the law and adopt grievance procedures that incorporate appropriate due process standards and provide for the prompt and equitable resolution of complaints alleging violations of 504 (34 C.F.R. § 104.7). Each school district also must take appropriate and continuing steps to notify students and their parents that it does not discriminate in its programs and activities on the basis of handicap (34 C.F.R. § 104.8).

Section 504 is antidiscrimination legislation; it is not a federal grant program. Unlike IDEA, Section 504 does not provide funds to schools. A state department of education may choose not to pursue monies available under federal grant statutes (e.g., IDEA-Part C funds for infants and toddlers with disabilities). School districts must comply with antidiscrimination legislation if they receive any federal funds for any purpose, however. OCR has the authority to remove federal funds from a district if it is not in compliance with 504.

Eligibility

With respect to public school educational services, Section 504 protections against discrimination apply to all pupils with handicaps who are of an age during which nonhandicapped pupils receive a public education, or who are eligible for educational services for handicapped pupils under state law or eligible for special education within the state under IDEA (34 C.F.R. § 104.3).

As noted previously, handicapped under Section 504 is defined more broadly than disability under IDEA. To be eligible for special education and related services under IDEA, pupils must be evaluated in accordance with procedures outlined in IDEA-Part B and found eligible under one of the 13 categories of disability, and they must need special education and related services because of that disability. The child's disability must affect his or her educational performance in order to receive special education and related services under Part B (see Chapter 5).

In contrast, under 504 a *handicapped person* is defined as any person who has a physical or mental impairment that substantially limits one or more of his or her major life activities (see Exhibit 6–1). *Physical impairment* means any physiological disorder or condition affecting one or more body systems. *Mental impairment* means any mental or psychological disorder, such as emotional or mental illness, or a specific learning disability. *Major life activities* means functions such as caring for one's self, performing manual tasks, walking, seeing, hearing, speaking, breathing, learning, and working. *Handicapped* individual includes persons with a history of impairment and those regarded as having an impairment who may, in fact, have no actual impairment. This last portion of the definition protects individuals from discriminatory action based on the perception of a handicap. For example, if a high school senior was denied admission to college solely on the basis of school records showing a history of special education placement, Section 504 safeguards would be triggered.

In sum, any student who has a physical or mental impairment that substantially limits a major life activity is handicapped within the meaning of Section 504. Section 504 prohibits schools from discriminating on the basis of handicap in providing aids, benefits, or services. Any student who has a condition or disorder that substantially limits his or her ability to participate in school programs and activities and who needs special assistance because of his or her limitations is eligible for special school accommodations under 504 (*Elizabeth S. v. Thomas K. Gilhool,* 1987). All students who are disabled under IDEA are considered to be handicapped and are, therefore, afforded the protections of Section

Exhibit 6–1. Section 504 Definition of Handicapped

(j) *Handicapped person.*(1) "Handicapped person" means any person who (i) has a physical or mental impairment which substantially limits one or more major life activities, (ii) has a record of such an impairment, or (iii) is regarded as having such an impairment.

(2) As used in paragraph (j)(1) of this section, the phrase:

(i) *Physical or mental impairment means* (A) any physiological disorder or condition, cosmetic disfigurement, or anatomical loss affecting one or more of the following body systems: neurological; musculoskeletal; special sense organs; respiratory, including speech organs; cardiovascular; reproductive, digestive, genito-urinary; hemic and lymphatic; skin; and endocrine; or (B) any mental or psychological disorder, such as mental retardation, organic brain syndrome, emotional or mental illness, and specific learning disabilities.

(ii) *Major life activities* means functions such as caring for one's self, performing manual tasks, walking, seeing, hearing, speaking, breathing, learning, and working.

(iii) *Has a record of such impairment* means has a history of, or has been misclassified as having, a mental or physical impairment that substantially limits one or more major life activities.

(iv) *Is regarded as having an impairment* means (A) has a physical or mental impairment that does not substantially limit major life activities but that is treated by a recipient as constituting such a limitation; (B) has a physical or mental impairment that substantially limits major life activities only as a result of the attitudes of others toward such impairment; or (C) has none of the impairments defined in paragraph (j)(2)(i) of this section but is treated by a recipient as having such an impairment.

Source: 34 C.F.R. § 104.3.

504. Students who are not disabled under IDEA may nevertheless be handicapped under 504.

Seven categories of children who might not be eligible for special education services under IDEA, but who *may* qualify under Section 504 are identified in Exhibit 6–2. They include students: (1) with ADD/ADHD, (2) who are learning-disabled but who do not exhibit a severe discrepancy between aptitude and achievement, (3) who are graduates of special education, (4) who are socially maladjusted and emotionally impaired, (5) with drug and alcohol dependency, (6) with health needs, and (7) with communicable diseases (adapted from Martin, 1992).

Evaluation of Pupils to Determine Eligibility

The evaluation regulations that implement Section 504 are difficult to interpret because they are limited in scope and detail. Although they specifically address evaluation with regard to *placement* in special or regular education,

Exhibit 6–2. Pupils Who May Qualify as Handicapped under Section 504

ADD/ADHD

ADD and ADHD are impairments under Section 504 if the condition substantially limits a major life activity, such as learning.

Learning Disabled without Discrepancy

504 regulations define mental impairment as any mental or psychological disorder including a learning disability. Pupils with learning disabilities (e.g., dyslexia) who do not show a severe discrepancy between achievement and ability are handicapped within the meaning of 504 if their condition substantially limits a major life activity, such as learning.

Graduates of Special Education

Section 504 protects students who graduate from special education and continue in regular education programs as well as those who graduate from high school and enter post-secondary settings.

Socially Maladjusted and Emotionally Impaired

504 regulations define mental impairment as any mental or psychological disorder including emotional or mental illness. Children who are socially maladjusted or who suffer an emotional impairment (e.g., school phobia) may qualify as handicapped under 504 if the condition substantially limits a major life activity, such as the capacity for normal peer relations or learning.

Drug and Alcohol Dependency

Students with alcohol or drug dependency are handicapped persons under 504 if their impairment substantially limits one or more of their major life activities. Individuals who have completed a supervised drug rehabilitation program are protected; however, those actively involved in drug abuse are not afforded 504 protections.

Health Needs

A number of schoolchildren have health conditions that substantially impair major life activities, such as caring for one's self, performing manual tasks, walking, seeing, hearing, speaking, breathing, or learning. Pupils with a wide range of health conditions (e.g., diabetes, asthma, severe allergies, disability from an accident, arthritis, epilepsy, sleep disorders, obesity) may qualify for accommodations under 504. A pupil with a temporary handicapping condition (e.g., broken limbs) also may qualify for accommodations.

Communicable Diseases

Students with communicable diseases, such as AIDS, are protected by Section 504. Schools are prohibited from discriminating against any "otherwise qualified" pupil with a communicable disease. This means that schools may not remove an infected child from the regular classroom unless a significant risk of transmission of the disease would still exist in spite of reasonable efforts by the school to accommodate the infected child (see also Chapter 9).

Source: Adapted from Martin (1992).

procedures for determining 504 eligibility or needed special accommodations are not clearly addressed. However since 1991, education law experts (Council of Administrators of Special Education, 1999; Hakola, 1992) and a series of OCR rulings have provided guidance in interpreting the evaluation regulations as they relate to the determination of whether a child is handicapped under 504 and the provision of appropriate school accommodations.

An evaluation of a student is required under 504 if it is believed that the pupil may qualify as handicapped and may need special school services or accommodations. Any child referred for evaluation because of a suspected disability under IDEA-Part B and who is not found eligible should be considered for possible eligibility as handicapped under Section 504 (Council of Administrators of Special Education, 1999).

Schools are required to advise students with handicaps and their parents of their rights and the school's duties under Section 504 (34 C.F.R. § 104.32). Schools must notify parents of their rights regarding the identification, evaluation, and placement of children with suspected handicaps prior to initiating a Section 504 evaluation. OCR has recommended that parents be notified of their procedural safeguard rights under 504 at the time the district requests parental permission for the evaluation (Cobb County [GA] School District, 1992). When a pupil is suspected of having a disability under IDEA, parent rights and school duties under both IDEA and 504 should be clearly identified.

The question of when an evaluation is triggered under Section 504 has been a source of confusion in many school districts. The 1991 DOE policy memorandum stated that a school must evaluate a pupil if the parents believe that their child is handicapped under 504, suggesting that schools must evaluate children on parental demand. In April 1993, OCR clarified this policy by stating that a school must evaluate a student only when the school has reason to believe a child has a suspected handicapping condition (Lim, 1993). Like IDEA, schools are not required to evaluate children based only on parental suspicion of a handicap. However, when a school does not agree with a parental request for evaluation, it must still inform parents of their right to contest that decision and the procedures for a fair and timely resolution of the evaluation dispute.

Martin (1992) interprets Section 504 evaluation regulations as requiring determination of the following: (a) Is there a physical or mental impairment? (b) Does that impairment substantially limit a major life activity? and (c) What kind of accommodations would be needed so that the student will be able to enjoy the benefits of the school program? Section 504 does not require a specific categorical diagnosis, only the determination of a handicapping condition that substantially impairs one or more major life activities at school and requires special accommodation by the school.

Under Section 504, schools are required to establish standards and procedures for the evaluation of pupils who, because of handicap, are believed to need special school accommodations. The 504 regulations regarding evaluation procedures (34 C.F.R. § 104.35) are almost identical to those implementing IDEA-Part B. Test and evaluation materials must have been validated for the purpose used, administered by trained personnel, and fair. The evaluation must be comprehensive enough to assess the nature and extent of the handicap and the needed accommodations and services. In interpreting data and in making placement decisions, schools must "draw upon information from a variety of sources," "establish procedures to ensure that information obtained from all such sources is documented and carefully considered," and ensure that decisions are made by a "group of persons, including persons knowledgeable about the child, the evaluation data, and the placement options" (34 C.F.R. § 104.35).

Timelines for the completion of an evaluation and determination of a child's needs are not specified in 504 regulations. OCR has held that although "504 does not specify the time periods permitted at each stage of the process of identification, evaluation, and placement, it is implicit that the various steps in the process will be completed within a reasonable time period" (Cobb County [GA] School District, 1992, p. 29). It also has held that it is reasonable to expect schools to complete evaluations under 504 within the same time frame outlined in state guidelines for completion of IDEA evaluations (East Lansing [MI] Public Schools, 1992).

Section 504 does not require re-evaluation of the student every three years, only periodic re-evaluation and re-evaluation prior to any significant change in placement (34 C.F.R. § 104.35). Courts have ruled that expulsion or long-term suspension (more than 10 days) of a student with a handicap is a change of placement requiring re-evaluation.

Free Appropriate Public Education

IDEA and Section 504 both require schools to provide a free appropriate public education to each student with handicaps regardless of the nature or severity of the handicap. *Appropriate education* is defined under 504 as "the provision of regular or special education and related aids and services (i) that are designed to meet individual educational needs of handicapped persons as adequately as the needs of nonhandicapped persons are met and (ii) are based on adherence to procedural safeguards" outlined in the law (34 C.F.R. § 104.33). Thus, under 504, appropriate education is more broadly defined than under IDEA-Part B (34 C.F.R. § 300.8), and it can consist of education in regular classes, education in regular class with the use of supplementary services, or special education and related services (see also Lake Washington [WA] School District No. 414, 1985).

Section 504, like IDEA, also requires schools to "educate, or provide for the education of, each qualified handicapped person in its jurisdiction with persons who are not handicapped to the maximum extent appropriate to the needs of the handicapped person" (34 C.F.R. § 104.34). Students with handicaps must be placed in the regular educational environment unless it is demonstrated by the school that the education of the student in the regular environment with the use of supplementary aids and services cannot be achieved satisfactorily. In providing or arranging for the provision of nonacademic services (e.g., lunch, recess) and extracurricular activities, schools must ensure that handicapped students participate with nonhandicapped students to the maximum extent appropriate to their needs. Students with handicaps also must be afforded opportunities to participate in after school activities and informed that those opportunities are available (34 C.F.R. § 104.34; 34 C.F.R. § 104.37; also Kenowa Hills [MI] Public Schools, 1992).

When Section 504 pupils are referred to or placed in a program not operated by the school district, the district retains responsibility for assuring that Section 504 rights and protections are afforded to the student placed elsewhere (34 C.F.R. § 104.33). When selecting a child's placement, proximity to the child's home must be considered (34 C.F.R. § 104.34). When school districts refer or place pupils with handicaps in programs not operated by the school itself, the placement must be at no cost to the parent. Schools also must ensure adequate transportation to the placement site at no greater cost to the parent than would be incurred if the student were placed in program operated by the school (34 C.F.R. § 104.33).

Accommodation Plan

Under Section 504, schools must provide a free and appropriate education (FAPE) for children with handicaps, designed to meet the individual education needs of handicapped children as adequately as those of nonhandicapped students. One means of meeting this requirement is through the implementation of an individualized education program developed in accordance with IDEA standards (34 C.F.R. § 104.33). Another option is to develop an accommodation plan for 504-only students (see Council of Administrators of Special Education, 1999).

Consistent with the recommended evaluation procedures, the student accommodation plan should be developed by a group of persons, including persons knowledgeable of the child and the evaluation data. The Council of Administrators of Special Education (1999) has suggested that this plan includes: (a) a description of the nature of the concern, (b) a description of the basis for the determination of the handicap, (c) a description of how the handicap affects a major life activity, (d) a description of the reasonable accommodations that are necessary,(e) the date when the plan will be reviewed or reassessed, and (f) the names and titles of the participants at the accommodation plan meeting. The accommodation plan should be included in the student's cumulative file and reviewed on the predetermined date.

Nature of the Required Accommodations

Section 504 requires the provision of regular or special education and related aids and services designed to meet the individual needs of pupils with handicapping conditions. DOE memoranda, OCR rulings, and court cases regarding school responsibilities to pupils who are handicapped within the meaning of 504 provide some guidance regarding the kinds of school accommodations required by the law. This portion of the chapter first summarizes school responsibilities to students with handicaps that affect classroom performance (e.g., learning, emotional, or behavior problems) and then discusses the types of accommodations that might be required under 504 for pupils with physical impairments or health conditions. It is important to note that specific accommodations for a child must always be determined by a group of persons and based on individual student need. What is provided here is an overview of the kinds of accommodations DOE or OCR have found acceptable or required.

The DOE memorandum on pupils with ADD/ADHD and several OCR rulings provide an explicit interpretation of school responsibilities to children who have handicaps that impair classroom performance but who do not qualify for special education and related services under IDEA. In its memorandum of 1991, DOE stated "Should it be determined that the child with ADD/ADHD is handicapped for purposes of Section 504 and needs only adjustments in the regular classroom, rather than special education, those adjustments are required by Section 504." DOE went on to state that through the use of appropriate adaptations and interventions in regular classes, schools effectively can address the instructional needs of many ADD/ADHD (504-only) children.

DOE identified more than 20 strategies available to meet the education needs of 504-only children with ADD/ADHD. It is important to note that the kinds of accommodations required by 504 for students with impairments that affect classroom performance are educational accommodations or strategies that a teacher, pupil assistance team, and/or school psychologist might recommend, and many of them are not overly costly. Possible adaptations in regular education programs suggested by DOE were as follows:

> providing a structured learning environment, repeating and simplifying instructions about in-class and homework assignments; supplementing verbal instructions with visual instructions; using behavioral management

techniques; adjusting class schedules; modifying test delivery; using tape recorders, computer-aided instruction, and other audio-visual equipment; selecting modified textbooks or workbooks, and tailoring homework assignments. (U.S. Department of Education, 1991)

Other provisions for 504-only children suggested by DOE ranged from:

consultation to special resources and may include reducing class size; use of one-on-one tutorials; classroom aides and note takers; involvement of a services coordinator to oversee implementation of special programs and services; and possible modification of nonacademic time such as lunchroom, recess, and physical education. (U.S. Department of Education, 1991)

DOE also stated that in meeting the needs of ADD/ADHD students, state educational agencies and school districts "should take the necessary steps to promote coordination between special and regular education programs." A question raised by parents of children with handicaps and school administrators is whether school districts may use special education programs and services in making accommodations for 504-only students with handicaps. The court ruling in *Lyons by Alexander v. Smith* (1993), OCR complaint investigation findings (for example, see Lake Washington [WA] School District No. 414, 1985), and OCR policy statements indicate that children with handicaps may have access to all IDEA programs and services, even if they do not qualify under IDEA. As the court noted in *Lyons* (1993), a school system may have to provide special education to a 504-only student if such services are necessary to prevent discrimination, that is, to meet the individual educational needs of the handicapped student as adequately as those of nonhandicapped students. Thus, school districts may use IDEA-supported school psychologists or other specialists to provide evaluation and accommodations for 504-only children with handicaps. However, school districts do not receive IDEA funds for 504-only students with handicaps.

Several administrative hearings and OCR investigations have addressed accommodations for students with emotional or behavior problems. These cases concerned students who did not qualify under IDEA-Part B as having a serious emotional disturbance but who were deemed to have a mental impairment that substantially affects a major life activity. For example, a Connecticut hearing officer held that an academically gifted student who experienced serious difficulties in peer relations qualified as handicapped under Section 504 and found acceptable the school's accommodation plan, which included having the school psychologist provide consultation to the teacher and parents and counseling for the student (In the Matter of a Child with Disabilities, 1992; see also Fairfield-Suisun Unified School District, 1989; Rialto Unified School District, 1989).

The court settlement in *Elizabeth S. v. Gilhool* (1987) provides guidance to schools regarding their responsibilities to physically handicapped and other health-impaired students who do not qualify under IDEA. This class action suit was initiated when a district refused to train school personnel to monitor the blood sugar levels of a 6-year-old with juvenile diabetes. It also addressed school responsibilities to a 6-year-old with spina bifida who walked with the assistance of braces and crutches. The court stated that the required school accommodations and services for students with physical or health impairments might include, but are not limited to, development of a plan to address any medical emergencies, school health services including monitoring of blood sugar levels, and arrangements for a child to take injections or medications, assistance with toileting, adjustment of class schedules, home instruction, use of an elevator or other accommodations to make school facilities accessible, adaptive transportation, and adaptive physical education and/or occupational therapy.

Case 6–2

Leigh Michels is a bright and academically talented ninth grader. Born with a mild form of cerebral palsy, she walks with a scissor-leg gait. Over Christmas vacation, Leigh had surgery to reduce the spasticity in her legs. Although temporarily confined to a wheelchair following the surgery, she was eager to return to school. When Mrs. Michels called the high school principal, Mr. Hershey, to arrange Leigh's school transportation, she was told she would have to take time off from her job to transport Leigh to school herself. Mr. Hershey stated that Leigh could not be transported in the special education van equipped with a wheelchair lift because Leigh did not qualify for special education under IDEA. Distressed at the prospect of losing more time from work, Mrs. Michels phoned her friend, Carrie Johnson, who works as a school psychologist in a neighboring district. Mrs. Michels then phoned the principal again and asked for a meeting to determine whether Leigh is handicapped within the meaning of Section 504 and, if eligible, to develop a school accommodation plan including adaptive transportation.

Case 6–2 is based on a real-life incident. When Mrs. Michels phoned the high school principal, Mr. Hershey, and began asking questions about school responsibilities to Leigh under Section 504, Mr. Hershey became so unnerved that he offered to personally transport Leigh to and from school during the weeks she was confined to a wheelchair ... and he did. This incident illustrates the fact that some school districts have not yet developed and implemented procedures to ensure compliance with Section 504 requirements. Additionally, many school administrators are not familiar with DOE policy that allows IDEA-supported special education services to be used in making accommodations for 504-only pupils.

Procedural Safeguards under Section 504

Procedural safeguards in Section 504 regulations are stated in more general terms than those in IDEA-Part B. Under 504, schools are required "to make available a system of procedural safeguards that permits parents to challenge actions regarding the identification, evaluation, or educational placement of their handicapped child whom they believe needs special education or related services" (DOE, 1991; also 34 C.F.R. § 104.36). The system of procedural safeguards must include "notice, an opportunity for the parents or guardian to examine relevant records, an impartial hearing with opportunity for participation by the person's parents or guardian and representation by counsel, and a review procedure" (34 C.F.R. § 104.36). Compliance with the procedural safeguards of IDEA-Part B is one means of fulfilling the Section 504 requirement. However, in an impartial due process hearing raising issues under Section 504, the impartial hearing officer must make a determination based on 504 regulations (Martin, 1992).

Parent Remedies

As noted, the Office of Civil Rights (OCR) is charged with investigating Section 504 complaints pertaining to DOE programs or activities. OCR investigates individual complaints, and a parent may trigger an investigation of school district compliance with 504 simply by filing a written complaint with OCR (Zirkel & Kincaid, 1993).

In addition, parents have the right to initiate a court action against the school on behalf of a child with handicaps if they believe the school has violated the provisions of Section 504 with respect to their child. In accordance with the Handicapped Children's Protection Act of 1986 (Pub. L. No. 99–372), if a Section 504 claim can be remedied under IDEA, parents must first attempt to remedy the problem under IDEA before filing a civil action on a Section 504 claim. Under IDEA, parents typically are required to exhaust administrative remedies (e.g., due process hearings) available to them before they pursue a court action. In contrast, parents are not required to exhaust administrative remedies before initiating a civil action under 504. The courts may award reasonable attorney fees as part of the costs to parents when they are the prevailing party in a Section 504 suit.

AMERICANS WITH DISABILITIES ACT OF 1990

Congress passed more than 20 laws prohibiting discrimination against individuals with disabilities between 1973 and 1990 (Burgdorf, 1991). The Americans with Disabilities Act of 1990 (ADA) (Pub. L. No. 101-336) is considered to be the most significant federal law ensuring the civil rights of all individuals with disabilities.

ADA was first introduced as a bill in Congress in 1988. In its statement of findings, Congress reported that "some 43,000,000 Americans have one or more physical or mental disabilities" (Pub. L. No. 101–336, § 2[a][1]). Congress found widespread discrimination against individuals with disabilities in all spheres of life, including employment, housing, public accommodations, education, transportation, communication, recreation, health services, and access to public services. Additionally, testimony to Congress documented a strong link between disability and poverty, joblessness, lack of education, and failure to participate in social and recreational opportunities (Burgdorf, 1991). President G. H. Bush signed ADA into law in 1990.

ADA guarantees equal opportunity to individuals with disabilities in employment, public services, transportation, state and local government services, and telecommunications. It differs from earlier laws in that it  extends to programs and activities outside the federal sphere and includes a detailed set of standards prohibiting discrimination (Burgdorf, 1991). Title II, Subtitle A, is the portion of the law pertaining to public schools.

The protections of ADA extend only to those persons who have a disability as defined by the law. Like Section 504, a disability is defined as a physical or mental impairment that substantially limits one or more major life activities, or a record of such an impairment, or being regarded as having such an impairment.

As noted in Chapter 5, IDEA-Part B requires schools to provide a statement of needed transition services for youth with disabilities beginning at age 16 (or younger if appropriate) as part of the individual education program (IEP). Transition services are a set of coordinated activities that promote movement from school to postschool activities. ADA promises to expand opportunities for youth with disabilities in their transition to postschool activities. School psychologists involved in planning transition services under IDEA need to be familiar with the protections against discrimination afforded by ADA in employment, education and training, transportation, recreation, and access to telecommunications. A detailed discussion of those portions of ADA is beyond the scope of this text. Readers are encouraged to consult Burgdorf (1991).

Title II, Subtitle A

Title II, Subtitle A, is the portion of ADA pertaining to public schools. Regulations implementing Title II appear at 28 *Code of Federal Regulations* (C.F.R.) Part 35. ADA prohibitions against discrimination in public schools are essentially the same as those outlined in Section 504: "No qualified individual with a disability shall, on the basis of disability, be excluded from participation in or be denied the benefits of the services, programs, or activities of a public entity, or be subjected to discrimination by any such entity" (28 C.F.R. § 35.130). *Qualified individual with a disability* under Title II means "an individual with a disability who, with or without reasonable modifications of rules, policies, or practices, the removal of architectural, communication, or transportation barriers, or the provision of auxiliary aids and services, meets the essential eligibility requirement for the receipt of services or the participation in programs or activities provided by the public entity" (28 C.F.R. § 35.104).

ADA thus prohibits discrimination against qualified individuals on the basis of disability in public school services, programs, or activities. ADA, like 504, also requires schools to make reasonable accommodations for students with disabilities:

> A public entity shall make reasonable modifications in policies, practices, or procedures when the modifications are necessary to avoid discrimination on the basis of disability, unless the public entity can demonstrate that making the modifications would fundamentally alter the nature of the service, program, or activity. (28 C.F.R. § 35.130)

ADA also requires that services, programs, and activities be provided in "the most integrated setting appropriate to the needs of qualified individuals with disabilities" (28 C.F.R. § 35.130).

In accordance with ADA, each school district must conduct a self-evaluation of its policies and practices with regard to individuals with disabilities and correct any that are not consistent with ADA (28 C.F.R. § 35.105). Like Section 504, ADA requires public schools to provide notice regarding the provisions of ADA and the school's responsibilities under the law (28 C.F.R. § 35.106). Schools must designate at least one employee to coordinate their efforts to comply with the law (28 C.F.R. § 35.107). School districts also must adopt and publish grievance procedures, providing for prompt and equitable resolution of complaints alleging violations of ADA (28 C.F.R. § 35.107).

There is much overlap between 504 and ADA in school responsibilities to students with disabilities. ADA regulations state that, unless otherwise noted, ADA "shall not be construed to apply a lesser standard" than 504 (28 C.F.R. § 35.103). Thus, ADA generally requires full compliance with 504, but at times it requires more than 504 in school obligations to students with disabilities. ADA stresses the removal of architectural barriers as a top priority (Martin, 1992; see also 28 C.F.R. Part 35, Appendix A).

The Office for Civil Rights within the U.S. Department of Education has been designated as the agency responsible for enforcing ADA with regard to public schools. Complaints regarding ADA violations may be filed with OCR. The "remedies" of Section 504 are the remedies of Title II of ADA. OCR may remove federal funds from schools not in compliance with ADA. ADA also allows private lawsuits against public schools, and administrative remedies (e.g., hearings) are not required to be exhausted prior to filing a lawsuit (28 C.F.R. § 35.172). The parents of a child with disabilities or an individual with disabilities may be awarded reasonable attorney fees if they prevail in any action filed under ADA (28 C.F.R. § 35.175).

Whistleblower's Protection

School psychologists also should be familiar with ADA's protection against retaliation or coercion for whistleblowers:

> (a) No private or public entity shall discriminate against any individual because that individual has opposed any act or practice made unlawful by this part or because that individual made a charge, testified, assisted, or participated in any manner in an investigation, proceeding or hearing under the Act or this part.
>
> (b) No private or public entity shall coerce, intimidate, threaten, or interfere with any individual in the exercise or enjoyment of, or on account of his having exercised or enjoyed, or on account of his or her having aided or encouraged any other individual in the exercise or enjoyment of, any right granted or protected by the Act or this part. (28 C.F.R. § 35.134)

This portion of the law was designed in part to protect individuals who advocate for the rights of the disabled from retaliation by the agency involved. Thus, if a school district failed to meet its obligations to pupils with disabilities under ADA, and a school employee assisted those students in obtaining their rights under the Act, the school district would be prohibited from retaliating against the employee. If the school did retaliate by firing or in some way demoting the employee, the employee would have the right to file a lawsuit against the school district under ADA's protection against retaliation. For example, in November, 2001, a federal jury awarded $1 million to a former special education teacher who was fired after persistently complaining that disabled students received less adequate time, equipment, and facilities for physical education than their nondisabled peers (Chestnut, 2001).

CONCLUDING COMMENTS

Some school districts have not yet developed a 504 service delivery model. In those districts, school psychologists have an important role to play in working with administrators, teachers, support staff, and parent representatives to develop policies and procedures for 504 referral, evaluation, and decision making, and to safeguard pupil and parent rights. Development and implementation of a practical and efficient 504 response model requires much cooperation among regular and special education personnel but will, it is hoped, result in greater school responsiveness to the needs of regular education students with handicapping conditions.

Much overlap exists between 504 and ADA in public school responsibilities to students with handicapping conditions. However, ADA protections against discrimination in employment, education and training, transportation, recreation, and access to telecommunications all promise to expand opportunities for youth with disabilities in their transition to postschool activities.

STUDY AND DISCUSSION

Questions for Chapter 6

1. What type of legislation is Section 504 of The Rehabilitation Act of 1973? How does it differ from IDEA in purpose, scope, and funding?
2. How is pupil eligibility determined under 504? Identify Martin's categories of students who may qualify as handicapped within the meaning of 504 but who might not be eligible for special education under IDEA.
3. Must a child have a permanent handicapping condition to be eligible for accommodations under 504?
4. What is the meaning of *free appropriate public education* within 504?
5. Describe the content of an accommodation plan under 504 and how one is developed.
6. Briefly describe the scope and purpose of ADA as it relates to public school children.

(Continued)

Discussion

What are some of the ways in which Section 504 can have a positive impact on schools and schoolchildren? See Jacob-Timm and Hartshorne (1994).

ACTIVITIES

Does your local school district distribute a handbook or pamphlet to parents outlining their rights and school responsibilities under Section 504 of The Rehabilitation Act of 1973? Obtain and review copies of informational materials given to parents.

Chapter 7

ETHICAL AND LEGAL ISSUES IN COUNSELING AND THERAPEUTIC INTERVENTIONS IN THE SCHOOLS

Based on a survey of members of the National Association of School Psychologists, Curtis, Hunley, Walker, and Baker (1999) reported that 86 percent of school practitioners engage in counseling of individual students, and about 53 percent conduct student group sessions. This chapter explores the ethical-legal issues associated with counseling and therapeutic interventions with individual students (see Corey, Corey, and Callanan, 1998, for information on the ethical-legal aspects of counseling students in groups). It begins with a discussion of pre-intervention responsibilities to the parent and pupil and intervention planning. The responsibilities of the school psychologist in situations involving danger to the student or others are addressed, followed by an overview of the legal issues associated with pregnancy and birth control counseling. Ethical-legal issues associated with behavioral interventions in the schools are then examined. We conclude with a brief discussion of issues associated with psychopharmacologic therapies in the school setting, using Ritalin as an example.

PRE-INTERVENTION RESPONSIBILITIES

School psychologists have a number of ethical and legal obligations to pupils and their parents prior to providing psychological treatment services.

Parent Involvement and Consent

As noted in Chapter 3, ethical codes, professional guidelines, and law are consistent in requiring parent consent (or the consent of an adult student) for school actions that may result in a significant intrusion on personal or family privacy beyond what might be expected in the course of ordinary classroom and school activities (Corrao & Melton, 1988). It is, however, generally viewed as permissible to provide emergency counseling without parent notice or consent in the event of a crisis situation in the schools (Canadian Psychological Association, 2000; NASP-PPE-III,C,#2; Pitcher & Poland, 1992). Consequently, with the exception of unusual situations, informed consent is obtained prior to the provision of psychological treatment. Bersoff and Hofer (1990) note that parental consent is implied for psychological interventions written in the child's individualized education program (IEP) under IDEA, but the psychologist may want, at times, to secure continued parental consent, particularly if the intervention changes over the course of treatment.

The provision of direct services to a minor child (e.g., the psychologist works with a child in overcoming a phobia) clearly requires parental consent. The situation is less clear-cut when the psychologist serves as a consultant to the teacher and the teacher serves as the behavior-change agent. DeMers and Bersoff (1985) suggest that parental consent probably is needed and desired if the focus of the consultation is a specific child, rather than the classroom, and the child may be treated differently from others as a result of the consultation to the teacher (also Reschly & Bersoff, 1999).

Responsibilities to the Pupil

Legally, in the school setting, informed consent for psychological services rests with the parents of a minor child. However, the practitioner is obligated ethically to respect the dignity, autonomy, and self-determination of the student/client. The decision to allow a student/client the opportunity to choose (or refuse) psychological treatment or intervention may involve consideration of a number of factors, including law, ethical issues (self-determination versus welfare of the client), the pupil's competence to make choices, and the likely consequences of affording choices (e.g., enhanced treatment outcomes versus choice to refuse treatment). We concur with Weithorn's (1983) suggestion that practitioners permit and encourage student/client involvement in treatment decision making to the maximum extent appropriate to the child and the situation.

Practitioners have an ethical obligation to inform the student/client of the scope and nature of the proposed intervention, whether they are given a choice about participating (NASP-PPE, III, B,#2). After children reach school age, the initial interview with the pupil also should include a discussion of the parameters of confidentiality.

Special Informed Consent Issues

Special informed consent issues include self-referrals for counseling, consent to experimental methods of treatment, and supervision and consultation release.

Self-Referrals for Counseling

Young children are unlikely to seek help or initiate a counseling relationship on their own. However, at the high school level, many referrals for counseling are self-referrals. Students may wish to see a school psychologist on the condition that their parents not be notified. This raises the question of whether students who are minors can ever be seen by the school psychologist for counseling without parental permission. We are not aware of any case law decisions that specifically address this question.

A reasonable, common sense approach to the issue of counseling minor students without parental consent was suggested by C. Osip in Canter (1989). Osip suggests allowing students one precounseling screening session without parental permission. This precounseling meeting could serve to ensure that the child is safe and not in danger. During this meeting, the psychologist could discuss the need for parental consent for further counseling sessions, offer to contact the parent on behalf of the student, or offer to meet jointly with the student and parents to discuss consent and ensure ongoing parent support. Unless there is a conflict with state law, we believe school districts should adopt written policies stating that students may be seen by the school psychologist or other mental health professional without parent notice or consent to ensure the student is not in danger (e.g., child abuse, suicidal), or if it is suspected the student may be a danger to others.

Practitioners should be aware that in some states, minors are given the right to access certain types of treatment independent of parental notice or consent under state law. However, these rights to access treatment usually are limited to conditions of a medical nature (e.g., drug abuse, venereal disease) and may not extend to the school setting. School psychologists need to consult their state laws to determine whether minors are given rights to seek treatment independent of parental notice or consent in their state, and under what conditions (Corrao & Melton, 1988).

Experimental Methods

In seeking informed consent for treatment, all experimental methods of treatment must be clearly indicated to prospective recipients (EP 10.01). Experimental methods of treatment may be either methods that are nonstandard practice in the profession, whose efficacy has not been established, or those that are new to the repertoire of the individual psychologist.

Supervision and Consultation Release

School psychologists, interns, and practicum students need to inform parents (and adult students) at the onset of the provision of services if they will be discussing information about their case with a supervisor or consultant (EP 10.01). As will be seen in Chapter 11, parents and adult students should be given the opportunity to make an informed choice whether to accept treatment services from a school psychology trainee. When treatment services are provided by a trainee, parents and adult students should be provided the name and phone number of the trainee's supervisor (Knapp & VandeCreek, 1997).

Planning Interventions

In recommending psychotherapeutic interventions, psychologists strive to propose a "set of options" for consideration by the student and others involved in intervention decision making (NASP-PPE, III, C, #1, #5). The proposed options should consider all resources (school and community) available to assist the student and family and take into account the objectives of the school and the classroom, the support and assistance that can be made available to the teacher, and the values and capabilities of the parents (NASP-PPE, III, C, #1, #3, #5). School psychologists "respect the wishes of parents who object to school psychological services and attempt to guide parents to alternative community resources (NASP-PPE, III, C, #4).

Psychologists also are obligated to recommend evidence-based intervention techniques, that is, those techniques "that the profession considers to be responsible, research-based practice" (NASP-PPE, I, C, #4; also EP 2.04). Consequently, they must keep abreast of the research literature on intervention strategies and their effectiveness.

Interventions with Culturally Diverse Clientele

Practitioners are obligated ethically to ensure that services are beneficial and respectful of the student-client. Consequently, practitioners have special obligations when working with students whose background characteristics are different from their own. First, psychologists need to be aware of how their own cultural heritage, gender, class, ethnic-racial identity, sexual orientation, and age cohort shape personal values and beliefs, including assumptions and biases related to those who are different (Hansen, Pepitone-Arreola-Rockwell, & Greene, 2000; Rogers et al., 1999). Second, psychologists need to learn about the student-client's background, values, beliefs, and worldview and how those cultural and experiential factors may influence development and behavior (Hansen et al., 1999; Lynch & Hanson, 1998; Ortiz & Flanagan, 2002). Third, in order to provide sensitive and effective services, practitioners must be able to demonstrate an understanding and respect for cultural and experiential differences in interacting with the student (APA, 1993; Hansen et al., 1999; Rogers et al., 1999; Lynch & Hanson, 1998). Fourth, practitioners are obligated to seek knowledge of best practices in selecting, designing, and implementing treatment plans for diverse clientele with learning or behavior problems (APA, 1993; Hansen et al., 1999, Rogers et al., 1999). And fifth, when working with diverse students, practitioners should assist the students and their parents to better understand the culture of the school and community so that they can make informed choices relevant to schooling and mental health services (Hays, 2001; Rogers et al., 1999).

Practitioners also are obligated to self-assess their own multicultural competence (Hansen et al., 1999). More specifically, they need to consider when circumstances (e.g., personal biases, lack of requisite knowledge, skills, or language fluency) may negatively influence professional practice and adapt accordingly; that is, by obtaining needed information, consultation, or supervision, or referring the student to a better qualified professional (APA, 1993; Hansen et al., 1999). (See Case 7–8 in this chapter and Appendix D.)

COUNSELING: ETHICAL AND LEGAL ISSUES

Tharinger and Stafford (1995) describe counseling in the schools as a process of ongoing, planned interactions between a student/client and a mental health professional. The school psychologist works to alleviate the student/client's distress by improving the child's psychological functioning and/or facilitating change in his or her environment, in particular the school and family systems. More specifically, the goals of counseling may include "alleviating the child's emotional and cognitive distress, changing the child's behavior, assisting with self-understanding, helping the child meet current developmental tasks successfully, supporting needed environmental changes, and promoting a more positive fit between the child and the systems in which she or he resides (e.g., school and family)" (p. 896).

In the next portion of the chapter, we explore ethical-legal issues in special counseling situations, such as working with students who are potentially dangerous to others or a threat to themselves. In responding to such situations, it is important for school psychologists to recognize that they are viewed differently in law than psychologists who work in non-school settings such as private practice. As noted in Chapter 2, school practitioners have a legal as well as a moral obligation to take reasonable steps to protect students from foreseeable harm. This obligation extends to all students, not just their own clients. Also, because many of the students they work with are minors, school practitioners must place a high priority on parent involvement.

Case 7–1

An 8-year-old girl, Celia, complained to her teacher that another child (a 13-year-old boy) was "playing games" with her. As it was apparent that the games involved inappropriate sexual contact, the teacher informed the school psychologist. The school psychologist counseled Celia without notifying her mother of the problem. The school principal was informed of the incidents and told the boy involved not to "bother" Celia any more. The principal also failed to notify Celia's mother about the incidents. Meanwhile, the assaults on Celia continued over a 3-month period, both on school premises and en route to school. Celia became increasingly despondent and withdrawn. The sexual assaults ultimately led to rape. The victim's mother, after learning what had happened, filed a lawsuit against the school psychologist, teacher, and principal.

The California Supreme Court ruled that the school had a mandatory duty to warn Celia's mother that her daughter was being sexually molested, a duty to report the assaults to a child protective agency, a duty to obtain written parent consent prior to psychological treatment dealing with matters of a sensitive sexual nature, and a duty to properly supervise the molesting student and ensure Celia's safety (adapted from Phillis P. v. Claremont Unified School District, *1986).*

Threat to Others

Schools are one of the safest places for children (Mulvey & Cauffman, 2001). However, violence in our schools is a concern of educators and parents. During the 1996–1997 school year, approximately 187,890 students were physically attacked or in a fight without a weapon; an additional 10,950 were attacked or in a fight involving a weapon (National Center for Education Statistics, 2001). Our focus here is on assessment of whether an individual student poses a danger to others; school-wide programs to identify students who may be at risk for violent acts are discussed in Chapter 9.

As noted previously, under state statutory law and case law, school personnel have a legal duty to protect pupils in their schools from reasonably foreseeable risk of harm. Also, in many states, therapists have a legal duty to take reasonable steps to prevent anticipated harm when their client is a danger to others (e.g., *Tarasoff v. Regents of California*, 1976). The assessment of whether a student poses a danger to others is not an easy task.

School personnel may become concerned about a student because of his or her aggressive, antisocial behavior (e.g., fighting, explosive temper). For such students, the task is to determine the risk for future violent acts and how to reduce the likelihood of future violence. Borum (2000) has provided guidelines regarding how to conduct a systematic assessment of violence potential in such situations. His approach takes into account the student's past violent acts, the precipitants to those acts, and the protective factors, that is—factors that would help the student avoid situations likely to trigger violent actions.

Students also may come to the attention of the school psychologist or other school personnel because they make direct or indirect threats to injure others. The term *targeted violence* is used to refer to situations in which both the potential perpetrator and target(s) are identifiable prior to a violent attack (Vossekuil, Reddy, Fein, Borum, & Modzeleski, 2000). As Borum (2000) notes, a different assessment approach is recommended in situations involving targeted violence.

When students make threats to injure others, such threats should be taken seriously (Reddy, Borum, Vossekuil, Fein, Berglund, & Modzeleski, 2001; *Mirand v. Board of Education of the City of New York*, 1994). A report sponsored by The Federal Bureau of Investigation recommends a multidisciplinary team approach to threat assessment (FBI Academy, 2000). This team might include mental health professionals, school administrators, and law enforcement professionals. In *Milligan et al. v. City of Slidell* (2000), a federal court ruled that it is permissible for school officials and police to detain and question a student thought to be planning an act of violence at school because the school's interest in deterring school violence outweighs a student's limited Fourth Amendment privacy rights in such situations.

The risk factors for targeted violence do not appear to be the same as the risk factors associated with general aggression and violence recidivism among youth (Reddy et al., 2001). Reddy et al. (2001) have outlined a model for evaluating whether a student is on a path toward targeted violence. Their model is based on three principles: (1) targeted violence is a result of an interaction among the student, situation, target, and setting; there is no single "type" of student prone to such acts; (2) evaluators must make a distinction between a student who makes threats vs. poses a threat; and (3) targeted violence is often the product of an understandable pattern of thinking and behavior. The model involves evaluating the student's behavior and pattern of conduct using information from multiple sources. Information gathering might involve interviewing the student, his or her family, teachers, and friends; and reviewing pupil records. Key questions that guide the threat assessment evaluation include the following: Does the student have ideas about or plans for targeted violence? Has the student shown an interest in violence, acts of violence by others, or weapons?

Has the student engaged in any attack-related behavior, including menacing, harassing, or stalking? Is the student cognitively and physically capable of carrying out a plan of violence? Has the student experienced a recent loss or loss of status and has this led to feelings of desperation and despair? And, what factors in the student's life and/or environment might increase or decrease the likelihood of the student becoming violent? (also see Borum, Fein, Vossekuil, & Berglund, 1999).

In making a decision whether a student is potentially dangerous, the psychologist is well advised to consult with other professionals (Waldo & Malley, 1992). In court decisions, therapists have not been held liable for failure to warn "when the propensity toward violence is unknown or would be unknown by other psychotherapists using ordinary skill" (Knapp & VandeCreek, 1982, p. 515).

Consistent with the guidelines for other situations involving danger, schools need to develop written procedures regarding when and how to notify school officials and legal authorities (e.g., police, the student's probation officer) if school staff become aware of a potentially assaultive student. These procedures should ensure that the intended victim is warned (see Case 7–1). If a student poses a threat to a minor child, the parents of the threatened child should be notified. Parents of a potentially assaultive student should be informed of the situation. The potentially violent student should be supervised in the school setting and at home, and steps should be taken to ensure there is no access to weapons. Mental health practitioners should be prepared to refer the family to a community mental health agency and be familiar with the procedures for voluntary or involuntary commitment of minors and adult students. Psychology practitioners should know and follow school policies regarding dangerous students and should document their actions in the management of a student who may become violent (Pitcher & Poland, 1992).

Practitioners also need to consider the long-range needs of students at risk for violence with regards to follow-up educational and mental health services. They need to ensure that the student receives well-coordinated assistance from the family, school, and community mental health professionals.

As is true of many mental health concerns in the school setting, efforts aimed at preventing student violence on a systemwide basis are preferable to the dilemmas of managing the assault-prone student. There appears to be a growing body of literature on this topic (see Brock, Lazarus, & Jimerson, 2002; also Chapter 9).

Threat to Self

Suicide is one of the three leading causes of death among adolescents (Center for Disease Control, 2001a). It is estimated that in 1997 there were approximately 9.5 completed suicides per 100,000 adolescents in the 15–19-year-old age group and 1.6 per 100,000 children in the 10–14-year-old age group (National Institute of Mental Health, 2001).

Case 7–2

Brian, a 14-year-old, confronted his teacher during class with a .38 caliber revolver. The teacher persuaded Brian to talk with the vice principal alone in an empty classroom. Brian showed the vice principal a suicide note he had written and asked to speak with his favorite teacher; he was not allowed to do so. When they left the classroom, Brian was confronted by a police officer who told him he was "in trouble with the law." Brian (still armed with the gun) entered the boy's restroom where he shot himself. Brian died later that morning (adapted from Kelson v. The City of Springfield, *1985).*

Case 7–3

"Nina," a 13-year-old middle-school student, became involved in Satanism and developed an obsessive interest in death. She told several friends that she intended to kill herself. Nina's friends reported her suicidal intentions to their school counselor (at a different school), who conveyed the information to Nina's school counselor. Both counselors met with Nina and questioned her about her statements concerning suicide, but she denied making them. Neither counselor informed Nina's parents or other members of the school staff about her suicidal statements. One week after telling her friends about her suicidal intentions, Nina and another 13-year-old girl consummated a murder-suicide pact in a public park some distance from the middle school she attended (adapted from Eisel v. Board of Education, *1991).*

School Response to Suicidal Intent

In *Kelson* (Case 7–2), Brian's parents filed a negligence suit against the school and city in state court and a Section 1983 lawsuit against the school and city in federal court, alleging that the state interfered with their constitutionally protected liberty interest in the companionship of their son.

When the Section 1983 lawsuit reached the U.S. Court of Appeals, the judge advised Brian's parents to file an amended claim against the school district after ruling on several legal questions raised by the case. In so doing, he raised the question of a possible relationship between school policy (namely, inadequate suicide training for its staff) and Brian's death.

In *Eisel v. Board of Education* (Case 7–3), Nina's father filed a negligence suit against the two school counselors, based on their failure to communicate information to him concerning Nina's contemplated suicide. Nina's father believed he could have prevented his daughter's death had he been told about her statements. The court held that a school has a special duty to protect a pupil from harm and that "school counselors have a duty to use reasonable means to attempt to prevent a suicide when they are on notice of a child or adolescent's suicidal intent" (*Eisel,* 1991, p. 456). The school counselors were viewed as having little discretion regarding whether to contact parents once information suggested a potential suicide.[1]

The *Eisel* and *Kelson* cases, among others (e.g., *Wyke v. Polk County School Board*, 1997), have been interpreted to suggest that schools should develop clear suicide prevention policies and procedures that include notifying parents and ensure adequate staff orientation to district policy and procedures. When it is suspected that a student is suicidal, the situation should be reported to the building principal and a designated staff member who has training in assessment of suicide lethality and suicide prevention. The school psychologist might serve as one of the designated staff members. The student should be assessed for the lethality of suicidal ideation because the degree of lethality determines the appropriate course of action (Poland, 1989). Most methods of assessing lethality involve seeking answers to a series of critical questions such as, Is there a preoccupation with death? Does the student have a suicide plan? Has the student made previous suicide attempts? Is the student involved with drugs? Has there been a precipitating event? And, why does the student want to die? (See Poland & Lieberman, 2002.)

Practitioners are not expected to be able to predict suicide attempts with perfect accuracy (Knapp, 1980), but they are expected to apply "skill and care in assessing suicidal potential and . . . a reasonable degree of care and skill in preventing the suicide" (1980, p. 609). Many psychologists recommend asking suicidal clients to sign a "no-suicide contract." Although "do no harm" contracts may be clinically useful, it is important to recognize that such contracts do not substitute for a careful risk assessment and appropriate intervention based on the assessed risk (Simon, 1999).

Parents must be contacted in all cases, whether the risk is determined to be low or high. As Poland (1989) notes, the question is not whether to

---

[1] This decision did not determine the school's liability; the decision only allowed action in another court to rule on the school's liability. The school counselors ultimately were not held liable for the $1 million in damages the father sought.

tell the parents, but how to elicit a supportive reaction from them. Parents of medium- or high-risk students should be contacted as soon as possible. The high-risk student should not be left alone, and his or her parents should be required to come to school for a conference and to pick up their child (Poland, 1989).

Poland (1989) recommends that two staff members conduct the parent notification conference and notes that some districts have parents sign a form acknowledging that they have been notified their child is suicidal. The psychologist needs to ensure that parents understand the seriousness of the situation, and parents should be advised to increase supervision at home and remove access to weapons and other means of self-harm (e.g., medications). The practitioner should be prepared to refer the family to a community mental health professional who has expertise in working with suicidal youth. Poland (1989) provides a number of recommendations for eliciting a supportive response from the parents. However, if parents are unwilling to follow through on treatment recommendations, Poland suggests it is appropriate to warn them that failure to seek assistance for their child is neglectful, and child protective services will be contacted.

Practitioners also need to consider the long-range needs of the suicidal student with regards to follow-up educational and mental health services. School personnel who work directly with a suicidal student should be informed so that they can provide adequate supervision (Poland, 1989).

Practitioners are well-advised to develop consultative relationships with clinicians who have expertise in suicide assessment and management whom they can contact for assistance in evaluating and managing a potential suicide situation (Jobes & Berman, 1993). Practitioners should document their actions regarding risk assessment and management of pupils who may be suicidal. They need to be familiar with community resources for referral, including the procedures for hospitalization of suicidal minors and adult students.

It has become increasingly important for school practitioners to obtain training to develop their professional competence in assessment and management of suicidal clients (Jobes & Berman, 1993). Additionally, psychologists who acquire special expertise in suicide prevention can play an important role in the development of the school's planned response to suicidal students. There is a growing body of literature on the development of suicide prevention programs (see Brock et al., 2002; Poland & McCormick, 1999).

Substance Abuse

A number of surveys suggest that substance abuse continues to be a problem in our schools. Alcohol is the substance most commonly abused by teenagers. In 2000, 52 percent of eighth graders, 71 percent of tenth graders, and 89 percent of twelfth graders reported having consumed alcohol within the year. In the same year, 27 percent of eighth graders, 46 percent of tenth graders, and 54 percent of twelfth graders reported using illicit drugs (National Institute on Drug Abuse, 2001). School psychologists (particularly those who work with middle and senior high students) need to be knowledgeable of drugs commonly used by adolescents and the symptoms of alcohol and drug abuse.

When substance abuse poses a threat to the student, it is appropriate to notify the parent of the problem and work with the parent in locating treatment resources (Forman & Randolph, 1987). Some states (e.g., Virginia) have enacted laws that require schools to report alcohol or substance abuse to parents. If the parent is uncooperative, the psychologist should explore treatment options that do not require parental consent. Every state has an agency responsible for coordinating substance abuse services that may be helpful in locating needed services (Forman & Randolph, 1987).

If knowledge of substance abuse involves other students in the school setting, the practitioner may need to discuss the situation with appropriate school authorities in order to ensure the safety of others. School psychologists must be cautious to avoid involvement in school disciplinary actions such as search and seizure, particularly if such activities are not part of their formal job responsibilities (see Chapter 2).

Case 7–4

Nick Greene, a member of the school's winning football team, made an appointment with the school psychologist, Sam Foster. He confided that he had been taking "supervitamins" to build up his muscles over the past year. A fellow high school student bought the vitamins at a local health club and sold them in the locker room to football team members. Nick had seen some TV news stories about steroids, and he thinks maybe the supervitamins "have some of that in it." He was worried because he also heard that steroids "could make a guy act queer," and he wanted to know if that could happen to him.

Sam Foster (Case 7–4) needs to work with Nick and his parents to ensure that Nick is seen by a physician to determine the nature of the substance taken, any harmful effects, and the appropriate course of treatment. He also needs to discuss his concerns about possible steroid abuse with high school officials (without disclosing Nick's identity) and explore ways to alert parents and students to the dangers of steroid use.

School psychologists can assume a leadership role in the development and implementation of school-based substance abuse programs, including educational programs for school staff and parents, prevention and intervention programs for students, and developing liaisons with community resources (see Cavell, Ennett, & Meehan, 2001).

Child Abuse

The Child Abuse Prevention, Adoption, and Family Services Act of 1988 defined child maltreatment as "the physical or mental injury, sexual abuse or exploitation, negligent treatment, or maltreatment of a child by a person who is responsible for the child's welfare, under circumstances which indicate that the child's health or welfare is harmed or threatened" (Pub. L. No. 100–294, § 14). States are required to use a similar definition of abuse in their reporting laws in order to be eligible for federal child protection funds. There is some variation among states, however, with regard to the way abuse is defined (see Kalichman, 1999). All 50 states have enacted legislation requiring school professionals to report suspected cases of child abuse to child welfare or protection agencies.

There were 2,822,829 investigations by Child Protective Services in 1999. An estimated 826,000 children were victims of child abuse or neglect that year (U. S. Department of Health and Human Services, 2001a). Most child abuse goes unreported, however. Researchers estimate that reported cases of child abuse constitute only about 40 percent of all cases (Kalichman, 1999).

Case 7–5

Pesce was a school psychologist providing services at the high school level. A female student (C. R.) gave him a note written to her by a male friend (J. D). The note included a statement made by J. D. expressing guilt and confusion about his sexual preference and possible hints of suicide. C. R. also informed Pesce that J. D. had visited the home of a male teacher where "something sexual" had occurred between them. Pesce urged C. R. to have J. D. get in touch with him to discuss these matters. Pesce did not notify anyone else of C. R.'s communications at that time.

Later the same day, J. D. visited Pesce in his office at school, and Pesce assured J. D. of the confidentiality of any information divulged and questioned him about issues raised by the letter. J. D. denied having any current suicidal intentions and denied that any sexual acts had occurred between the male teacher and him but stated that the teacher had once shown him "pictures" when he

Case 7–5 *(Continued)*

visited the teacher's home. J. D. also expressed a desire to have help in addressing his confusion over sexual preference. Pesce arranged for J. D. to see a therapist.

Pesce reached a professional judgment that it was in J. D.'s best interest for Pesce to honor their confidential relationship and not inform school authorities about J. D.'s communications without his consent. After considering relevant state laws, school regulations, the guidelines of the American Psychological Association, and consulting with an attorney and a colleague, Pesce chose not to notify a child protection agency or any school officials of the rumored sexual activity or suicidal tendencies.

During the following week, J. D. kept two appointments with the therapist Pesce had recommended but canceled a third. Pesce then met jointly with J. D. and the therapist. During that meeting, J. D. revealed that he and the male teacher had engaged in a sexual act. J. D. then agreed with Pesce that it would be best to reveal the information to school authorities. Pesce promptly did so.

After making his report to school officials, Pesce was given a five-day disciplinary suspension for "failure promptly to report J. D.'s possible suicidal tendencies and the alleged sexual misconduct of a male teacher" (p. 790).

Pesce filed a suit against school officials alleging (among other claims) that the state's requirement for reporting suspected child abuse infringed unconstitutionally on his right of confidentiality in the professional relationship (derived from the student's right to privacy). The court noted that, as a school psychologist, Pesce may well be able to claim a right to confidentiality in his professional relationships with his clients. However, even if there is such a right to confidentiality, there is a greater compelling interest, namely to protect children from abuse. The court found that "the Illinois requirement that Pesce and others in similar positions of responsibility promptly report child abuse to a state agency does not unconstitutionally infringe on any federal right of confidentiality" (p. 798) (adapted from Pesce v. J. Sterling Morton High School District 201, *Cook County, Illinois, 1987).*

School psychologists legally are required to report all cases of suspected child abuse. All states provide immunity from civil or criminal action for making such a report, as long as it is made in good faith. Penalties for not reporting may include civil liability and loss of certification or license. In *State v. Gover* (1989), the court held that it is not necessary that school personnel be certain that the abuse took place, only that there is reason to suspect abuse. In *Phillis P.* (Case 7–1), the California Supreme Court held that the school psychologist had a mandatory duty to report a student who was sexually molesting another student to the state child protection agency. In *Pesce* (Case 7–5), the court held that the duty to protect schoolchildren by reporting suspected child abuse outweighs any right to confidentiality of the psychologist–client relationship.[2]

School psychology practitioners must be familiar with the signs of abuse and neglect. They must know the procedures for reporting and familiarize themselves with the designated agency and its procedures for handling reports (see Horton & Cruise, 2001). It is the responsibility of the child protection agency, not school personnel, to confirm or disconfirm the existence of abuse or neglect.

Most child abuse occurs in the context of the family, rather than the school. One concern about making a report about suspected abuse might be the loss of rapport with the student or with the family as a result of making a report. However, based on a review of the available studies, Kalichman concludes that "… little evidence exists to support the popular perceptions that reporting abuse has detrimental effects on the quality and efficacy of professional services. In fact, studies specifically addressing these issues in clinical settings find that reporting sometimes benefits the treatment process" (1999, p. 61). He goes on to note, however, that additional research is needed in this area. Similarly, Meddin and Rosen note that, "After their initial and appropriate anger at the intervention of the agency, most parents feel a sense of relief that the problems has [sic] been identified, and they are usually very willing to work toward a solution" (1986, p. 30).

School psychologists can assume an important role in the prevention, identification, and reporting of child abuse and in the treatment of abused children (see Horton & Cruise, 2001; Kalichman, 1999).

Pregnancy and Birth Control Information

In the following paragraphs we provide a brief overview of the legal issues associated with student pregnancy and birth control counseling.

---

[2] The case of *Pesce* is a curious one for a number of reasons. First, no mention is made of parent involvement. Second, school officials also failed to notify protective services after Pesce notified them of his concerns. The reader may wish to consider alternative decisions that might be made in handling a situation like the one that confronted Pesce and the possible consequences of various actions for the parties involved.

Pregnancy

Recent years have witnessed a slight decline in adolescent pregnancies. In 1997, there were an estimated 321,300 pregnancies in the 15–17-year-old age group, and 23,700 for girls under age 15 (Center for Disease Control, 2001b). In the U.S., an estimated 15.3 million new cases of sexually transmitted disease occur each year, at least a quarter of them are among teenagers (National Institute of Allergy and Infectious Diseases, 2001).

Case 7–6

Tamara Jones, a high school English teacher, referred a 15-year-old student, Brenda, to the school psychologist for a precounseling screening. Mrs. Jones is concerned because Brenda's grades have declined markedly, and although she has discussed this with Brenda's parents, she sees no improvement. Charlie Maxwell, the school psychologist, meets with Brenda and explains both confidentiality and its limits at the onset of their meeting. He also explains to Brenda that if they decide to work together, he will need the consent of Brenda's parents for their counseling sessions. Brenda, visibly quite shaken, explains that she has been sexually active and thinks she might be pregnant. She is afraid to tell her parents.

Brenda (Case 7–6) suspects she is pregnant. Charlie Maxwell needs to refer Brenda to a physician or clinic to confirm or disconfirm the pregnancy. School psychologists who work with adolescents must be knowledgeable of area physicians and family planning clinics that provide teens with sensitive and supportive care. Parent notification or consent is not needed for a minor to visit a family planning clinic (Brooks-Gunn & Furstenberg, 1989). It is important, however, to refer students to a neutral agency, not one perceived as an abortion clinic (Hummel et al., 1985).

With parental consent, the psychologist may continue to work with a minor student on pregnancy management. This phase of pregnancy counseling should prepare the student for the emotional issues associated with having to make decisions regarding pregnancy alternatives (Ross-Reynolds & Hardy, 1985; Stoiber, 1997). Psychologists involved in pregnancy counseling must be knowledgeable of their state laws regarding access to abortion for minors.

Numerous court cases have involved minors and access to abortion; only a few will be mentioned here. In *Planned Parenthood of Central Missouri v. Danforth* (1976), the Supreme Court held that a Missouri statute requiring parental consent prior to an abortion in the case of an unmarried minor was unconstitutional. At this time, parental consent is required in some states, but parental permission may be required only if the law provides for a judicial bypass procedure, that is,

> ... an alternative procedure whereby authorization for the abortion can be obtained. A pregnant minor is entitled to such a proceeding to show either (1) that she is mature enough and well enough informed to make her abortion decision, in consultation with her physician, independently of her parents' wishes; or (2) that even if she is not able to make this decision independently, the desired abortion would be in her best interests. (*Bellotti v. Baird*, 1979, p. 4973)

More recently, in *Planned Parenthood of Southeastern Pennsylvania v. Casey* (1992), the Supreme Court reaffirmed that a state "may require a minor seeking an abortion to obtain the consent of a parent or guardian, provided that there is an adequate judicial bypass procedure" (p. 4813).

Some states have laws requiring the physician to notify the parents of a girl who is a minor prior to an abortion. In *H.L. Etc., Appellant v. Scott M. Matheson* (1981), the Court upheld a Utah law requiring the physician to notify the parents in certain circumstances, namely, when the girl is dependent on her parents, she is not emancipated, and she makes no claim that she is mature enough to make the decision alone or that parental notice would adversely affect her relationship with her parents. Supreme Court decisions since 1981 have not modified the earlier holdings regarding parental notice. In *Hodgson v. Minnesota* (1989), the Supreme Court held that the two-parent notice requirement in Minnesota's abortion statute is constitutionally invalid. However, because the Minnesota statute provides for a judicial bypass procedure, under which a minor may obtain an abortion without parental notice, the statute as a whole was found to be valid. In *Ohio v. Akron Center for Reproductive Health* (1989), the Court upheld a one-parent notice law that also provides for judicial bypass.

Birth Control Information

The issue of school involvement in the provision of family planning information is highly controversial and involves deep-rooted family and community values. School policies run the gamut from those that forbid discussion of birth control with individual students, to experimental programs that allow easy student access to family planning information and contraceptives (e.g., health clinics on or adjacent to school grounds).

Practitioners who work with adolescents must be knowledgeable of state law and local school policy regarding the provision of birth control information by school staff and be sensitive to community and family values. Providing competent advice on contraception to a minor in the school setting is probably permissible unless it conflicts with state or local policies (Fischer & Sorenson, 1996).

Prevention Efforts

School psychologists can play an important role in encouraging the development of programs to prevent teen pregnancies and reduce the incidence of sexually transmitted diseases among teenagers. Interested readers are referred to Meyers and Landau (2002) and Stoiber (1997).

Summary

Within the protection of a confidential relationship, students may report any number of behaviors that, although not immediately dangerous, have that potential. Such actions as failure to take prescribed medications, eating disorders, criminal activity, and engaging in unprotected sex and sexual promiscuity might all fall into this category.

Anticipating all possible circumstances in counseling that may prove to be a problem is not possible. The keys to dealing with most cases successfully are, first, a candid discussion of confidentiality and its limits at the onset of offering services; second, a good working relationship with the student; third, knowledge of state laws and regulations as well as school policies; fourth, familiarity with resources in the community and how to access them; and fifth, dealing openly and honestly with the student about your concerns and possible courses of action.

Competence and Responsibility

Consistent with the principle of responsible caring, school psychologists are obligated to "recognize the strengths and limitations of their training and experience, engaging only in practices for which they are qualified" (NASP-PPE, II, A, #1; also EP 2.01). A problem for the practitioner is to determine what constitutes an acceptable and recognized level of competency. Seeking assistance through supervision, consultation, and referral are appropriate strategies for handling a difficult case (NASP-PPE, II, A, #1). It is necessary and appropriate for Sam Foster to refer Nick Greene to a physician knowledgeable of the problems of steroid abuse (Case 7–4). However, practitioners who plan to introduce new counseling techniques or expand the scope of their services must complete appropriate and verifiable training before offering such services (EP 2.01).

Case 7–7

Carrie Johnson, school psychologist, has developed expertise in eating disorders and has successfully counseled a number of students on a one-to-one basis. She became interested in providing a counseling group for students with eating disorders and attended a one-day workshop on using group-counseling methods with anorexic and bulimic teens. She is now using this group counseling technique with students in her schools.

Is Carrie (Case 7–7) competent to provide group counseling to teens with eating disorders? The question of her competence relates to both the adequacy of the workshop she attended as well as her background. If she has had extensive training in group counseling, including prior supervised experience, she is able to claim more competence to attempt this new technique than if this workshop was her first exposure to the group counseling process. Group counseling techniques require a high degree of skill and prior supervised experience (Fischer & Sorenson, 1996).

Case 7–8

Tamika, a new student in Mr. March's fifth-grade class, recently transferred from an inner-city school located in a poverty-ridden neighborhood. She came to live with her grandparents after her mother's death. She is one of only a few African-American students in her new school, which, along with her Black English, sets her apart from her classmates. Tamika's records from her previous school indicated that she was an average student, and there is no mention of disciplinary problems. According to Mr. March, Tamika appears to be scared and angry. She refuses to talk in class, has made no friends, and does not complete assignments. Her classmates complain that she is "mean;" that she shoves or punches when no teachers are in sight. When Hannah Cook, the school psychologist, phoned Tamika's grandparents to discuss her school adjustment and invite them in for a conference, Tamika's grandmother responded, "The Lord brought Tamika to us, and He will show us the way." She declined to come in for a conference but agreed to allow Hannah to work with Tamika to identify possible interventions. Hannah has received training in helping children cope with grief and loss, but she has little experience working with African-American students or their families, particularly students from low-income, inner-city homes who may be mistrusting of white school professionals.

Practitioners also must evaluate their competence to provide services to students whose background characteristics are outside the scope of their supervised experience. Is Hannah competent to provide psychological counseling to Tamika (Case 7–8)? Ignoring or minimizing the importance of client characteristics such as race, ethnicity, sexual orientation, or socioeconomic background may result in approaches that are ineffective (Hansen et al., 2000; Rogers et al., 1999). (See Appendix D.)

An issue related to the question of competence is whether the school psychologist is the most competent professional available to provide the counseling service. NASP's code of ethics states "School psychologists recognize the competence of other professionals. They encourage and support the use of all resources to best serve the interests of students and clients" (NASP-PPE, III, E, #2). Charlie (Case 7–6) may have some knowledge of pregnancy management counseling, but he must consider whether Brenda might benefit more from counseling provided by another professional. Hannah (Case 7–8) may have some expertise in helping children cope with loss. However, she should consider whether Tamika might benefit more from counseling provided by a professional who has experience working with African-American children and their families.

School psychologists also are ethically obligated "to refrain from any activity in which their personal problems or conflicts may interfere with professional effectiveness" (NASP-PPE, II, A, #5). When a potential conflict of interest exists, practitioners ask their supervisor to assign a different psychologist. If that is not feasible, the practitioner should attempt to guide the family to alternative community resources (NASP-PPE, III, A, #5, C, #4).

Responsibility

NASP's code of ethics states "School psychologists develop interventions which are appropriate to the presenting problems and are consistent with data collected. They modify or terminate the treatment plan when the data indicate the plan is not achieving the desired goals" (NASP-PPE, IV, C, #6). In providing counseling services, the practitioner may recognize that he or she is unable to help the client. The APA code of ethics states "Psychologists terminate therapy when it becomes reasonably clear that the client/patient ... is not likely to benefit, or is being harmed by continued service" (EP 10.10). If the practitioner determines that he or she is not able to be of professional assistance to the client, the psychologist should "suggest alternative service providers as appropriate" (EP 10.10).

BEHAVIORAL INTERVENTION

For many years, school psychologists have provided consultation to teachers regarding how to use behavior change techniques. As noted in Chapter 5, special education law now requires the use of behavioral interventions to address problem behaviors of children with disabilities when those behaviors impede the child's learning or that of others (34 C.F.R. § 300.346). For the purpose of this discussion, behavioral intervention means the planned and systematic use of learning principles, particularly operant techniques and modeling theory, to change the behavior of individual students either by working with the student directly, or in collaboration or consultation with the teacher (or parent) who serves as the primary change agent. The following discussion of ethical-legal issues associated with behavioral interventions focuses on issues associated with the stages of problem identification, intervention, and evaluation.

Problem Clarification

During the problem clarification stage, the practitioner clarifies the nature and extent of the behavioral concern, identifies child and environmental factors associated with the problem behavior, and assists in the selection of behavior change goals.

Goal Selection

An ethical concern that arises during the problem clarification stage is whether or not the goals of intervention are in the best interests of the child. Classroom behavior modification programs introduced in the late 1960s often focused on teaching children to "be still, be quiet, and be docile" (Winett & Winkler, 1972), what Conoley and Conoley (1982) later referred to as "dead man behaviors." Such goals may assist the teacher in maintaining a quiet, orderly classroom, but they are not likely to improve learning or foster the healthy personal-social development of children (Winett & Winkler, 1972). The psychologist is obligated ethically to ensure replacement behaviors are selected that "enhance the long-term well-being of the child" (Harris & Kapche, 1978, p. 27) and are consistent with the long-range goal of self-management—that is, goals must be selected to ensure that the pupil will develop appropriate adaptive behaviors and not just suppress inappropriate ones (Van Houten et al., 1988).

It also is important to set goals that are realistic for the student and his or her situation. "Setting unrealistic goals is a disservice to students and to their parents, as well as a source of frustration to teachers and other staff" (Alberto & Troutman, 1982, p. 42).

Functional Behavioral Assessment

When children with disabilities evidence problem behaviors that interfere with learning, IDEA requires the school to conduct an assessment to determine the function the problem behavior serves for the child (Yell, Drasgow, & Ford, 2000). Two assessment methodologies have been developed to assist in identifying the functions served by a behavior. *Functional assessment* is based on naturalistic observations and involves direct observation and the use of informants (e.g., teacher interviews and rating scales to gather information). *Functional analysis* involves controlled observation—that is, the factors that are believed to maintain the behavior are experimentally manipulated (Martens, Witt, Daly, & Vollmer, 1999). Both assessment strategies allow evaluation of the child and the environmental factors associated with the problem behavior, including examination of the setting events, antecedents, and consequences of behavior (Yell et al., 2000).

Intervention

There is considerable research support for the practice of selecting treatments based on a systematic diagnosis of the function a problem behavior serves for the child (Tilly, Knoster, & Ikeda, 2000). After identifying the functions served by a problem behavior, IDEA requires the IEP team to develop a behavior intervention plan. School psychologists are obligated ethically to select (or assist in the selection of) change procedures that have demonstrated effectiveness. Practitioners also are obligated to select the least drastic procedures and those that minimize the risk of adverse side effects that are likely to be effective. The notion of least-drastic procedures grew out of the legal doctrine of least-restrictive alternative (see Chapter 5). Consistent with these ethical obligations, IDEA requires the IEP team to consider *positive* behavioral interventions to address problem behaviors of children with disabilities (34 C.F.R. § 300.346).

The literature reflects some consensus about the acceptability of various behavior change procedures. First choice (Level I) strategies are based on differential reinforcement (e.g., reinforcing appropriate behaviors incompatible with problem behaviors). Second choice (Level II) strategies are based on extinction (withdrawing of reinforcement for undesired behavior). Third choice (Level III) strategies include removal of desirable stimuli (e.g., time-out procedures). The least acceptable (Level IV) strategies are those that involve presentation of aversive stimuli (from Alberto & Troutman, 1982, p. 206).

In the 1970s, a number of behavioral control or change procedures came under the scrutiny of the courts. These early cases concerned youth in juvenile corrections facilities (e.g., *Morales v. Turman,* 1974; *Pena v. New York State Division for Youth,* 1976) or residential mental health facilities (e.g., *New York State Association for Retarded Children v. Carey,* 1975). These cases provide some insight into the minimal standards that must be adhered to in the use of behavioral methods so as not to violate the constitutional rights of the children involved. More specifically, these cases suggest that behavioral control methods must not deprive pupils of their basic rights to food; water; shelter, including adequate heat and ventilation; sleep; and exercise periods. Several more recent court cases have looked more directly at the use of behavioral methods in the public schools (e.g., *Dickens by Dickens v. Johnson County Board of Education* 1987, and *Hayes v. Unified School District No. 377,* 1987).

Differential Reinforcement

The systematic use of differential reinforcement is considered to be a first-choice strategy. Access to privileges (use of the classroom computer to play games), special luxuries (colorful stickers), and social reinforcers (smiles and praise) are types of reinforcers that typically present no special concerns. However, the early court rulings cited have been interpreted to suggest that not all types of reinforcers are acceptable. Some classroom teachers use token economies to manage behavior. In token economies, tokens or points may be earned for appropriate behavior, and the tokens subsequently are exchanged for rewards. The use of token economies should not result in denial of food, water, adequate shelter, or rest and exercise periods, and students should not be denied educational opportunities that are part of the child's expected program (e.g., gym, art) (Hindman, 1986).

Removal of Desirable Stimuli

Certain types of Level III interventions have come under legal scrutiny. Time-out is a popular behavior management strategy. Harris (1985) identified three different types of time-out: (a) nonexclusion, which involves removing the child from the reinforcing situation, but still allowing the child to observe the on-going activity; (b) exclusion, which involves removing the child from the reinforcing situation but not from the room; and (c) isolation, which involves the removal of the child from the reinforcing situation and placing him or her in a different area or room (see Turner & Watson, 1999). Discussion here focuses primarily on the use of exclusion and isolation time-out procedures.

Two legal challenges to the use of time-out in the public schools found it to be an acceptable procedure to safeguard other students from disruptive behavior (*Dickens,* 1987; *Hayes,* 1987; see also *Honig v. Doe,* 1988).[3] In *Dickens,* the court noted that "judicious use of behavioral modification techniques such as 'time-out' should be favored over expulsion in disciplining disruptive students, particularly the handicapped" (1987, p. 158).

However, the use of time-out must meet reasonable standards safeguarding the rights and welfare of pupils. In finding the use of time-out permissible, the judge in *Dickens* also noted, "This is not to say that educators may arbitrarily cage students in a corner of the classroom for an indeterminate length of time" (1987, p. 158). The court considerations in *Dickens, Hayes,* and earlier cases suggest some general parameters for the use of time-out: School personnel must monitor a secluded student to ensure his or her well-being. The room must have adequate ventilation (*Morales,* 1974); the time-out room itself must not present a fire or safety hazard (*Hayes,* 1987); students must be permitted to leave time-out for appropriate reasons (*Dickens,* 1987); and the door to the time-out room must remain unlocked (*New York State Association for Retarded Children v. Carey,* 1975).

Students should be given prior notice about the types of behaviors that will result in being placed in time-out (*Hayes,* 1987), and school personnel must ensure that time-out, when used as punishment, is "not unduly harsh or grossly disproportionate" to the offense (*Dickens,* 1987, p. 158). Placement in time-out should not result in "a total exclusion from the educational process for more than a trivial period" (*Goss v. Lopez,* 1975, p. 575). Use of time-out combined with instruction in the time-out room, or requiring the child to do schoolwork while segregated or secluded, is recommended (*Dickens,* 1987). (See Turner & Watson, 1999, for a review of research-based best practices in the use of time-out.)

Presentation of Aversive Stimuli

A highly controversial area in behavioral intervention is the use of aversive conditioning, in which a discomforting stimulus is presented contingent upon the child's undesirable behavior. Some psychologists and educators believe that aversive conditioning must never be used; others believe its use may be justified in the treatment of extremely self-injurious or dangerous aggressive behaviors. It is beyond the scope of

---

[3] In *Dickens*, time-out procedures involving having the child sit at a desk placed inside a three-sided refrigerator carton in the corner of the classroom, where the child could not see classmates, but could hear the teacher and sometimes see the teacher and chalkboard. *Hayes* involved removing the child to a different room.

this book to explore the controversy fully; interested readers are referred to Jacob-Timm (1996), National Institutes of Health (1991), and Repp and Singh (1990).

Evaluation of Treatment Effectiveness

Consistent with our code of ethics, practitioners continually assess the impact of any behavioral treatment plan, "and modify or terminate the treatment plan when the data indicate that the plan is not achieving the desired goals" (NASP-PPE, IV, B, #6).

Competence

As Alberto and Troutman have observed, because "many applied behavior analysis procedures seem so simple, they are often misused by persons who do not adequately understand them" (1982, p. 40). The misapplication of behavioral techniques may result in potential harm to the child, and teachers and parents may conclude that "behavior modification doesn't work." Practitioners interested in using behavioral interventions in the schools need verifiable training in applied behavior analysis that includes supervised practice. Ongoing consultation with an experienced behavior therapist is recommended until a high level of expertise is attained (Alberto & Troutman, 1982).

PSYCHOPHARMACOLOGIC INTERVENTIONS IN THE SCHOOLS

In the 1990s, there was an increase in the use of psychotropic agents to treat a variety of mental disorders in children (Jensen, 1998). As Jensen notes (1998), this rise in the use of psychotropic agents occurred despite the fact that many of these medications have not been adequately tested for safety and effectiveness in children. This portion of the chapter alerts the practitioner to ethical and legal issues associated with the use of medications to treat children with school learning or behavior problems. Discussion here is limited to the use of Ritalin (methylphenidate hydrochloride), a drug that has been approved by the Food and Drug Administration for the treatment of Attention Deficit Hyperactivity Disorder (ADHD) in children age 6 years and older (*Physicians Desk Reference*, 2001). Ritalin is widely prescribed for schoolchildren in the United States (Marshall, 2000), and it provides an excellent example of both the promise and potential pitfalls of drug therapy.

Case 7–9

In 1980, a California court approved the settlement of a lawsuit filed by 18 students and their parents against the school district. In the suit, the parents made claims against the school district and staff (including the school psychologist) stemming from the district's intrusion into the decision whether or not a child should take Ritalin to control what the schools alleged was hyperactive behavior. The parents contended that they had been subjected to extremely strong pressure to agree to the administration of the drug. One parent reported being called in before an array of school district staff and told that she would be a "foolish parent" if she refused to give the drug to her son. Others were told that their children could not possibly succeed in school without the drug or that they would not be able to remain in regular classes unless they took it. Nothing was mentioned about the potentially dangerous side effects of the drug; and when parents asked about this, they were told that the drug was as harmless as aspirin. Only the most superficial of medical examinations of the children were done prior to prescribing or recommending the drug, and no follow-up monitoring at all was done. No efforts were made to alter any environmental factors (such as poor teaching) that might have contributed to the child's difficult behavior.

The suit was filed after two of the children experienced their first grand mal epileptic seizures while taking the drug. Other children complained of aches and pains, insomnia, loss of appetite, apathy, moodiness, nosebleeds, and other problems associated with the drug Ritalin. Expert witnesses for the parents testified that many of the children were perfectly normal and should never have been candidates for drug therapy, and that the school's procedures for diagnosis and prescription were woefully inadequate.

The settlement agreement ordered by the court included a lump-sum of $210,000.00, which the court allocated among the plaintiffs according to the severity of harm each child suffered. In addition, the settlement agreement set forth a number of policy clarifications that precluded the school district from diagnosing hyperactivity or recommending in any way that a child take behavior modification drugs. (Adapted from Benskin v. Taft City School District, *1980).*

Substantial research has shown that stimulant medication is effective in the treatment of ADHD (Angold, Erkanli, Egger, & Costello, 2000;

DuPaul, Barkley, & Connor, 1998). Many school psychology practitioners and teachers have witnessed the dramatic improvements that occur for some children after they are placed on Ritalin. However, the use of Ritalin or other drugs to treat difficulties such as ADHD places the child at risk for physical or psychological harm because of the problems of potential misdiagnosis and drug side effects. A number of different types of hyperactivity exist, and stimulant medication is not appropriate for all types. Some children may be placed on Ritalin because of misdiagnosis, and use of the drug may consequently mask the child's true problems (Angold et al., 2000; Marshall, 2000).

Although Ritalin is generally considered safe, harm can result from its side effects. Potential side effects include nervousness, insomnia, anorexia, nausea, dizziness, headache, cardiac arrythmia, blood pressure changes, skin rash, abdominal pain, and growth suppression. Although rare, toxic psychosis, the development of Tourette Syndrome, abnormal liver function, and cerebral arteritis (inflammation) also have been reported (*Physicians' Desk Reference,* 2001).

A number of lawsuits have been filed against the public schools and physicians by parents of children prescribed Ritalin. In many of these suits, children suffered physical (e.g., Tourette Syndrome) and/or psychological harm (e.g., suicidal behavior) as a result of drug treatment recommended to them by school personnel (see Case 7–9). In some instances, parents report that they were pressured by school officials to seek drug treatment for their son or daughter with threats of exclusion from school if they failed to comply (*Valerie J. v. Derry CO-OP School District,* 1991).

Based on our experiences in the schools, we believe that school personnel are sometimes too quick to suggest medication for children whose high activity level is a problem for the teacher. Correct diagnosis of ADHD is based on *DSM-IV-TR* criteria (American Psychiatric Association, 2000) following a comprehensive psychological assessment and pediatric medical examination (Barkley & Edwards, 1998). The psychological evaluation should be based on multiple assessment methods across settings, including teacher, parent, and child interviews; behavior rating scales; cognitive and educational assessment; direction observation in the classroom; and functional behavioral assessment (Barkley & Edwards, 1998; Hoff, Doepke, & Landau, 2002).

DuPaul et al. (1998) provide a list of child, family, and situational factors that should be examined when drug therapy is under consideration, and it is likely that the school psychologist can play a valuable role in collecting this information. However, *decisions to prescribe drugs must be made by a physician (a point that should be clearly communicated to parents), and parents must be free to choose or refuse the use of such medication without pressure from the school.* In *Valerie J. v. Derry CO-OP School District* (1991), the court held that a school may not require a pupil to take

Ritalin as a precondition for attendance. In 2001, Connecticut became the first state to enact legislation prohibiting school personnel from suggesting psychiatric medication of a child to any parent. The purpose of the law is to ensure "the *first* mention of drugs comes from a physician" (Hoff et al., 2002, p. 1134).

The court settlement in *Benskin* provides some guidance for school policies regarding drug treatment. Drug treatment requires careful physician–school–parent collaboration. The school should ensure that the use of drug therapy is based on informed parental consent that includes a description of the potential benefits (e.g., enhanced academic productivity, reduced disruptive behavior), and risks (e.g., drug side effects and adverse reactions). Through cooperative efforts with the physician, the school must ensure that careful monitoring of the child is undertaken. School psychologists can assist in the documentation of the effectiveness or noneffectiveness of drug treatments and, thereby, provide important feedback to the physician and parents (see DuPaul et al., 1998; Kubiszyn, Brown, & DeMers, 1997).

Research suggests drug treatment such as Ritalin is generally effective in improving the academic productivity of children with ADHD (DuPaul et al., 1998). However, individualized instruction may be needed to translate improved productivity into enhanced academic achievement. Based on their review of the research, Henker and Whalen (1989) conclude that most children with ADHD need tailored educational programs along with help in their social development, whether they are given medication. Thus, the practitioner's involvement does not end with the prescription of medication.

CONCLUDING COMMENTS

> Teenaged parents. Academic failure. Substance abuse. Youth suicide. Divorce. AIDS. Childhood depression. Juvenile delinquency. Sexual abuse. The list of problems facing students in our schools today continues to grow and seemingly is endless. Yet, our time and resources remain limited. (Zins & Forman, 1988, p. 539)

Today we must add terrorism and school shootings.

In this chapter, we focused on the ethical-legal issues associated with counseling and therapeutic interventions in the schools. Partly in response to court decisions and high profile crisis events, many schools are beginning to recognize the importance of a planned response to crisis situations, and many are beginning to place a greater emphasis on the prevention of mental health problems.

STUDY AND DISCUSSION

Questions for Chapter 7

1. When a school psychologist becomes aware of a potentially assaultive student, what actions are appropriate?
2. When a school psychologist becomes aware of a potentially suicidal student, what actions are appropriate?
3. When a school psychologist suspects child abuse or child neglect, what actions are appropriate?
4. Develop a list of guidelines for teachers on how to safeguard the ethical and legal rights of pupils when behavioral interventions are planned and implemented.
5. May a school require a child to take medication as a precondition for school attendance? Identify the ethical-legal issues associated with the use of medications to treat school children with learning and behavior problems.

Discussion

1. How do you distinguish substance use from abuse? How will you decide whether the use of alcohol or illegal drugs poses a threat to a student and that it is necessary to notify the parent? See Forman and Pfeiffer (1997).
2. How do you determine when a professional hunch becomes reasonable suspicion of child abuse? See Horton and Cruise (2001) and Kalichman (1999) for discussion of the issues associated with reporting suspected child maltreatment.

VIGNETTES

1. Mrs. McClure, a kindergarten teacher, stopped by Wanda Rose's office. "Wanda," she said, I need your advice. Mr. and Mrs. Clifford came in to see me about their son, Kyle, who is in my kindergarten class. Kyle is a sweet, effeminate boy who prefers to play with the girls in the doll corner rather than play with the boys. 'Dad' isn't comfortable with Kyle's girlishness, so the Cliffords now have a psychologist from downstate working with them to change Kyle's feminine behaviors. They want me to carry out a behavior change program in class similar to the one they are using at home—I'm to give Kyle blue poker chips when he shows masculine behavior and red ones for feminine behavior. The Cliffords will then reward Kyle for the blue chips—minus the red ones—he brings home from school. Wanda, I'm just not comfortable with this. What do you think I should do? What should I tell the Cliffords?"

How should Wanda respond to this situation? What are the ethical issues involved? (See LeVay, 1996, pp. 97–102.)

2. Sam Foster, school psychologist, developed good rapport with Frank Green, a tenth grader, when he counseled Frank about some problems in adjusting to a new stepfather. Later in the year, Frank makes an appointment to see Sam and reports that things seem to be going better at home. He confides that he stopped by to talk with Sam because he is worried about a girl in his woodshop class named "Heidi." Heidi is a friendly 16-year-old who is mentally retarded. Recently, three boys in the woodshop class began to show a special interest in her. Frank saw the boys take Heidi into a storeroom near the woodshop on two occasions after class, and he thinks the boys are doing something bad to Heidi. How should Sam handle this situation?

3. Cindy, a troubled 14-year-old whom Hannah has seen previously for counseling, comes to her without an appointment. She is upset because two of her best friends, Tara and Trisha, have made plans to "ambush and beat up" another girl after school because of an argument about a boy. She knows that Tara and Trisha have been in trouble at school before for fighting, and she is worried they will be kicked out of school if they follow through on their plans, and that they may really hurt their intended victim. How should Hannah respond to this situation? What are the ethical-legal issues involved?

4. Nora Hudson, a 16-year-old, makes an appointment to see Charlie Maxwell, the school psychologist. Nora confides that she is worried that her friend Jason may be planning to kill himself. She reports that Jason has been upset since his parents announced their plans for divorce several weeks ago and that he has been talking about "ending it all" because life isn't worth living. Recently Jason gave her several books from his prized collection of science fiction because he "won't be needing them anymore." How should Charlie handle this situation?

ACTIVITIES

Role-play the following situations:

1. A teenager (age 14) has made an appointment for a counseling session with you, the school psychologist. Role-play the initial meeting during which the psychologist defines the parameters of confidentiality and discusses parent consent issues.

2. A parent, Mrs. Fox, has made an appointment with you to discuss her concerns about Bill, her 15-year-old son. She reports that Bill has become moody and difficult and that his grades have recently declined markedly. She would like you to meet with Bill to see whether you can discover what the problems are and report your findings back to her. Role-play this initial meeting, including a discussion of consent and confidentiality issues.

3. During a precounseling screening session, Joan Bellows, a 16-year-old, confides in you that she might be pregnant. Role-play how you might handle this situation.

Chapter 8

INDIRECT SERVICES I: ETHICAL-LEGAL ISSUES IN WORKING WITH TEACHERS AND PARENTS

Based on their survey of National Association of School Psychologists (NASP) members, Curtis, Hunley, Walker, and Baker (1999) reported that most school psychologists engage in consultation (97%) and most present in-service education programs (78%). Reschly and Wilson (1995) also surveyed NASP members and found that practitioners devote an average of seven hours per week to problem-solving consultation, defined as working with consultees (teachers or parents) with students as clients, but that they desired an increase in time for consultation activity.

In Chapters 8 and 9, we focus on ethical and legal issues associated with indirect services. In the first portion of this chapter, we discuss ethical issues associated with professional-to-professional consultation, focusing on teachers as consultees. The second portion of the chapter addresses issues in working with parents. In Chapter 9, we address special topics in systems-level consultation.

CONSULTATION WITH TEACHERS

In this chapter, we use the term *consultation* to refer to a voluntary, nonsupervisory relationship between the consultant (school psychologist) and consultee (teacher or other school professional) established to remediate learning or behaviors problems of the student-client, and/or to improve the professional skills of the consultee (Conoley & Conoley, 1982; Gutkin & Curtis, 1999). By voluntary, we mean that the consultant makes an informed choice to enter the consultative relationship. Unlike supervision, consultation is nonhierarchical; the consultant and consultee share coordinate status (see Chapter 11). The consultee remains an autonomous professional and retains the right to accept or reject suggestions made by the consultant. Although the consultee retains responsibility for decisions, the consultant encourages alternative solutions until a resolution of problems is achieved. Like supervision, the goals of consultation in the schools should be work-related (Conoley & Conoley, 1982; Gutkin & Curtis, 1999; Zins & Erchul, 2002).

Integrity in Consultative Relationships with Teachers

In providing school-based consultative services, the school psychologist is working within a network of relationships. Consistent with the broad ethical principle of integrity in professional relationships, the psychologist-consultant strives to be honest and straightforward in interactions with the consultee. Consultants define the direction and nature of their personal loyalties, objectives, and competencies and advise and inform all persons of these commitments (NASP-PPE, III, E, #3).

Gutkin and Curtis (1999) suggest that the consultation role be clearly defined to the school community prior to offering consultative services (EP 3.11; NASP-PPE, IV, B, #3). Discussions of consultative services should include role definition, the process of goal setting during consultation, the responsibilities of the consultant and consultee, and the parameters of confidentiality. Although initially this may occur at the level of the school, the same entry stage issues subsequently are discussed with individual teachers at the beginning of a consultative relationship.

A means of ensuring a mutual understanding of the parameters of a consultative relationship is through contracting. "A contract is a verbal or written agreement between the consultant and the consultee that specifies the parameters of the relationship" (Conoley & Conoley, 1982, p. 115). The contract might include the following elements: (a) general goals of consultation and how specific goals will be selected; (b) tentative time frame; (c) consultant responsibilities (services to be provided, methods to be used, time commitment, how the success of the consultation will be evaluated); (d) the nature of consultee responsibilities; and (e) confidentiality rules (adapted from Gallessich, 1982, pp. 272–273).

Respect for the Dignity of Persons (Welfare of the Consultee and Client)

When providing consultation to teachers, the broad principle of respect for the dignity of persons encompasses the obligation to safeguard consultee and client autonomy and self-determination, to make known and respect boundaries of confidentiality, and to promote understanding across culturally diverse consultant-consultee-client groups.

Client Welfare, Autonomy, and Self-Determination

Although in consultation the teacher is the recipient of services, pupil welfare "must be of primary importance to a school-based consultant" (Davis & Sandoval, 1982).

Student-client. School psychologists consider the pupil-clients to be their primary responsibility and act as advocates for their rights and welfare. The psychologist is obligated to work with the teacher to ensure that consultation goals and intervention strategies are selected that are likely to be ultimately beneficial to the student(s) (NASP-PPE, E, #1).

Because consultation is an indirect service, the ethical responsibility for the impact of their services on pupils raises certain practical difficulties for consultants (Newman, 1993). A number of strategies can be used for safeguarding student welfare, autonomy, and self-determination when providing consultative services. These include involving the student(s) as much as feasible in the selection of goals and change strategies and selecting goals to promote student self-management. Consultants also must consider the ethical adequacy of particular intervention approaches (Newman, 1993).

Teacher-consultee. Although the student is seen as the primary client, psychologists also strive to safeguard the dignity and rights of other recipients of services (NASP-PPE, IV, A, #1, #2). In providing consultation to the teacher, the teacher-consultee remains an autonomous professional and retains the right to accept or reject suggestions made by the consultant. The psychologist discourages teacher dependence on the consultant (Fanibanda, 1976). The consultant also is careful to avoid stepping into the role of counselor/therapist to the consultee (Gutkin & Curtis, 1999).

Consultants must be keenly sensitive to the ethical issues of manipulation and control of the consultee in providing consultative services to teachers (Hughes, 1986). The psychologist and teacher have differing fields of specialization, and they may have differing values. It is important that, as consultants, we "sufficiently understand the values of the community, institution, consultee, and clients with whom we work so that we will not merely impose our values on them" (Davis & Sandoval, 1982, p. 545; also NASP-PPE, IV, B, #1). As Fanibanda (1976) points out, our obligation to the welfare of the student may require us to advocate for certain decisions even if they conflict with the apparent value orientation of the consultee. Candid discussion of values and goals throughout consultation is a safeguard for teacher autonomy (Brown, Pryzwansky, & Schulte, 1987).

Consistent with our ethical codes, school psychologists work in full cooperation with teachers in a relationship based on *mutual respect* (NASP-PPE, III, E, #1). It is important to remember that teachers are our most important resource in helping children in the school setting.

Informed Consent

In offering consultative services to the teacher, the use of a verbal or written contract helps to ensure his or her informed consent for services.

Informed consent of the parent is needed if an intervention is planned for a student that diverges from ordinary, expected schooling.

Confidentiality

Confidentiality in providing consultative services to the teacher can be problematic. The parameters of confidentiality must be discussed at the onset of the delivery of services, and at a minimum, teachers should clearly understand what and how information will be used, by whom, and for what purposes (Newman, 1993; EP 4.02; NASP-PPE, III, A, #11). In general, in consultation to the teacher or other school staff, the guarantees of client confidentiality apply to the consultant–consultee relationship (Fanibanda, 1976). All that is said between the psychologist and consultee is kept confidential by the psychologist, unless the consultee requests information be disclosed to others (Davis & Sandoval, 1982). Violation of confidentiality in consultation with teachers or other staff is likely to result in a loss of trust in the psychologist and may impair his or her ability to work with the consultee and others.

Is there ever a duty to breach the confidentiality of the consultant–consultee relationship to safeguard the welfare of the student(s)? In providing consultative services to teachers, ethical responsibility requires that limits to the promise of confidentiality be identified (Conoley & Conoley, 1982; Hughes, 1986; Newman, 1993). Thus, for example, the practitioner may want to ensure a prior agreement that the consultant may breach confidentiality in those unusual instances when the consultee "chronically and stubbornly" persists in unethical activities (Conoley & Conoley, 1982, p. 216).

However, "Before breaching confidentiality, the consultant must have expended all resources at influencing the consultee to take collaborative action" (Hughes, 1986, p. 491). Such a breach of confidentiality should be given careful consideration and *would only be appropriate when the consultee's actions are harmful or potentially harmful to the student-client.* "The consultee's approach toward the client actually must be detrimental to the child rather than a less than optimal approach" (Hughes, 1986, p. 491). The consultant is obligated to discuss the need to disclose confidential information with the consultee prior to disclosure.

Fairness and Nondiscrimination

The broad ethical principle of respect for the dignity of persons also encompasses the values of fairness and nondiscrimination. School psychologists deal justly and impartially with each consultee regardless of his or her personal, political, cultural, racial, or religious characteristics.

However, as noted in Chapter 1, the school psychologist's responsibility goes beyond striving to be impartial and unprejudiced in the delivery of services. Practitioners have an ethical obligation to become knowledgeable of the values, beliefs, and worldview of the consultee and client groups they encounter in their schools so as to be able to provide consultative services in a culturally sensitive manner (NASP-PPE,III,A,#2; APA, 1993a).

Case 8–1

In the 1980s, there was a change in the ethnic-racial composition of Littlefield Elementary, one of Charlie Maxwell's schools, from 60 percent white to almost 90 percent African-American and Hispanic students. Littlefield now has a dynamic African-American principal and a staff composed of many new teachers of diverse racial and ethnic backgrounds as well as older white teachers. Charlie is concerned because a white second-grade teacher, Mrs. Dolan, recommends five or six of her students for grade retention each year, all African-American boys. (Adapted from Rogers et al., 1999.)

Providing consultation across culturally diverse consultant-consultee-client groups can pose special challenges. In order to provide consultation services that foster school success for all students, Charlie Maxwell (Case 8–1) needs to ensure that Mrs. Dolan and other teachers understand the background, culture, and learning styles of the African-American and Hispanic students who now attend Littlefield and how to select materials and modify instruction as needed to meet their needs. He also can help families new to Littlefield better understand the culture and expectations of the school and work to assist parents in supporting their child's achievement. Conceptual frameworks for cross-cultural consultation and best practices in providing services across culturally diverse consultant-consultee-clients groups recently have been addressed in the literature (see Ingraham & Meyers, 2000).

Responsible Caring

Psychologists are obligated ethically to provide consultation only within the boundaries of their competence, to evaluate the impact of consultative services on consultees and clients, and to modify consultative plans as needed to ensure effectiveness.

Professional Responsibility in Teacher Consultation

Practitioners accept responsibility for their decisions and the consequences of their actions (EP Principles A and B; NASP-PPE, III, A, #1), and they work to offset any harmful consequences of decisions made. School psychologists "modify or terminate the treatment plan when the data indicate the plan is not achieving the desired goals" (NASP-PPE, IV, C, #6).

Models of consultation typically include four stages: an entry phase and the stages of problem identification/clarification, intervention/problem solution, and evaluation. The fourth stage of the consultation process, evaluation, encourages professional responsibility on the part of both the psychologist and consultee. During this stage, the consultant and consultee assess whether the intervention was successful in meeting the agreed-on goals, and if not, the consultant and consultee "recycle" back to the stage of problem identification/clarification or intervention/solution.

However, in the course of the consultative process, it may become apparent to the psychologist that he or she is unable to assist the consultee. If so, he or she is obligated ethically to refer the consultee to another professional. This could occur when the consultee has emotional difficulties that interfere with effective functioning. As noted earlier, the practitioner generally must avoid the dual roles of consultant and counselor/therapist to the teacher (Gutkin & Curtis, 1999). It may also become apparent during the consultative process that another professional is better able to assist the consultee (e.g., another psychologist with different skills, or perhaps a well-respected teacher with special expertise in the problem area) (NASP-PPE, III, E, #2).

Special problems with regard to professional responsibility sometimes occur when the practitioner steps into the role of *consultant-trainer* and provides in-service to teachers in the school or district. Although at first it might seem that the use of "informational methods" such as in-service raises no special ethical concerns, problems may arise when there is no planned follow-up on the ways in which the information provided is understood and used by teachers or other staff.

For example, a number of writers have noted that brief workshop methods of teaching applied behavior analysis techniques to teachers are inadequate and may result in unintended harmful consequences for pupils. As Conoley and Conoley suggest, consultant-trainers are well-advised to view in-service training as "a *means*, not an *end*" (1982, p. 134). A number of options exist for follow-up consultation that help to ensure new ideas and techniques introduced during in-service training are used appropriately in the classroom (see Hansen et. al., 1990, for suggestions).

Competence

Ethically, school psychology practitioners are obligated to provide services only within areas of competency (NASP-PPE, II, A, #1; also EP 2.01). Brown et al. (1987) suggest that the following competencies are necessary to provide effective consultative services: knowledge of models of consultation, organizational theory, and change strategies; skills in communication, relationship building, contracting, mediating, and group leadership; and judgmental competencies with regard to problem identification and solution. In addition, the personal characteristics of the consultant are important in successful school-based consultation (see Conoley & Conoley, 1982). In order to provide consultative services effectively, practitioners also must be knowledgeable of the organization, philosophy, goals, and methodology of their school (NASP-PPE, IV, B, #1), and they must be familiar with the areas of competence of other professionals in their setting. In addition, Rogers et al. (1999) provide a list of recommended competencies for consulting across multiculturally diverse consultant-consultee-clients groups.

SPECIAL ISSUES IN WORKING WITH PARENTS

Family-school partnerships have been linked to improved student achievement and higher academic aspirations, higher rates of academic engagement and attendance, and a reduction of suspensions and early school withdrawals (Christenson, 1995; Pelco, Jacobson, Ries, & Melka, 2000). A national survey by Pelco et al. (2000) found that school psychologists support the concept of parent involvement in education and more than 80 percent reported working with parents to improve pupil learning, behavior, parenting practices, and build parent-school cooperation. Parents too generally support the concept of a "partnership" with professionals (Christenson, Hurley, Sheridan, & Fenstermacher, 1997).

Respect for the Dignity of Persons

We will again utilize the framework provided by the code of ethics of the Canadian Psychological Association (2000) to discuss the issues involved in working with parents and families.

Autonomy and Self-Determination

Historically, prior to the 1970s, parents were expected to simply be passive recipients of decisions made by professionals. They were often considered to be the source of their child's problems and treated poorly. Today, however, parents are viewed as collaborative partners in parent-professional relationships (Fish, 2002; Turnbull & Turnbull, 2001). Sheridan, Cowan, and Eagle (2000) define collaboration as "a student-centered, dynamic framework that endorses collegial, interdependent, and co-equal styles of interaction between families and educators who work jointly together to achieve common goals" (2000, p. 314).

If parents are to assume the role of "equal and full partners with educators and school systems" (Turnbull & Turnbull, 2001, p. 13), however, schools must actively encourage and enable parents to do so. Psychologists, along with other school personnel, may need to help parents acquire the knowledge and competencies "necessary to solve problems, meet needs, realize personal projects, or otherwise attain goals" (Dunst & Trivette, 1987, p. 451). Practitioners also must know the rights of parents under federal and state law and ensure that parents are informed of those rights.

As a result of advocacy efforts by parents and court rulings, the presumption that parents should be viewed as collaborators in educational decision-making for their child has been incorporated into our codes of ethics and education law (Fish, 2002). The Individuals with Disabilities Act (IDEA) 1997 places greater emphasis on parent involvement in special education decision making than previous versions of the law (Sheridan et al., 2000). In addition, according to NASP's code of ethics, when a pupil experiences school difficulties, practitioners encourage and promote parent involvement in all phases of the problem identification and remediation process (NASP-PPE, III, C). They clearly explain their services so that they are understood by parents (NASP-PPE, III, C, #1), and "respect the wishes of parents who object to school psychological services," guiding them to alternative community resources (NASP-PPE, III, C, #4). Findings and recommendations are communicated to parents in language that they can understand (NASP-PPE, IV, D, #2), and when an interpreter is used, psychologists adhere to the ethical guidelines regarding their use (see EP 2.05). Furthermore, practitioners propose alternative recommendations to parents, ensuring that options take into account the values, cultural background, family circumstances, and capabilities of the parent (NASP-PPE, III, C, #1).

It is important to recognize, however, that not all educators are willing to grant parents a partnership role. Furthermore, because of individual and cultural differences, not all parents may wish to assume a co-equal role, and some are not capable of doing so (Webb, 2001b). In such situations, because the psychologist's "greatest responsibility is to those persons in the most vulnerable position," practitioners have a special obligation to speak up for the rights and wishes of the parent and student (CPA, Principle I).

Managing the Conflicting Interests of Parent, Child, and School

How do psychologists provide guidance, advice, and intervention while respecting parent autonomy and encouraging parent empowerment? What if the wishes of the parent do not coincide with the psychologist's view of what is best for child? How do psychologists balance the needs of the particular parent or family with the larger needs of the school (Friedman, Helm, & Marrone, 1999)? The problem of conflicting interests of multiple clients (parent, pupil, school) can arise in a variety of contexts (Jacob-Timm, 1999). We provide two examples here that focus on special education decision making.

Case 8–2

Charlie Maxwell is asked to conduct a re-evaluation of a girl, Jane, diagnosed as developmentally disabled, who will be entering the junior high next fall. Consistent with parental wishes Jane has been in an inclusive setting since kindergarten. Following his assessment, Charlie feels very strongly that Jane will receive much greater academic benefit from an outstanding self-contained program in the junior high. However, the parents have made it clear that they wish to continue with an inclusive program for their daughter.

In Case 8–2, consistent with the principle of respect for autonomy, Charlie should encourage the parents to exercise their right to make their wishes known and understood. One way to foster parent autonomy and safeguard their legal rights in special education decision-making is to ensure that parents understand the assessment findings, alternative recommendations, the process of decision-making (including factors the team is legally required to consider), and their role in that process. For example, at the beginning of the IEP team meeting to determine Jane's placement, Charlie might remind all team members that, as educators and parents, they share the goal of developing the best possible program the district can offer Jane—a program that, at a minimum, meets the legal standard of reasonably designed to confer meaningful educational benefit. In addition, Charlie might summarize issues that must be considered by the team under IDEA in making the placement decision: The presumption is placement in regular education with supplementary supports and services and placement in a more restrictive setting must be justified on the basis of greater academic or social benefit, the presence of behavior that interferes with the learning of others in the regular classroom, or costs of supporting placement in regular education that are significantly more expensive than alternative placements (see Chapter 5). The goal of providing such information is to put parents on equal footing with other team members in the decision making process.

Charlie must ensure that Jane's parents understand the benefits and shortcomings of the alternative decisions. However, he must take care not to usurp their right to an independent opinion and voice about desired services for their child. Hartshorne (2002) recommends that professionals "encourage parents to choose the right answers for themselves, with the understanding there may be no absolute right answer or any way to find one. Parents can be supported in having made the best decisions they can given what is known. Of course, professionals can also encourage parents to investigate all available information." Friedman et al. (1999), on the other hand, state that "it is proper and ethical and, in fact, supportive of the concept of consumer or patient autonomy for the professional to actively seek to influence the decisions and actions of the person(s) being helped" (p. 355). They argue that professionals have a greater base of knowledge and skills than do parents and that equal and mutual relationships naturally involve attempts to influence the other.

Case 8–3

The parents of a five-year-old boy with developmental disabilities have requested that their child be fully included in the kindergarten at his neighborhood school. Because of the child's unique needs, Sam Foster, the school psychologist, and the boy's parents believe he should be in a full-day program. Consequently, the parents have requested that their son be in both sections of kindergarten, morning and afternoon. Prior to the boy's IEP meeting, the school district's assistant superintendent contacted Sam. She heard about the possible request for a full-day kindergarten placement, and is concerned because by teacher contract a child with special needs counts as two children in a classroom. This boy would take the space of four children in kindergarten. Because this is a desirable school in the district, this means that three children will be turned away by the school and assigned to other elementary schools in the district.

How do psychologists balance the needs of the particular family with the larger needs of the school? NASP's code of ethics recognizes that school psychologists serve multiple clients including children, parents, and systems and state that practitioners should support conclusions that are in the best interests of the child (NASP-PPE.IV, A, #1, #2; also CPA, Principle I). Sam, in Case 8–3, like Charlie in Case 8–2, may want to remind IEP team members of the legal parameters of the placement decision at the IEP team meeting. A full-day program must be provided if that is what is necessary to confer meaningful benefit. Then, Sam should advocate for the full-day kindergarten program he believes meets the intent of IDEA and is in the best interests of the child, even if it puts him in conflict with district wishes.

Privacy and Confidentiality

School psychologists respect family privacy and do not seek information that is not needed in the provision of services. Practitioners must be sensitive to cultural differences regarding the concept of privacy and recognize that, in some cultures, discussing personal problems with individuals outside of the family is "taboo" (Webb, 2001, p. 343). In such situations, it is critically important that practitioners follow culturally appropriate protocols to build a relationship with family members before initiating discussion of the pupil's difficulties. Practitioners also should discuss confidentiality and its limits with family members before seeking information from them, carefully identifying the types of information that might be shared with other school personnel or outside agencies, for what purpose, and under what circumstances. The concept of confidentiality may not be familiar to parents from some cultures; whereas parents from other backgrounds may be very concerned that information will not be held in confidence (Webb, 2001).

Responsible Caring

Consistent with the principle of beneficence (responsible caring), school psychologists practice within the boundaries of their competence and accept responsibility for their actions. Practitioners must consider whether they are competent to provide services in light of family characteristics (e.g., language, cultural background) and the nature of the concern, or whether the family might benefit more from services provided by another professional (see, for example, Case 7–8). Webb (2001) reviewed the available research on "cultural matching" of psychologist and client, and reported that, for some groups, racial matching between practitioner and client results in more positive outcomes (Webb, 2001; also Behring,

Cabello, Kushida, & Murguia, 2000). Webb goes on to note, however, that for most clients who participated in these studies, *"the practitioner's personal qualities of sensitivity and competence were more important than was similarity of ethnicity and race"* (p. 344).

Case 8–4

Pearl Meadows received a referral for evaluation of a first grader, Brent, because of his slow academic progress in reading and math. Brent lives in a trailer with his grandparents and two-year-old brother in a small rural community known for its high unemployment and poverty. His mother is in prison, convicted of burglary and arson. Brent is initially slow to warm up to Pearl but becomes quite talkative during their second meeting. Brent shares that he recently got in "big trouble" with his grandpa because he snuck out his bedroom window after being put to bed and went to play with older boys who live down the road. He goes on to explain how grandpa went "WHACK, WHACK, WHACK, WHACK, WHACK" on his rear with a wooden paddle when he got home.

In responsible practice, practitioners discern the potential harm as well as benefits of their work with families. They must be concerned about the effects of their actions on parents, other caregivers, and siblings, as well as pupil-clients. Pearl (Case 8–4) is obligated ethically to be sensitive to cultural and generational differences in the use of physical punishment in discipline but is obligated legally to report suspected child abuse (Williams-Gray, 2001). She must consider what actions, if any, might by appropriate in responding to Brent's disclosure and the possible consequences of each alternative course of action for Brent, his brother, and grandparents.

Integrity in Relationships with Parents

Parent partnerships are ideally based on honesty, trust, shared responsibility, and mutual support (Sheridan et al., 2000). Practitioners must avoid conflicts of interest (EP Principle B)—that is, they refrain from taking on a professional role when their own interests (personal, professional, legal, financial) could reasonably be expected to impair their objectivity, competence, or effectiveness or expose clients to harm or exploitation (EP 3.06; NASP-PPE, III, A, #6, #7). In situations where there is a potential conflict of interest, practitioners ask their supervisor to assign a different psychologist. If that is not feasible or acceptable, the practitioner should attempt to guide the parents to alternative community resources (NASP-PPE, III, A, #5, C, #4).

School psychologists also must consider potential problems associated with multiple relationships. In working with parents, multiple relationships occur when the psychologist is in a professional role with the parents and at the same time has a relationship with a person closely associated with or related to the parents (EP 3.05). For example, the psychologist might be dating a divorced parent's ex-spouse, or the parent with whom the school psychologist is consulting might also be the school teacher for the psychologist's own child. Psychologists refrain from entering into a multiple relationship if the relationship could reasonably be expected impair the psychologist's performance, or otherwise risks exploitation or harm to the person with whom the professional relationship exits (EP 3.05). Again, in such situations, the parent(s) should be offered the services of another psychologist in the district, and if that is not feasible or acceptable, the practitioners should attempt to guide them to alternative community resources. "Multiple relationships that would not reasonably be expected to cause impairment or risk exploitation or harm are not unethical" (EP 3.05). If, due to unforseen circumstances, a potentially harmful multiple relationship arises, the psychologist attempts to revolve it with due regard for the best interests of the client and others involved (EP 3.05, NASP-PPE, III, #4).

Case 8–5

Hannah Cook is trying to establish a working partnership with a Puerto Rican family whose 15-year-old daughter is pregnant. The family has appreciated Hannah's openness with them and recently invited her to the girl's babyshower. Should Hannah attend? (Situation suggested by Congress, 2001.)

For many years, psychotherapists were cautioned to avoid social or other nonprofessional contacts with their patients because a blurring of professional boundaries can impair the therapist's objectivity or effectiveness. More recently, however, codes of ethics have been modified to recognize that not all social contact between psychologists and their clients poses a risk of harm. Social contacts with families may, in fact, improve parent-school relations. For example, with Hispanic families relationships may be expected to involve *personalismo*, or warm, friendly relationships based on a real concern for the individual. Making a personal connection with the family may be the only way to establishing a partnership (Congress, 2001). Hannah (Case 8–5) should consider both the potential benefits and disadvantages of social interaction with her student-client and family in deciding whether to attend the babyshower.

Diversity Issues

School psychologists are obligated ethically to provide services to students and their families that are respectful of diverse backgrounds and circumstances (EP 2.01). Living in a multicultural society makes this challenging. Webb (2001) identified four themes related to strains and obstacles in culturally diverse practice (also see Ortiz & Flanagan, 2002). One is "The practitioner's lack of understanding about the multidimensional reality and stresses of the client's situation in the context of the client's specific cultural and family environment" (p. 339). School psychologists must strive to understand family circumstances; they cannot assume that the parents' reality is the same as theirs.

Case 8–6

Charlie Maxwell receives a referral for an African-American boy, Adam, who is experiencing difficulty learning to read. Charlie arranges to meet with Adam's teacher, Mrs. Barbos, who reports that Adam does not seem to be able to distinguish different phonemes. Adam has a "non-stop" runny nose and congestion, and Mrs. Barbos wonders if he is experiencing ear infections and possible hearing difficulties. Mrs. Barbos goes on to explain that Adam's parents did not show up for school open house or fall conferences. She has tried to contact them by phone many times after school and at night, but no one answers. Exasperated, she comments, "How can we be expected to help these kids when their parents don't care?"

When Charlie is able to contact Adam's mother (Case 8–6), he learns that she is a widow who works the second shift as a press operator in a stamping plant. Adam and his sisters go home to a neighbor's house after school where she picks them up after midnight. She noticed that Adam has had some congestion but did not want to take him out of school to see the doctor and cannot afford to miss work. Now that she knows he is having problems at school, she promises to take him to the doctor and contact the teacher.

A second theme concerns difficulties in "engaging, communicating, and agreeing about the problem" (Webb, 2001, p. 339). Practitioners must be able to establish rapport with parents and communicate the school's concerns in culturally sensitive ways and seek to understand how the parents' view their child's development, learning, and behavior, and the school's concerns. In some school districts, considerably more children are diagnosed as emotionally disturbed than in other districts. This is likely due in part to different understandings of particular behavior. When the community becomes diverse culturally, these understandings can create considerable confusion.

A third theme describes "different ideas about seeking help and dealing with the problem situation" (Webb, 2001, p. 339). School psychologists should examine their systems for making services available to families to ensure that they are usable by persons from different cultural groups. In addition, it is likely that cultural modifications in the psychologist's approach will be needed to work effectively with families from different backgrounds. For some families, attempts to establish a collaborative partnership may not be culturally appropriate (Behring et al., 2000; Lynch & Hanson, 1998). For example, some families with Asian roots place great importance on expert opinion and prefer a directive rather than a collaborative approach (Behring et al., 2000).

It is also important to recognize that many families prefer to seek and receive help from other family members, friends, or religious leaders rather than schools or social service agencies. Some mistrust school personnel (Webb, 2001). Practitioners are obligated ethically to identify alternative sources of assistance available in the community (NASP-PPE, III, C, #5) and should work to support, rather than supplant, existing community-based helping relationships.

The final theme concerns the "different values and worldviews of the practitioner and the client" (Webb, 2001, p. 339). School psychologists should recognize that the way they prioritize needs and services may differ considerably from the way this is done by parents.

Lopez and Rogers (2001) developed a comprehensive list of cross-cultural competencies for school psychologists. Four apply to working with parents and would seem important practice for school psychologists who wish to be respectful of and sensitive to cultural differences of the families they work with. These are being aware "of roles parents play in child's country of origin," "understanding of differences in child rearing practices due to cultural differences," respecting "values that clash with dominant culture," and being aware "of the value placed in education by the parents of the client" (p. 302). (Also see Appendix D).

Case 8–7

The principal has asked Pearl Meadows to attend a conference with the parents of a first-grade girl, Sally. When Pearl enters the conference room, she is greeted by two women who introduce themselves as Sally's mother Fran and Sally's mother Lynnly, who then go on to identify themselves as lesbians. Fran explains that they requested a meeting because, although Sally has been accepted by her classmates, she is harassed repeatedly on the school bus and playground by older boys who call her "Dyke Tyke" and other names. They hope the principal and staff will take action to stop the harassment.

A greater number of sexual minority parents are identifying themselves to school personnel than in past years. Unfortunately, as Ryan and Martin (2000) have observed, "At present there are few school systems that have the information, experience, comfort level, or even willingness to address the needs of lesbian, gay, bisexual and transgender-parented families" (p. 207). To form effective home-school partnerships with families headed by lesbian and gay parents, practitioners must discard "any traditional notions about what a family constellation should optimally be" (p. 208). Practitioners are encouraged to seek specialized knowledge of the social obstacles faced by families with sexual minority parents and their needs in the school system (Ryan & Martin, 2000; also Bahr, Brish, & Croteau, 2000).

In an interview study with sexual-minority headed families, respondents identified both benefits and risks of disclosure of their family constellation to school personnel. Some choose not to disclose that they are sexual minority parents because they fear discrimination in housing or employment, social rejection or harassment of their children, loss of child custody because of sexual orientation, and/or because they feel they will not be welcome at school (Ryan & Martin, 2000). Others, such as Sally's mothers in Case 8–7, choose to disclose their family constellation in hopes of opening channels of communication with the school and directly addressing any problems that may arise.

In Case 8–7, the school principal, teachers, Pearl, and other school staff must work cooperatively to address the immediate issue of teasing and harassment (see Henning-Stout, James, & Macintosh, 2000). Pearl will also seek ways to promote positive partnerships with these and other gay-parented families and to foster a school climate that encourages acceptance of diversity of family constellation. It will be a challenging task (see Ryan & Martin, 2000).

Responsibility to Community and Society

As noted in Chapter 1, school psychologists have an ethical obligation to use psychological knowledge to benefit students and the larger school community. Parent-school partnerships have been found to enhance the success of students. Practitioners can assist in developing a school environment that is welcoming to all parents, identifying parent-involvement activities appropriate to their own school-community, and implementing and evaluating school-parent partnership efforts (Christenson et al., 1997). An increasing number of resources are available to assist practitioners in pursuing these goals (e.g., Elizalde-Utnick, 2002; Esler, Godber, & Christenson, 2002; Lynch & Hanson, 1998; Ryan & Martin, 2000; Sheridan et al., 2000).

CONCLUDING COMMENTS

Effective problem-solving and intervention for students who are experiencing difficulties in social or emotional development, school learning, or behavior depends on using the combined skills and resources of teachers, other professionals, and the family (Hubbard & Adams, 2002). School psychologists can play an important role in drawing together the resources of the school, family, and community to bring about positive change for individual pupils, classrooms, and schools.

STUDY AND DISCUSSION

Questions for Chapter 8

1. What information should be provided in describing the consultant's role to the school community and individual consultees?
2. Under what circumstances, if any, might it be appropriate for the psychologist-consultant to breach the confidentiality of a consultative relationship with a teacher?
3. Although the idea that parents should be viewed as collaborators in educational decision-making has been incorporated into education law and our codes of ethics, it is not always realized in practice. Identify two barriers to parents assuming the role of "equal and full partners with educators and school systems."

(Continued)

4. Throughout the text, the authors have stressed the idea that the school psychologist's responsibility goes beyond being impartial and unprejudiced in the delivery of services. Identify some of the practitioner's special obligations in working with families from backgrounds different than their own.

VIGNETTES

1. Pearl Meadows received a referral for evaluation of a first grader, Chad, because of his slow academic progress in reading and math. Chad lives with his parents and two-year-old brother in an attractive ranch-style home near school. His father is a social studies teacher, his mother a nurse-supervisor at the local hospital. Chad is initially slow to warm up to Pearl but becomes quite talkative during their second meeting. Chad shares that he recently got in "big trouble" with his parents because he snuck out his bedroom window after being put to bed and went to play with older boys who live around the block. He goes on to explain how his dad went "WHACK, WHACK, WHACK, WHACK, WHACK" on his rear with a wooden paddle when he got home.

When does spanking become abuse? What actions, if any, should Pearl consider in response to Chad's disclosure, and what are the possible consequences of those actions for the parties involved? Did the information regarding social class influence your beliefs regarding appropriate actions in the case of Brent and his grandfather (Case 8–4) versus Chad and his father? In what ways? (For additional information, see Horton and Cruise, 2001).

2. Mrs. French, a middle-school English teacher, stops by to see the school psychologist, Charlie Maxwell. Mrs. French is upset about a love note she intercepted between two students in one of her classes. The note was written by a 14-year-old boy named Derek to another boy in the class. Derek knows that Mrs. French has read and kept the note, but she has not spoken with him about the matter. Mrs. French wants Charlie to confront Derek with the note and talk with Derek's parents so that he will "get help to cure him of this sick stuff before it's too late." How should Charlie respond to this situation? (Adapted from Eversole, 1993; also see *Sterling v. Minersville* [2000] in Chapter 2).

3. Victor and Margaret Lee attend school in Pearl Meadow's district. Their father, who speaks almost no English, is the cook at their family-owned Chinese restaurant, while their mother, who is fluent in English, manages the restaurant and is very actively involved in her children's education. One Monday morning, Pearl is saddened to hear of Mrs. Lee's unexpected death over the weekend. While Margaret, in eighth grade, slowly adjusts to her loss, Victor, a fifth grader, continues to struggle with his grief many months after his mother's death, and he has begun to show signs of serious depression. Pearl would like to meet with Mr. Lee to discuss Victor's depression. The principal suggests that Margaret serve as the interpreter during the conference. What are the ethical issues regarding choice and use of interpreters? (See APA's Ethical Principles, 2.05; also Rogers et al., 1999). Evaluate the appropriateness of the principal's suggestion in light of the hierarchical family structure of many Asian families (see Webb, 2001, p. 342), and the psychologist's ethical obligations to Victor.

ACTIVITIES

Role-play the following situation:

Mrs. Finch, a first grade teacher, is known to have a punitive classroom management style. One parent recently complained to the principal after Mrs. Finch spanked her son. Mrs. Finch has asked you (probably as a result of the principal's urging) to help her develop a more positive classroom discipline style. Role-play your initial meeting with Mrs. Finch during which you offer your consultative services, and define the parameters of the consultant-consultee relationship.

Chapter 9

INDIRECT SERVICES II: SPECIAL TOPICS IN SCHOOL CONSULTATION

Based on their national survey, Reschly and Wilson (1995) reported that school practitioners devote an average of two hours each week to systems/organizational consultation, but an increase in time for this type of indirect service was desired. We use the term *systems-level consultation* to refer to cooperative problem-solving between the school psychologist (consultant) and consultee(s) (e.g., principal, teachers, district-level administrators) with a goal of improving school policies, practices, and/or programs so as to better serve the mental health and educational needs of students. Consultation goals might focus on facilitating change in classrooms, grades, buildings, or at the district level (Curtis & Stollar, 2002). According to Curtis and Stollar (2002), to be competent to provide systems-level consultation, school psychologists need expertise in understanding human behavior from a social systems perspective, well-developed skills in collaborative planning and problem-solving procedures, and knowledge of principles for organizational change.

We concur with Prilleltensky's suggestion that, consistent with the principle of responsibility to community and society, "school psychologists have a moral responsibility to promote not only the well-being of their clients but also of the environments where their clients function and develop" (1991, p. 200). In the first portion of the chapter, we summarize the ethical and legal issues associated with the following special topics in school consultation: school testing and assessment programs, grade retention, grouping pupils for instructional purposes, school discipline, school violence prevention and response, and pupil harassment and discrimination. The chapter closes with a brief discussion of issues associated with public schooling for three additional groups of children with special needs: children with limited English proficiency, gifted and talented pupils, and students with serious communicable diseases. The National Association of School Psychologists (NASP) has adopted position statements on a number of these topics. (NASP statements can be found at http://www.nasponline.org/.) These position statements are resolutions by the Association to advocate for certain practices seen as promoting the mental health and education needs of children and youth. Interested readers are encouraged to consult them.

SCHOOL TESTING AND ASSESSMENT PROGRAMS

A heightened emphasis on school accountability has given impetus to the development of statewide pupil assessment programs. The No Child Left Behind Act of 2001 requires each state to develop challenging academic content standards for mathematics, reading or language arts, and science and measurable achievement standards expected of all children for those content areas (Pub. L. No. 107–110 § 1111[a][1]). Each state also must implement a set of high-quality, yearly student academic assessments that include, at a minimum, assessment in mathematics, reading or language arts, and science, which will be used as the primary means of determining yearly performance of the state, school district, and school. The assessments must meet nationally recognized technical standards for reliability and validity. Statewide reading and mathematics tests must be administered annually in grades 3–8 beginning in 2005–2006, and in science beginning in 2007–2008 (Pub. L. No. 107–110 § 1111[b][3]). Each state must attain academic proficiency for all students within 12 years, and districts must document progress toward that goal each year. Districts must make public school choice available to pupils in schools that fail to demonstrate progress for two consecutive years and offer supplemental tutoring after a third year of failure to demonstrate progress. The Individuals with Disabilities Education Act of 1997 (IDEA) requires children with disabilities to participate in state and districtwide assessment programs (with appropriate accommodations in testing), but children who cannot participate in such assessments are allowed to participate in alternative assessments.

Unfortunately, statewide testing programs can encourage school practices that are not in the best interests of children. Braden (2002) uses the term *high stakes* testing to refer to situations in which test outcomes have a direct impact on the lives of stakeholders. Results of statewide programs have been used to evaluate the performance of individual teachers and schools. Low-scoring schools may suffer negative publicity and increased external scrutiny and control, while high-scoring schools receive public praise, increased autonomy, and, in some states, financial rewards (Braden, 2002). Allington and McGill-Franzen (1992) found that, in response to high-stakes testing, schools may attempt to inflate overall district scores by placing more children in special education, categorizing more children as limited English proficient, and retaining more students in the early grades. Psychologists must speak out against such practices.

School psychologists can play a positive role in improving school test performance by assisting districts in evaluating the consistency among their goals, curriculum, and the test demands; promoting quality evidence-based instructional practices; and providing consultation to improve student test-taking skills (see Braden, 2002). School psychologists also can assist districts by identifying reasonable test accommodations for students with disabilities (see Council for Exceptional Children, 2000).

In addition to statewide pupil evaluation programs, many districts have their own testing programs. Such testing programs can serve a number of purposes, including screening, student evaluation for instructional planning, and program evaluation and research. In many districts, the school psychologist is the professional with the greatest expertise in measurement. Consequently, practitioners may be asked to help administrators and teachers make decisions regarding whether a testing program is needed, clarify the purposes of a testing program, help select tests and assessment tools that are technically adequate and valid for the intended purpose, develop guidelines for appropriate test interpretation and use of results, and assist in reporting data to parents and the community. The *Standards for Educational and Psychological Testing* or *Standards* (American Educational Research Association, American Psychological Association, and National Council on Measurement in Education, 1999), provides guidelines for school testing programs (pp. 51–54) (also see Vanderwood & Powers, 2002).

Minimum competency testing and the use of developmental/readiness screening test results in the schools pose special ethical-legal concerns.

Minimum Competency Testing

Minimum competency testing is the practice of requiring a student to achieve a certain score on a standardized test in order to be promoted or to receive a high school diploma (Medway & Rose, 1986). Minimum competency tests are usually criterion-referenced tests that evaluate whether students have mastered important skills. Such tests create a high stakes situation for individual students. There have been a number of legal challenges to the policy of requiring students to pass an examination before they are awarded a high school diploma. *Debra P. v. Turlington* (1984) is probably the most important decision in this area.

In Florida, high school seniors are required to pass a state-mandated competency test to receive a high school diploma. Students unable to pass the test are typically awarded a certificate of attendance. *Debra P.* was a class action suit filed on behalf of African-American students in the state of Florida. The plaintiffs claimed to have a property interest in receiving a diploma and that use of the competency exam was a denial of the equal protection clause of the 14th Amendment because the test was discriminatory against African Americans.

The court ultimately upheld the right of the state to require students to pass a competency test to receive a diploma. The court identified several issues that must be addressed in evaluating whether minimum competency tests are legally permissible. The first is whether adequate notice exists, that is, an adequate phase-in period before the test is used to determine award of a diploma. Other issues are whether the test has adequate curricular validity and whether the school can document acceptable instructional validity. Curricular validity addresses the question of whether the curriculum of the school matches what is measured by the test. Instructional validity is whether the students are, in fact, taught what is outlined in the curriculum, that is, whether the curriculum is implemented (Fischer & Sorenson, 1996; also *Debra P.*, 1984, p. 1408).

Legally, pupils with disabilities also may be required to pass a competency test to receive a high school diploma. The school must ensure that tests used with disabled students are a valid measure of school achievement and that no student is penalized due to his or her disability (Fischer & Sorenson, 1996). Medway and Rose (1986) suggest that special education students who might be able to pass a high school competency test have appropriate instructional goals outlined in their individualized education programs (IEP) and that teachers be able to document that adequate instruction was provided.

Developmental/Readiness Screening Tests

Many public school districts implemented prekindergarten developmental/readiness screening programs in the 1970s. Developmental screening tests are designed to determine quickly and tentatively whether a child's progress is age-appropriate (Lichtenstein, 1981). Children classified as having potential school problems on the basis of screening test results then are referred for a more comprehensive evaluation to reject or confirm the suspected problem and plan for appropriate intervention, if indicated.

Screening test scores alone do not have adequate reliability and validity for educational decision making about individual pupils and should be used only for identifying children in need of further evaluation, or for decisions that are tentative and easily reversed. Unfortunately, our experiences suggest many schools have used screening test scores to deny or delay kindergarten entry or as the sole criterion for assigning a child to a developmental classroom (e.g., developmental kindergarten). Because of the limited technical adequacy of screening tests, decisions to assign a child to a developmental classroom are best made in cooperation with the parent, based on the consideration of a combination of factors (e.g., physical, cognitive, personal-social development).

SCHOOL ENTRY AND GRADE RETENTION DECISIONS

Teachers and principals occasionally recommend delayed school entry for pupils who appear to be "not ready" to begin school, and grade repetition often is recommended for pupils who demonstrate poor academic achievement. We now explore the legal and ethical issues associated with these practices.

School Entry

We are aware that many public school districts persist in the practice of advising or encouraging parents to postpone school entry an extra year. Such practices often stem from a misunderstanding of compulsory school attendance laws. Compulsory school attendance laws identify the ages (e.g., 7–16 years) during which the state (school) can compel school attendance; the school may hold the parent responsible for ensuring that his or her child receives schooling during those years in accordance with state requirements (Reutter, 1994).

However, after a child reaches the age of school eligibility, the child has a property interest (created by the state or local school board) in receiving a public school education. The legal reasoning of *Pennsylvania Association for Retarded Citizens v. Commonwealth of Pennsylvania* (*P.A.R.C.*) (1972) consent decree can be seen to apply in all school districts (Kirp, 1973); that is, public school districts must offer an education program for all children who are age-eligible for school entry in their district under the equal protection clause of the 14th Amendment. No child can be turned away. If a child is not ready for regular kindergarten, the school must offer an alternative educational program at public school expense (see *P.A.R.C.*, 1972, p. 1262).

Case 9–1

Tommy Fields was administered a developmental screening test by Wanda Rose, the school psychologist, during the district's annual spring prekindergarten screening program. On the basis of the screening test results and the fact that Tommy had a summer birthday only a few months before the kindergarten entry cutoff date, Wanda Rose informed Tommy's mother that he was "not ready" for kindergarten and suggested she keep him at home "for another year to grow." Mrs. Fields, a single parent with a full-time job, was distressed by the screening test results and recommendation and the prospect of paying for another year of full-time day care for Tommy.

Because Tommy (Case 9–1) is old enough for the local school kindergarten program, the school must provide some sort of program at district expense (e.g., preschool or developmental kindergarten). (See Rafoth, 2002, for an additional discussion of delayed school entry.)

Grade Retention

Grade retention, or nonpromotion, is the popular practice of requiring a student to repeat a grade due to poor academic achievement. A number of studies have found no lasting beneficial effect of grade retention (see Jimerson, 2001, and Rafoth, 2002, for reviews). Some research suggests that grade retention actually may be detrimental, especially in the areas of student self-concept, and personal and social adjustment.

In general, the courts have preferred not to interfere with school promotion or retention decisions (Sales, Krauss, Sacken, & Overcast, 1999). However, the court considerations in *Sandlin v. Johnson* (1981) suggest that a decision to retain a child cannot be arbitrary; that is, the method for assignment to a particular grade must be reasonably related to the purpose of providing appropriate instruction and furthering education. Furthermore, any method of determining pupil retention that has a disproportionate impact on minorities may be scrutinized more closely as a possible denial of equal educational opportunities.

School psychologists have an important role to play in promoting early identification and intervention for pupils with school difficulties and in ensuring that retention is not used inappropriately. Alternatives to retention are discussed in Rafoth (2002).

INSTRUCTIONAL GROUPING

With the landmark *Brown v. Board of Education* decision in 1954, the courts ruled that school segregation by race was a denial of the right to equal protection (equal educational opportunity) under the 14th Amendment. Following this decision, the courts began to scrutinize school practices that suggested within-school segregation—that is, where minority children were segregated and treated differently within the schools. A number of court cases were filed against the public schools in which minority group children were overrepresented in the lower educational tracks (ability groups) and special education classes (see Chapter 5).

Grouping and Minority Students

Hobson v. Hanson (1967, 1969) was the first significant challenge to the disproportionate assignment of minority group (African American) children to lower ability tracks. The judge in this case noted that the tracking system was rigid, the lower tracks offered inferior educational opportunities, and children were grouped on the basis of racially biased group ability tests. He ruled that the tracking system was a violation of the equal protection clause of the 14th Amendment and ordered the system abolished. He did not find that ability grouping was *per se* unconstitutional (see also *McNeal v. Tate County School District,* 1975).

Court rulings in more recent cases also found that ability grouping is not *per se* unconstitutional (*Georgia State Conference of Branches of NAACP v. State of Georgia,* 1985; *Simmons v. Hooks,* 1994). In these cases, the courts held that ability grouping that results in within-school segregation may be permissible if the school district can demonstrate that their grouping practices will remedy the results of past segregation by providing better educational opportunities for children. *Georgia* was a class action suit decided on behalf of African-American students in Georgia because of their disproportionate assignment to the lower achievement groups, resulting in intraschool racial segregation. In this case, information about grouping practices showed that students typically were assigned to achievement rather than ability groups on the basis of a combination of factors including assessment of skill level in a basal series, achievement test results, and teacher recommendations. In defending their grouping practices, the schools noted that the achievement groupings were flexible (i.e., students could move easily from one group to another) and likely to benefit students as instruction was matched to skill level. They also presented achievement data to show that pupils in the lower tracks did, in fact, benefit from the instructional grouping. The schools consequently were able to show that their grouping practices resulted in enhanced educational opportunities for African-American students. The court found in favor of the schools.

Simmons v. Hooks (1994) involved a school district in which students were placed in whole-class ability tracks in kindergarten through third grade, with a disproportionate number of African-American students placed in the low ability classes. In grades 4 through 6, students were placed in heterogeneous classes, with within-class instructional grouping for reading, math, and language arts. The district was not able to show that whole-class ability grouping resulted in better educational opportunities for pupils in grades kindergarten through 3, and the court found this practice unconstitutionally segregative. The court did not find heterogeneous class assignment with within-class grouping for reading, math, and language arts unconstitutionally segregative.

Instructional Grouping and Children's Needs

As noted in *Simmons v. Hooks* (1994), a number of different types of instructional grouping practices exist. The grouping practice that has raised the most concern is ability-grouped class assignment, in which pupils are assigned to self-contained classes based on homogeneity of ability. Research suggests that assignment to self-contained classes based on ability level does not improve school achievement and may result in lowered self-esteem and educational aspirations for students placed in the lower tracks (Ross & Harrison, 1997). School psychologists are encouraged to be knowledgeable of the literature on classroom grouping and to promote alternatives that are in the best interests of all children (Dawson, 1995; Ross & Harrison, 1997).

In concluding this section, it is important to note that these cases concerning within-school grouping should not draw attention away from the sad fact that, today, many children of color attend underfunded, inferior, segregated schools in poverty-pockets of the country. As Kozol observed, our "... nation, for all practice and intent, has turned its back on the moral implications, if not yet the legal ramifications, of the *Brown* decision" (1991, p. 4). In many cities, the racial segregation of schools is largely ignored and uncontested; the presence of dilapidated, ill-equipped, inadequately staffed ghetto schools has been accepted as a "permanent American reality" (p. 4).

SCHOOL DISCIPLINE

Under the general mandate to operate the public school, school officials have been given "a wide latitude of discretion" to fulfil their duty to maintain order, ensure pupil safety, and educate children (*Burnside v. Byars*, 1966, p. 748). Historically, school administrators and teachers were allowed to function quite autonomously in maintaining school and classroom discipline. In recent years, however, the courts have been called on to consider the constitutionality of school rules and of school disciplinary methods.

In considering the constitutionality of school rules, the courts generally have held that school rules and regulations must be a reasonable exercise of the power and discretion of the school authorities, related to the purpose of maintaining order and discipline (*Burnside v. Byars*, 1966), and enforced in a non-discriminatory manner. The courts also have generally held that school rules should be clearly stated, and the consequences for conduct code violations should be reasonably explicit. Students should be informed of expectations for appropriate conduct through written statements or instruction (Reutter, 1994). The methods of school discipline that frequently have been the focus of judicial scrutiny include corporal punishment, suspension, and expulsion.

School discipline is the job responsibility of the building principal, not the school psychologist. However, because of their role as consultant to principals and teachers regarding mental health principles and pupils with behavior problems, practitioners need a sound working knowledge of the ethical-legal aspects of disciplinary practices.

Corporal Punishment

> Why is it that school children remain the last Americans that can be legally beaten? (Messina, 1988, p. 108)

Corporal punishment generally is defined as the infliction of pain on the body by the teacher or other school official as a penalty for conduct disapproved of by the punisher. Forms of corporal punishment include spanking, beating, whipping, gagging, punching, shoving, knuckle rapping, arm twisting, shaking, and ear and hair pulling, among others (Messina, 1988).

Some social science evidence suggests that corporal punishment in the schools is psychologically harmful to children and that alternative approaches to maintaining school discipline are preferable and more effective (Messina, 1988; Purcell, 1984). Furthermore, children throughout the country have suffered severe and sometimes permanent physical injuries as a result of corporal punishment administered in the schools, including injuries to the head, neck, spine, kidneys, and genitals; perforated eardrums and hearing loss; facial and body scars; and chipped teeth (Hyman, 1990). Unfortunately, the use of corporal punishment in the schools is based on "social norms which are seeded deep within American culture" (Purcell, 1984, p. 188) and disciplinary practices which are deep-seeded within the American schools (Messina, 1988).

In the text that follows, case law and statutory law regarding corporal punishment are summarized. The role of the school psychologist in promoting alternatives to corporal punishment then is discussed.

Case Law

Historically, English common law viewed teachers as having the authority to use corporal punishment under the doctrine of *in loco parentis*. According to this doctrine, a child's father delegated part of his parental authority to the tutor or schoolmaster. The tutor or schoolmaster then "stood in the place of the parent" and was permitted to use "restraint and correction" as needed to teach the child (Zirkel & Reichner, 1986). In the United States, the notion that educators have the authority to use corporal punishment under the common law doctrine of *in loco parentis* dates back to Colonial times, but it has been replaced gradually with the view that the state (school) has the right to administer corporal punishment because of the school's legitimate interest in maintaining order for the purpose of education.

Baker v. Owen (1975) raised the question of whether the parent can "undelegate," or take away, the school's authority to use corporal punishment. In this case, Mrs. Baker told the school principal she did not want her son, Russell, corporally punished as he was a fragile child. Following a minor school infraction, his teacher took a drawer divider and spanked him twice, causing some bruises. Mrs. Baker filed a complaint in federal court alleging that her fundamental right to the care, control, and custody of her child had been violated when the school used corporal punishment despite her prohibition.

The court in *Baker* held that the school's interest in maintaining order by the use of reasonable corporal punishment outweighs parental rights to determine the care and control of their child, including how a child shall be disciplined. Under this ruling, schools were free to use reasonable corporal punishment for disciplinary purposes, despite parental objections to the practice.

In *Ingraham v. Wright,* a 1977 Supreme Court ruling, the parents of two schoolchildren contended that corporal punishment was a violation of a child's basic constitutional rights. The Court in *Ingraham* agreed to consider whether corporal punishment in the schools is "cruel and unusual punishment" under the Eighth Amendment, the extent to which paddling is constitutionally permissible, and whether paddling requires due process protection under the 14th Amendment.

The Court found that corporal punishment to maintain discipline in the schools does not fall under the "cruel and unusual punishment" prohibition of the Eighth Amendment because the Amendment was designed to protect those accused of crimes. The Court noted that "the schoolchild has little need for the protection of the Eighth Amendment" because the openness of the schools and supervision by the community afford significant safeguards from the abuse of corporal punishment by teachers (*Ingraham v. Wright,* 1977, p. 1412).

Justice Powell, who wrote the majority opinion, acknowledged that the 14th Amendment protects the right to be free from unjustified intrusions on personal security and that liberty interests are "implicated" if punishment is unreasonable. However, he went on to state that "there can be no deprivation of substantive rights as long as disciplinary corporal punishment is within the limits of common law privilege" (p. 1415) and held that due process safeguards do not apply. Thus, the Court in *Ingraham* found that corporal punishment of schoolchildren is not unconstitutional *per se*. However, the opinion left unanswered the question of whether corporal punishment *is ever* unconstitutional.

Several more recent court decisions at the level of the U.S. Circuit Court of Appeals suggest that excessive corporal punishment is likely to be viewed as unconstitutional. In *Hall v. Tawny* (1980) and *Garcia by Garcia v. Miera* (1987), for example, the parents of schoolchildren filed Section 1983 civil rights lawsuits against school officials after their children were severely beaten as a part of disciplinary actions. The actions of the school personnel in these cases were seen as a violation of the substantive rights of the child to be free of state intrusions into realms of personal privacy and bodily security through means the court viewed as "brutal and demeaning."

Statutory Law

As of 1994, 27 states had adopted legislation or issued regulations banning the use of corporal punishment in public schools (Hyman, Barrish, & Kaplan, 1997). Most state laws that prohibit corporal punishment allow teachers and others in the school setting to use reasonable physical restraint as necessary to protect people from immediate physical danger, or to protect property. Michigan's law, for example, allows an individual to use reasonable physical force for self-defense and in defense of others, to prevent self-injury, to obtain a weapon, and to restrain or remove a disruptive student who refuses to refrain from further disruptive behaviors when told to do so (Public Act 521 as amended by Act No. 6 of the Public Acts of 1992). The Paul D. Coverdell Teacher Protection Act of 2001, part of the No Child Left Behind Act (Pub. L. No.. 107-110 §§ 2361-2368), provides a limitation on liability for teachers, principals, or other school professionals when they undertake reasonable actions to maintain order, discipline, and an appropriate educational environment (see Chapter 2).

Promoting Alternatives

School psychology practitioners can work to abolish corporal punishment by sensitizing teachers to the negative consequences of corporal punishment, promoting alternatives to its use through in-service and consultation, and by advocating state legislation and school board policies banning the use of corporal punishment for school disciplinary purposes (see Hyman et al., 1997).

School psychologists also may serve an important role by sensitizing school staff to the potential legal sanctions for the use of corporal punishment. The use of corporal punishment can be costly to the principal or teacher in terms of time and legal defense fees, even if they are ultimately found innocent of any wrongdoing. In districts that have banned the use of corporal punishment, its use is likely to result in disciplinary action by the local school board, possibly including suspension or loss of employment. Even in states that allow the use of corporal punishment in the schools, parents who are upset by its use with their child may pursue several courses of legal action. The majority of corporal punishment cases are filed in state courts under charges of battery, assault and battery, or negligent battery. Parents also may file a complaint under state child abuse laws. In addition, a number of parents have filed actions in federal court under Section 1983 (Henderson, 1986).

Suspension and Expulsion

Schools have been given the authority to suspend or expel students to maintain order and carry out the purpose of education. Short-term suspension typically is defined as an exclusion of 10 days or less from school or from participation in classes and activities (in-school suspension). In most districts, school principals are given the authority to suspend students. Expulsion means exclusion of the student for a period longer than 10 consecutive school days or the equivalent, with "equivalent" determined by factors such as the number and proximity of excluded days (Hindman, 1986; Lohrmann & Zirkel, 1995). Student expulsion usually requires action by the school board.

The specific grounds for disciplinary suspensions and expulsions vary from state to state. School codes are likely to allow suspension or expulsion of students guilty of persistent noncompliance with school rules and directives, weapon and drug-related offenses, repeated use of obscene language, stealing or vandalizing property on school grounds, and using violence or encouraging the use of violence (Hindman, 1986; Reutter, 1994). The No Child Left Behind Act of 2001 includes "The Gun-Free Schools Act" (Pub. L. No.. 107-110 § 4141). This portion of the legislation requires each state receiving federal funds under the Act to have in effect a state law requiring schools to expel for a period of not less than one year a student who brings a firearm to school. However, the law must allow the chief school administrator to modify the expulsion requirement on a case-by-case basis, and States may allow students expelled from their regular school to receive educational services in an alternative setting. The Act also requires that incidents of students bringing firearms or weapons to school be reported to the juvenile or criminal justice system.

In 1975, *Goss v. Lopez* was decided by the Supreme Court. This case was filed on behalf of several high school students suspended without any sort of informal due process hearing. The Court ruled that because education is a state-created property right, the school may not suspend or expel pupils without some sort of due process procedures to protect students from arbitrary or wrongful infringement of their interests in schooling. In writing the majority opinion, Justice White outlined the minimal due process procedures required for suspensions of 10 days or less:

> Students facing temporary suspension have interest qualifying for protection of the Due Process Clause, and due process requires, in connection with a suspension of 10 days or less, that the student be given oral or written notice of the charges against him and, if he denies them, an explanation of the evidence the authorities have and an opportunity to present his side of the story. The Clause requires at least these rudimentary precautions against unfair or mistaken findings of misconduct and arbitrary exclusion from school (*Goss v. Lopez,* 1975, p. 740).

Justice White further noted that "longer suspensions or expulsions for the remainder of the school term, or permanently, may require more formal procedures" (p. 741). He also noted that, generally, the notice and hearing should precede the removal of the pupil from the school. However, pupils "whose presence poses a continuing danger to persons or property or an ongoing threat of disrupting the academic process may be immediately removed from school. In such cases, the necessary notice and rudimentary hearing should follow as soon as practicable" (*Goss v. Lopez,* 1975, p. 740).

When immediate removal of a student is under consideration, it is important to remember that suspension may serve as a trigger for suicide attempts or violence against others. Consequently, parents should be notified if it is necessary to remove their child from school, and students who are suspended during the school day should not be sent home to an empty house (see *Armijo v. Wagon Mound School District*, 1998).

Students with Disabilities

When Congress passed Pub. L. 94-142 in 1975, it was recognized that schools might rely on suspension and expulsion policies to exclude children with disabilities from public schools, particularly students with emotional and behavioral difficulties. Consequently, IDEA includes special protections with regard to disciplinary removals of children with disabilities.

Short Term Disciplinary Removals. IDEA allows school officials to remove a child with a disability from the child's current placement for not more than 10 school days for any violation of school rules to the extent such a removal would be applied to children without disabilities. Education services need not be provided to a student removed for 10 days or less *in a given school year* if services are not provided to a child without disabilities who has been similarly removed (34 C.F.R. § 300.121). Parents should be notified of any disciplinary removals, and they must be advised of all procedural safeguards.

IDEA also permits additional removals for not more than 10 consecutive school days in the same school year for separate incidents of misconduct as long as those removals do not constitute a change of placement

(34 C.F.R. § 300.520). After a child with a disability has been removed from his or her current placement for more than 10 school days in the same school year, during any subsequent days of removal the school must provide education services to the extent necessary to enable the child to progress in the general curriculum and appropriately advance toward achieving the goals set out in the child's IEP (34 C.F.R. § 300.121). School personnel may determine appropriate services in consultation with the child's special education teacher. A *change of placement* occurs if the disciplinary removal from the child's current educational placement is for more than 10 consecutive school days; or the child is subjected to a series of removals that constitute a pattern because they cumulate to more than 10 school days in a school year, and because of factors such as length of each removal, the total amount of time the child is removed, and the proximity of the removals to one another (34 C.F.R. § 300.519). A change of placement requires an IEP meeting (see "Behavioral Plan Required").

Placement in an Interim Alternative Educational Setting. School officials may order placement of a child with a disability into an appropriate interim alternative educational setting (IAES) for the same amount of time that a child without a disability would be subject to discipline, but for not more than 45 days, if the child carries a weapon to school or to a school function, or the child knowingly possesses or uses illegal drugs or sells or solicits the sale of a controlled substance while at school or a school function (34 C.F.R. § 300.520).

In addition, a hearing officer may order a change in the placement of a child with a disability to an IAES for not more than 45 days if the hearing officer determines, in an expedited due process hearing, that the school has demonstrated by substantial evidence that maintaining the current placement of a child with a disability is substantially likely to result in injury to the child or to others. In ordering a change of placement, the officer must consider the appropriateness of the child's current placement, whether the school has made reasonable efforts to minimize the risk of harm in the child's current placement (including the use of supplementary aids and services), and the appropriateness of the alternative setting for the child (34 C.F.R. § 300.521).

Determination of Setting. The interim alternative educational setting (IAES) must be selected so as to enable the child to continue to participate in the general curriculum (although in another setting) and to receive the services and modifications that will enable the child to meet his or her current IEP goals. The IAES also must be selected to ensure that the child will receive services and modifications designed to address the problem behavior so that it does not recur (34 C.F. R. § 300.522).

Behavioral Plan Required. Either before or not later than 10 days after either first removing the child for more than 10 school days in a school year or commencing a removal that constitutes a change of placement, the school must convene an IEP team meeting. If the child had a behavioral intervention plan prior to the disciplinary action, the IEP team is required to review the plan and modify it as necessary to address the problem behavior. If no behavioral plan existed prior to the disciplinary action, the school must convene an IEP team meeting to develop an assessment plan to address the problem behavior, conduct a functional behavioral assessment, and implement a behavioral intervention plan for the child to address the behavior that resulted in the disciplinary action (34 C.F.R. § 300.520) (also see Chapter 7).

Manifest Determination Review. If a disciplinary action is contemplated as a result of weapons, drugs, or potential injury to self or others, or if a disciplinary action involving a change of placement for more than 10 days is contemplated for a child with a disability who engaged in behavior that violated any school rule or code, a manifest determination review must be conducted. This review is conducted by the IEP team and other qualified personnel immediately after the disciplinary decision is made if possible, but no later than 10 school days after the date on which the decision to take that action was made. This review examines the relationship between the child's disability and the behavior that resulted in the disciplinary action (34 C.F. R. § 300.523).

IDEA 1997 outlines a number of requirements for finding that behavior is or is not a manifestation of the child's disability. The IEP team may determine that the behavior of the child was not a manifestation of the child's disability only if it first considers, in terms of the behavior that led to the disciplinary action, all relevant information, including evaluation and diagnostic results, information supplied by the parents of the child, observations of the child, and the child's IEP and placement; and then determines that (a) in relationship to the behavior subject to the disciplinary action, the child's IEP and placement were appropriate and the special education services, supplementary aids and services, and behavior intervention strategies were provided consistent with the child's IEP and placement; (b) the child's disability did not impair the ability of the child to understand the impact and consequences of the behavior subject to disciplinary action; and (c) the child's disability did not impair the ability of the child to control the behavior subject to disciplinary action. If the IEP team and other qualified personnel determine that any of these standards were not met, the behavior must be considered a manifestation of the child's disability (34 C.F.R. § 300.523).

If the result of the review (described in the proceeding paragraph) is a determination that the behavior of the child with a disability was not a manifestation of the child's disability, the relevant disciplinary procedures applicable to children without disabilities may be applied to the child in the same manner that they would be applied to other children (e.g., long-term suspension), except that children with disabilities under IDEA must continue to receive a free appropriate public education. Schools must provide services to the extent necessary to enable the child to appropriately advance toward achieving the goals set out in the child's IEP (34 C.F.R. § 300.121). Services are determined by the IEP team. Schools may discontinue educational services to 504-only students (those protected by 504 but not eligible under IDEA) as long as nonhandicapped students receive identical treatment ("Discipline Under Section 504," 1996).

Parent Appeals. Parents who disagree with a determination that a child's behavior was not a manifestation of his or her disability, or with any decision regarding disciplinary placement, may request an expedited hearing (34 C.F.R. § 300.525). The child remains in the IAES pending the decision of the hearing officer or until the expiration of the time limit, whichever comes first, unless the parent and school agree otherwise. If the child is placed in an IAES and the school proposes to change the child's placement after expiration of the IAES, the child remains in the current placement (prior to the IAES) during any proceeding to challenge the proposed change of placement. If, however, the school maintains that it is dangerous for the child to be in the current placement, the school may request an expedited hearing (34 C.F.R. § 300.526).

A child who has not been determined to be eligible for special education and who engaged in behavior that violated any school rule or code may seek IDEA protections by asserting that the school knew the child had a disability before the behavior leading to disciplinary action occurred. The school is deemed to have knowledge that a child has a disability if (a) the parent had expressed concern in writing that their child is in need of special education (concern may be expressed orally if the parent does not know how to write or has a disability that prevents a written statement), (b) the behavior or performance of the child demonstrates the need for such services, (c) the parent has requested an evaluation of the child, or (d) the teacher or other school personnel have expressed concern about the child to the special education director or by making a referral. If a request is made for evaluation of a child during the time the child is subjected to disciplinary measures, the evaluation will be conducted in an expedited manner, and if found eligible, the child will receive special education and related services (34 C.F.R. § 300.527). (See Kublick, Bard, and Perry, 2000, for additional information.)

Referral and Action by Law Enforcement. IDEA 1997 clarifies that school personnel may report a crime committed by a child with a disability to appropriate authorities, and nothing in the law prevents law enforcement and judicial authorities from exercising their duties with regard to crimes committed by a child with a disability. The school that reports a crime must ensure that copies of the special education and disciplinary records of the child are transmitted for consideration by the authorities (34 C.F.R. § 300.529).

Monitoring of Suspension and Expulsion Rates. Under IDEA, states are required to collect and examine data to determine whether significant discrepancies are occurring in the rate of long-term suspensions and expulsions of children with disabilities among school districts or compared to the rates for children without disabilities. If discrepancies are occurring, the SEA must review and, if appropriate, revise policies, procedures, and practices related to the development and implementation of IEPs, the use of behavioral interventions, and procedural safeguards (34 C.F.R. § 300.146).

SCHOOL VIOLENCE PREVENTION

> Despite the fact that schools remain one of the safest places for youths to be, schools are beginning to adopt identification systems to determine which students could be future killers. The methods used to accomplish this not only are unproven but are inherently limited in usefulness and often do more harm than good for both the children and the school setting. (Mulvey & Cauffman, 2001, p. 797)

This portion of the chapter focuses on schoolwide efforts to prevent violent student behaviors; practitioner responsibilities in the management of a student who may pose a threat to others are discussed in Chapter 7. Exhibit 9–1 outlines recommendations for schools regarding violence prevention and response. These suggestions were based on a review of statutory and case law, recommendations from school attorneys, U.S. Department of Education policy recommendations, and expert opinion. (For additional information about the history and legal underpinnings of these recommendations, see Feinberg and Jacob, 2002).

Districtwide efforts to create violence-free school environments have often included the development of safe school plans and crisis response teams. Specific components of safe school plans vary. Some components of safe school plans (e.g., use of metal detectors) raise legal concerns (see

Exhibit 9–1. Preventing and Responding to School Violence[1]

1. All school districts should have a comprehensive safe school plan that addresses violence prevention, intervention, and response (see Stephens, 1994). The plan should describe the procedures and personnel available to respond in the event that a crisis occurs, be developed by a school-community team, take into account the resources available to the district; and be consistent with federal, state, and local laws (Dwyer, Osher, & Warger, 1998).

2. As part of its safe school plan, districts should ensure student discipline policies and practices foster a positive school climate and minimize the likelihood of student alienation and mistrust. School rules and regulations must be a reasonable exercise of the power of school authorities, related to the purpose of maintaining order and discipline, and be enforced in a fair and nondiscriminatory manner. Policies should be clearly stated and publicized, must not violate the legal rights of pupils or their parents, and should be implemented in ways that are respectful of the rights and dignity of individual students (Jacob & Feinberg, 2002; Mulvey & Cauffman, 2001; Sales et al., 1999).

3. Every district should establish an incident reporting and tracking system to determine the nature and scope of crime and violence in their schools and monitor progress towards reducing crime (Rapp, Carrington, & Nicholson, 1992). Schools should implement policies that encourage staff and students to report incidents and concerns. The nature and scope of school crimes should be documented prior to the implementation of any safety measures that may compromise student freedoms. For example, if metal detectors are introduced, but challenged in court, the school must demonstrate that use of metal detectors is justified by state (school) interests compelling enough to override students' privacy interests (e.g., a history of weapons incidents at school).

4. Districts should ensure adequate staff orientation to district violence prevention and response policies and procedures and provide on-going training for staff to improve violence prevention efforts through curricular and other interventions. Pulliam (1999) and Pitcher and Poland (1992) recommend that the violence prevention component of a safe school plan include training for administrators and staff on how to recognize and defuse potential violence.

5. The violence prevention component should include written policies that protect students from harassment and specifically harassment and hate crimes based on race, color, national origin, sex, disability, and sexual orientation. The policy should specify how students, staff, and parents can report concerns about harassment and identify the school personnel responsible for ensuring reasonable steps are taken to stop harassment and prevent future occurrences (see U.S. Department of Education & Bias Crimes Task Force of the National Association of Attorneys General, 1999).

6. The intervention component of the safe school plan should include written procedures for school personnel to follow if they suspect that a student is potentially dangerous to others, to self, or is a victim of abuse. Threats of violence and suicide should be taken seriously. When it is suspected a student is suicidal, the student should be seen by a mental health professional with training in assessment of suicide lethality. When a student makes threats to harm others, procedures should ensure that the student is seen for evaluation by professionals knowledgeable of threat assessment. District policies should state that students may be seen by the school

[1]From Feinberg & Jacob, 2002. Copyright 2002 by the National Association of School Psychologists. Reprinted by permission of the publisher.

Exhibit 9–1. *(Continued)*

psychologist or other mental health professional without parent consent to determine whether the pupil is dangerous or in danger. If a pupil is determined to be a threat to self or others, school procedures should ensure that appropriate parties are informed of the situation (e.g., parents of a suicidal youth) and that there is a coordinated response, drawing on the resources of the school, family, and community as needed.

7. The job descriptions of school personnel should be written to include their likely roles in school violence prevention and crisis response (Pitcher & Poland, 1992). School employees are more likely to be shielded from liability in lawsuits if they are acting within the scope of their authority.

8. School personnel who are expected to assume special roles in violence prevention or response (e.g., psychologists who assess suicide lethality) should receive verifiable training to assume those roles and be encouraged to consult with experts in situations where the appropriate course of action is not clear.

9. The crisis response component of the safe school plan should identify a school-based core team responsible for crisis management, trained to respond to unforeseeable events (Dwyer et al., 1998; *Kelson v. City of Springfield*, 1985). The plan should identify the individuals (or their alternates) who will be expected to take responsibility in a crisis situation, and how to contact medical, fire, and police emergency assistance, and community mental health providers (Pulliam, 1999).

10. The crisis response plan should be coordinated carefully with law enforcement. When a crime occurs on school grounds, the police are in charge. School officials should be prepared to assist police in their efforts to define and secure the crime zone (e.g, preserve evidence) (Pulliam, 1999).

11. The crisis response plan should identify a trained spokesperson responsible for answering questions from the media to ensure that there is no disclosure of confidential information and that pupil, staff, and family privacy are respected (Pitcher & Poland, 1992).

12. The plan should emphasize the need for careful documentation of all steps taken to prevent a crisis situation, as well as the steps taken by the crisis team in the aftermath of a crisis. Such documentation can assist in improving crisis response procedures and serves as a record in the event there is a legal action against the school following a crisis event.

Jacob & Feinberg, 2002). Discussion here is limited to the ethical and legal problems associated with districtwide programs to identify pupils "at risk" for targeted violence.

A number of organizations have published lists of characteristics common among students prone to violence (e.g., American Psychological Association, 1999; Dwyer, Osher, & Warger, 1998; National School Safety Center, 1999). Information about the early warning signs that relate to troubling behaviors can be used to educate staff, students, and parents about what to look for so that pupils in need of assistance can receive help early, before their problems become severe (Dwyer et. al., 1998). However, some districts have implemented screening programs in an effort to identify students "at risk" for targeted violence that raise legal and ethical concerns. Key concerns are inappropriate labeling and stigmatization, invasion of pupil and family privacy without informed consent, and misuse of results.

Checklists have been used in a number of school districts to identify pupils as "dangerous or potentially dangerous" ("School Psychologists," 1999). However, no simple checklists or tests can accurately identify pupils who will become school killers. Furthermore, because the base rate for acts of planned, targeted violence is low, it is not likely there will ever be instruments that can accurately identify students who will attempt such acts. Consequently, schools that label pupils "potentially violent" on the basis of checklists or other such instruments are violating a pupil's constitutional right to be free from arbitrary stigmatization by the state (see Chapter 2). In their attempts to identify troubled youth, schools also are cautioned against asking students to complete surveys or questionnaires that are intrusive of personal or family privacy without informed parent consent (Bradley, 1998; *Merriken v. Cressman*, 1973).

Screening results also may be misused in planning interventions. According to one (hopefully erroneous) news report, a midwestern school district used results of a behavior checklist as the basis for placement of students in an alternative education program or expulsion ("School Psychologists," 1999). In our opinion, when students come to the attention of school staff because of warning signs or troubling behaviors, ethically and legally the most appropriate course of action is to work with parents to ensure their son or daughter is seen for evaluation by a qualified professional. Intervention with youth at risk for violence should be planned by professionals with expertise in working with troubled youth, in collaboration with the parents and the student. Removal of students from their regular education environment or denying school access on the basis of a checklist would likely be viewed as impermissible in a court of law.

We concur with Mulvey and Cauffmann's conclusion that efforts to reduce the likelihood of school crime and violence should focus on fostering a positive, supportive school climate and healthy student-school relationships, rather than unproven and potentially harmful attempts to identify future school shooters. "Students who are committed to school, feel that they belong, and trust the administration are less likely to commit violent acts than those who are uninvolved, alienated, or mistrustful" (2001, p. 800). Furthermore, when students feel connected to school and an atmosphere of mutual trust and respect exists among students, teachers, and administrators, the "critical link between those who often know when trouble is brewing and those who can act to prevent it" has a chance to develop (Mulvey & Cauffmann, 2001, p. 801). (Also see Brock, Lazarus, & Jimerson, 2002.)

HARASSMENT AND DISCRIMINATION

Federal antidiscrimination law protects students from harassment and hate crimes based on race, color, national origin, sex, and disability. Title VI of the Civil Rights Act of 1964 prohibits discrimination based on race, color, or national origin in programs or activities receiving federal financial assistance and makes schools responsible for taking reasonable steps to remedy racial harassment of students. Similarly, Title IX of the Education Amendments of 1972 prohibits discrimination on the basis of gender and makes schools responsible for taking reasonable steps to remedy sexual harassment of students. Section 504 and the Rehabilitation Act of 1964 and Title II of the Americans with Disabilities Act of 1990 prohibit discrimination based on disability. Federal statutory law does not currently protect public school students from discrimination or harassment based on sexual orientation. However, as evident from the ruling in *Nabozny v. Podlesny* (Case 9–4), harassment on the basis of sexual orientation may violate state laws or the U.S. Constitution.

Exhibit 9–2 summarizes three court cases involving the failure of schools to protect students from harassment and discrimination in school.

Exhibit 9–2. Three Cases Involving Harassment and Discrimination

Case 9–2

In 1999, the U.S. Supreme Court heard Davis v. Monroe County Board of Education, *a lawsuit filed against a school district under Title IX. The case was brought by the mother of a girl who, as a fifth grader, was subjected to a prolonged pattern of sexual harassment by one of her classmates. The unwanted sexual advances included attempts to touch the girl's breasts and genital areas and statements such as "I want to get in bed with you" and "I want to feel your boobs" (p. 1666). The girl reported each incident to her mother and classroom teacher. The teacher and school administrators did not respond to complaints from the mother; the school did not take steps to stop the harassment by disciplining the boy or separating the two (e.g., changing the girl's seat in class so she did not have to sit next to him); and the teacher did not allow other girls to report their complaints about the boy to the principal. The boy eventually was charged and convicted in juvenile court of sexual battery against the girl.*

Exhibit 9–2. *(Continued)*

Case 9–2 *(Continued)*

The Supreme Court ruled that Title IX applies to student-on-student sexual harassment. In her opinion, Justice O'Connor stated that "damages are not available for simple acts of teasing and name-calling among school children" but rather for behavior "so severe, pervasive, and objectively offensive" (p. 1675) that it denies its victims the equal access to education as guaranteed under Title IX. She went on to state that the school officials must have known of the harassment and, acting with "deliberate indifference," failed to take reasonable steps to stop it. The case was returned to a lower court for determination of the school district's liability.

Case 9–3

In 1998, the United States District Court for the Central District of California issued a ruling in Davison v. Santa Barbara High School, *a case in which the school district was sued because of alleged racial discrimination in violation of Title VI and Section 1983 and subsequently moved to have the case dismissed. This lawsuit concerned an 11th grade African-American student, Cheron, who was the target of racial harassment at school. For example, classmates placed a drawing of an African-American person hanging from a tree by a rope around the neck on Cheron's desk, with "Sharoon" (a combination of "Cheron" and "coon") written next to the hanging body. When Cheron and her parents complained to the vice principal, they were promised an investigation, but nothing was done. The school had a history suggesting a racially hostile environment. Prior incidents included racially offensive graffiti on students lockers, racially derogatory remarks to other students, and the circulation of racist literature by white supremacist groups on campus. Furthermore, evidence suggested that school administrators knew about the racially hostile environment, but the district failed to take any action to remedy the problems. The Court determined not to dismiss Cheron's Title VI claim and that the district was not immune from liability for claims under Title VI.*

Exhibit 9–2. *(Continued)*

Case 9–4

In 1996, the United States Court of Appeals for the Seventh Circuit issued its ruling in Nabozny v. Podlesny. *This case concerned Jamie, a boy who was harassed continually and physically abused by his fellow students throughout his middle school and high school years because he is homosexual. Classmates referred to him as "faggot" and "queer." In seventh grade, two students performed a "mock rape" on him in science class in front of 20 other students who looked on and laughed. When Jamie reported the incident, the principal told him that "boys will be boys" and that he should expect such treatment from his fellow students if he is going to be openly gay. No action was taken against the students involved. In eighth and ninth grades, Jamie suffered assaults in the school bathroom, including an incident in which he was pushed into a urinal and urinated on by his attackers. In tenth grade, he was pelted with steel nuts and bolts. That same year, he was beaten in school by 8 boys while other students looked on and laughed. When Jamie reported the incident, the school official in charge of discipline laughed and told him that he deserved such treatment because he is gay. Jamie later collapsed from internal bleeding that resulted from the beating. Although a school counselor encouraged administrators to take steps to protect Jamie and discipline the perpetrators, nothing was done.*

For more than four years, Jamie and his parents repeatedly asked school officials to protect him and to punish his assailants. Despite the fact that the school had a policy of investigating and punishing student-on-student sexual harassment, the administrators turned a deaf ear to Jamie's requests. Jamie eventually filed suit against several school officials and the district under Section 1983 alleging, among other claims, that his 14th Amendment rights to equal protection had been violated by school officials because they denied him the protection extended to other students. The court concluded that it would allow a lawsuit for damages against school officials because, if the facts presented were true, school officials had violated Jamie's 14th Amendment right to equal protection by failing to protect him from harassment to the same extent as other students because he is gay. The court also concluded that the law establishing the defendant's liability was sufficiently clear for the defendants to know that their conduct was unconstitutional.

The Supreme Court ruling in *Davis* (Case 9–2) along with the court ruling in *Davidson* (Case 9–3) suggest that, to avoid liability under federal antidiscrimination legislation, schools must take reasonable steps to prevent student-on-student harassment based on race, color, national origin, sex, and disability. The court in *Nabozny* (Case 9–4) indicated that, under the 14th Amendment of the Constitution, school personnel must take reasonable steps to prevent student-on-student harassment based on sexual orientation. Such preventative actions are necessary to ensure an environment in which all children have equal opportunities to learn, and because student-on-student harassment may be a precursor to even more serious acts of sexual assault or physical violence (see U.S. Department of Education & Bias Crimes Task Force of the National Association of Attorneys General, 1999).

Consistent with these court rulings, federal antidiscrimination legislation, and ethical principles regarding nondiscrimination, safe school plans should include policies to ensure that students and staff are free from verbal abuse and intimidation based on race, color, national origin, sex, disability, and sexual orientation. However, in developing and applying policies to prevent harassment, schools must take care to avoid violating student First Amendment rights to free speech and expression. (See U.S. Department of Education & Bias Crimes Task Force of the National Association of Attorneys General, 1999, for guidance in developing appropriate policies.)

As noted in Chapter 1, school psychologists have an ethical responsibility to help ensure that all youth can attend school, learn, and develop their personal identity in an environment free from discrimination, harassment, violence, and abuse (NASP, 1999). As systems-level consultants, school psychologists can help to develop and implement school policies, procedures, and programs to protect students from harassment and discrimination. Through advocacy and education of staff and students, we can work to foster a school climate that promotes not only understanding and acceptance of, but a respect for and valuing of individual differences. (For additional information, see U.S. Department of Education & Bias Crimes Task Force of the National Association of Attorneys General, 1999; and Henning-Stout, James, & Macintosh, 2000).

OTHER PUPILS WITH SPECIAL NEEDS

In the last portion of this chapter, we discuss the ethical-legal issues associated with public schooling for three other groups of pupils with special needs: children with limited English proficiency, gifted and talented pupils, and students with communicable diseases.

Children with Limited English Proficiency

In 1974, the Supreme Court decided a landmark case, *Lau v. Nichols,* concerning the education of children with limited English proficiency (LEP). This case was based on a class action suit filed by non-English-speaking Chinese students in the San Francisco Unified School District. At that time, more than half of the LEP Chinese pupils were taught solely in English, with no supplemental instruction in the English language. Furthermore, proficiency in English was a requirement for high school graduation. The plaintiffs in this case claimed that the school's practice was a denial of equal opportunity under the 14th Amendment.

The case was decided on statutory grounds (Civil Rights Act of 1964), rather than the equal protection clause of the 14th Amendment. The 1964 Civil Rights Act prohibits discrimination in programs receiving federal assistance. In his decision in favor of the plaintiffs, Justice Douglas wrote "there is no equality of treatment merely by providing students with the same facilities, textbooks, teachers, and curriculum; for students who do not understand English are effectively foreclosed from meaningful education" (*Lau v. Nichols,* 1974, p. 566).

Lau v. Nichols has been interpreted to mean that schools must provide assistance or "take affirmative steps" to ensure that children with limited English proficiency have access to a meaningful education. It is *not* seen as requiring bilingual instruction for each LEP child.

Thus, no federal mandate requires bilingual education for the LEP child. However, in 1968, the Bilingual Education Act was added as an amendment to the Elementary and Secondary Education Act of 1965 (Pub. L. No. 100-297), providing funds for bilingual education. Title III of the No Child Left Behind Act of 2001 now provides funds for language instruction for limited English proficient and immigrant students. Part A of Title III is the English Acquisition, Language Enhancement, and Academic Achievement Act (Pub. L. No. 107-110 §§ 3101-2102). The purpose of this portion of the statute is to provide funds to help children develop proficiency in English while meeting state academic content and achievement standards. Each state is given the flexibility to implement the research-based language instructional programs it believes to be most effective for teaching English, with the goal of preparing students to enter all-English instruction settings. It requires schools to demonstrate increased English proficiency of limited-English-proficient children each year.

School psychologists who serve children with limited English proficiency need to maintain up-to-date knowledge of best practices in assessment and instruction of the LEP child (see Lopez & Gopaul-McNicol, 1997; Paredes Scribner, 2002).

Gifted and Talented Pupils

No federal legislation requires schools to provide specialized education to gifted and talented students. In 1988, the Jacob K. Javits Gifted and Talented Students Education Act was passed (part of ESEA). This legislation provided funds for programs and projects designed to meet the special instructional needs of gifted and talented students. The new Jacob K. Javits Gifted and Talented Students Education Act of 2001 (Pub. L. No. 107-110 §§ 5461-5466) reaffirms the purposes of the 1988 Act. The identification and provision of services to gifted and talented students who may not be identified and served through traditional assessment methods is a funding priority (e.g., pupils with limited English proficiency and those from economically disadvantaged backgrounds). The Act also establishes a National Research Center for Research for the Education of Gifted and Talented Children and Youth.

Many disagreements exist about how to identify gifted and talented children and how to provide them effective educational programs (see Callahan, 1997; Rizza & McIntosh, 2001). School psychologists involved in the identification of gifted and talented students and the development of instructional programs are obligated to keep abreast of current literature in this area.

Students with Communicable Diseases

State and local school boards have the power and authority to adopt regulations to safeguard the health and safety of students. Schools may require vaccinations or immunizations prior to school attendance, and they may deny school access to children who pose a health threat to others (Reutter, 1994). The difficulty with serious long-term communicable diseases is in determining whether the health threat posed by the infected child is significant enough to outweigh the child's right to schooling in the least restrictive and most normal setting. Because of current interest and concern, the discussion here focuses on students with acquired immunodeficiency syndrome (AIDS)/human immunodeficiency virus (HIV), but the issues raised are pertinent to other communicable diseases (e.g., hepatitis B). We discuss AIDS/HIV as a handicapping condition under Section 504 of the Rehabilitation Act of 1973 and IDEA, and the obligation of school personnel to safeguard the privacy of pupils with communicable diseases.

AIDS and the Rehabilitation Act of 1973

Initially, some disagreement existed about whether Section 504 provides protection against discriminatory treatment for an individual with a communicable disease. However, in *School Board of Nassau County, Florida v. Arline* (1987), the Supreme Court made it clear that a person with a communicable disease is eligible for protection under Section 504. *Arline* was a case concerning a teacher dismissed from her job after she suffered a relapse of tuberculosis. In *Arline,* the Supreme Court judged it necessary to conduct a two-step individualized inquiry to determine whether a person with a communicable disease is otherwise qualified under Section 504 (1987, p. 1131).

The two-step inquiry outlined in *Arline* suggests that in determining whether a pupil is otherwise qualified, it is first necessary to evaluate whether the student poses *a significant risk of transmission* of the disease to others in the school setting. This part of the inquiry must be based on medical judgment and include consideration of the nature, duration, and severity of the risk and the probabilities the disease will be transmitted and cause varying degrees of harm. The second step in evaluating whether a student with a contagious disease is "otherwise qualified" is to evaluate, in light of the medical findings, whether the school can reasonably accommodate the pupil. A pupil who poses a significant risk of communicating an infectious disease to others in school is not otherwise qualified to be placed in the regular school setting if reasonable accommodation will not eliminate that risk.

At this time, court rulings have specifically found that pupils with AIDS or AIDS-related complex are handicapped within the meaning of Section 504 (e.g., *Doe v. Belleville Public School District No. 118,* 1987; *Martinez v. The School Board of Hillsborough County, Florida,* 1987; *Thomas v. Atascadero Unified School District,* 1987). Thus, schools that receive federal assistance may not discriminate against any otherwise qualified school child with AIDS/HIV. *If a significant risk of transmission would still exist in spite of reasonable efforts by the school to accommodate the infected child, then the pupil is not "otherwise qualified," and removal from the normal classroom setting is permissible* (*Thomas,* 1987).

Arline and other court rulings (e.g., *District 27 Community School Board v. Board of Education of the City of New York,* 1986) suggest that the decision of whether a child with AIDS or similar communicable disease should be excluded from the normal school setting must be made on a case-by-case basis. There appears to be some consensus among the Centers for Disease Control (CDC), National Education Association, and APA's Task Force on Pediatric AIDS regarding the appropriate decision-making process. All recommend a team approach to decision making. CDC suggests the team be composed of the child's physician and parent or guardian, along with school health personnel.

The CDC's recommended guidelines for prevention of HIV transmission in day care, school, and athletics can be retrieved from their Web site (http://www.cdc.gov/; also Simmonds & Chanock, 1993). Simmonds and Chanock, authors of the recommended guidelines, suggest consideration of the following factors in placement decisions: the child's propensity for aggressive biting, the likelihood of uncontrollable bleeding episodes, the presence of oozing skin lesions that cannot be covered, and the child's immune function. No cases of HIV transmission in day-care settings or schools have been reported and, worldwide, only one case of HIV transmission attributed to sports has been reported. Simmonds and Chanock conclude that, for most school-age children with HIV infection, the normal classroom setting is appropriate. Decisions regarding participation in contact sports should be made on a case-by-case basis (see CDC guidelines for considerations).

AIDS and IDEA

Children with AIDS/HIV do not qualify for special education and related services under the "other health impairment" classification of IDEA-Part B unless the disease adversely affects educational performance. As noted in *Doe v. Belleville Public School District No. 118* (1987), "Based on the Department of Education's opinions and the tenor of the statutory language, the Court concludes that EAHCA [IDEA] would apply to AIDS victims *only* if their physical condition is such that it adversely affects their educational performance (i.e., their ability to learn and to do the required classroom work)" (p. 345) (also *District 27*, 1986).

Pupil Privacy

Schools must protect the privacy of students with AIDS or other communicable diseases. Knowledge that a student is infected should be confined to those persons with a direct need to know. School personnel also must keep abreast of state policies regarding the disclosure of information about students with communicable diseases. In Michigan, for example, the passing of information about a person with a serious communicable disease by school personnel is a felony punishable by a prison term of up to three years and a $5,000 fine, or both (Public Act 488, Section 5131 [10]).

The School Psychologist and Pupils with AIDS/HIV

School psychologists potentially can serve a number of important consultation roles with regard to students with AIDS/HIV or other serious communicable diseases. School psychologists can work closely with school and community health professionals in promoting AIDS education and, more generally, health education in the schools. Practitioners also may develop expertise on the psychological aspects of serious childhood disease and provide consultation to teachers as well as supportive counseling to enhance the psychological well-being of infected children and their families. (For additional information, see Wodrich, Swerdlik, Chenneville, & Landau, 1999).

CONCLUDING COMMENTS

As Dawson observed some time ago, "school psychologists are often in a position to influence educational policy and administrative practices" (1987, p. 349). Maintaining up-to-date knowledge of school policies and practices that have an impact on the welfare of children and sharing that expertise in consultation with school principals and other decision makers, "may enable school psychologists to effect organizational change that can have a positive impact on large numbers of children" (Dawson, 1987, p. 348).

STUDY AND DISCUSSION

Questions for Chapter 9

1. Under IDEA, must special education students participate in statewide assessment programs? May schools require special education students to pass a minimum competency test prior to the award of a high school diploma?
2. Is the use of paddling (spanking) for disciplinary purposes in the schools constitutionally permissible?
3. What strategies does a school have under IDEA for handling a special education student who violates school rules? What is a manifest determination review?
4. Are public schools required to provide bilingual instruction under federal law?
5. Do gifted children have a right to an individualized and appropriate education under federal law?
6. Do children with AIDS/HIV qualify for special education? Under what circumstances does Section 504 allow schools to remove students with AIDS from the regular classroom?

Chapter 10

RESEARCH IN THE SCHOOLS: ETHICAL AND LEGAL ISSUES

In this chapter we explore the ethical and legal aspects of research in the schools. There are a number of sources of guidance in the conduct of research with human participants. The codes of ethics of both the American Psychological Association (APA) and the National Association of School Psychologists (NASP) include standards for research. In recognition of some of the special problems posed by research with children, the Society for Research in Child Development (SRCD) also developed ethical standards specifically for research with children (SRCD, 1990/1991). *Ethical Principles in the Conduct of Research with Human Participants* (RHP) (APA, 1982), published by APA, is an older text, but it continues to be a useful resource for identifying and understanding fundamental principles. More recently, APA published *Ethics in Research with Human Participants* (Sales & Folkman, 2000), a book with chapters contributed by experts in research ethics. Chapter topics include moral foundations, planning research, recruitment of participants, informed consent, privacy and confidentiality, and authorship, among others.

The National Research Act of 1974 (Pub. L. No. 93-348) outlines federal policies for research with human participants. It is interesting to note that the basic elements of APA's *Ethical Principles in the Conduct of Research with Human Participants* and federal policies for research with human participants can be traced back to the Nuremberg Code, a judicial summary made at the war trials of Nazi physicians who conducted medical experiments on war prisoners and were indicted for crimes against humanity (Keith-Spiegel, 1983).

The National Research Act mandated the formation of the National Commission for the Protection of Human Subjects of Biomedical and Behavioral Science Research. One of the charges to the commission was to identify the basic ethical principles that should underlie the conduct of research involving human subjects; its second charge was to develop guidelines to assure that research involving human participants is conducted in accordance with those principles. In 1979, the commission published *The Belmont Report: Ethical Principles and Guidelines for the*

Protection of Human Subjects of Biomedical and Behavioral Research. In *The Belmont Report,* three broad ethical principles relevant to research with human subjects were identified:

1. *Respect for persons*—the obligation to respect the autonomy of individuals and protect individuals with diminished autonomy;
2. *Beneficence*—the obligation to do no harm, to maximize possible benefits and minimize possible harm; and
3. *Justice*—the obligation to ensure that all persons share equally in the burdens and benefits of research.

The Belmont Report also included specific guidelines for the protection of human subjects. These guidelines were the basis for the regulations regarding the protection of human research participants issued by the Department of Health and Human Services (HHS) in 1981. Additional protections for children were added to the regulations in 1983 (45 C.F.R. Subtitle A, Part 46). Only institutions receiving federal research support are legally required to comply with the rules and regulations drafted under the National Research Act. However, as DeMers and Bersoff note, researchers should be familiar with the Act's regulations because they "reflect current legal opinion" of appropriate conduct in research activity (1985, p. 333).

COMPETENCE, RESPONSIBILITY, AND WELFARE OF PARTICIPANTS

The broad ethical principles of professional competence and responsibility (responsible caring) and respect for the dignity and welfare of persons provide the foundation for ethical decision making in the conduct of research in the schools.

Professional Competence and Responsibility

In all types of data-gathering activities, whether it is decision-oriented action research or more basic research, school psychologists are ethically obligated to conduct research "as well as they know how" (RHP, p. 15). As Koocher and Keith-Spiegel (1998) have noted, poorly designed research is likely to result in invalid and perhaps misleading findings. Misleading findings may result in the introduction or continuation of ineffective practices and a potential disservice to children, teachers, parents, and others. Poorly designed studies also are unfair to research participants who volunteer in hopes of contributing to the knowledge base of psychology and education.

For these reasons, school psychologists with limited expertise in research design should consult with experienced researchers to assure a planned study is methodologically sound.

In conducting research, the responsibility for the ethical treatment of study participants rests with the individual research investigator. He or she is responsible for the actions of all members of the research team (collaborators and assistants), although each team member also bears responsibility for his or her own actions (SRCD Introduction).

Welfare of the Participant

In planning research and data collection, priority must always be given to the welfare of the participant (RHP, p. 18; SRCD, Introduction). The researcher is obligated ethically to identify any potential risks for the research participants and collect data in ways that will avoid or minimize such risks (RHP, p. 17; also SRCD Principle 1; 45 C.F.R. § 46.111). The five major types of risk are physical, psychological, social, legal, and economic. Potential risks of research participation may include pain or physical injury, exposure to stressful procedures and possible emotional discomfort or harm, invasion of privacy, loss of community standing, exposure to criminal prosecution, loss of employment or potential monetary gain, denial of potentially beneficial treatment, and violations of confidentiality.

Ethical and legal standards for research are consistent in recommending that the researcher ask the advice of others regarding the acceptability of proposed research procedures (NASP-PPE, IV, F, #2). The greater the potential risks, the greater the obligation to seek advice and observe stringent safeguards. The SRCD recommends peer review of any and all research involving children (SRCD Introduction). Consistent with guidelines outlined in The National Research Act, colleges and universities typically have an institutional review board (IRB) that evaluates the ethical acceptability of research proposed by faculty and students. Policies and procedures regarding review and approval of research activities in the public schools vary; some school districts have research review boards. School psychologists are well advised to consult with principals, teachers, parents, and others about the acceptability of proposed studies, and obtain formal school district approval of proposed research through appropriate administrative channels.

This chapter explores informed consent for research; the risks of invasion of privacy, exposure to stress or harm and denial of beneficial treatment; post data-collection responsibilities; concealment and deception; confidentiality of data; research with ethnic and linguistic minority populations; and scientific misconduct.

Informed Consent

Case 10–1 is a summary of the circumstances that prompted Sylvia Merriken, the mother of an eighth grader named Michael, to file a complaint against the school system that was subsequently decided in a federal district court in Pennsylvania in 1973. Although this incident occurred 30 years ago, it is not hard to imagine the occurrence of similar events today as school districts continue to struggle with the problem of substance abuse.

Case 10–1

School administrators, teachers, and members of the school board were alarmed by reports of high levels of drug abuse by students in the school district. They decided to hire a private consultant in hopes of developing an effective drug abuse prevention program for junior high students. The initial phase of the program involved research to identify eighth graders at risk for drug abuse. As part of the research phase, questionnaires were administered to eighth graders, their teachers and classmates. Students were asked to rate themselves on a number of personality variables, such as level of self-confidence, and they were asked about their relationship to their parents. (For example, Did one or both of your parents hug and kiss you goodnight when you were small? Do they make you feel unloved?) Teachers were asked to identify students with antisocial behavior patterns, and students were asked to identify classmates with problem behavior patterns. The private consultant planned to collect and analyze the data and prepare a list of "potential drug abusers" for the school superintendent that could be used to identify pupils in need of drug prevention therapy. The therapy program would use peer-pressure techniques to combat potential drug abuse, and teachers would serve as the therapists. A letter was sent to parents informing them of the diagnostic testing and prevention program and assuring confidentiality of the results. Parent silence in response to the letter was construed as consent for their child to participate (adapted from Merriken v. Cressman, 1973; Bersoff, 1983).

Sylvia Merriken's complaint alleged that the school's drug abuse prevention program, particularly the research phase, violated her constitutional rights and those of her son, including the right to privacy. A central issue in this case was the school's failure to seek informed consent for the collection of personal, private information about Michael and his family. As mentioned in Chapter 3, case law and government regulations concur that waiver of an individual's rights, such as the right to privacy, must be based on informed consent. The key elements of informed consent are that it must be knowing, competent, and voluntary. The court held that the school's program violated Sylvia Merriken's right to privacy, and an injunction was issued.

Consent Must Be Knowingly Given

Informed consent in research is a written agreement between the researcher and research participant that outlines the obligations and responsibilities of each party. The investigator informs the participant of all aspects of the research that may be expected to influence willingness to participate and answers all questions about the nature of the research procedures (EP 8.02; SRCD 2, 3; 45 C.F.R. § 46.116).

Who Gives Consent?

The individual giving consent to volunteer for research must be legally competent to do so (Bersoff, 1983). In the HHS protections for children involved as research subjects, a distinction is made between *consent,* what a person may do autonomously, and *permission,* what a person may do on behalf of another, as when a parent or guardian grants permission for a child to participate in research (46 C.F.R. § 46.402). When research involves children (minors) as study participants, legal standards (HHS) and codes of ethics (SRCD 2, 3) suggest the researcher seek informed consent or permission of the parent or legal guardian for the child to participate, and the child's assent to participate, if appropriate. Assent is defined as "a child's affirmative agreement to participate in research" (46 C.F.R. § 46.402). This means that the child "shows some form of agreement to participate without necessarily comprehending the full significance of the research necessary to give informed consent" (SRCD 2). HHS regulations note that a child's ability to make informed decisions about participation in research depends on his or her age and maturity (46 C.F.R. § 46.408).

Ferguson (1978) has observed that individual level of cognitive development and the complexity of the research situation must be taken into account in determining a child's capacity to make choices regarding research participation. She suggests that informed parental permission is both necessary and sufficient for research with infants and toddlers. The preschool-age child, however, is able to understand explanations stated in here-and-now concrete terms, with a straightforward description of what participation means for the child. The researcher is consequently obligated to seek both parental permission and affirmative assent for the child of preschool age or older. Ferguson provides some helpful guidelines for explaining research to children of various ages (1978, pp. 118–120).

SRCD suggests that the informed consent of any person whose interaction with the child is the subject of the study also be obtained (Principle 4). For example, a study of the association between children's positive or negative feelings about their classroom teacher and academic achievement would require parental permission, the child's assent to participate, and the teacher's informed consent.

Freedom from Coercion

The third characteristic of informed consent is that it must be voluntary. HHS guidelines specify that each research participant (the parent or legal representative in the case of a minor child) should be given "sufficient opportunity" to decide whether or not to choose to participate in the research, and should be informed that they may refuse to participate without incurring any penalty (46 C.F.R. § 46.116). The investigator also must respect the individual's freedom to discontinue participation at any time (EP 8.02; SRCD 2, 3, 4; 45 C.F.R. § 46.116). Consistent with the values of respect for self-determination and autonomy, researchers must attract consent and assent without coercion, duress, pressure, or undue enticement or influence (Koocher & Keith-Spiegel, 1998; also EP 8.06).

In the school setting, it is important to allow potential volunteers (e.g., pupils, teachers) the opportunity to decline to participate without embarrassment (SRCD 2, 3, 4). In the *Merriken v. Cressman* decision, Judge Davis noted that the school did not afford the students an opportunity to decline to participate without being marked for "scapegoating" and unpleasant treatment by peers (1973, p. 915).

It also is important to remember that researchers may not promise benefits from research participation unless they are able to ensure the promised outcomes (SRCD 8). For example, a researcher may not guarantee that participation in an experimental counseling group for overweight teens will result in weight loss for each participant, although weight loss might be identified as a possible benefit from participation.

Minimal Risk Research

Informed consent is not always needed for research in the schools. Whether it is needed depends on a number of factors including the purpose of the study, the research design and methodology, the protections afforded research participants, and the nature of the relationship between the investigator and the school system. Legal standards suggest that minimal risk research in public school settings probably does not require informed consent as long as information is recorded and reported in a way that individuals cannot be identified. Minimal risk research generally means that the study poses little likelihood of invasion of privacy, exposure to stress, or psychological or physical harm as a result of participation in the study.

HHS regulations exempt the following types of research from its informed consent requirements: "research conducted in established or commonly accepted educational settings, *involving normal educational practices*" and research involving "the use of *educational tests* (cognitive, diagnostic, aptitude, achievement)" if information taken from these sources is recorded in such a manner that subjects cannot be identified [italics added] (45 C.F.R. § 46.101). Similarly, RHP states that "Research participation that is incidental to systematic study of the effects of normal variations in a regular institutional program appears not to raise serious ethical concerns even when the principle of informed consent is compromised" (p. 45). Note that research involving psychological tests is not exempt from informed consent requirements under HHS regulations (DeMers & Bersoff, 1985). HHS regulations require informed parental consent before a pupil can be instructed to submit to psychological testing for research purposes.

The Protection of Pupil Privacy Act (PPRA) (as amended by Pub. L. No. 107–110 § 1061) requires local school districts that receive *any* federal funds to develop policies, in consultation with parents, to notify parents when the school intends to request one or more of the following types of information from students, or if nonemergency invasive physical examinations of students will be conducted: (1) political affiliations or beliefs of the student or the student's parent; (2) mental and psychological problems potentially embarrassing to the student or his or her family; (3) sex behavior and attitudes; (4) illegal, antisocial, self-incriminating, and demeaning behavior; (5) critical appraisals of other individuals with whom respondents have close family relationships; (6) legally recognized privileged and analogous relationships; (7) religious practices, affiliations, or beliefs of the student or student's parent; or (8) income, other than required by law to determine eligibility for participation in a program or for receiving financial assistance under a program. The parent of a student must be given the opportunity to inspect the survey, upon request, prior to its distribution. Parents also must be given the opportunity to have their student "opt out" of the information-gathering activity or physical examination. The standard for research activities funded by the Department of Education is more stringent: researchers may not gather the types of information listed above without written informed parent consent.

Research involving the study of existing school records also would be viewed as minimal risk research under HHS regulations as long as information is recorded in such a manner that subjects cannot be identified directly or through identifiers linked to the subjects (45 C.F.R. § 46.101). Similarly, under the Family Educational Rights and Privacy Act of 1974 (FERPA), organizations conducting studies *on behalf of the school* do not need parental consent for access to educational records for research purposes. However, under FERPA, informed parental consent is needed for the release of personally identifiable information from educational records if the research is not being conducted on behalf of the school.

As a general rule, when we put children at risk or treat them differently than one would normally expect in the schools, then the possibility of a "legally cognizable injury" is created, and informed consent must be obtained (DeMers & Bersoff, 1985, p. 332).

The Components of the Informed Consent Agreement

HHS has outlined a number of requirements for informed consent for research (46 C.F.R. § 46.116). The consent agreement is a written agreement but it may be presented orally to the individual giving consent. Oral presentation should be witnessed by a third party. The informed consent information must be presented in a language understandable to the participant or guardian granting permission for the child to participate, and the researcher may not include language that implies a release from ethical and legal responsibility to the subjects of the study.

The basic components of the informed consent agreement include the following: (a) a description of the nature and purpose of the research and the procedures and expected duration of participation; (b) a description of "any reasonably foreseeable risks or discomforts" for the participant; (c) a description of any potential benefits to the participant that can reasonably be expected; (d) a description of available alternative treatments that might be advantageous; (e) a description of the extent to which confidentiality of information will be maintained; (f) instructions concerning whom may be contacted to answer questions about the research; (g) a statement that participation is voluntary and that the participant may discontinue the study at any time without penalty; and (h) for studies that involve more than minimal risk, a description of any compensation and medical treatment available if injury occurs as a result of participation. SRCD guidelines also suggest that the professional and institutional affiliation of the researcher be identified (Principle 3). The consent form should be signed by the parent or guardian of a minor child, or the research participant if age 18 or older. Grunder (1978) recommends using reading-level determination formulas to evaluate the readability of the consent form to assure it is understandable.

EXPOSURE TO STRESS OR HARM AND DENIAL OF BENEFICIAL TREATMENT

Consistent with the principle of responsible caring, researchers take steps to protect study participants from physical and emotional discomfort, harm, and danger (RHP, p. 51; SRCD 1). We can think of no ethically permissible studies by school psychologists that involve exposing a study participant to harm and danger. Research on the use of medications in treatment of behavior or learning problems (e.g., the use of Ritalin in the treatment of hyperactivity) exposes the child to potentially dangerous medical side effects (see Chapter 7). Although data regarding the effects of medications might be gathered in the school setting, any research involving the administration of drugs must be conducted under the supervision of a physician knowledgeable of the necessary medical and legal safeguards (see RHP, 57–58).

Prior to beginning a study, the researcher is obligated to determine whether proposed research procedures are stressful and to explore ways to avoid or minimize stress by modifying the research methodology (SRCD 1). Psychological discomfort is likely to result from failure experiences; temptations to lie, cheat, or steal; or if the investigator asks the research participant to reveal personal information that is embarrassing, or perform disturbing tasks such as rating parents (RHP, pp. 58–59). The survey questions for students in the *Merriken* case, for example, were likely to be quite stressful for some eighth graders (see also Case 1–1).

In evaluating the acceptability of a study that places the participants at risk for discomfort, the researcher is obligated to seek the advice of others and carefully consider whether the potential benefits of the study outweigh the risks, often called a risk-benefit analysis (SRCD Introduction). The researcher must obtain fully informed consent for any study that exposes the subjects to potential discomfort or harm (RHP, p. 53). HHS guidelines suggest informed consent be sought for any research that exposes volunteers to risks greater than those ordinarily encountered in daily life (46 C.F.R. § 46.102).

Assessing the potential risks of research participation for children can be a difficult and complex task. The researcher is obligated to consider developmental factors, prior experiences, and individual characteristics of the study participants in evaluating children's vulnerability to research risk. The likelihood of distress, embarrassment, and diminished self-esteem should be evaluated within a developmental context. For example, after age 7 or 8, children have greater self-awareness and capacity to make inferences about the meaning of others' behavior, and consequently they become increasingly more sensitive to both explicit and implied judgments of their performance in research situations. There also are developmental changes with regard to embarrassment from intrusions on privacy. The privacy concerns of young children center on their bodies and possessions. As children mature, privacy concerns extend to include informational privacy, namely, a desire to keep private information about their peer group, activities, and interests. Adolescents are highly sensitive to privacy intrusions, and may view requests for personal information as intrusive and threatening (Thompson, 1990).

The researcher also must be alert to the fact that the data collection procedures may result in unanticipated discomfort or harm. It is important to monitor the research procedures, particularly when research involves children (SRCD, Introduction). Children are likely to be highly sensitive to failure, and "seemingly innocuous" questions may be stressful for some children (RHP, p. 59). If a research participant appears to show a stressful reaction to the procedures, the researcher is obligated "to correct these consequences" and should consider altering the data-collection procedures (SRCD 10).

In planning research investigations on the effectiveness of new treatments or interventions, school psychologists are obligated to select an alternative treatment known to be beneficial (a contrast group), rather than using a no-treatment control group, if at all feasible. If the new or experimental intervention is found to be effective, contrast or control group participants should be given access to the new treatment (RHP, p. 68; also see EP 8.02).

POST–DATA COLLECTION RESPONSIBILITIES

The investigator is obligated to end the data collection session with "a positive and appropriate debriefing" (RHP, p. 67). After the data are collected, the investigator provides the participant with information about the nature of the study and attempts to remove any misconceptions that participants may have (EP 8.08). The investigator also is obligated to remove or correct any undesirable consequences that result from research participation (RHP, p. 66; SRCD 10, 12). As Holmes (1976) has observed, stress is likely to occur when participants acquire an awareness of their own inadequacies and weaknesses as a result of participation in research. Researchers are obligated to introduce procedures to desensitize participants when this occurs; that is, the investigator must eliminate any distress that results from self-knowledge acquired as a result of research (Holmes, 1976).

As APA notes, there are special postexperimental responsibilities in research with children. The investigator must "ensure that the child leaves the research situation with no undesirable aftereffects of participation" (RHP, p. 66). This may mean "that certain misconceptions should not be removed or even that some new misconceptions should be induced. If children erroneously believe that they have done well on a research task, there may be more harm than good in trying to correct this misconception than in permitting it to remain" (RHP, p. 66). When children feel that they have done poorly, corrective efforts are needed. Such efforts might include introducing a special experimental procedure "to guarantee the child a final success experience" (RHP, p. 66).

Investigators also are obligated to consider any long-range after-effects from participation in research. Research that introduces the possibility of irreversible after-effects should not be conducted (RHP, p. 59). In *Merriken,* Judge Davis admonished the school for its failure to acknowledge the risks of harm introduced by its drug prevention program. He noted that, on the basis of responses to an unvalidated survey, a student could be erroneously labeled as a "potential drug abuser," possibly resulting in stigma, peer rejection, or a self-fulfilling prophesy and be subjected to group therapy sessions conducted by untrained and inexperienced therapists (1973, p. 920).

CONCEALMENT AND DECEPTION

Case 10–2 provides an illustration of deception and concealment in research.

Case 10–2

Carrie Johnson, school psychologist, decided to conduct a study of differences in teacher behaviors toward regular education and mainstreamed special education pupils to fulfill the research requirements for her Psy.D. degree. She planned to observe time-samples of reading instruction in five second-grade classrooms in the district and code the number of positive and negative comments the teachers made to regular and special education pupils. She was concerned that knowledge of the purpose of the study might alter teacher behavior, so she misinformed the teachers that

Case 10–2 *(Continued)*

the purpose of the research was to study the peer interaction patterns of special education students. The findings from her study showed that all teachers observed gave special education students more negative and fewer positive comments during reading instruction when compared with their regular education classmates. Carrie placed a xeroxed form letter in the faculty mailbox of each teacher-participant and building principal, thanking them for their help and briefly summarizing her findings. Two of the teacher-participants were angry about the deception. They demanded their observation data be destroyed, and they complained to the school administration. A third teacher was dismayed and embarrassed by her biased treatment of students with disabilities and considered abandoning her career in teaching.

Concealment

The nature and purpose of a study may require a compromise of the principle of fully informed consent (RHP, p. 36; SRCD 6). The term concealment is used to refer to studies in which the investigator gathers information about individuals without their knowledge or consent; that is, the study subject may not know he or she has participated in a research study (RHP, p. 36). These studies often involve covert (hidden) or unobtrusive observation. The National Research Act regulations and APA's code of ethics (EP 8.5; RHP, p. 39) suggest that covert or unobtrusive observational studies can be considered minimal risk research and exempt from informed consent requirements as long as data are recorded so that subjects cannot be identified directly or indirectly, the behaviors observed are "public," the research does not deal with sensitive or illegal behaviors (sexual behaviors, drug abuse), the experience of the person is not affected by the research (i.e., the research procedures are nonreactive), and the person is not put at risk in the event of a breach of confidentiality (criminal or civil liability, financial damage or loss of employment) (45 C.F.R. § 46.101; RHP, pp. 36–39). The research described in Case 10–2 appears to present minimal risk for the pupils observed in the study.

Deception

The term deception is typically used to refer to studies in which the participants are misinformed about the purpose of the study or the meaning of the participant's behavior (RHP, p. 40). Carrie Johnson's study illustrates the use of deception with the teacher-participants; she deliberately misinformed them of the purpose of the study so as to avoid altering their typical teaching behaviors.

Studies that involve deception are controversial. The investigator has a responsibility to seek peer review and carefully evaluate whether the use of deception is justified by the value of the study and to consider alternative procedures (EP 8.07; RHP, p. 41; SRCD 6). Fisher and Fryberg (1994) suggest researchers ask nonparticipants from the same subject pool about the acceptability of the deception before proceeding with the study. Another alternative is forewarning subjects; that is, gaining the informed consent of participants to use deception as part of the research procedure. Some researchers maintain that the intentional use of deception with children is never justified as "children may be left with the distinct impression that lying is an *appropriate* way for adults to achieve their goals" (Keith-Spiegel, 1983, p. 201).

If, after consultation with others, it is determined that the use of deception is necessary and justified by the value of the study, the researcher incurs additional obligations to the study participants. After the completion of the data collection, the researcher must fully inform each participant of the nature of the deception, detect and correct any stressful after-effects, and provide an opportunity for the participant to withdraw from the study after the deception is revealed (RHP, p. 41). In studies involving deception, the postexperimental debriefing involves explaining to participants that they were deceived as part of the research procedures (EP 8.08, SRCD 6) and dealing with any resultant feelings.

In the incident described, Carrie did not fulfill her postexperimental obligations to the teacher-participants. An individual or small group meeting was needed to explain the nature of the deception, introduce appropriate desensitization procedures, and assure the confidentiality of the data gathered. It would have been beneficial for the teacher-participants to know that their differential treatment of low-achieving students is "normal" teacher behavior and most likely an unconscious response to student behavior—that is, student behavior may condition teacher behavior (Brophy & Good, 1974). Offering to work with teachers to help modify these behaviors would have been appropriate and in the best interests of everyone involved.

CONFIDENTIALITY OF DATA

Codes of ethics, case law, and legal regulations are consistent in requiring a clear prior agreement between the investigator and research participant about who will have access to information gathered during research and what types of information, if any, will be shared with others. "Information obtained about the research participant during the course of an investigation is confidential unless otherwise agreed on in advance. When the possibility exists that others may obtain access to such information, this possibility, together with the plans for protecting confidentiality, is explained to the participants as part of the procedure for obtaining informed consent" (RHP, p. 70; also SRCD 11).

In his *Merriken* decision, Judge Davis noted that the school made a blanket promise to parents that survey results would be confidential. However, documents describing the program indicated that, to the contrary, it was anticipated that a "massive data bank" would be developed, and information would be shared with guidance counselors, athletic coaches, PTA officers, and school board members, among others (p. 916). The judge also noted that the list of "potential drug abusers" could be subpoenaed by law enforcement authorities. Investigators are obligated to forewarn research participants of any such risks of violation of confidentiality.[1]

RHP recommends removing identifying information from research protocols immediately (p. 82). If a coding key that links the individual to his or her data is necessary because of the nature of the research, it should be kept in a secure location. The use of any permanent recordings during data collection (e.g., videotapes) increases the risk of loss of anonymity. The researcher should seek informed consent to create and maintain such records (RHP, p. 37; also EP 8.03).

Codes of ethics and standards do not prohibit the sharing of research information if informed consent to do so is obtained. Information obtained in the course of research (e.g., test scores) may be helpful in educational planning for an individual child. However, it is of critical importance that researchers in the schools have a clear prior understanding with all parties involved (pupils, parents, teachers, administrators, support staff) regarding what research information will be shared and with whom and what information will not be disclosed (RHP, pp. 70–71). School administrators may believe they have a legitimate right to information gathered about individual teachers, and parents are likely to believe they have a right to information about their child's performance in a research situation unless they are advised ahead of time that the research information gathered will be confidential.

Student researchers are advised against offering to share information from psychological tests with parents or teachers. The interpretation of

[1] Investigators planning research on sensitive topics such as drug abuse may apply to HHS for a confidentiality certificate to protect subject identity from disclosure in legal proceedings. (See Folkman, 2000.)

psychological tests by students outside the supervised internship setting raises ethical-legal questions regarding the independent practice of psychology without certification or licensure (see also SRCD 13).

In unusual circumstances, a researcher may choose to disclose confidential information deliberately for the protection of the research participant or the protection of others. "The protection afforded research participants by the maintenance of confidentiality may be compromised when the investigator discovers information that serious harm threatens the research participant or others" (RHP, 1982, p. 69). The researcher may uncover information about the participant that has important implications for his or her well-being, such as emotional or physical problems. Such situations are most likely rare in school settings. If deliberate disclosure is warranted, however, the research volunteer (parent or guardian of a minor child) should be counseled about the problem identified by someone qualified to interpret and discuss the information gathered and handle any resultant distress. If disclosure of information to a third party is anticipated, this also should be discussed with the research participant (or parent or guardian) (RHP, 1982, p. 72; also SRCD 9).

School psychologists must be sensitive to potential loss of confidentiality as a result of presentation or publication of research findings. As APA notes, there are rarely problems with loss of confidentiality when data on groups are published (RHP, p. 73). However, school psychology practitioners may be interested in presenting or publishing case studies. Often the data from case studies were obtained as part of the treatment plan and follow-up, and informed consent to use the data for research was not obtained. If a psychologist plans to present or publish case information, this should be discussed with the individuals involved (pupils, parents, teachers) and informed consent should be obtained. The researcher also should make a sincere effort to disguise the identity of the research participants (EP 4.07; SRCD 11).

It is usually appropriate to offer research participants a brief summary of the findings from the study based on the data from all study participants. This summary should preserve the anonymity of the participants and the confidentiality of the data gathered from individual participants.

RESEARCH WITH ETHNIC AND LINGUISTIC MINORITY POPULATIONS

In conducting research that involves ethnic and linguistic minority groups, researchers must give special consideration to the selection and recruitment of research participants, research methodology, evaluation of potential risks and benefits, and reporting of results. In the 1960s, a number of research investigations came to the attention of the U.S.

Congress in which poor, minority, and other vulnerable groups carried the burden of research, but were often denied its benefits. Perhaps the best known of these was the Tuskegee Study, conducted by the U.S. Public Health Service, in which 400 African American men with syphilis were observed until autopsy to determine the natural course of the disease. The study lasted from 1932 to 1972. The men were left untreated even when penicillin became available. According to White (2000), the facts of the Tuskegee Study were more complex than presented in the public forum (e.g., penicillin treatment typically was limited to early syphilis although many study participants had late-latent syphilis). However, growing concern about this and other research studies gave impetus to the formation of the National Commission for the Protection of Human Subjects of Biomedical and Behavior Science research (discussed earlier), and heightened awareness of the importance of the ethical principle of justice, namely, the obligation to ensure that all persons share equally in the burdens and benefits of research. In accordance with this principle, researchers must select and recruit participants in an equitable manner, or for reasons directly related to the research question, instead of selecting subjects because of their easy availability or tractability.

Researchers also have special obligations when planning research studies of ethnic and linguistic minorities. Non-minority researchers must be sensitive to the ways in which their own background and biases may impact how they conceptualize and design research studies (Rogers et al., 1999). In addition, it is critically important for researchers to have or to acquire knowledge of the culture of the minority group under study, including an understanding of how to convey respect for that culture in the conduct of research. Researchers are advised to seek input from members of the group being studied in planning the research project. This can help to ensure that the research targets the needs of the study population, that research questions and methods are culturally appropriate, and that risks and benefits are evaluated in light of the special circumstances of the group participating in the study (Gil & Bob, 1999).

In addition, researchers must be cautious in interpretation of findings. According to Atkinson, "we each have our own way of interpreting data based on the cultural lenses through which we view the world" (1993, p. 220). Again, seeking to understand the experiences and worldview of the study group, and seeking input from members of that group regarding the possible meaning of data, may help the researcher avoid inaccurate and biased interpretation (Gil & Bob, 1999). Also, in the dissemination of research, researchers should consider how their findings might be misrepresented, and how to minimize the likelihood their findings will result in unintended harm (Sieber, 2000).

SCIENTIFIC MISCONDUCT

Scientific misconduct here refers to reporting research findings in a biased or misleading way, fabricating or falsifying data, plagiarism, or taking credit for work that is not your own. Consistent with APA and NASP codes of ethics, school psychologists strive to collect and report research information so as to make an honest contribution to knowledge and minimize the likelihood of misinterpretation and misunderstanding. In publishing reports of their research, they acknowledge the limitations of their study, the existence of disconfirming data, and identify alternate hypotheses and explanations of their findings (EP Principle C; NASP-PPE, IV, F, #4).

The publication of scientific misinformation based on false or fabricated data is a serious form of misconduct that can potentially result in harm to others. In November 1988, Dr. Stephen Breuning, a psychopharmacologist, pleaded guilty to charges of fabricating research data. The charges followed an investigation of his research that reported improved functioning for mentally retarded children treated with Ritalin or Dexedrine, research that "helped shape drug treatment policy for mentally retarded" individuals in several states (Hostetler, 1988). This was the nation's first federal conviction for falsifying scientific data. Breuning was ordered to pay over $11,000.00 in restitution and was sentenced to 60 days in jail and 5 years probation (Coughlin, 1988). Breuning's case triggered much discussion of the need to protect the public from misinformation. Psychologists and others involved in investigating the case hoped that it would serve as a warning to others about the seriousness of falsifying data in scientific research (Hostetler, 1988, p. 5).

Another type of scientific misconduct is plagiarism. *Plagiarism* "occurs when the words, ideas, or contributions of others are appropriated in writing or speech without proper citation or acknowledgment" (McGue, 2000, p. 83). Psychologists are ethically and legally obligated to acknowledge the sources of their ideas when publishing or making a professional presentation (NASP-PPE, IV, F, #7; also EP 8.11; McGue, 2000). Both published and unpublished material that influenced the development of the manuscript or presentation materials must be acknowledged.

Finally, psychologists take credit "only for work they have actually performed or to which they have contributed" (EP 8.12). "Principal authorship and other publication credits accurately reflect the relative scientific or professional contributions of the individuals involved ... Minor contributions to the research or to the writing for publications are acknowledged appropriately, such as in footnotes or in an introductory statement" (EP 8.12). (See McGue, 2000)

CONCLUDING COMMENTS

As in other areas of service delivery, school psychologists can most likely avoid ethical-legal dilemmas in research by maintaining an up-to-date knowledge of relevant guidelines, careful planning of proposed research activities, and seeking consultation and advice from others when questions arise. School psychologists conducting research need to be knowledgeable of the organization and methodology of the school and to work within the organizational framework, taking care to build and maintain good public relations within and outside of the school community during all phases of a research project.

STUDY AND DISCUSSION

Questions for Chapter 10

1. Identify the key codes of ethics and legal documents that provide guidelines for research.
2. What is the single most important ethical consideration in conducting research?
3. Identify five types of potential risks for research participants.
4. What are the key elements of informed consent for research?
5. What is the difference between consent and assent for research participation?
6. We do not always seek children's assent for the provision of psychological services. Why should we seek their assent to participate in psychological research?
7. Do we always need informed parent consent for research in the schools? What is minimal risk research?

Discussion

In 2001, third and fifth graders in a California school participated in a study conducted by a school therapist as part of her graduate degree requirements. The consent form sent home to parents said nothing about the survey's content. Angry parents contacted the school after learning the survey asked children questions such as whether they were "thinking about having sex," "touching my private parts too much," and "thinking about touching other people's private parts"(Bowman, 2002).

(Continued)

What are the ethical and legal issues associated with this research situation? What risks for children are associated with participation in this study? What mechanisms to protect schoolchildren in human subjects research apparently failed in this situation? What are some ways researchers can evaluate whether their research designs and data gathering instruments are developmentally appropriate and appropriate in light of special characteristics (e.g., pupils with learning difficulties) that may heighten vulnerability to research risks? (See Thompson, 1990.)

VIGNETTES

1. Christa Jones, a second-year student in a school psychology program, administered IQ tests to children in area nursery schools as part of her thesis research. Two months after she completed the data collection, the director of one of the nursery schools requested IQ test information for a pupil she feels is delayed developmentally as a first step toward requesting a full evaluation of the child's developmental status and learning potential. How should Christa respond? What are the ethical-legal issues involved?

2. After seeing a newspaper article on how Internet chat rooms reduced feelings of isolation for some sexual minority youth, Brad Gilman, a school psychology student, decided to conduct his masters thesis research on the life stories of gay teens. To gather his data, he pretended to be a gay teen, entered several chat rooms popular among lesbian, gay, and bisexual youth, asked questions to prompt chat-room participants to share information about their lives, and then recorded their conversations verbatim. In his thesis write-up, he identified the chat rooms he had visited and included many direct quotes, attributing quotes to the speaker's undisguised online pseudonym. What are the ethical issues involved in this research project? (See Frankel & Siang, 1999.)

3. Marrisa Garcia, a school psychologist, was concerned about the failure of her district to successfully involve Hispanic families in home-school collaboration efforts. After receiving approval from her district and a small research grant from a private corporation, she began an interview study with Hispanic families to identify the barriers to their participation in school meetings, parent conferences, and school outreach activities.

Perhaps because she was of Hispanic descent and quite fluent in Spanish, Marrisa was able to establish rapport with families, gain their trust, and solicit their informed consent for research participation. During the interviews, Marrisa was surprised to learn that several of the families avoided involvement with the schools because one or more family member had entered the country illegally, and they feared detection. What are the ethical and legal issues associated with this research situation? (See Henning-Stout, 1996.)

4. In order to complete the requirements for her specialist degree, Shantelle Brown decided to conduct a study of the effectiveness of a drug education program in reducing substance abuse at the middle school level. She plans to individually interview middle school students to ask about their patterns of drug use before and after their participation in the new drug education program. What are the ethical and legal issues associated with a study of this type?

ACTIVITIES

If you are required to complete a research project as part of your program of graduate studies and the project will involve human subjects, obtain a copy of the application you must complete for review and approval of research by your university Institutional Review Board (IRB). Gather sample consent and assent forms from faculty who have conducted research projects with children.

Chapter 11

ETHICAL AND LEGAL ISSUES IN SUPERVISION

Supervision can occur in a variety of settings (school, hospital, university) and for a variety of different purposes (McIntosh & Phelps, 2000). For example, school psychologists may serve as supervisors of interns, of practitioners seeking full certification or licensure, and, in larger school districts with more than one psychologist, they may assume a supervisory role as lead psychologist or director of psychological services (Harvey & Struzziero, 2000). The goal of this chapter is to provide an introduction to some of the ethical and legal issues associated with field-based supervision of interns and beginning practitioners in a school setting. For comprehensive treatment of the topic of supervision in school psychology, readers are referred to Harvey and Struzziero's (2000) *Effective Supervision in School Psychology*.

For the purposes of the chapter, we will adopt McIntosh and Phelps' definition of supervision:

> Supervision is an interpersonal interaction between two or more individuals for the purpose of sharing knowledge, assessing professional competencies, and providing objective feedback with the terminal goals of developing new competencies, facilitating effective delivery of psychological services, and maintaining professional competencies (2000, pp. 33–34).

Unlike consultation, in supervision the supervisor has ultimate responsibility for client welfare (Knapp & VandeCreek, 1997). The supervisor assumes authority to direct and control services provided by the supervisee, and has responsibility "for all professional practices of the supervisee" (NASP-PPE, III, F, #1). In accordance with the ethical codes of the National Association of School Psychologists (NASP) and the American Psychological Association (APA), the supervisor is obligated to take reasonable steps to ensure that supervisees "perform services responsibly, competently, and ethically" (Knapp & VandeCreek, 1997; also NASP-PPE, III, F, #3, #4). Some differences exist, however, in the supervisor's role and duties depending on the type of supervision. The supervisor assumes greater control and is obligated to provide more intensive supervision to interns and other psychologists-in-training (e.g., practitioners with a preliminary credential to practice who are pursuing full certification or licensure) than to fully credentialed practitioners (Knapp & VandeCreek, 1997).

Supervision may include both professional development functions (e.g., working with the supervisee to promote skill development) and administrative functions (e.g., hiring, delegating work assignments, evaluation of job performance for contract renewal) (Harvey & Struzziero, 2000). Some psychologists routinely assume both roles, particularly those who serve as lead psychologist or director of psychological services. Numerous legal issues are associated with hiring employees, employee performance evaluation, and contract renewal or nonrenewal that are beyond the scope of this text. Interested readers are referred to Reutter (1994).

PROFESSIONAL STANDARDS FOR SUPERVISION

Both NASP and the APA include guidelines pertinent to supervision in their codes of ethics (see, for example, NASP-PPE, III, F; EP 7.06). In addition, both NASP (2000a) and APA (1981) have published recommended professional standards for supervision in school psychology. NASP's *Guidelines for the Provision of School Psychological Services* (2000a) Unit Guideline 5 addresses supervision, and outlines the following criteria for being a supervisor of school psychological services: supervisors must be state and nationally certified (or eligible for national certification), have three years of experience as a practicing school psychologist, and be identified by the agency or school as a supervisor (*Guidelines* 5.1). The *Guidelines* also require "that practica and internship experiences occur under conditions of appropriate supervision" (*Guidelines* 5.7) and that interns and beginning school psychologists receive a minimum of two hours of supervision per week (*Guidelines* 5.2). NASP *Guidelines* (5.5) go on to state that supervision should be ongoing, and not simply restricted to students in training.

NASP's *Standards for Training and Field Placement Programs in School Psychology* (2000b) specify standards for field experiences and internships that must be met by school psychology training programs to receive NASP training program approval. Similarly, APA's Committee on Accreditation publishes standards for internships that must be met to be eligible for doctoral training program and internship accreditation (APA's Committee on Accreditation, 2002). In addition, NASP's *Standards for the Credentialing of School Psychologists* (2000b) outlines recommended pre-degree and post-degree supervision requirements for states to consider when developing their standards for credentialing of school psychologists, and describes the required supervised field experiences to become a Nationally Certified School Psychologist (NCSP).

PROFESSIONAL DISCLOSURE STATEMENT AND INDIVIDUALIZED LEARNING PLAN

Consistent with the ethical principles of integrity in professional relationships and respect for the supervisee's right to make informed choices, Cobia and Boes (2000) recommend the parameters of the supervisory relationship be outlined in a *professional disclosure statement*. This written agreement is similar to an informed consent agreement between school psychologist and client (Chapter 3) or a consultative contract between psychologist and teacher-consultee (Chapter 8).

The professional disclosure statement is a means of ensuring a mutual understanding between the supervisor and supervisee with regard to rights and responsibilities of all parties, and helps to ensure the supervisee is able to make an informed choice about entering the supervisor-supervisee relationship. The professional disclosure statement might include the following components: (a) description of the supervision site, clientele, and types of services typically provided; (b) credentials of the supervisor; (c) general goals of supervision and how specific objectives will be selected; (d) time frame, frequency and length of supervision contacts, and type of supervision provided (i.e., individual vs. group supervision); (e) rights and responsibilities of supervisor and supervisee; (f) potential risks and benefits of supervision; (g) parameters of confidentiality; (h) record-keeping; and (i) methods of evaluation (Cobia & Boes, 2000; also NASP-PPE, III, F, #2).

In addition to a professional disclosure statement, it is recommended that the supervisee, in cooperation with his or her supervisor, develop a written *individualized learning plan* outlining his or her learning objectives, activities for the achievement of those objectives (e.g., supervised experiences, reading, attending workshops), and how progress towards mastery of objectives will be evaluated. This individualized learning plan provides further clarification of the expectations and responsibilities of both the supervisor and supervisee, and sets the stage for the establishment of a collaborative supervisory relationship (Cobia & Boes, 2000; NASP-PPE, III, F, #2). The plan should be reviewed and modified periodically, and serve as the basis for on-going feedback to the supervisee.

While the professional disclosure statement and individualized learning plan clarify rights and responsibilities of supervisors and supervisees, a written university-internship site affiliation agreement is advisable in those settings where school psychologists provide field supervision for student interns. This agreement outlines the duties of the university as well as the internship site with regard to an intern's field experience (see NASP's *Standards for Training and Field Placement Programs in School Psychology*, 2000b, III).

ETHICAL PRINCIPLES AND SUPERVISION

Ethical principles and standards pertinent to supervision in school psychology are discussed in the text that follows.

Respect for the Dignity of Persons (Welfare of the Client and Supervisee)

In providing supervision, the supervisor must consider the rights and welfare of multiple parties (pupil-client, parents, teachers, other pupils, the supervisee). However, protecting the welfare of the pupil-client is of primary importance.

Case 11–1

Wanda Rose agreed to supervise a school psychology intern, Morgan LaLone, who is interested in infant assessment and intervention. Morgan administered the Bayley Scales a number of times as part of her university practicum experience but feels she is not yet ready to conduct an infant assessment on her own. Consequently, in preparing Morgan's individualized learning plan, Wanda and Morgan agree they will conduct a number of infant assessments together before Morgan undertakes such evaluations independently. This will afford Morgan the opportunity to observe Wanda interact with babies and their parents, as well as practice administration of infant scales, before she begins conducting infant assessments on her own.

In Case 11–1, Wanda and Morgan have mutually agreed on a plan that ensures infants and their parents will receive psychological services that meet high professional standards while Morgan is gaining competence in infant assessment and working with parents.

A number of issues should receive attention early in supervision to help safeguard the well being of student-clients and others. Supervisees should receive explicit instructions regarding how and under what circumstances to contact their supervisor immediately (Knapp & VandeCreek, 1997). They should receive verifiable training in the school district's crisis prevention and response procedures, including written instructions regarding what to do in situations in which it is suspected a pupil might be a danger to self, a danger to others, or in danger (e.g., child abuse) (see Chapter 10). Additionally, it is important to remind interns not to leave pupils unsupervised after they remove them from their classes for assessment or treatment.

Consistent with ethical obligations and the legal requirements of most states, supervisors review and co-sign psychological reports prepared by interns and supervisees who do not yet hold a credential to practice in the state (NASP-PPE, D, #4).

Case 11–2

When Carrie Johnson's cooperative special services unit hired a new school psychologist, Ben Pennington, Carrie agreed to serve as supervisor for his first year. A year of supervision by a certified school psychologist was required for Ben to be eligible for full rather than preliminary certification under state law. Carrie also recognized the importance of providing professional support for her new colleague. During one of their weekly meetings, Carrie learned that the assistant principal and special education coordinator in one of Ben's three schools had assigned Ben the responsibility of scheduling all IEP team meetings in the building. Carrie was angry because IEP scheduling was part of the job description of the building special education coordinator, not the school psychologist. It appears the assistant principal is attempting to take advantage of a new employee.

Although welfare of the client is of primary importance, the supervisor is also obligated to consider the welfare of the supervisee. Supervisors are in a position of greater power than supervisees, and are expected to advocate for the welfare of the supervisee (Knapp & VandeCreek, 1997). In Case 11–2, Carrie needs to work with Ben to chose a course of action that will relieve Ben of the inappropriately assigned duties but still make in possible for him to have a positive working relationship with the assistant principal involved. Practitioners new to a school district may feel overwhelmed by requests for assistance from teachers and others, particularly when faced with a backlog of referrals. Consequently, it is advisable for supervisors to introduce beginning practitioners and interns at a school staff meeting, and to clarify their role and how work assignments will be delegated and prioritized (NASP-PPE, III, E, IV, B, #3).

Autonomy and Self-Determination

The use of a professional disclosure statement is a means of ensuring that the supervisee makes an informed choice when entering a supervisor-supervisee relationship. As described previously, this statement should include a description of the general goals of supervision. There is currently some consensus in the literature that a supervisor's training responsibilities encompass four broad areas: (1) competency; (2) ethical sensitivity, knowledge, decision making, and behavior; (3) understanding of and respect for individual and cultural differences; and (4) emotional awareness and personal functioning (Conoley & Sullivan, 2002; Lamb, Cochran, & Jackson, 1991; Vasquez, 1992). In addition, consistent with the principle of autonomy and self-determination, the supervisor and supervisee should work together to identify specific objectives and experiences to include in the supervisee's individualized learning plan, taking into account the supervisee's current and desired competencies.

Psychologists also have an obligation to ensure that student-clients and their parents have an opportunity to make an informed choice about whether to accept services provided by an intern or practitioner under supervision, and parents should be provided the name and phone number of the supervisor to contact in the event they are not satisfied with the services provided (Knapp & VandeCreek, 1997; NASP-PPE, III, C, #1). In addition, written parent consent and pupil assent should be obtained prior to audio- or video-taping pupils as part of supervision process, and, unless parents agree otherwise, such tapes should be destroyed as soon as they are no longer needed for supervision purposes (EP 4.03; Harvey & Struzziero, 2000).

Privacy and Confidentiality

In general, the guarantees of client confidentiality apply to the supervisor-supervisee relationship. However, supervision often involves evaluations of supervisee performance that must be shared with others (e.g., the university intern supervisor). Consequently, the professional disclosure statement should identify the circumstances under which information regarding the performance of the supervisee will be disclosed to others and the nature and types of information that may be disclosed. Furthermore, supervisees should be informed that supervisors have a duty to breach confidentiality if such action is necessary to safeguard the welfare of clients.

Supervisors are well-advised to review ethical and legal principles with supervisees regarding respect for privacy and maintaining client confidentiality, and to discuss district policies regarding privacy of pupil records. In a study of ethical transgressions of school psychology graduate students, Tryon (2000) found that failure to maintain the privacy and confidentiality of others was an area of difficulty for students.

Fairness, Nondiscrimination, and Diversity Issues

Psychologists are ethically obligated to be respectful of cultural, individual, and role differences in providing supervision to interns and employees (EP Principle E; also NASP-PPE, III, A, #2). Like consultation across culturally diverse groups, supervision across culturally diverse supervisor-supervisee-client groups can be challenging, particularly with regard to building understanding and trust.

Case 11–3

Charlie Maxwell was pleased when asked to provide field-based supervision for an African-American intern. His district has had difficulty recruiting African-American school psychologists, and he is hopeful that his new intern, Donita, might be interested in future employment with his district. Donita came to the internship with strong assessment and intervention skills for an entry-level practitioner. She had grown up in the inner city and was able to establish a warm, positive rapport with a number of African-American parents who were previously uninvolved with the school. However, Sam received several negative evaluations of Donita from principals and teachers because they were unable to understand the Black English she used when conversing with parents during meetings.

While Donita (Case 11–3) has been able to open channels of communication with African-American parents, she has inadvertently alienated some teachers and administrators. Charlie (Case 11–3) needs to share the feedback he received from principals and teachers with Donita regarding their inability to understand her speech patterns, and explore strategies (such as speaking more slowly) to make sure all persons involved in parent meetings understand what is being said. His feedback and guidance are necessary to ensure Donita will be able to build a good working relationship with school staff and provide effective services to teachers, pupils, and their families.

Responsible Caring in Supervision

In order to foster the supervisee's professional development and safeguard the well being of clients, supervisors should offer and provide supervision only within the areas of their own competence (Cobia & Boes, 2000). The supervisor is obligated to be forthcoming and accurate in describing to potential supervisees the areas in which he or she is qualified to provide supervision, and may wish to include this information in the professional disclosure statement (NASP-PPE, III, F, #1). As illustrated by Case 11–4, supervision by another professional with appropriate credentials, training, and skills should be arranged if the supervisee would like to gain experience in areas outside of the competence of the supervisor; otherwise such experiences should not be offered.

Case 11–4

Sam Foster's district accepted a school psychology intern, Roberto Otero, for the upcoming academic year. Roberto is Hispanic and bilingual and would like to gain supervised experience working with pupils and families whose native language is Spanish and consulting with teachers in the district's ESL (English as a second language) classrooms. Because Sam is not competent to provide psychological services to bilingual students, he has arranged for Roberto to receive supervision from the district's Spanish-bilingual psychologist for the second half of his internship year.

Also with regard to supervisor competence, it is important to note that few school psychology supervisors receive formal training in how to supervise (Ward, 2001). Harvey and Struzziero have outlined the basic skills needed for supervision (2000, pp. 5–7; also Conoley & Sullivan, 2002). School psychologists who wish to provide supervision should assess their competence to do so, and possibly seek training in effective supervisory methods. Furthermore, supervisors should seek feedback from former supervisees regarding the effectiveness of their supervision methods.

The supervisor also is obligated to ensure that client welfare is not compromised because of the supervisee's lack of competence. In her study of school psychology graduate students, Tryon (2000) found that, in addition to respecting privacy and confidentiality, working within the boundaries of competence was also an area of difficulty. Supervisors must "delegate responsibilities carefully and deliberately to their supervisees" (Knapp & VandeCreek, 1997, p. 591; NASP-PPE, F, #1). The supervisor has a duty to carefully assess the skill level of the supervisee by review of past training and experiences; face-to-face discussion; evaluation of work samples; use of audio and videotape and direct observation; and inviting feedback from recipients of the supervisee's services (Conoley & Sullivan, 2002; Harvey & Struzziero, 2000). As in Wanda's supervision of her intern

Morgan (Case 11–1), it may be appropriate and necessary for the supervisor to work very closely with the supervisee in certain practice areas before allowing the supervisee to function more autonomously in providing services.

As Bosk (1979) has observed, there are dilemmas inherent in the supervisor's role of selecting and assigning responsibilities to the beginning practitioner. In order to master new skills and situations, beginners must be given the opportunity to try new experiences and learn from their successes and mistakes. At the same time, the supervisor must protect the client from the supervisee's errors, and make sure the supervisee is not overly discouraged by his or her mistakes. *Technical* errors occur when trainees are performing their role conscientiously, but their skills fall short of what the task requires. Similarly, *judgmental* errors occur when trainees are performing conscientiously, but select an incorrect strategy or treatment. Supervisors should assure trainees that technical errors and errors in professional judgment are "inevitable and forgivable" during training, and seek to create an atmosphere in which supervisee's can openly admit and discuss such mistakes without fear. Open discussion of errors encourages trainees to learn from their mistakes and take responsibility for them (Bosk, 1979).

In contrast, *normative errors* constitute a more serious failure, possibly resulting in the need for reprimand, probation, or dismissal (Bosk, 1979). Normative errors occur when the supervisee fails to discharge his or her role responsibilities conscientiously, or violates fundamental expectations for proper conduct in the profession, such as covering up mistakes. Normative errors are a breach of psychologist-client and supervisor-supervisee trust.

Consistent with the principle of responsible caring, supervision must be provided "on a scheduled basis with additional supervision available as needed," and supervisees should be provided timely and straightforward evaluations of their progress (Knapp & VandeCreek, 1997, p. 593). Supervisors are ethically obligated to use "objective, accurate, and fair" methods for evaluating their supervisees (NASP-PPE, III, F, #5; EP 7.06; also see Conoley & Sullivan, 2002; Harvey & Struzziero, 2000, pp. 93–98). As recommended by Cobia and Boes (2000), the professional disclosure statement should outline the methods and timetable for evaluation. Such evaluations should occur early and often enough in supervision to make and implement modifications in the individualized learning plan if the supervisee is not making the desired progress towards goals and objectives. As Knapp and VandeCreek suggest, the final evaluation of supervisee performance should "never come as a surprise to a supervisee" (p. 594).

Records of supervisee performance should be maintained on an ongoing basis and with sufficient detail to provide support for summative appraisals and any final recommendations (e.g., for or against approval for state certification, employment renewal). Supervisors should maintain a record of supervisory contacts to document supervision was provided as promised in the professional disclosure statement and consistent with professional standards.

Sometimes it is necessary to terminate a supervisory relationship before the end of the agreed on supervision period. In such situations, supervisors "should summarize the progress made by the supervisee, discuss the supervisee's additional need for supervision and training, draw generalizations from the supervision, resolve interpersonal issues, review the written evaluation with the supervisee in a personal interview, and bring supervision to a closure" (Harvey & Struzziero, 2000, p. 43).

School psychology practitioners are ethically obligated to engage in continuing professional development (NASP-PPE, II, A, #4). The individualized learning plan can provide a mechanism whereby the supervisor can teach self-supervision to the supervisee (Harvey & Struzziero, 2000). By periodic review of the learning plan, supervisees gain practice in self-assessing their own skills, pinpointing areas in need further development, and identifying strategies to remediate skill deficit areas.

Integrity in Supervisor-Supervisee Professional Relations

Supervisory relationships are ideally based on honesty, objectivity, and mutual respect. Supervisors "must be continually careful not to abuse the inherent power in the supervisor-supervisee relationship" (Vasquez, 1992, p. 200). Practitioners refrain from taking on a supervisory role when their own interests (personal, professional, legal, financial) could reasonably be expected to impair their objectivity, competence, or effectiveness in providing supervision, or place the supervisee at risk for exploitation or harm (EP Principles A and B; NASP-PPE, IV, C, #2; D, #4). Supervisors are cautioned not to step into the dual role of therapist and supervisor to the supervisee. "While it is the responsibility of supervisors to help supervisees identify personal issues that interfere with their work, it is up to the supervisee to obtain appropriate help to resolve them" (Harvey & Struzziero, 2000, p. 14).

Psychologists also must consider potential problems associated with multiple relationships. In working with supervisees, multiple relationships occur when the psychologist is in a supervisory role and at the same time has a relationship with a person closely associated with or related to the supervisee (EP 3.05). For example, a practitioner to might be asked to accept the daughter or son of a close personal friend as a supervisee. School psychologists are obligated to refrain from entering into a multiple relationship if the relationship could reasonably be expected to impair their performance as a supervising psychologist, or otherwise risks exploitation or harm to the supervisee (EP 3.05). School psychologists also are prohibited "from engaging in sexual relationships with their students, supervisees, trainees, or past or present clients" (NASP-PPE, II, A, #6; also EP 3.02, 3.08).

Case 11–5

Jack Western was a capable and conscientious intern during his first semester as Pearl Meadow's supervisee. After Christmas vacation, however, Jack was often late to school, sporadically absent due to illness, and appeared disorganized and unprepared for meetings. When Pearl expressed concern about this change in his performance, Jack apologized, attributed his tardiness and disorganization to the stress of completing his master's thesis and promised to do better. The following week, however, when reviewing a pupil assessment he completed, Pearl noticed that Jack failed to record any of the child's verbatim responses on the Vocabulary and Comprehension WISC-III subtests and that his report was poorly written, with little attention to integration and interpretation of findings. Then, after lunch that day, Pearl thought she smelled alcohol on his breath. When Pearl queried Jack about the incomplete WISC-III protocol and hastily written report during their supervision meeting, Jack disclosed that his wife had left him over Christmas and that he was devastated by their separation. He had never administered all the WISC-III subtests and had simply fabricated the scores. When asked whether alcohol was a problem, he confided that he had been drinking heavily.

As Cobia and Boes (2000) and others (e.g., Harvey and Struzziero, 2000) have observed, the role of supervisor in psychology often involves the dual roles of evaluator and growth facilitator of the supervisee, and balancing these two roles may cause "ethical tugs" for the supervisor. As part of the supervision process, supervisors encourage supervisees to be open and self-disclosing, particularly regarding strengths and difficulties in professional functioning. However, as in Case 11–5, it is possible that the supervisee, as a result of the supervisor's encouragement, may disclose material that leads to the conclusion that the supervisee has serious skill deficits or personal problems, and is perhaps not suited for the professional role of school psychologist (Cobia & Boes, 2000). Pearl (Case 11–5) may feel she has betrayed Jack's trust because, after encouraging his self-disclosure, she must now terminate his internship on the basis of the information disclosed.

However, in supervision, ethical priority must always be given to the welfare of current and future clients (Cobia & Boes, 2000). Knapp and VandeCreek distinguish between supervisee *distress* and *impairment*. A supervisee may be experiencing stress and discomfort, but still be "able to perform his or her job responsibly" (1997, p. 591). In such situations, the supervisee is able to provide services adequately, and, with the support and guidance of the supervisor, make progress towards internship goals. *Impairment* refers to the inability of the supervisee "to fulfil minimal responsibilities of their profession because of a mental or physical disability" (p. 591), thus placing the client at risk for misdiagnosis, inappropriate and inadequate treatment, and possible harm. When a supervisee is suffering from an impairment or engages in serious normative errors, it is ethically appropriate and necessary for the supervisor to recommend a failing internship grade, suspend or terminate the internship, deny endorsement for state credentialing, and/or recommend nonrenewal of an employment contract or immediate termination of employment. These risks, along with the potential benefits of supervision, should be outlined in the professional disclosure statement (Sherry, 1991).

LIABILITY ISSUES

It is well established in common law that psychologists in independent practice or health care settings may be held liable for their own actions or the actions of supervisees that result in harm to clients (Knapp & VandeCreek, 1997; also see *Tarasoff*, Chapter 3). The legal principle of *respondent superior* ("let the master answer" for the wrongful acts of his servant) provides the foundation for liable suits against a supervisor when the actions of supervisee result in harm to a client (Black, 1983). As discussed in Chapter 2, however, whether a school employee can be sued is a complicated matter, determined by state legislation and case law. Many states hold individual school employees immune from liability under state law during the performance of duties within the scope of their employment. The provision of supervision to school psychology trainees or employees should be included in the job description of practitioners who provide such services.

Some, but not all, states permit tort actions against school districts and allow recovery up to the limits of the school's liability insurance. Consequently, inappropriate actions by a supervisee that result in harm to a student could trigger a negligence suit against the school under state law, and possibly result in reprimand or suspension of employment of the supervisor if it is determined the supervisor failed to provide proper supervision to the supervisee. Supervisees should be reminded that they have a legal duty to take steps to protect pupils from reasonably foreseeable risk of harm, and, as noted previously, supervisees should receive verifiable training regarding how to respond to situations that suggest a potential danger to students or others. In addition, if a supervisee violates a pupils's constitutional rights or other rights under federal law, parents could file suit against the supervisor and supervisee under Section 1983 of the Civil Rights Act of 1871.

Also, parents who are not satisfied with the identification, evaluation, or placement of their child with a disability under IDEA may request mediation, a hearing, and pursue court action when administrative remedies are exhausted. Supervisors are advised to select their cases for interns and beginning practitioners carefully, avoiding those that might be expected to trigger difficult school-parent disagreements.

Although the likelihood of an intern being involved in a lawsuit in the school setting is probably small, we encourage supervisors and interns to consider purchasing professional liability insurance. Interns may not be covered by the school district's liability insurance if they are not also employees of the district (see Chapter 2).

CONCLUDING COMMENTS

Quality supervision helps to ensure that practitioners are trained and prepared to provide school psychological services that meet high professional standards. Unfortunately, several studies have found that school psychology practitioners often do not receive as much supervision as other mental health practitioners. Furthermore, there is not as much research literature on effective supervision in school psychology as in counseling or clinical psychology (Fischetti & Crespi, 1999; McIntosh & Phelps, 2000). Consequently, school psychologists should consider ways in which they can contribute to the field by providing quality supervision to interns and beginning practitioners, and ways in which they might contribute to our knowledge of effective supervision practices by conducting or participating in research on supervision.

STUDY AND DISCUSSION

Reread Case 11–5 about Pearl and her supervisee, Jack. What information do you think Pearl should share with Jack's university supervisor, and why? What information should Pearl disclose to the school district regarding the termination of Jack's internship, and why? Do you believe Pearl should recommend to the university that Jack be permanently dismissed from his graduate training program? Or, do you believe Jack should be allowed to complete an internship after he has received treatment for alcohol abuse and personal problems? What are the ethical reasons for or against each course of action? See Lamb et al. (1991) for a discussion of suggested procedures for identifying and responding to a supervisee's problematic behaviors or impairment.

Epilogue

ETHICS, PROFESSIONAL STANDARDS, AND ADVOCACY

According to NASP's code of ethics, school psychologists act as advocates for the rights and welfare of pupils (NASP-PPE, IV, A, #1, #2, #3). Consistent with the general ethical principle of responsibility to community and society, practitioners promote school policies to enhance the welfare of students, and they may work as advocates for change at the state and national level to better protect the interests and rights of children.

Throughout this book, we have advanced the view that the primary purpose of our codes of ethics is *to protect the public.* Codes of ethics were not created to protect the professional (Wonderly, 1989). However, in this epilogue we illustrate how our codes of ethics and professional standards can be a source of support for the practitioner when advocacy for the rights and educational needs of children brings the psychologist in conflict with the school. This is particularly likely to occur if, in the face of limited resources, the school is resistant to providing legally mandated services.

In the case of *Forrest v. Ambach* (1980, 1983), Forrest, a school psychologist, claimed that she was fired from her position for actions that were ethically and legally mandated. For example, she claimed to have been criticized for conducting full and comprehensive evaluations and writing comprehensive reports. Also, she was allegedly criticized for recommending services the child needed as opposed to services the schools offered. She also claimed to have been criticized for discussing her conclusions with parents and for dissenting from the views of other professionals during staffings. This is a case where ethics and law are clearly on the side of the school psychologist, serving to defend the nature of her practice. The *amici curiae* brief written by Bersoff (1981) for the American Psychological Assocation, and filed in support of her case, is an outstanding example of how law and ethics can serve to support a high quality of professional service by the practitioner.

The judge in her initial appeal (1980) wrote, "The ethical standards of any professional employed by a school board cannot be cavalierly dismissed as irrelevant to the employer-employee relationship" (p. 122). The judge went on, "If, in fact, petitioner was dismissed solely due to her attempt to adhere to statutory mandates and her own professional standards as a psychologist, then her dismissal by said school board would be arbitrary, capricious, and unconstitutional" (p. 123).

Despite the fact that the state commissioner of education ultimately found that her dismissal was not based on these actions, and her firing was upheld, school psychologists should be encouraged by the judge's ruling in the case. By adhering to professional standards in the delivery of services, school psychologists may increase their freedom to utilize best practices in the field, as well as provide themselves with protection when advocacy for children brings them in conflict with the school.

CONCLUDING COMMENTS

In attempting to write as current a book as we could, we have been impressed by the speed with which law and ethics can change. You, the school psychologist, must take it from here. This means maintaining your currency regarding new developments in ethics and law and also working proactively for school policies and law to better serve the interests and rights of children.

STUDY AND DISCUSSION

Discussion

School psychologists at times face ethical dilemmas because of their dual functions as client advocate and employee (Helton, Ray, & Biderman, 2000; Jacob-Timm, 1999). In times of limited school resources, school psychologists may experience an increase in pressure to practice unethically. For example, when resources are limited, psychologists may be encouraged to recommend inexpensive, rather than appropriate, placements and interventions and limit information provided to parents, rather than fully inform them of their rights and choices.

What strategies will you use to avoid conflicts between your ethical responsibilities to the client and administrative pressure to make decisions that are not in the best interests of the client? How will you successfully resist administrative pressures to practice unethically? (See EP 1.03, 3.07, 3.11; Helton, Ray, & Biderman, 2000)

Appendix A

NASP'S PRINCIPLES FOR PROFESSIONAL ETHICS[1]

I. INTRODUCTION

The formal principles that elucidate the proper conduct of a professional school psychologist are known as *Ethics*. By virtue of joining the Association, each NASP member agrees to abide by the *Ethics*, acting in a manner that shows respect for human dignity and assuring a high quality of professional service. Although ethical behavior is an individual responsibility, it is in the interest of an association to adopt and enforce a code of ethics. If done properly, members will be guided toward appropriate behavior, and public confidence in the profession will be enhanced. Additionally, a code of ethics should provide due process procedures to protect members from potential abuse of the code. The NASP *Principles for Professional Ethics* have been written to accomplish these goals.

The principles in this manual are based on the assumptions that: 1) school psychologists will act as advocates for their students/clients, and 2) at the very least, school psychologists will do no harm. These assumptions necessitate that school psychologists "speak up" for the needs and rights of their students/clients even at times when it may be difficult to do so. School psychologists also are constrained to provide only those services for which they have acquired an acknowledged level of experience, training, and competency. Beyond these basic premises, judgment is required to apply the ethical principles to the fluid and expanding interactions between school and community.

There are many different sources of advice for the proper way to behave; local policies, state laws, federal laws, credentialing standards, professional association position statements, and books that recommend "Best Practices" are just a few. Given one's employment situation and the array of recommendations, events may develop in which the ethical course of action is unclear.

The Association will seek to enforce the Ethical Principles with its members. NASP's *Guidelines for the Provision of School Psychological Services* are typically not enforced, although all members should work toward achieving the hallmarks of quality services delivery that are described therein. Similarly, "position statements" and "best practices" documents are not adjudicated. The guidance of the Ethical Principles is intentionally broad to make it more enduring than other documents that reflect short-term opinions about specific actions shaped by local events, popular trends, or recent developments in the field. The member must use judgment to infer the situation-specific rule from the

[1] Copyright 2000 by the National Association of School Psychologists. Reprinted by permission of the publisher.

general ethical principle. The lack of a specific reference to a particular action does not indicate permission or provide a defense against a charge of unethical practice. (For example, the document frequently refers to a school psychologist's relationship with a hypothetical "student/client." Therefore, one should apply *Ethical Principles* in all professional situations, realizing that one is not released from responsibility simply because another individual is not strictly a "student" or a "client.")

The principles in this manual are organized into several sections as a result of editorial judgment. Therefore, principles discussed in one section may also apply to other sections. Every school psychologist, regardless of position (e.g., practitioner, researcher, university trainer, supervisor, state or federal consultant, administrator of psychological services) or setting (e.g., public or private school, community agency, hospital, university, private practice) should reflect upon the theme represented in each ethical principle to determine its application to her or his individual situation. For example, although a given principle may specifically discuss responsibilities toward "clients," the intent is that the standards would also apply to supervisees, trainees, and research participants. At times, the *Ethics* may require a higher standard of behavior than the prevailing policies and pertinent laws. Under such conditions, members should adhere to the *Ethics*. Ethical behavior may occasionally be forbidden by policy or law, in which case members are expected to declare their dilemma and work to bring the discrepant regulations into compliance with the *Ethics*. To obtain additional assistance in applying these principles to a particular setting, a school psychologist should consult with experienced school psychologists and seek advice from the National Association of School Psychologists or the state school psychology association. Throughout the *Principles for Professional Ethics,* it is assumed that, depending upon the role and setting of the school psychologist, the client could include children, parents, teachers and other school personnel, other professionals, trainees, or supervisees.

Procedural guidelines for filing an ethical complaint and the adjudication of ethical complaints are available from the NASP office or Web site (www. naspweb. org).

II. PROFESSIONAL COMPETENCY

A. General

1. School psychologists recognize the strengths and limitations of their training and experience, engaging only in practices for which they are qualified. They enlist the assistance of other specialists in supervisory, consultative, or referral roles as appropriate in providing services. They must continually obtain additional training and education to provide the best possible services to children, families, schools, communities, trainees, and supervisees.
2. Competency levels, education,training, and experience are declared and accurately represented to clients in a professional manner.
3. School psychologists do not use affiliations with persons, associations, or institutions to imply a level of professional competence that exceeds that which has actually been achieved.
4. School psychologists engage in continuing professional development. They remain current regarding developments in research, training, and professional practices that benefit children, families, and schools.
5. School psychologists refrain from any activity in which their personal problems or conflicts may interfere with professional effective-

ness. Competent assistance is sought to alleviate conflicts in professional relationships.

6. School psychologists know the *Principles for Professional Ethics* and thoughtfully apply them to situations within their employment setting or practice. Ignorance or misapplication of an ethical principle is not a reasonable defense against a charge of unethical behavior.

III. PROFESSIONAL RELATIONSHIPS

A. General

1. School psychologists are committed to the application of their professional expertise for the purpose of promoting improvement in the quality of life for children, their families, and the school community. This objective is pursued in ways that protect the dignity and rights of those involved. School psychologists accept responsibility for the appropriateness of their professional practices.
2. School psychologists respect all persons and are sensitive to physical, mental, emotional, political, economic, social, cultural, ethnic and racial characteristics, gender, sexual orientation, and religion.
3. School psychologists in all settings maintain professional relationships with children, parents, and the school community. Consequently, parents and children are to be fully informed about all relevant aspects of school psychological services in advance. The explanation should take into account language and cultural differences, cognitive capabilities, developmental level, and age so that it may be understood by the child, parent, or guardian.
4. School psychologists attempt to resolve situations in which there are divided or conflicting interests in a manner that is mutually beneficial and protects the rights of all parties involved.
5. School psychologists are responsible for the direction and nature of their personal loyalties or objectives. When these commitments may influence a professional relationship, school psychologists inform all concerned persons of relevant issues in advance, including, when applicable, their direct supervisor for consideration of reassignment of responsibilities.
6. School psychologists do not exploit clients through professional relationships or condone these actions in their colleagues. No individuals, including children, clients, employees, colleagues, trainees, parents, supervisees, and research participants, will be exposed to deliberate comments, gestures, or physical contacts of a sexual nature. School psychologists do not harass or demean others based on personal characteristics. School psychologists do not engage in sexual relationships with their students, supervisees, trainees, or past or present clients.
7. Dual relationships with clients are avoided. Namely, personal and business relations with clients may cloud one's judgment. School psychologists are aware of these situations and avoid them whenever possible.
8. School psychologists attempt to resolve suspected detrimental or unethical practices on an informal level. If informal efforts are not

productive, the appropriate professional organization is contacted for assistance, and procedures established for questioning ethical practice are followed:

a. The filing of an ethical complaint is a serious matter. It is intended to improve the behavior of a colleague that is harmful to the profession and/or the public. Therefore, school psychologists make every effort to discuss the ethical principles with other professionals who may be in violation.
b. School psychologists enter into the complaint process thoughtfully and with concern for the well-being of all parties involved. They do not file or encourage the filing of an ethics complaint that is frivolous or motivated by revenge.
c. Some situations may be particularly difficult to analyze from an ethical perspective. School psychologists consult ethical standards from related fields and seek assistance from knowledgeable, experienced school psychologists and relevant state/national associations to ascertain an appropriate course of action.
d. School psychologists document specific instances of suspected ethical violations (i.e., date, time, relevant details) as well as attempts to resolve these violations.

9. School psychologists respect the confidentiality of information obtained during their professional work. Information is revealed only with the informed consent of the child, or the child's parent or legal guardian, except in those situations in which failure to release information would result in clear danger to the child or others. Obsolete confidential information will be shredded or otherwise destroyed before placement in recycling bins or trash receptacles.
10. School psychologists discuss confidential information only for professional purposes and only with persons who have a legitimate need to know.
11. School psychologists inform children and other clients of the limits of confidentiality at the outset of establishing a professional relationship.

B. Students

1. School psychologists understand the intimate nature of consultation, assessment, and direct service. They engage only in professional practices that maintain the dignity and integrity of children and other clients.
2. School psychologists explain important aspects of their professional relationships in a clear, understandable manner that is appropriate to the child's or other client's age and ability to understand. The explanation includes the reason why services were requested, who will receive information about the services provided, and the possible outcomes.
3. When a child initiates services, school psychologists understand their obligation to respect the rights of a child to initiate, participate in, or discontinue services voluntarily (See III-C-2 for further clarification). When another party initiates services, the school psychologist will make every effort to secure voluntary participation of the child.

4. Recommendations for program changes or additional services will be discussed with appropriate individuals, including any alternatives that may be available.

C. Parents, Legal Guardians, and Appointed Surrogates
   1. School psychologists explain all services to parents in a clear, understandable manner. They strive to propose a set of options that takes into account the values and capabilities of each parent. Service provision by interns, practicum students, or other trainees should be explained and agreed to in advance.
   2. School psychologists recognize the importance of parental support and seek to obtain that support by assuring that there is direct parent contact prior to seeing the child on an ongoing basis. (Emergencies and "drop-in" self-referrals will require parental notification as soon as possible. The age and circumstances under which children may seek services without parental consent varies greatly; be certain to comply with III-D5.) School psychologists secure continuing parental involvement by a frank and prompt reporting to the parent of findings and progress that conforms to the limits of previously determined confidentiality.
   3. School psychologists encourage and promote parental participation in designing services provided to their children. When appropriate, this includes linking interventions between the school and the home, tailoring parental involvement to the skills of the family, and helping parents gain the skills needed to help their children.
   4. School psychologists respect the wishes of parents who object to school psychological services and attempt to guide parents to alternative community resources.
   5. School psychologists discuss with parents the recommendations and plans for assisting their children. The discussion includes alternatives associated with each set of plans, which show respect for the ethnic/cultural values of the family. The parents are informed of sources of help available at school and in the community.
   6. School psychologists discuss the rights of parents and children regarding creation, modification, storage, and disposal of confidential materials that will result from the provision of school psychological services.

D. Community
   1. School psychologists also are citizens, thereby accepting the same responsibilities and duties as any member of society. They are free to pursue individual interests, except to the degree that those interests compromise professional responsibilities.
   2. School psychologists may act as individual citizens to bring about social change in a lawful manner. Individual actions should not be presented as, or suggestive of, representing the field of school psychology or the Association.
   3. As employees or employers, in public or independent practice domains, school psychologists do not engage in or condone practices that discriminate against children, other clients, or employees (if applicable) based on race, disability, age, gender, sexual orientation, religion,

national origin, economic status, or native language.

4. School psychologists avoid any action that could violate or diminish the civil and legal rights of children and other clients.
5. School psychologists adhere to federal, state, and local laws and ordinances governing their practice and advocacy efforts. If regulations conflict with ethical guidelines, school psychologists seek to resolve such conflict through positive, respected, and legal channels, including advocacy efforts involving public policy.

E. Other Professionals

1. To best meet the needs of children and other clients, school psychologists cooperate with other professional disciplines in relationships based on mutual respect.
2. School psychologists recognize the competence of other professionals. They encourage and support the use of all resources to best serve the interests of children and other clients.
3. School psychologists should strive to explain their field and their professional competencies, including roles, assignments, and working relationships to other professionals.
4. School psychologists cooperate and coordinate with other professionals and agencies with the rights and needs of children and other clients in mind. If a child or other client is receiving similar services from another professional, school psychologists promote coordination of services.
5. The child or other client is referred to another professional for services when a condition or need is identified which is outside the professional competencies or scope of the school psychologist.
6. When transferring the intervention responsibility for a child or other client to another professional, school psychologists ensure that all relevant and appropriate individuals, including the child/client when appropriate, are notified of the change and reasons for the change.
7. When school psychologists suspect the existence of detrimental or unethical practices by a member of another profession, informal contact is made with that person to express the concern. If the situation cannot be resolved in this manner, the appropriate professional organization is contacted for assistance in determining the procedures established by that profession for examining the practices in question.
8. School psychologists who employ, supervise, or train other professionals, accept the obligation to provide continuing professional development. They also provide appropriate working conditions, fair and timely evaluation, and constructive consultation.

F. School Psychologist Trainees and Interns

1. School psychologists who supervise interns are responsible for all professional practices of the supervisees. They assure children and other clients and the profession that the intern is adequately supervised as designated by the practice guidelines and training standards for school psychologists.
2. School psychologists who conduct or administer training programs provide trainees and prospective

trainees with accurate information regarding program sponsorships/endorsements/accreditation, goals/objectives, training processes and requirements, and likely outcomes and benefits.
3. School psychologists who are faculty members in colleges or universities or who supervise clinical or field placements apply these ethical principles in all work with school psychology trainees. In addition, they promote the ethical practice of trainees by providing specific and comprehensive instruction, feedback, and mentoring.
4. School psychology faculty members and clinical or field supervisors uphold recognized standards of the profession by providing training related to high quality, responsible, and research-based school psychology services. They provide accurate and objective information in their teaching and training activities; identify any limitations in information; and acknowledge disconfirming data, alternative hypotheses, and explanations.
5. School psychology faculty members and clinical or field supervisors develop and use evaluation practices for trainees that are objective, accurate, and fair.

IV. PROFESSIONAL PRACTICES—GENERAL PRINCIPLES

A. Advocacy
1. School psychologists typically serve multiple clients including children, parents, and systems. When the school psychologist is confronted with conflicts between client groups, the primary client is considered to be the child. When the child is not the primary client, the individual or group of individuals who sought the assistance of the school psychologist is the primary client.
2. School psychologists consider children and other clients to be their primary responsibility, acting as advocates for their rights and welfare. If conflicts of interest between clients are present, the school psychologist supports conclusions that are in the best interest of the child. When choosing a course of action, school psychologists take into account the rights of each individual involved and the duties of school personnel.
3. School psychologists' concerns for protecting the rights and welfare of children are communicated to the school administration and staff as the top priority in determining services.
4. School psychologists understand the public policy process to assist them in their efforts to advocate for children, parents, and systems.

B. Service Delivery
1. School psychologists are knowledgeable of the organization, philosophy, goals, objectives, and methodologies of the setting in which they are employed.
2. School psychologists recognize that an understanding of the goals, processes, and legal requirements of their particular workplace is essential for effective functioning within that setting.
3. School psychologists attempt to become integral members of the

client service systems to which they are assigned. They establish clear roles for themselves within that system.

4. School psychologists who provide services to several different groups may encounter situations in which loyalties are conflicted. As much as possible, the stance of the school psychologist is made known in advance to all parties to prevent misunderstandings.
5. School psychologists promote changes in their employing agencies and community service systems that will benefit their clients.

C. Assessment and Intervention

1. School psychologists maintain the highest standard for educational and psychological assessment and direct and indirect interventions.
   a. In conducting psychological, educational, or behavioral evaluations or in providing therapy, counseling, or consultation services, due consideration is given to individual integrity and individual differences.
   b. School psychologists respect differences in age, gender, sexual orientation, and socioeconomic, cultural, and ethnic backgrounds. They select and use appropriate assessment or treatment procedures, techniques, and strategies. Decision-making related to assessment and subsequent interventions is primarily data based.
2. School psychologists are knowledgeable about the validity and reliability of their instruments and techniques, choosing those that have up-to-date standardization data and are applicable and appropriate for the benefit of child.
3. School psychologists use multiple assessment methods such as observations, background information, and information from other professionals, to reach comprehensive conclusions.
4. School psychologists use assessment techniques, counseling and therapy procedures, consultation techniques, and other direct and indirect service methods that the profession considers to be responsible, research-based practice.
5. School psychologists do not condone the use of psychological or educational assessment techniques, or the misuse of the information these techniques provide, by unqualified persons in any way, including teaching, sponsorship, or supervision.
6. School psychologists develop interventions that are appropriate to the presenting problems and are consistent with data collected. They modify or terminate the treatment plan when the data indicate the plan is not achieving the desired goals.
7. School psychologists use current assessment and intervention strategies that assist in the promotion of mental health in the children they serve.

D. Reporting Data and Conference Results

1. School psychologists ascertain that information about children and other clients reaches only authorized persons.
   a. School psychologists adequately interpret information so that the recipient can better help the child or other clients.
   b. School psychologists assist agency recipients to establish procedures to properly safeguard confidential material.

2. School psychologists communicate findings and recommendations in language readily understood by the intended recipient. These communications describe potential consequences associated with the proposals.
3. School psychologists prepare written reports in such form and style that the recipient of the report will be able to assist the child or other clients. Reports should emphasize recommendations and interpretations; unedited computer-generated reports, pre-printed "check-off" or "fill-in-the-blank" reports, and reports that present only test scores or global statements regarding eligibility for special education without specific recommendations for intervention are seldom useful. Reports should include an appraisal of the degree of confidence that could be assigned to the information. Alterations of previously released reports should be done only by the original author.
4. School psychologists review all of their written documents for accuracy, signing them only when correct. Interns and practicum students are clearly identified as such, and their work is co-signed by the supervising school psychologist. In situations in which more than one professional participated in the data collection and reporting process, school psychologists assure that sources of data are clearly identified in the written report.
5. School psychologists comply with all laws, regulations, and policies pertaining to the adequate storage and disposal of records to maintain appropriate confidentiality of information.

E. Use of Materials and Technology
   1. School psychologists maintain test security, preventing the release of underlying principles and specific content that would undermine the use of the device. School psychologists are responsible for the security requirements specific to each instrument used.
   2. School psychologists obtain written prior consent or they remove identifying data presented in public lectures or publications.
   3. School psychologists do not promote or encourage inappropriate use of computer-generated test analyses or reports. In accordance with this principle, a school psychologist would not offer an unedited computer report as his or her own writing or use a computer-scoring system for tests in which he or she has no training. They select scoring and interpretation services on the basis of accuracy and professional alignment with the underlying decision rules.
   4. School psychologists maintain full responsibility for any technological services used. All ethical and legal principles regarding confidentiality, privacy, and responsibility for decisions apply to the school psychologist and cannot be transferred to equipment, software companies, or data-processing departments.
   5. Technological devices should be used to improve the quality of client services. School psychologists will resist applications of technology that ultimately reduce the quality of service.
   6. To ensure confidentiality, student/client records are not transmitted electronically without a guarantee of privacy. In line with

this principle, a receiving FAX machine must be in a secure location and operated by employees cleared to work with confidential files, and e-mail messages must be encrypted or else stripped of all information that identifies the student/client.

7. School psychologists do not accept any form of remuneration in exchange for data from their client data base without informed consent.

F. Research, Publication, and Presentation

1. When designing and implementing research in schools, school psychologists choose topics and employ research methodology, subject selection techniques, data-gathering methods, and analysis and reporting techniques that are grounded in sound research practice. School psychologists clearly identify their level of training and graduate degree on all communications to research participants.
2. Prior to initiating research, school psychologists working in agencies without review committees should have at least one other colleague, preferably a school psychologist, review the proposed methods.
3. School psychologists follow all legal procedures when conducting research, including following procedures related to informed consent, confidentiality, privacy, protection from harm or risks, voluntary participation, and disclosure of results to participants. School psychologists demonstrate respect for the rights of and well-being of research participants.
4. In publishing reports of their research, school psychologists provide discussion of limitations of their data and acknowledge existence of disconfirming data, as well as alternate hypotheses and explanations of their findings.
5. School psychologists take particular care with information presented through various impersonal media (e.g., radio, television, public lectures, popular press articles, promotional materials). Recipients should be informed that the information does not result from or substitute for a professional consultation. The information should be based on research and experience within the school psychologists's recognized sphere of competence. The statements should be consistent with these ethical principles and should not mistakenly represent the field of school psychology or the Association.
6. School psychologists uphold copyright laws in their publications and presentations and obtain permission from authors and copyright holders to reproduce other publications or materials. School psychologists recognize that federal law protects the rights of copyright holders of published works and authors of non-published materials.
7. When publishing or presenting research or other work, school psychologists do not plagiarize the works or ideas of others and acknowledge sources and assign credit to those whose ideas are reflected.
8. School psychologists do not publish or present fabricated or falsified data or results in their publications and presentations.

9. School psychologists make available data or other information upon which conclusions and claims reported in publications and presentations are based, provided that the data are needed to address a legitimate concern or need and that the confidentiality and other rights of all research participants are protected.
10. If errors are discovered after the publication or presentation of research and other information, school psychologists make efforts to correct errors by publishing errata, retractions, or corrections.
11. School psychologists accurately reflect the contributions of authors and other individuals in publications and presentations. Authorship credit and the order in which authors are listed are based on the relative contributions of the individual authors. Authorship credit is given only to individuals who have made substantial professional contributions to the research, publication, or presentation.
12. School psychologists only publish data or other information that make original contributions to the professional literature. School psychologists do not publish the same finding in two or more publications and do not duplicate significant portions of their own previous publications without permission of copyright holders.
13. School psychologists who participate in reviews of manuscripts, proposals, and other materials for consideration for publication and presentation respect the confidentiality and proprietary rights of the authors. School psychologists who review professional materials limit their use of the materials to the activities relevant to the purposes of the professional review. School psychologists who review professional materials do not communicate the identity of the author, quote from the materials, or duplicate or circulate copies of the materials without the author's permission.

V. PROFESSIONAL PRACTICE SETTINGS—INDEPENDENT PRACTICE

A. Relationship with Employers

1. Some school psychologists are employed in a variety of settings, organizational structures, and sectors and, as such, may create a conflict of interest. School psychologists operating in these different settings recognize the importance of ethical standards and the separation of roles and take full responsibility for protecting and completely informing the consumer of all potential concerns.
2. School psychologists dually employed in independent practice and in a school district may not accept any form of remuneration from clients who are entitled to the same service provided by the school district employing the school psychologist. This includes children who attend the non-public schools within the school psychologist's district.
3. School psychologists in independent practice have an obligation to inform parents of any school psychological services available to them at no cost from the public or private schools prior to delivering such services for remuneration.
4. School psychologists working in both independent practice and

employed by school districts conduct all independent practice outside of the hours of contracted public employment.

5. School psychologists engaged in independent practice do not use tests, materials, equipment, facilities, secretarial assistance, or other services belonging to the public sector employer unless approved in advance by the employer.

B. Service Delivery

1. School psychologists conclude a financial agreement in advance of service delivery.
   a. School psychologists ensure to the best of their ability that the client clearly understands the agreement.
   b. School psychologists neither give nor receive any remuneration for referring children and other clients for professional services.
2. School psychologists in independent practice adhere to the conditions of a contract until service thereunder has been performed, the contract has been terminated by mutual consent, or the contract has otherwise been legally terminated.
3. School psychologists in independent practice prevent misunderstandings resulting from their recommendations, advice, or information. Most often, direct consultation between the school psychologist in private practice and the school psychologist responsible for the student in the public sector will resolve minor differences of opinion without unnecessarily confusing the parents, yet keep the best interest of the student or client in mind.
4. Personal diagnosis and therapy are not given by means of public lectures, newspaper columns, magazine articles, radio and television programs, or mail. Any information shared through mass media activities is general in nature and is openly declared to be so.

C. Announcements/Advertising

1. Appropriate announcement of services, advertising, and public media statements may be necessary for school psychologists in independent practice. Accurate representations of training, experience, services provided, and affiliation are done in a restrained manner. Public statements must be based on sound and accepted theory, research, and practice.
2. Listings in telephone directories are limited to the following: Name/names, highest relevant degree, state certification/licensure status, national certification status, address, telephone number, brief identification of major areas of practice, office hours, appropriate fee information, foreign languages spoken, policy regarding third-party payments, and license number.
3. Announcements of services by school psychologists in independent practice are made in a formal, professional manner using the guidelines of V-C-2. Clear statements of purposes with unequivocal descriptions of the experiences to be provided are given. Education, training, and experience of all staff members are appropriately specified.
4. School psychologists in independent practice may use brochures in the announcement of services. The

brochures may be sent to other professionals, schools, business firms, governmental agencies, and other similar organizations.

5. Announcements and advertisements of the availability of publications, products, and services for sale are professional and factual.
6. School psychologists in independent practice do not directly solicit clients for individual diagnosis, therapy, and for the provision of other school psychological services.
7. School psychologists do not compensate in any manner a representative of the press, radio, or television in return for personal professional publicity in a news item.

Appendix B

ETHICAL PRINCIPLES OF PSYCHOLOGISTS AND CODE OF CONDUCT[1]

INTRODUCTION AND APPLICABILITY

The American Psychological Association's (APA's) Ethical Principles of Psychologists and Code of Conduct (hereinafter referred to as the Ethics Code) consists of an Introduction, a Preamble, five General Principles (A–E), and specific Ethical Standards. The Introduction discusses the intent, organization, procedural considerations, and scope of application of the Ethics Code. The Preamble and General Principles are aspirational goals to guide psychologists toward the highest ideals of psychology. Although the Preamble and General Principles are not themselves enforceable rules, they should be considered by psychologists in arriving at an ethical course of action. The Ethical Standards set forth enforceable rules for conduct as psychologists. Most of the Ethical Standards are written broadly, in order to apply to psychologists in varied roles, although the application of an Ethical Standard may vary depending on the context. The Ethical Standards are not exhaustive. The fact that a given conduct is not specifically addressed by an Ethical Standard does not mean that it is necessarily either ethical or unethical.

This Ethics Code applies only to psychologists' activities that are part of their scientific, educational, or professional roles as psychologists. Areas covered include but are not limited to the clinical, counseling, and school practice of psychology; research; teaching; supervision of trainees; public service; policy development; social intervention; development of assessment instruments; conducting assessments; educational counseling; organizational consulting; forensic activities; program design and evaluation; and administration. This Ethics Code applies to these activities across a variety of contexts, such as in person, postal, telephone, internet, and other electronic transmissions. These activities shall be distinguished from the purely private conduct of psychologists, which is not within the purview of the Ethics Code.

Membership in the APA commits members and student affiliates to comply with the standards of the APA Ethics Code and to the rules and procedures used to enforce them. Lack of awareness or misunderstanding of an Ethical Standard is not itself a defense to a charge of unethical conduct.

The procedures for filing, investigating, and resolving complaints of unethical conduct are described in the current Rules and Procedures of the APA Ethics Committee. APA may impose sanctions on its members for violations of the standards of the Ethics Code, including termination of APA membership, and may notify other bodies and individuals of its actions. Actions that violate the standards of the Ethics Code may also lead to the imposition of sanctions on psychologists or students whether or not they are APA members by bodies other than APA, including state psychological associations, other professional groups, psychology boards, other state or federal agencies, and payors for health services. In addition, APA may take action against a member after his or her conviction of a felony, expulsion or suspension from an affiliated state psychological association, or suspension or loss of licensure.

The Ethics Code is intended to provide guidance for psychologists and standards of professional conduct that can be applied by the APA and by other bodies that choose to adopt them. The Ethics Code is not intended to be a basis of civil liability. Whether a psychologist has violated the Ethics Code does not by itself determine whether the psychologist is legally liable in a court action, whether a contract is enforceable, or whether other legal consequences occur.

The modifiers used in some of the standards of this Ethics Code (e.g., *reasonably*, *appropriate*, *potentially*) are included in the standards when they would (1) allow professional judgment on the part of psychologists, (2) eliminate injustice or inequality that would occur without the modifier, (3) ensure applicability across the broad range of activities conducted by psychologists, or (4) guard against a set of rigid rules that might be quickly outdated. As used in this Ethics Code, the term *reasonable* means the prevailing professional judgment of psychologists engaged in similar activities in similar circumstances, given the knowledge the psychologist had or should have had at the time.

PREAMBLE

Psychologists are committed to increasing scientific and professional knowledge of behavior and people's understanding of themselves and others and to the use of such knowledge to improve the condition of individuals, organizations, and society. Psychologists respect and protect civil and human rights and the central importance of freedom of inquiry and expression in research, teaching, and publication. They strive to help the public in developing informed judgments and choices concerning human behavior. In doing so, they perform many roles, such as researcher, educator, diagnostician, therapist, supervisor, consultant, administrator, social interventionist, and expert witness. This Ethics Code provides a common set of principles and standards upon which psychologists build their professional and scientific work.

This Ethics Code is intended to provide specific standards to cover most situations encountered by psychologists. It has as its goals the welfare and protection of the individuals and groups with whom psychologists work and the education of members, students, and the public regarding ethical standards of the discipline.

The development of a dynamic set of ethical standards for psychologists' work-related conduct requires a personal commitment and lifelong effort to act ethically; to encourage ethical behavior by students, supervisees, employees, and colleagues; and to consult with others concerning ethical problems.

GENERAL PRINCIPLES

This section consists of General Principles. General Principles, as opposed to Ethical Standards, are aspirational in nature. Their intent is to guide and inspire psychologists toward the very highest ethical ideals of the profession. General Principles, in contrast to Ethical Standards, do not represent obligations and should not form the basis for imposing sanctions. Relying upon General Principles for either of these reasons distorts both their meaning and purpose.

PRINCIPLE A: BENEFICENCE AND NON-MALEFICENCE

Psychologists strive to benefit those with whom they work and take care to do no harm. In their professional actions, psychologists seek to safeguard the welfare and rights of those with whom they interact professionally and other affected persons, and the welfare of animal subjects of research. When conflicts occur among psychologists' obligations or concerns, they attempt to resolve these conflicts in a responsible fashion that avoids or minimizes harm. Because psychologists' scientific and professional judgments and actions may affect the lives of others, they are alert to and guard against personal, financial, social, organizational, or political factors that might lead to misuse of their influence. Psychologists strive to be aware of the possible effect of their own physical and mental health on their ability to help those with whom they work.

PRINCIPLE B: FIDELITY AND RESPONSIBILITY

Psychologists establish relationships of trust with those with whom they work. They are aware of their professional and scientific responsibilities to society and to the specific communities in which they work. Psychologists uphold professional standards of conduct, clarify their professional roles and obligations, accept appropriate responsibility for their behavior, and seek to manage conflicts of interest that could lead to exploitation or harm. Psychologists consult with, refer to, or cooperate with other professionals and institutions to the extent needed to serve the best interests of those with whom they work. They are concerned about the ethical compliance of their colleagues' scientific and professional conduct. Psychologists strive to contribute a portion of their professional time for little or no compensation or personal advantage.

PRINCIPLE C: INTEGRITY

Psychologists seek to promote accuracy, honesty, and truthfulness in the science, teaching, and practice of psychology. In these activities psychologists do not steal, cheat, or engage in fraud, subterfuge, or intentional misrepresentation of fact. Psychologists strive to keep their promises and to avoid unwise or unclear commitments. In situations in which deception may be ethically justifiable to maximize benefits and minimize harm, psychologists have a serious obligation to consider the need for, the possible consequences of, and their responsibility to correct any resulting mistrust or other harmful effects that arise from the use of such techniques.

PRINCIPLE D: JUSTICE

Psychologists recognize that fairness and justice entitle all persons to access to and benefit from the contributions of psychology and to equal quality in the processes, procedures, and services being conducted by psychologists. Psychologists exercise reasonable judgment and take precautions to ensure that their potential biases, the boundaries of their competence, and the limitations of their expertise do not lead to or condone unjust practices.

PRINCIPLE E: RESPECT FOR PEOPLE'S RIGHTS AND DIGNITY

Psychologists respect the dignity and worth of all people, and the rights of individuals to privacy, confidentiality, and self-determination. Psychologists are aware that special safeguards may be necessary to protect the rights and welfare of persons or communities whose vulnerabilities impair autonomous decision making. Psychologists are aware of and respect cultural, individual, and role differences, including those based on age, gender, gender identity, race, ethnicity, culture, national origin, religion, sexual orientation, disability, language, and socioeconomic status and consider these factors when working with members of such groups. Psychologists try to eliminate the effect on their work of biases based on those factors, and they do not knowingly participate in or condone activities of others based upon such prejudices.

ETHICAL STANDARDS

1. RESOLVING ETHICAL ISSUES

1.01 Misuse of Psychologists' Work

If psychologists learn of misuse or misrepresentation of their work, they take reasonable steps to correct or minimize the misuse or misrepresentation.

1.02 Conflict Between Ethics and Law, Regulations, or Other Governing Legal Authority

If psychologists' ethical responsibilities conflict with law, regulations, or other governing legal authority, psychologists make known their commitment to the Ethics Code and take steps to resolve the conflict. If the conflict is unresolvable via such means, psychologists may adhere to the requirements of the law, regulations, or other governing legal authority.

1.03 Conflicts Between Ethics and Organizational Demands

If the demands of an organization with which psychologists are affiliated or for whom they are working conflict with this Ethics Code, psychologists clarify the nature of the conflict, make known their commitment to the Ethics Code, and to the extent feasible, resolve the conflict in a way that permits adherence to the Ethics Code.

1.04 Informal Resolution of Ethical Violations

When psychologists believe that there may have been an ethical violation by another psychologist, they attempt to resolve the issue by bringing it to the attention of that individual, if an informal resolution appears appropriate and the intervention does not violate any confidentiality rights that may be involved. (See also Standard 1.02, Conflicts Between Ethics and Law, Regulations, or Other Governing Legal Authority, and 1.03, Conflicts Between Ethics and Organizational Demands.)

1.05 Reporting Ethical Violations

If an apparent ethical violation has substantially harmed or is likely to substantially harm a person or organization and is not appropriate for informal resolution under Standard 1.04, Informal Resolution of Ethical Violations, or is not resolved properly in that fashion, psychologists take further action appropriate to the situation. Such action might include referral to state or national committees on professional ethics, to state licensing boards, or to the appropriate institutional authorities. This standard does not apply when an intervention would violate confidentiality rights or when psychologists have been retained to review the work of another psychologist whose professional conduct is in question. (See also Standard 1.02, Conflicts Between Ethics and Law, Regulations, or Other Governing Legal Authority.)

1.06 Cooperating With Ethics Committees

Psychologists cooperate in ethics investigations, proceedings, and resulting requirements of the APA or any affiliated state psychological association to which they belong. In doing so, they address any confidentiality issues. Failure to cooperate is itself an ethics violation. However, making a request for deferment of adjudication of an ethics complaint pending the outcome of litigation does not alone constitute noncooperation.

1.07 Improper Complaints

Psychologists do not file or encourage the filing of ethics complaints that are made with reckless disregard for or willful ignorance of facts that would disprove the allegation.

1.08 Unfair Discrimination Against Complainants and Respondents

Psychologists do not deny persons employment, advancement, admissions to academic or other programs, tenure, or promotion, based solely upon their having made or their being the subject of an ethics complaint. This does not preclude taking action based upon the outcome of such proceedings or considering other appropriate information.

2. COMPETENCE

2.01 Boundaries of Competence

(a) Psychologists provide services, teach, and conduct research with populations and in areas only within the boundaries of their competence, based on their education, training, supervised experience, consultation, study, or professional experience.

(b) Where scientific or professional knowledge in the discipline of psychology establishes that an understanding of factors associated with age, gender, gender identity, race, ethnicity, culture, national origin, religion, sexual orientation, disability, language, or socioeconomic status is essential for effective implementation of their services or research, psychologists have or obtain the training, experience, consultation, or supervision necessary to ensure the competence of their services, or they make appropriate referrals, except as provided in Standard 2.02, Providing Services in Emergencies.

(c) Psychologists planning to provide services, teach, or conduct research involving populations, areas, techniques, or technologies new to them undertake relevant education, training, supervised experience, consultation, or study.

(d) When psychologists are asked to provide services to individuals for whom appropriate mental health services are not available and for which psychologists have not obtained the competence necessary, psychologists with closely related prior training or experience may provide such services in order to ensure that services are not denied if they make a reasonable effort to obtain the competence required by using relevant research, training, consultation, or study.

(e) In those emerging areas in which generally recognized standards for preparatory training do not yet exist, psychologists nevertheless take reasonable steps to ensure the competence of their work and to protect clients/patients, students, supervisees, research participants, organizational clients, and others from harm.

(f) When assuming forensic roles, psychologists are or become reasonably familiar with the judicial or administrative rules governing their roles.

2.02 *Providing Services in Emergencies*

In emergencies, when psychologists provide services to individuals for whom other mental health services are not available and for which psychologists have not obtained the necessary training, psychologists may provide such services in order to ensure that services are not denied. The services are discontinued as soon as the emergency has ended or appropriate services are available.

2.03 *Maintaining Competence*

Psychologists undertake ongoing efforts to develop and maintain their competence.

2.04 *Bases for Scientific and Professional Judgments*

Psychologists' work is based upon established scientific and professional knowledge of the discipline. (See also Standards 2.01e, Boundaries of Competence, and 10.01b, Informed Consent to Therapy.)

2.05 *Delegation of Work to Others*

Psychologists who delegate work to employees, supervisees, or research or teaching assistants or who use the services of others, such as interpreters, take reasonable steps to (1) avoid delegating such work to persons who have a multiple relationship with those being served that would likely lead to exploitation or loss of objectivity; (2) authorize only those responsibilities that such persons can be expected to perform competently on the basis of their education, training, or experience, either independently or with the level of supervision being provided; and (3) see that such persons perform these services competently. (See also Standards 2.02, Providing Services in Emergencies; 3.05, Multiple Relationships; 4.01, Maintaining Confidentiality; 9.01, Bases for Assessments; 9.02, Use of Assessments; 9.03, Informed Consent in Assessments; and 9.07, Assessment by Unqualified Persons.)

2.06 *Personal Problems and Conflicts*

(a) Psychologists refrain from initiating an activity when they know or should know that there is a substantial likelihood that their personal problems will prevent them from performing their work-related activities in a competent manner.

(b) When psychologists become aware of personal problems that may interfere with their performing work-related duties adequately, they take appropriate measures, such as obtaining professional consultation or assistance, and determine whether they should limit, suspend, or terminate their work-related duties. (See also Standard 10.10, Terminating Therapy.)

3. HUMAN RELATIONS

3.01 *Unfair Discrimination*

In their work-related activities, psychologists do not engage in unfair discrimination based on age, gender, gender identity, race, ethnicity, culture, national origin, religion, sexual orientation, disability, socioeconomic status, or any basis proscribed by law.

3.02 *Sexual Harassment*

Psychologists do not engage in sexual harassment. Sexual harassment is sexual solicitation, physical advances, or verbal or nonverbal conduct that is sexual in nature, that occurs in connection with the psychologist's activities or roles as a psychologist, and that either (1) is unwelcome, is offensive, or creates a hostile workplace or educational environment, and the psychologist knows or is told this or (2) is sufficiently severe or intense to be abusive to a reasonable person in the context. Sexual harassment can consist of a single intense or severe act or of multiple persistent or pervasive acts. (See also Standard 1.08, Unfair Discrimination Against Complainants and Respondents.)

3.03 *Other Harassment*

Psychologists do not knowingly engage in behavior that is harassing or demeaning to persons with whom they interact in their work based on factors such as those persons' age, gender, gender identity, race, ethnicity, culture, national origin, religion, sexual orientation, disability, language, or socioeconomic status.

3.04 *Avoiding Harm*

Psychologists take reasonable steps to avoid harming their clients/patients, students, supervisees, research participants, organizational clients, and others with whom they work, and to minimize harm where it is foreseeable and unavoidable.

3.05 *Multiple Relationships*

(a) A multiple relationship occurs when a psychologist is in a professional role with a person and (1) at the same time is in another role with the same person, (2) at the same time is in a relationship with a person closely associated with or related to the person with whom they have the professional relationship, or (3) promises to enter into another relationship in the future with the person or a person closely associated with or related to the person.

A psychologist refrains from entering into a multiple relationship if the multiple relationship could reasonably be expected to impair the psychologist's objectivity, competence, or effectiveness in performing his or her functions as a psychologist, or otherwise risks exploitation or harm to the person with whom the professional relationship exists.

Multiple relationships that would not reasonably be expected to cause impairment or risk exploitation or harm are not unethical.

(b) If a psychologist finds that, due to unforeseen factors, a potentially harmful multiple relationship has arisen, the psychologist takes reasonable steps to resolve it with due regard for the best interests of the affected person and maximal compliance with the Ethics Code.

(c) When psychologists are required by law, institutional policy, or extraordinary circumstances to serve in more than one role in judicial or administrative proceedings, at the outset they clarify role expectations and the extent of confidentiality and thereafter as changes occur. (See also Standards 3.04, Avoiding Harm, and 3.07, Third-Party Requests for Services.)

3.06 *Conflict of Interest*

Psychologists refrain from taking on a professional role when personal, scientific, professional, legal, financial, or other interests or relationships could reasonably be expected to (1) impair their objectivity, competence, or effectiveness in performing their functions as psychologists or (2) expose the person or organization with whom the professional relationship exists to harm or exploitation.

3.07 *Third-Party Requests for Services*

When psychologists agree to provide services to a person or entity at the request of a third party, psychologists attempt to clarify at the outset of the service the nature of the relationship with all individuals or organizations involved. This clarification includes the role of the psychologist (e.g., therapist, consultant, diagnostician, or expert witness), an identification of who is the client, the probable uses of the services provided or the information obtained, and the fact that there may be limits to confidentiality. (See also Standards 3.05, Multiple Relationships, and 4.02, Discussing the Limits of Confidentiality.)

3.08 *Exploitative Relationships*

Psychologists do not exploit persons over whom they have supervisory, evaluative, or other authority such as clients/patients, students, supervisees, research participants, and employees. (See also Stan-dards 3.05, Multiple Relationships; 6.04, Fees and Financial Arrange-ments; 6.05, Barter with Clients/ Patients; 7.07, Sexual Relationships with Students and Supervisees; 10.05, Sexual Intimacies With Current Therapy Clients/Patients; 10.06, Sexual Intimacies with Relatives or Significant Others of Current Therapy Clients/Patients; 10.07, Therapy With Former Sexual Partners; and 10.08, Sexual Intimacies With Former Therapy Clients/Patients.)

3.09 Cooperation with Other Professionals

When indicated and professionally appropriate, psychologists cooperate with other professionals in order to serve their clients/patients effectively and appropriately. (See also Standard 4.05, Disclosures.)

3.10 Informed Consent

(a) When psychologists conduct research or provide assessment, therapy, counseling, or consulting services in person or via electronic transmission or other forms of communication, they obtain the informed consent of the individual or individuals using language that is reasonably understandable to that person or persons except when conducting such activities without consent is mandated by law or governmental regulation or as otherwise provided in this Ethics Code. (See also Standards 8.02, Informed Consent to Research; 9.03, Informed Consent in Assessments; and 10.01, Informed Con-sent to Therapy.)

(b) For persons who are legally incapable of giving informed consent, psychologists nevertheless (1) provide an appropriate explanation, (2) seek the individual's assent, (3) consider such persons' preferences and best interests, and (4) obtain appropriate permission from a legally authorized person, if such substitute consent is permitted or required by law. When consent by a legally authorized person is not permitted or required by law, psychologists take reasonable steps to protect the individual's rights and welfare.

(c) When psychological services are court ordered or otherwise mandated, psychologists inform the individual of the nature of the anticipated services, including whether the services are court ordered or mandated and any limits of confidentiality, before proceeding.

(d) Psychologists appropriately document written or oral consent, permission, and assent. (See also Standards 8.02, Informed Consent to Research; 9.03, Informed Consent in Assessments; and 10.01, Informed Consent to Therapy.)

3.11 Psychological Services Delivered To or Through Organizations

(a) Psychologists delivering services to or through organizations provide information beforehand to clients and when appropriate those directly affected by the services about (1) the nature and objectives of the services, (2) the intended recipients, (3) which of the individuals are clients, (4) the relationship the psychologist will have with each person and the organization, (5) the probable uses of services provided and information obtained, (6) who will have access to the information, and (7) limits of confidentiality. As soon as feasible, they provide information about the results and conclusions of such services to appropriate persons.

(b) If psychologists will be precluded by law or by organizational roles from providing such information to particular individuals or groups, they so inform those individuals or groups at the outset of the service.

3.12 Interruption of Psychological Services

Unless otherwise covered by contract, psychologists make reasonable efforts to plan for facilitating services in the event that psychological services are interrupted by factors such as the psychologist's illness, death, unavailability, relocation, or retirement or by the client's/patient's relocation or financial limitations. (See also Standard 6.02c, Maintenance, Dissemination, and Disposal of Confidential Records of Professional and Scientific Work.)

4. PRIVACY AND CONFIDENTIALITY

4.01 Maintaining Confidentiality

Psychologists have a primary obligation and take reasonable precautions to protect confidential information obtained through or stored in any medium, recognizing that the extent and limits of confidentiality may be regulated by law or established by institutional rules or professional or scientific relationship. (See also Standard 2.05, Delegation of Work to Others.)

4.02 Discussing the Limits of Confidentiality

(a) Psychologists discuss with persons (including, to the extent feasible, persons who are legally incapable of giving informed consent and their legal representatives) and organizations with whom they establish a scientific or professional relationship (1) the relevant limits of confidentiality and (2) the foreseeable uses of the information generated through their psychological activities. (See also Standard 3.10, Informed Consent.)

(b) Unless it is not feasible or is contraindicated, the discussion of confidentiality occurs at the outset of the relationship and thereafter as new circumstances may warrant.

(c) Psychologists who offer services, products, or information via electronic transmission inform clients/patients of the risks to privacy and limits of confidentiality.

4.03 Recording

Before recording the voices or images of individuals to whom they provide services, psychologists obtain permission from all such persons or their legal representatives. (See also Standards 8.03, Informed Consent for Recording Voices and Images in Research; 8.05, Dispensing with Informed Consent for Research; and 8.07, Deception in Research.)

4.04 Minimizing Intrusions on Privacy

(a) Psychologists include in written and oral reports and consultations, only information germane to the purpose for which the communication is made.

(b) Psychologists discuss confidential information obtained in their work only for appropriate scientific or professional purposes and only with persons clearly concerned with such matters.

4.05 Disclosures

(a) Psychologists may disclose confidential information with the appropriate consent of the organizational client, the individual client/patient, or another legally authorized person on behalf of the client/patient unless prohibited by law.

(b) Psychologists disclose confidential information without the consent of the individual only as mandated by law, or where permitted by law for a valid purpose such as to (1) provide needed professional services, (2) obtain appropriate professional consultations, (3) protect the client/patient, psychologist, or others from harm, or (4) obtain payment for services from a client/patient, in which instance disclosure is limited to the minimum that is necessary to achieve the purpose. (See also Standard 6.04e, Fees and Financial Arrangements.)

4.06 Consultations

When consulting with colleagues, (1) psychologists do not disclose confidential information that reasonably could lead to the identification of a client/patient, research participant, or other person or organization with whom they have a confidential relationship unless they have obtained the prior consent of the person or organization or the disclosure cannot be avoided, and (2) they disclose information only to the extent necessary to achieve the purposes of the consultation. (See also Standard 4.01, Maintaining Confidentiality.)

4.07 *Use of Confidential Information for Didactic or Other Purposes*

Psychologists do not disclose in their writings, lectures, or other public media, confidential, personally identifiable information concerning their clients/patients, students, research participants, organizational clients, or other recipients of their services that they obtained during the course of their work, unless (1) they take reasonable steps to disguise the person or organization, (2) the person or organization has consented in writing, or (3) there is legal authorization for doing so.

5. ADVERTISING AND OTHER PUBLIC STATEMENTS

5.01 *Avoidance of False or Deceptive Statements*

(a) Public statements include but are not limited to paid or unpaid advertising, product endorsements, grant applications, licensing applications, other credentialing applications, brochures, printed matter, directory listings, personal resumes or curricula vitae, or comments for use in media such as print or electronic transmission, statements in legal proceedings, lectures and public oral presentations, and published materials. Psychologists do not knowingly make public statements that are false, deceptive, or fraudulent concerning their research, practice, or other work activities or those of persons or organizations with which they are affiliated.

(b) Psychologists do not make false, deceptive, or fraudulent statements concerning (1) their training, experience, or competence; (2) their academic degrees; (3) their credentials; (4) their institutional or association affiliations; (5) their services; (6) the scientific or clinical basis for, or results or degree of success of, their services; (7) their fees; or (8) their publications or research findings.

(c) Psychologists claim degrees as credentials for their health services only if those degrees (1) were earned from a regionally accredited educational institution or (2) were the basis for psychology licensure by the state in which they practice.

5.02 *Statements by Others*

(a) Psychologists who engage others to create or place public statements that promote their professional practice, products, or activities retain professional responsibility for such statements.

(b) Psychologists do not compensate employees of press, radio, television, or other communication media in return for publicity in a news item. (See also Standard 1.01, Misuse of Psychologists' Work.)

(c) A paid advertisement relating to psychologists' activities must be identified or clearly recognizable as such.

5.03 *Descriptions of Workshops and Non-Degree-Granting Educational Programs*

To the degree to which they exercise control, psychologists responsible for announcements, catalogs, brochures, or advertisements describing workshops, seminars, or other non-degree-granting educational programs ensure that they accurately describe the audience for which the program is intended, the educational objectives, the presenters, and the fees involved.

5.04 *Media Presentations*

When psychologists provide public advice or comment via print, internet, or other electronic transmission, they take precautions to ensure that statements (1) are based on their professional knowledge, training, or experience in accord with appropriate psychological literature and practice, (2) are otherwise consistent with this Ethics Code, and (3) do not indicate that a professional relationship has been established with the recipient. (See also Standard 2.04, Bases for Scientific and Professional Judgments.)

5.05 *Testimonials*

Psychologists do not solicit testimonials from current therapy clients/patients or other persons who because of their particular circumstances are vulnerable to undue influence.

5.06 *In-Person Solicitation*

Psychologists do not engage, directly or through agents, in uninvited in-person solicitation of business from actual or potential therapy clients/patients or other persons who because of their particular circumstances are vulnerable to undue influence. However, this prohibition does not preclude (1) attempting to implement appropriate collateral contacts for the purpose of benefiting an already engaged therapy client/patient or (2) providing disaster or community outreach services.

6. RECORD KEEPING AND FEES

6.01 *Documentation of Professional and Scientific Work and Maintenance of Records*

Psychologists create, and to the extent the records are under their control, maintain, disseminate, store, retain, and dispose of records and data relating to their professional and scientific work in order to (1) facilitate provision of services later by them or by other professionals, (2) allow for replication of research design and analyses, (3) meet institutional requirements, (4) ensure accuracy of billing and payments, and (5) ensure compliance with law. (See also Standard 4.01, Maintaining Confidentiality.)

6.02 *Maintenance, Dissemination, and Disposal of Confidential Records of Professional and Scientific Work*

(a) Psychologists maintain confidentiality in creating, storing, accessing, transferring, and disposing of records under their control, whether these are written, automated, or in any other medium. (See also Standards 4.01, Maintaining Confidentiality, and 6.01, Documentation of Professional and Scientific Work and Maintenance of Records.)

(b) If confidential information concerning recipients of psychological services is entered into databases or systems of records available to persons whose access has not been consented to by the recipient, psychologists use coding or other techniques to avoid the inclusion of personal identifiers.

(c) Psychologists make plans in advance to facilitate the appropriate transfer and to protect the confidentiality of records and data in the event of psychologists' withdrawal from positions or practice. (See also Standards 3.12, Interruption of Psychological Services, and 10.09, Interruption of Therapy.)

6.03 *Withholding Records for Nonpayment*

Psychologists may not withhold records under their control that are requested and needed for a client's/patient's emergency treatment solely because payment has not been received.

6.04 *Fees and Financial Arrangements*

(a) As early as is feasible in a professional or scientific relationship, psychologists and recipients of psychological services reach an agreement specifying compensation and billing arrangements.

(b) Psychologists' fee practices are consistent with law.

(c) Psychologists do not misrepresent their fees.

(d) If limitations to services can be anticipated because of limitations in financing, this is discussed with the recipient of services as early as is feasible. (See also Standards 10.09, Interruption of Services, and 10.10, Terminating Therapy.)

(e) If the recipient of services does not pay for services as agreed, and if psychologists intend to use collection agencies or legal measures to collect the fees, psychologists first inform the person that such measures will be taken and provide that person an opportunity to make prompt payment. (See also Standards 4.05, Disclosures; 6.03, Withholding Records for Nonpayment; and 10.01, Informed Consent to Therapy.)

6.05 Barter with Clients/Patients

Barter is the acceptance of goods, services, or other nonmonetary remuneration from clients/patients in return for psychological services. Psychologists may barter only if (1) it is not clinically contraindicated, and (2) the resulting arrangement is not exploitative. (See also Standards 3.05, Multiple Relationships, and 6.04, Fees and Financial Arrangements.)

6.06 Accuracy in Reports to Payors and Funding Sources

In their reports to payors for services or sources of research funding, psychologists take reasonable steps to ensure the accurate reporting of the nature of the service provided or research conducted, the fees, charges, or payments, and where applicable, the identity of the provider, the findings, and the diagnosis. (See also Standards 4.01, Maintaining Confidentiality; 4.04, Minimizing Intrusions on Privacy; and 4.05, Disclosures.)

6.07 Referrals and Fees

When psychologists pay, receive payment from, or divide fees with another professional, other than in an employer-employee relationship, the payment to each is based on the services provided (clinical, consultative, administrative, or other) and is not based on the referral itself. (See also Standard 3.09, Cooperation with Other Professionals.)

7. EDUCATION AND TRAINING

7.01 Design of Education and Training Programs

Psychologists responsible for education and training programs take reasonable steps to ensure that the programs are designed to provide the appropriate knowledge and proper experiences, and to meet the requirements for licensure, certification, or other goals for which claims are made by the program. (See also Standard 5.03, Descriptions of Workshops and Non-Degree-Granting Educational Programs.)

7.02 Descriptions of Education and Training Programs

Psychologists responsible for education and training programs take reasonable steps to ensure that there is a current and accurate description of the program content (including participation in required course- or program-related counseling, psychotherapy, experiential groups, consulting projects, or community service), training goals and objectives, stipends and benefits, and requirements that must be met for satisfactory completion of the program. This information must be made readily available to all interested parties.

7.03 Accuracy in Teaching

(a) Psychologists take reasonable steps to ensure that course syllabi are accurate regarding the subject matter to be covered, bases for evaluating progress, and the nature of course experiences. This standard does not preclude an instructor from modifying course content or requirements when the instructor considers it pedagogically necessary or desirable, so long as students are made aware of these modifications in a manner that enables them to fulfill course requirements. (See also Standard 5.01, Avoidance of False or Deceptive Statements.)

(b) When engaged in teaching or training, psychologists present psychological information accurately. (See also Standard 2.03, Maintaining Competence.)

7.04 *Student Disclosure of Personal Information*

Psychologists do not require students or supervisees to disclose personal information in course- or program-related activities, either orally or in writing, regarding sexual history, history of abuse and neglect, psychological treatment, and relationships with parents, peers, and spouses or significant others except if (1) the program or training facility has clearly identified this requirement in its admissions and program materials or (2) the information is necessary to evaluate or obtain assistance for students whose personal problems could reasonably be judged to be preventing them from performing their training- or professionally related activities in a competent manner or posing a threat to the students or others.

7.05 *Mandatory Individual or Group Therapy*

(a) When individual or group therapy is a program or course requirement, psychologists responsible for that program allow students in undergraduate and graduate programs the option of selecting such therapy from practitioners unaffiliated with the program. (See also Standard 7.02, Descriptions of Education and Training Programs.)

(b) Faculty who are or are likely to be responsible for evaluating students' academic performance do not themselves provide that therapy. (See also Standard 3.05, Multiple Relationships.)

7.06 *Assessing Student and Supervisee Performance*

(a) In academic and supervisory relationships, psychologists establish a timely and specific process for providing feedback to students and supervisees. Information regarding the process is provided to the student at the beginning of supervision.

(b) Psychologists evaluate students and supervisees on the basis of their actual performance on relevant and established program requirements.

7.07 *Sexual Relationships with Students and Supervisees*

Psychologists do not engage in sexual relationships with students or supervisees who are in their department, agency, or training center or over whom psychologists have or are likely to have evaluative authority. (See also Standard 3.05, Multiple Relationships.)

8. RESEARCH AND PUBLICATION

8.01 *Institutional Approval*

When institutional approval is required, psychologists provide accurate information about their research proposals and obtain approval prior to conducting the research. They conduct the research in accordance with the approved research protocol.

8.02 *Informed Consent to Research*

(a) When obtaining informed consent as required in Standard 3.10, Informed Consent, psychologists inform participants about (1) the purpose of the research, expected duration, and procedures; (2) their right to decline to participate and to withdraw from the research once participation has begun; (3) the foreseeable consequences of declining or withdrawing; (4) reasonably foreseeable factors that may be expected to influence their willingness to participate such as potential risks, discomfort, or adverse effects; (5) any prospective research benefits; (6) limits of confidentiality; (7) incentives for participation; and (8) whom to contact for questions about the research and research participants' rights. They provide opportunity for the prospective participants to ask questions and receive answers. (See also Standards 8.03, Informed Consent for Recording Voices and Images in Research; 8.05, Dispensing with Informed Consent for Research, and 8.07, Deception in Research.)

(b) Psychologists conducting intervention research involving the use of experimental treatments, clarify to participants at the outset of the research (1) the experimental nature of the treatment; (2) the services that will or will not be available to the control group(s) if appropriate; (3) the means by which assignment to treatment and control groups will be made; (4) available treatment alternatives if an individual does not wish to participate in the research or wishes to withdraw once a study has begun; and (5) compensation for or monetary costs of participating including, if appropriate, whether reimbursement from the participant or a third-party payor will be sought. (See also Standard 8.02a, Informed Consent to Research.)

8.03 Informed Consent for Recording Voices and Images in Research

Psychologists obtain informed consent from research participants prior to recording their voices or images for data collection unless (1) the research consists solely of naturalistic observations in public places, and it is not anticipated that the recording will be used in a manner that could cause personal identification or harm or (2) the research design includes deception, and consent for the use of the recording is obtained during debriefing. (See also Standard 8.07, Deception in Research.)

8.04 Client/Patient, Student, and Subordinate Research Participants

(a) When psychologists conduct research with clients/patients, students, or subordinates as participants, psychologists take steps to protect the prospective participants from adverse consequences of declining or withdrawing from participation.

(b) When research participation is a course requirement or opportunity for extra credit, the prospective participant is given the choice of equitable alternative activities.

8.05 Dispensing With Informed Consent for Research

Psychologists may dispense with informed consent only (1) where research would not reasonably be assumed to create distress or harm and involves (a) the study of normal educational practices, curricula, or classroom management methods conducted in educational settings; (b) only anonymous questionnaires, naturalistic observations, or archival research for which disclosure of responses would not place participants at risk of criminal or civil liability or damage their financial standing, employability, or reputation, and confidentiality is protected; or (c) the study of factors related to job or organization effectiveness conducted in organizational settings for which there is no risk to participants' employability and confidentiality is protected or (2) where otherwise permitted by law or federal or institutional regulations.

8.06 Offering Inducements for Research Participation

(a) Psychologists make reasonable efforts to avoid offering excessive or inappropriate financial or other inducements for research participation when such inducements are likely to coerce participation.

(b) When offering professional services as an inducement for research participation, psychologists clarify the nature of the services, as well as the risks, obligations, and limitations. (See also Standard 6.05, Barter With Clients/Patients.)

8.07 *Deception in Research*

(a) Psychologists do not conduct a study involving deception unless they have determined that the use of deceptive techniques is justified by the study's significant prospective scientific, educational, or applied value and that effective nondeceptive alternative procedures are not feasible.

(b) Psychologists do not deceive prospective participants about research that is reasonably expected to cause physical pain or severe emotional distress.

(c) Psychologists explain any deception that is an integral feature of the design and conduct of an experiment to participants as early as is feasible, preferably at the conclusion of their participation, but no later than at the conclusion of the data collection, and permit participants to withdraw their data. (See also Standard 8.08, Debriefing.)

8.08 *Debriefing*

(a) Psychologists provide a prompt opportunity for participants to obtain appropriate information about the nature, results, and conclusions of the research, and they take reasonable steps to correct any misconceptions that participants may have of which the psychologists are aware.

(b) If scientific or humane values justify delaying or withholding this information, psychologists take reasonable measures to reduce the risk of harm.

(c) When psychologists become aware that research procedures have harmed a participant, they take reasonable steps to minimize the harm.

8.09 *Humane Care and Use of Animals in Research*

(a) Psychologists acquire, care for, use, and dispose of animals in compliance with current federal, state, and local laws and regulations, and with professional standards.

(b) Psychologists trained in research methods and experienced in the care of laboratory animals supervise all procedures involving animals and are responsible for ensuring appropriate consideration of their comfort, health, and humane treatment.

(c) Psychologists ensure that all individuals under their supervision who are using animals have received instruction in research methods and in the care, maintenance, and handling of the species being used, to the extent appropriate to their role. (See also Standard 2.05, Delegation of Work to Others.)

(d) Psychologists make reasonable efforts to minimize the discomfort, infection, illness, and pain of animal subjects.

(e) Psychologists use a procedure subjecting animals to pain, stress, or privation only when an alternative procedure is unavailable and the goal is justified by its prospective scientific, educational, or applied value.

(f) Psychologists perform surgical procedures under appropriate anesthesia and follow techniques to avoid infection and minimize pain during and after surgery.

(g) When it is appropriate that an animal's life be terminated, psychologists proceed rapidly, with an effort to minimize pain and in accordance with accepted procedures.

8.10 Reporting Research Results

(a) Psychologists do not fabricate data. (See also Standard 5.01a, Avoidance of False or Deceptive Statements.)

(b) If psychologists discover significant errors in their published data, they take reasonable steps to correct such errors in a correction, retraction, erratum, or other appropriate publication means.

8.11 Plagiarism

Psychologists do not present portions of another's work or data as their own, even if the other work or data source is cited occasionally.

8.12 Publication Credit

(a) Psychologists take responsibility and credit, including authorship credit, only for work they have actually performed or to which they have substantially contributed. (See also Standard 8.12b, Publication Credit.)

(b) Principal authorship and other publication credits accurately reflect the relative scientific or professional contributions of the individuals involved, regardless of their relative status. Mere possession of an institutional position, such as department chair, does not justify authorship credit. Minor contributions to the research or to the writing for publications are acknowledged appropriately, such as in footnotes or in an introductory statement.

(c) Except under exceptional circumstances, a student is listed as principal author on any multiple-authored article that is substantially based on the student's doctoral dissertation. Faculty advisors discuss publication credit with students as early as feasible and throughout the research and publication process as appropriate. (See also Standard 8.12b, Publication Credit.)

8.1 Duplicate Publication of Data

Psychologists do not publish, as original data, data that have been previously published. This does not preclude republishing data when they are accompanied by proper acknowledgment.

8.14 Sharing Research Data for Verification

(a) After research results are published, psychologists do not withhold the data on which their conclusions are based from other competent professionals who seek to verify the substantive claims through reanalysis and who intend to use such data only for that purpose, provided that the confidentiality of the participants can be protected and unless legal rights concerning proprietary data preclude their release. This does not preclude psychologists from requiring that such individuals or groups be responsible for costs associated with the provision of such information.

(b) Psychologists who request data from other psychologists to verify the substantive claims through reanalysis may use shared data only for the declared purpose. Requesting psychologists obtain prior written agreement for all other uses of the data.

8.15 Reviewers

Psychologists who review material submitted for presentation, publication, grant, or research proposal review respect the confidentiality of and the proprietary rights in such information of those who submitted it.

9. ASSESSMENT

9.01 Bases for Assessments

(a) Psychologists base the opinions contained in their recommendations, reports, and diagnostic or evaluative statements, including forensic testimony, on information and techniques sufficient to substantiate their findings. (See also Standard 2.04, Bases for Scientific and Professional Judgments.)

(b) Except as noted in 9.01 c, psychologists provide opinions of the psychological characteristics of individuals only after they have conducted an examination of the individuals adequate to support their statements or conclusions. When, despite reasonable efforts, such an examination is not practical, psychologists document the efforts they made and the result of those efforts, clarify the probable impact of their limited information on the reliability and validity of their opinions, and appropriately limit the nature and extent of their conclusions or recommendations. (See also Standards 2.01, Boundaries of Competence, and 9.06, Interpreting Assessment Results.)

(c) When psychologists conduct a record review or provide consultation or supervision and an individual examination is not warranted or necessary for the opinion, psychologists explain this and the sources of information on which they based their conclusions and recommendations.

9.02 Use of Assessments

(a) Psychologists administer, adapt, score, interpret, or use assessment techniques, interviews, tests, or instruments in a manner and for purposes that are appropriate in light of the research on or evidence of the usefulness and proper application of the techniques.

(b) Psychologists use assessment instruments whose validity and reliability have been established for use with members of the population tested. When such validity or reliability has not been established, psychologists describe the strengths and limitations of test results and interpretation.

(c) Psychologists use assessment methods that are appropriate to an individual's language preference and competence, unless the use of an alternative language is relevant to the assessment issues.

9.03 Informed Consent In Assessments

(a) Psychologists obtain informed consent for assessments, evaluations, or diagnostic services, as described in Standard 3.10, Informed Consent, except when (1) testing is mandated by law or governmental regulations; (2) informed consent is implied because testing is conducted as a routine educational, institutional, or organizational activity (e.g., when participants voluntarily agree to assessment when applying for a job); or (3) one purpose of the testing is to evaluate decisional capacity. Informed consent includes an explanation of the nature and purpose of the assessment, fees, involvement of third parties, and limits of confidentiality and sufficient opportunity for the client/patient to ask questions and receive answers.

(b) Psychologists inform persons with questionable capacity to consent or for whom testing is mandated by law or governmental regulations about the nature and purpose of the proposed assessment services, using language that is reasonably understandable to the person being assessed.

(c) Psychologists using the services of an interpreter obtain informed consent from the client/patient to use that interpreter, ensure that confidentiality of test results and test security are maintained, and include in their recommendations, reports, and diagnostic or evaluative statements, including forensic testimony, discussion of any limitations on the data obtained. (See also Standards 2.05, Delegation of Work to Others; 4.01, Maintaining Confidentiality; 9.01, Bases for Assessments; 9.06, Interpreting Assessment Results; and 9.07, Assessment by Unqualified Persons.)

9.04 *Release of Test Data*

(a) The term *test data* refers to raw and scaled scores, client/patient responses to test questions or stimuli, and psychologists' notes and recordings concerning client/ patient statements and behavior during an examination. Those portions of test materials that include client/patient responses are included in the definition of *test data*. Pursuant to a client/patient release, psychologists provide test data to the client/patient or other persons identified in the release. Psychologists may refrain from releasing test data to protect a client/patient or others from substantial harm or misuse or misrepresentation of the data or the test, recognizing that in many instances release of confidential information under these circumstances is regulated by law. (See also Standard 9.11, Maintaining Test Security.)

(b) In the absence of a client/patient release, psychologists provide test data only as required by law or court order.

9.05 *Test Construction*

Psychologists who develop tests and other assessment techniques use appropriate psychometric procedures and current scientific or professional knowledge for test design, standardization, validation, reduction or elimination of bias, and recommendations for use.

9.06 *Interpreting Assessment Results*

When interpreting assessment results, including automated interpretations, psychologists take into account the purpose of the assessment as well as the various test factors, test-taking abilities, and other characteristics of the person being assessed, such as situational, personal, linguistic, and cultural differences, that might affect psychologists' judgments or reduce the accuracy of their interpretations. They indicate any significant limitations of their interpretations. (See also Standards 2.01 b and c, Boundaries of Competence, and 3.01, Unfair Discrimination.)

9.07 *Assessment by Unqualified Persons*

Psychologists do not promote the use of psychological assessment techniques by unqualified persons, except when such use is conducted for training purposes with appropriate supervision. (See also Standard 2.05, Delegation of Work to Others.)

9.08 *Obsolete Tests and Outdated Test Results*

(a) Psychologists do not base their assessment or intervention decisions or recommendations on data or test results that are outdated for the current purpose.

(b) Psychologists do not base such decisions or recommendations on tests and measures that are obsolete and not useful for the current purpose.

9.09 *Test Scoring and Interpretation Services*

(a) Psychologists who offer assessment or scoring services to other professionals accurately describe the purpose, norms, validity, reliability, and applications of the procedures and any special qualifications applicable to their use.

(b) Psychologists select scoring and interpretation services (including automated services) on the basis of evidence of the validity of the program and procedures as well as on other appropriate considerations. (See also Standard 2.01 b and c, Boundaries of Competence.)

(c) Psychologists retain responsibility for the appropriate application, interpretation, and use of assessment instruments, whether they score and interpret such tests themselves or use automated or other services.

9.10 Explaining Assessment Results

Regardless of whether the scoring and interpretation are done by psychologists, by employees or assistants, or by automated or other outside services, psychologists take reasonable steps to ensure that explanations of results are given to the individual or designated representative unless the nature of the relationship precludes provision of an explanation of results (such as in some organizational consulting, preemployment or security screenings, and forensic evaluations), and this fact has been clearly explained to the person being assessed in advance.

9.11. Maintaining Test Security

The term *test materials* refers to manuals, instruments, protocols, and test questions or stimuli and does not include *test data* as defined in Standard 9.04, Release of Test Data. Psychologists make reasonable efforts to maintain the integrity and security of test materials and other assessment techniques consistent with law, contractual obligations, and in a manner that permits adherence to this Ethics Code.

10. THERAPY

10.01 Informed Consent to Therapy

(a) When obtaining informed consent to therapy as required in Standard 3.10, Informed Consent, psychologists inform clients/patients as early as is feasible in the therapeutic relationship about the nature and anticipated course of therapy, fees, involvement of third parties, and limits of confidentiality and provide sufficient opportunity for the client/patient to ask questions and receive answers. (See also Standards 4.02, Discussing the Limits of Confidentiality, and 6.04, Fees and Financial Arrangements.)

(b) When obtaining informed consent for treatment for which generally recognized techniques and procedures have not been established, psychologists inform their clients/patients of the developing nature of the treatment, the potential risks involved, alternative treatments that may be available, and the voluntary nature of their participation. (See also Standards 2.01e, Boundaries of Competence, and 3.10, Informed Consent.)

(c) When the therapist is a trainee and the legal responsibility for the treatment provided resides with the supervisor, the client/patient, as part of the informed consent procedure, is informed that the therapist is in training and is being supervised and is given the name of the supervisor.

10.02 Therapy Involving Couples or Families

(a) When psychologists agree to provide services to several persons who have a relationship (such as spouses, significant others, or parents and children), they take reasonable steps to clarify at the outset (1) which of the individuals are clients/patients and (2) the relationship the psychologist will have with each person. This clarification includes the psychologist's role and the probable uses of the services provided or the information obtained. (See also Standard 4.02, Discussing the Limits of Confidentiality.)

(b) If it becomes apparent that psychologists may be called on to perform potentially conflicting roles (such as family therapist and then witness for one party in divorce proceedings), psychologists take reasonable steps to clarify and modify, or withdraw from, roles appropriately. (See also Standard 3.05c, Multiple Relationships.)

10.03 Group Therapy

When psychologists provide services to several persons in a group setting, they describe at the outset the roles and responsibilities of all parties and the limits of confidentiality.

10.04 Providing Therapy to Those Served by Others

In deciding whether to offer or provide services to those already receiving mental health services elsewhere, psychologists carefully consider the treatment issues and the potential client's/patient's welfare. Psychologists discuss these issues with the client/patient or another legally authorized person on behalf of the client/patient in order to minimize the risk of confusion and conflict, consult with the other service providers when appropriate, and proceed with caution and sensitivity to the therapeutic issues.

10.05 Sexual Intimacies With Current Therapy Clients/Patients

Psychologists do not engage in sexual intimacies with current therapy clients/patients.

10.06 Sexual Intimacies with Relatives or Significant Others of Current Therapy Clients/Patients

Psychologists do not engage in sexual intimacies with individuals they know to be close relatives, guardians, or significant others of current clients/patients. Psychologists do not terminate therapy to circumvent this standard.

10.07 Therapy With Former Sexual Partners

Psychologists do not accept as therapy clients/patients persons with whom they have engaged in sexual intimacies.

10.08 Sexual Intimacies With Former Therapy Clients/Patients

(a) Psychologists do not engage in sexual intimacies with former clients/patients for at least two years after cessation or termination of therapy.

(b) Psychologists do not engage in sexual intimacies with former clients/patients even after a two-year interval except in the most unusual circumstances. Psychologists who engage in such activity after the two years following cessation or termination of therapy and of having no sexual contact with the former client/patient bear the burden of demonstrating that there has been no exploitation, in light of all relevant factors, including (1) the amount of time that has passed since therapy terminated; (2) the nature, duration, and intensity of the therapy; (3) the circumstances of termination; (4) the client's/patient's personal history; (5) the client's/patient's current mental status; (6) the likelihood of adverse impact on the client/patient; and (7) any statements or actions made by the therapist during the course of therapy suggesting or inviting the possibility of a post-termination sexual or romantic relationship with the client/patient. (See also Standard 3.05, Multiple Relationships.)

10.09 Interruption of Therapy

When entering into employment or contractual relationships, psychologists make reasonable efforts to provide for orderly and appropriate resolution of responsibility for client/patient care in the event that the employment or contractual relationship ends, with paramount consideration given to the welfare of the client/patient. (See also

Standard 3.12, Interruption of Psychological Services.)

10.10 Terminating Therapy

(a) Psychologists terminate therapy when it becomes reasonably clear that the client/patient no longer needs the service, is not likely to benefit, or is being harmed by continued service.

(b) Psychologists may terminate therapy when threatened or otherwise endangered by the client/patient or another person with whom the client/patient has a relationship.

(c) Except where precluded by the actions of clients/patients or third-party payors, prior to termination psychologists provide pretermination counseling and suggest alternative service providers as appropriate.

History and Effective Date Footnote

This version of the APA Ethics Code was adopted by the American Psychological Association's Council of Representatives during its meeting, August 21, 2002, and is effective beginning June 1, 2003. Inquiries concerning the substance or interpretation of the APA Ethics Code should be addressed to the Director, Office of Ethics, American Psychological Association, 750 First Street, NE, Washington, DC 20002-4242. The Ethics Code and information regarding the Code can be found on the APA web site, www.apa.org/ethics. The standards in this Ethics Code will be used to adjudicate complaints brought concerning alleged conduct occurring on or after the effective date. Complaints regarding conduct occurring prior to the effective date will be adjudicated on the basis of the version of the Ethics Code that was in effect at the time the conduct occurred.

The APA has previously published its Ethics Code as follows:

American Psychological Association. (1953). Ethical standards of psychologists. Washington, DC: Author.

American Psychological Association. (1959). Ethical standards of psychologists. American Psychologist, 14, 279-282.

American Psychological Association. (1963). Ethical standards of psychologists. American Psychologist, 18, 56-60.

American Psychological Association. (1968). Ethical standards of psychologists. American Psychologist, 23, 357-361.

American Psychological Associa-tion. (1977, March). Ethical standards of psychologists. APA Monitor, 22-23.

American Psychological Association. (1979). Ethical standards of psychologists. Washington, DC: Author.

American Psychological Association. (1981). Ethical principles of psychologists. American Psychologist, 36, 633-638.

American Psychological Association. (1990). Ethical principles of psychologists (Amended June 2, 1989). American Psychologist, 45, 390-395.

American Psychological Association. (1992). Ethical principles of psychologists and code of conduct. American Psychologist, 47, 1597-1611.

Request copies of the APA's Ethical Principles of Psychologists and Code of Conduct from the APA Order Department, 750 First Street, NE, Washington, DC 20002-4242, or phone (202) 336-5510.

Appendix C

GUIDELINES FOR THE PROVISION OF SCHOOL PSYCHOLOGICAL SERVICES[1]

INTRODUCTION

The *Guidelines for the Provision of School Psychological Services* represents the position of the National Association of School Psychologists regarding the delivery of appropriate and comprehensive school psychological services. First written in 1978, revised in 1984, 1992, 1997, and 2000, the *Guidelines* serve as a guide to the organization and delivery of school psychological services at the federal, state, and local levels. The *Guidelines* provide direction to school psychologists, students, and trainers in school psychology, administrators of school psychological services, and consumers of school psychological services regarding excellence in professional school psychology. They also delineate what services might reasonably be expected to be available from most school psychologists and, thus, should help to further define the field. In addition, they are intended to educate the profession and the public regarding appropriate professional practices and, hopefully, will stimulate the continued development of the profession.

A principal objective of the *Guidelines* is to inform policy- and decision-makers of the major characteristics of comprehensive school psychological services. The first section presents the responsibilities of the individual school psychologist. The second section outlines responsibilities that should be assumed by the unit responsible for providing psychological services within an organization (e.g., school district, community agency) that employs school psychologists. The "unit" is defined as the entity (e.g., the single school psychologist in a small district, a psychological services unit in a large district, a district that contracts with an agency for psychological services) that is responsible for ensuring that schools, students, and families receive comprehensive psychological services.

Not all school psychologists or school psychological service units will be able to meet every standard contained within this document. Nevertheless, it is anticipated that these guidelines will serve as a model of "good practice" for program development and professional practice on a federal, state, and local level.

[1] Copyright 2000 by the National Association of School Psychologists. Reprinted by permission of the publisher.

School psychologists will perceive that it is in their own best interest—and that of the agencies, parents, and children they serve—to adhere to and support these *Guidelines*. NASP encourages state and federal legislators, local school boards, and the administrative leaders of federal, state, and local education agencies to support the concepts contained within these *Guidelines*.

NASP acknowledges that the *Guidelines* set requirements for services not presently mandated by federal law or regulation and not always mandated in state laws and administrative rules. Future amendments of such statues and rules, and the state and local plans resulting from them, should incorporate the suggestions contained in this document. Furthermore, NASP understands that school psychological services are provided within the context of ethical and legal mandates. Nothing in these *Guidelines* should be construed as superseding such relevant rules and regulations.

The *Guidelines* provide flexibility, permitting agencies and professionals to develop procedures, policies, and administrative organizations that meet both the needs of the agency and the professional's desire to operate within recognized professional standards of practice. At the same time, the *Guidelines* have sufficient specificity to ensure that services will be provided appropriately and adequately.

PRACTICE GUIDELINES

Practice Guideline 1

School psychologists use a decision-making process in collaboration with other team members to (a) identify academic and behavior problems, (b) collect and analyze information to understand the problems, (c) make decisions about service delivery, and (d) evaluate the outcomes of the service delivery.

School psychologists must (a) utilize current professional literature on various aspects of education and child development, (b) translate research into practice through the problem-solving process, and (c) use research design and statistics skills to conduct investigations to develop and facilitate effective services.

1.1 School psychologists define problems in ways that (a) identify desired goals (e.g., academic/behavioral), (b) are measurable, (c) are agreed upon by those involved, and (d) are linked appropriately to assessment strategies.

1.2 School psychologists select assessment methods(s) that are validated for the problem area under consideration including formal and informal assessment procedures, as appropriate, and include data collected from all settings and persons necessary and appropriate to complete the problem-solving process.

1.3 School psychologists develop and implement effective interventions that are based upon the data collected and related directly to the desired outcomes of those interventions.

1.4 School psychologists use appropriate assessment information to evaluate interventions to determine their effectiveness, their need for modification, or their need for redevelopment. Effectiveness is determined by the relationship between the actual outcome of the intervention and the desired goal articulated in the problem-solving process.

1.5 School psychologists apply the problem-solving process to broader research- and systems-level problems that result in the identification of factors that influence learning and behavior, the evaluation of the outcomes of classroom, building, and system initiatives and the implementation of decision-making practices designed to meet general public accountability responsibilities.

Practice Guideline 2

School psychologists must have the ability to listen well, participate in discussions, convey information, and work together with others at an individual, group, and systems level. School psychologists must understand the degree to which policy influences systems, systems influence programs, programs and interventions impact consumers, and the methods to facilitate organizational development through strategic change.

2.1 School psychologists use decision-making skills and are proficient in systems consultation to facilitate communication and collaboration with students and school personnel, community professionals, agencies, and families/schools.

2.2 School psychologists participate in public policy discussions and understand the process by which public policy influences systems. By applying decision-making methods to public policy determination, school psychologists facilitate organization development and change.

2.3 School psychologists must be able to present and disseminate information to diverse communities, such as parents, teachers, school boards, policy makers, business leaders, and fellow school psychologists in a variety of contexts, in an organized and meaningful manner.

2.4 School psychologists facilitate the development of healthy learning environments and reduce divisiveness through the use of conflict resolution and negotiation skills.

2.5 School psychologists function as change agents, using their skills in communication, collaboration, and consultation to promote necessary change at the individual student, classroom, building, and district local, state, and federal levels.

Practice Guideline 3

School psychologists (in collaboration with others) develop challenging but achievable cognitive and academic goals for all students, provide information about ways in which students can achieve these goals, and monitor student progress towards these goals.

3.1 School psychologists apply current empirically based theory and knowledge of learning theory and cognitive processes to the development of effective instructional strategies to promote student learning and social and emotional development.

3.2 School psychologists incorporate assessment information to the development of instructional strategies to meet the individual learning needs of children.

3.3 School psychologists use appropriate and applicable assessment techniques to assess progress toward academic goals and assist in revising instructional methodology as necessary.

3.4 School psychologists assist in facilitating and implementing a variety of research-based instructional methods (e.g., cooperative learning, class-wide peer tutoring, cognitive strategy training) to enhance learning of students at the individual, group, and systems level.

3.5 School psychologists assist in the design and delivery of curriculum to help students develop behaviors to support effective learning such as study skills, self-regulation and self-monitoring, planning/organization, time management skills, and making choices that maintain physical and mental health.

3.6 School psychologists promote the principles of student-centered learning to help students develop (when appropriate) their individual ability to be self-regulated learners, including the ability to set individual learning goals, design a learning process to achieve those goals, and assess outcomes to determine whether the goals were achieved.

3.7 School psychologists are informed about advances in curriculum and instruction and share this knowledge with educators, parents, and the community at large to promote improvement in instruction, student achievement, and healthy lifestyles.

Practice Guideline 4

School psychologists make decisions based on multiple theoretical perspectives and translate current scientific information to develop effective behavioral, affective, or adaptive goals for all students, facilitate the implementation of programs/interventions to achieve these goals, and monitor progress towards these goals.

4.1 School psychologists use decision-making models (e.g., functional behavioral assessment) that consider the antecedents, consequences, functions, and potential causes of behavioral problems experienced by students with disabilities, which may impair learning or socialization.

4.2 School psychologists identify factors that facilitate the development of optimal learning environments. Optimal learning environments are characterized as settings where all members of the school or agency community treat one another with respect and dignity. Optimal learning environments are characterized as settings where students' basic needs are assured so that learning can occur and health and mental health are systematically evaluated.

4.3 School psychologists facilitate the development and implementation of strategies that result in instructional environments which foster learning and high rates of academic-engaged time and reduce the presence of factors that promote alienation and impact learning and behavioral progress.

4.4 School psychologists demonstrate appropriate knowledge of treatment acceptability and treatment integrity by including these principles in the development, implementation, and evaluation of interventions.

4.5 School psychologists apply the principles of generalization and transfer of training in the development of interventions in such a way that, when appropriate, interventions can be implemented across settings—school, home, and community.

4.6 School psychologists develop and implement behavior change programs (individual, group, classroom) that demonstrate the use of alternative, appropriate approaches (e.g., positive reinforcement, social skills training, academic interventions) to student discipline, ecological and behavioral approaches to classroom management, and awareness of classroom climate.

4.7 School psychologists assist parents and other adult caregivers in the development, implementation, and evaluation of behavior change programs in the home in order to facilitate the learning and behavioral growth of their child.

4.8 School psychologists incorporate appropriate strategies when developing and delivering intervention programs to facilitate successful transitions of students from one environment to another environment. These programs include program to program, early childhood to school, school to school, and school to work transitions.

4.9 School psychologists evaluate interventions (learning/behavioral) for individuals and groups. These include the skills necessary both to evaluate the extent to which the intervention contributed to the outcome and to identify what constitutes a "successful" outcome.

Practice Guideline 5

School psychologists have the sensitivity, knowledge, and skills to work with individuals and groups with a diverse range of strengths and needs from a variety of racial, cultural, ethnic, experiential, and linguistic backgrounds.

5.1 School psychologists develop academic and behavioral interventions. They recognize that interventions most likely to succeed are those which are adapted to the individual needs and characteristics of the student(s) for whom they are being designed.

5.2 School psychologists recognize (in themselves and others and in the techniques and instruments that they use for assessment and intervention) the subtle racial, class, gender, and cultural biases they may bring to their work and the way these biases influence decision-making, instruction, behavior, and long-term outcomes for students. School psychologists work to reduce and eliminate these biases where they occur.

5.3 School psychologists promote practices that help children of all backgrounds feel welcome and appreciated in the school and community.

5.4 School psychologists incorporate their understanding of the influence of culture, background, and individual learning characteristics when designing and implementing interventions to achieve learning and behavioral outcomes.

Practice Guideline 6

School psychologists demonstrate their knowledge of schools (or other institutional settings) as systems when they work with individuals and groups to facilitate structure and public policies that create and maintain schools and other systems as safe, caring, and inviting places for all persons in that system.

6.1 School psychologists use their knowledge of development, learning, family, and school systems to assist schools and communities to develop policies and practices related to discipline, decision-making, instructional support, staff training, school improvement plans, program evaluation, transition plans, grading, retention, and home-school partnerships.

6.2 School psychologists use their knowledge of organizational development and systems theory to assist in creating climates that result in mutual respect and caring for all individuals in the system, an atmosphere of decision-making and collaboration, and a commitment to quality services.

6.3 School psychologists regularly participate in the development of policies and procedures that advocate for effective programs and services.

6.4 School psychologists are actively involved in the development of systems change plans (such as school improvement plans) that directly impact the programs and services available to children, youth, and their families and that directly impact the ways in which school psychologists deliver their services.

6.5 School psychologists assist in the development of policies and procedures to ensure that schools are safe and violence free. School psychologists participate in the implementation and evaluation of programs that result in safe and violence-free schools and communities.

6.6 School psychologists are actively involved in public policy at the local, state, and federal levels as a means of creating systems of effective educational services.

6.7 School psychologists are aware of funding mechanisms that are available to school and communities that support health and mental health services. School psychologists participate in the development of funding strategies to assure that needed services are available to students and their families.

Practice Guideline 7

School psychologists shall appropriately utilize prevention, health promotion, and crisis intervention methods based on knowledge of child development, psychopathology, diversity, social stressors, change, and systems.

7.1 School psychologists shall apply knowledge of child development, psychopathology, diversity, social stressors, change, and systems to the identification and recognition of behaviors that are precursors to school dropouts or the development of mental health disorders such as conduct disorders or internalizing disorders.

7.2 School psychologists shall provide direct counseling and indirect interventions through consultation for students with disabilities and suspected disabilities who experience mental health problems that impair learning and/or socialization.

7.3 School psychologists shall develop, implement, and evaluate prevention and intervention programs based on recognized factors that are precursors to development of severe learning and behavioral problems.

7.4 School psychologists shall collaborate with school personnel, parents, students, and the community to provide competent mental health support during and after crises (for example, suicide, death, natural disasters, murder, bombs or bomb threats, extraordinary violence, and sexual harassment).

7.5 School psychologists promote wellness by (a) collaborating with other health care professionals to provide a basic knowledge of behaviors that lead to good health for children; (b) facilitating environmental changes conducive to good health and adjustment of children; and (c) accessing resources to address a wide variety of behavioral, learning, mental, and physical needs.

Practice Guideline 8

School psychologists have knowledge of family influences that affect students' wellness, learning, and achievement and are involved in public policy that promotes partnership between parents, educators, and the community.

8.1 School psychologists design and implement and evaluate programs to promote school-family partnerships for the purpose of enhancing academic and behavioral goals for students. These might include (but are not limited to) developing parent education programs, establishing drop-in centers for parents, establishing homework hotlines, or providing other supports for parents to help them parent successfully and to help them enhance the academic and psychological development of their children.

8.2 School psychologists help parents feel comfortable participating in school functions or activities. These might include providing support for them when participating on special education and I.E.P. teams, encouraging parental involvement in school-wide committees such as school improvement teams, *and* facilitating home-school communication when problems arise and includes assisting parents in accessing community-based services for their family.

8.3 School psychologists educate the school community regarding the influence of family involvement on school achievement and advocate for parent involvement in school governance and policy development whenever feasible.

8.4 School psychologists help create linkages between schools, families, and community agencies, and help coordinate services when programming for children involves multiple agencies.

8.5 School psychologists are knowledgeable about the local system of care and related community services available to support students and their families.

8.6 School psychologists work with parent organizations to promote public policy that empowers parents to be competent consumers of the local system of services.

8.7 School psychologists are active participants in public policy by serving on committees, participating in work groups and task forces, and in responding to proposed legislation and rules.

GUIDELINES FOR THE ORGANIZATION AND OPERATION OF THE UNIT

Unit Guideline 1: Organization of Service Delivery

School psychological services are provided in a coordinated, organized fashion and are delivered in a manner that ensures the provision of a comprehensive and seamless continuum of services. Services are delivered following the completion of a strategic planning process based on the needs of the consumers and an empirically supported program evaluation model.

1.1 School psychological services are available and accessible to all students and clients served by the agency and are in proportion to the needs of the client.

1.2 School psychological services are available to all students on an equal basis and are not determined by a specific funding source. Services are provided to students based on their need, not based on their eligibility to generate specific funding.

1.3 School psychological services are integrated with other school and community services. Students and their families should not be responsible for the integration of these services based on funding, setting, or program location. Therefore, school psychological and mental health services are provided through a "seamless" system of care.

1.4 School psychological services units ensure that the services delivered by the unit and provided directly by the school psychologist to consumers are based on a strategic plan. The plan is developed based on the collective needs of the district and community with the primary focus being the specific needs of the population served by individual practitioners.

1.5 School psychological services units conduct regular evaluations of the collective services provided by the unit as well as those services provided by individual practitioners. The evaluation process focuses on both the nature and extent of the services provided (process) and the student/family focused outcomes of those services (product).

1.6 The school psychological services unit provides a range of services to their clients. These consist of direct and indirect services that require involvement with the entire educational system as well as other services systems in the community. The consumers of and participants in these services include: students, teachers, administrators, other school personnel, families, caretakers, other community and regional agencies, and resources that support the educational process.

Unit Guideline 2: Climate

It is the responsibility of the unit to create a climate in which school psychological services can be delivered with mutual respect for all parties. Employees of the unit have the freedom to advocate for the services that are necessary to meet the needs of consumers and are free from artificial, administrative, or political constraints that might hinder or alter the provision of appropriate services.

2.1 Providers of school psychological services maintain a cooperative relationship with colleagues and co-workers in the best mutual interests of clients. Conflicts are resolved in a professional manner.

2.2 The potential negative impact of administrative constraints on effective services is kept to a minimum. The school psychologist will advocate for administrative policies that support the school psychologist in seeking the needed services and will provide mechanisms for referral and consultation regarding unmet health and mental health needs.

2.3 Members of the unit advocate in a professional manner for the most appropriate services for their clients without fear of reprisal from supervisors or administrators.

2.4 School psychological service units are aware of the impact of work environment on the job satisfaction of unit employees and on the quality of services provided to consumers. Measures of work climate are included when the unit conducts self-evaluations.

2.5 School psychological service units promote and advocate for balance between professional and personal lives of unit employees. Unit supervisors monitor work and stress levels of employees and take steps to reduce pressure when the well-being of the employee is at risk. Supervisors are available to employees to problem solve when personal factors may adversely affect job performance and when job expectations may adversely affect the personal life of the employee.

Unit Guideline 3: Physical, Personnel, and Fiscal Support Systems

School psychological services units ensure that (a) an adequate recruitment and retention plan for employees exists to ensure adequate personnel to meet the needs of the system; (b) all sources of funding, both public and private, are used and maximized to ensure the fiscal support necessary to provide adequate services; (c) all employees have adequate technology, clerical services, and a physical work environment; and (d) employees have adequate personnel benefits necessary to support the work of the unit including continuing educational professional development.

3.1 School psychological services units assume the professional responsibility and accountability for services provided through the recruitment of qualified and diverse staff and the assurance that staff members function only in their areas of competency.

3.2 School psychological services units support recruitment and retention of qualified staff by advocating for appropriate ratios of school psychology services staff to students. The ratio of staff to students should not exceed one staff person for every 1000 sttudents.

3.3 School psychological services units utilize advanced technologies (e.g., computer-assisted) in time management, communication systems, data management systems, and service delivery.

3.4 School psychological services unit have access to adequate clerical assistance, appropriate professional work materials, sufficient office and work space, adequate technology support (e.g., e-mail, computer) and general working conditions that enhance the delivery of effective services. Included are test materials, access to private telephone and office, secretarial services, therapeutic aids, and professional literature.

Unit Guideline 4: Communication and Technology

The school psychological services unit ensures that policies and practices exist which result in positive, proactive communication and technology systems both within the unit, its central organizational structure, and those organizational structures with which the unit interacts.

4.1 School psychological service units provide opportunities for members of the unit to communicate with each other about issues of mutual professional interest on a regular basis.

4.2 School psychological services units maintain a formal system of communication channels with other units within the parent organization and between the unit and other agencies with whom it interacts on behalf of clients. The unit engages in decision-making and strategic planning with other units and agencies in order to ensure optimal services are provided to mutual clients.

4.3 School psychological services units ensure that staff members have access to the technology necessary to perform their jobs adequately and to maintain communication with service providers and clients within and outside the unit. The requirement for confidentiality is respected, with adequate resources available to service providers to ensure confidential communication.

4.4 School psychological services units' policy on student records is consistent with state and federal rules and laws and ensures the protection of the confidentiality of the student and his or her family. The policy specifies the types of data developed by the school psychologist that are classified as school or pupil records. The policy gives clear guidance regarding which documents belong (consistent with FERPA or similar state/court regulations) to the school and the student/guardian and which documents (such as clinical notes) are the personal property of the school psychologist.

4.5 Parents may inspect and review any personally identifiable data relating to their children that were collected, maintained, or used in his/her evaluation. Although test protocols are part of the student's record, school psychologists protect test security and observe copyright restrictions. Release of records and protocols is done consistent with state/federal regulations.

Unit Guideline 5: Supervision

The school psychological services unit ensures that all personnel have levels and types of supervision adequate to ensure the provision of effective and accountable services. Supervision is provided through an ongoing, positive, systematic, collaborative process between the school psychologist and the school psychology supervisor. This process focuses on promoting professional growth and exemplary professional practice leading to improved performance by all concerned including the school psychologist, supervisor, students, and the entire school community.

5.1 A supervisor of a school psychological services unit holds or meets the criteria for the Nationally Certified School Psychologist (NCSP) credential and has been identified by an employing agency and/or school psychological service unit as a supervisor responsible for school psychology services in the agency or unit. Supervisors hold a state school psychologist credential and have a minimum of three years of experience as a practicing school psychologist. Training and/or experience in the supervision of school personnel are desirable.

5.2 When supervision is required for interns, beginning school psychologists, or others for whom supervision is necessary, such supervision will be provided at least two hours per week for persons employed full time.

5.3 Supervisors lead school psychological services units in developing, implementing, and evaluating a coordinated plan for accountability and evaluation of all services provided in order to maintain the highest level of effectiveness. Such plans include specific, measurable objectives pertaining to the planned effects of services. Evaluation is both formative and summative. Supervisors provide leadership by promotion of innovative service delivery systems that reflect best practices in the field of school psychology.

5.4 Supervisors lead school psychological services units in developing, implementing, and evaluating a coordinated plan for accountability and evaluation of all services provided by individual staff members and by the unit as a whole in order to maintain the highest level of services. Such plans include specific, measurable objectives pertaining to the planned effects of services on all relevant elements of the system and the students it serves. Evaluation is both formative and summative.

5.5 The school psychological services unit continues to provide supervision or peer review for its school psychologists after their first year of employment to ensure continued professional growth and development and support for complex or difficult cases.

5.6 Supervisors coordinate the activities of the school psychological services unit with other professional services units through review and discussion of 1) intervention planning and outcomes; 2) comprehensive, systemic procedures and special concerns; and 3) discrepancies among views of various professional service providers or employing agencies.

5.7 Supervisors ensure that practica and internship experiences occur under conditions of appropriate supervision including 1) access to professional school psychologists who will serve as appropriate role models, 2) provision of supervision by an appropriately credentialed school psychologist, and 3) provision of supervision within the guidelines of the training institution and NASP *Standards for Training and Field Placement Programs in School Psychology*.

5.8 Supervisors provide professional leadership through participation in school psychology professional organizations and active involvement in local, state and federal public policy development.

Unit Guideline 6: Professional Development and Recognition Systems

Individual school psychologists and the school psychological services unit develop professional development plans annually. The school psychological services unit ensures that continuing professional development of its personnel is both adequate for and relevant to the service delivery priorities of the unit and that recognition systems exist to reflect the continuum of professional development activities embraced by its personnel.

6.1 All school psychologists within the unit actively participate in activities designed to continue, enhance, and upgrade their professional training and skills to help ensure quality service provision.

6.2 The school psychological services unit provides support (e.g., funding, time, supervision) to ensure that school psychologists have sufficient access to continuing professional development and supervision activities at a minimal level necessary to maintain the NCSP.

6.3 School psychologists develop a formal professional development plan and update this plan annually. The goals, objectives, and activities of the plan are influenced by the following factors in order of priority: (1) the most pressing needs of the population and community served; (2) the knowledge, skills, and abilities required to implement initiatives sponsored by the unit; and (3) the individual interest areas of the school psychologists employed by the unit.

6.4 School psychologists seek and use appropriate types and levels of supervision as they acquire new knowledge, skills, and abilities through the professional development process.

6.5 School psychologists document the type, level, and intensity of their professional development activities. The school psychological services unit provides technology and personnel resources to assist in these activities.

6.6 School psychologists individually seek appropriate levels of advanced recognition (e.g., advanced degrees, levels established by district, state, or national recognition bodies) to reflect ongoing professional development.

6.7 School psychological services units provide levels of recognition (e.g., salary, opportunity to use new skills) within the unit that reflect the professional development of the school psychologists in the unit.

Unit Guideline 7: Contracted/ Independent Provider Services

The school psychological services unit is responsible for providing psychological services. These services can come from district-employed school psychologists, from psychologists employed in independent practice, or through other agencies. Regardless of whether personnel are employed or contracted, it is the responsibility of the unit to ensure the same level and quality of services as those provided by personnel from within the unit.

7.1 Contractual school psychological services encompass the same comprehensive continuum of services as is provided by regularly employed school psychologists. These services include opportunities for follow-up and continuing consultation appropriate to the needs of the student. Individual contracts for services may be limited as long as the school psychological services unit ensures comprehensive services overall.

7.2 Contractual school psychological services are not used as a means to decrease the amount and quality of school psychological services provided by an employing agency. They may be used to augment and enhance programs, as in the case of retaining needed expertise, to coordinate with other community health services, and to assure that services are available to students and their families.

7.3 Contracted services may be used as a mechanism to maximize available resources. However, any such models of service must provide comprehensive psychological services and assure quality services of equal or greater value when compared to services provided by school-based personnel.

7.4 Contractual school psychological services are provided in a manner that protects the due process rights of students and their parents as defined by state and federal laws and regulations.

7.5 Psychologists providing contractual school psychological services provide those services in a manner consistent with these *Guidelines*, NASP *Principles for Professional Ethics*, and other relevant professional guidelines and standards.

7.6 Persons providing contractual psychological services are fully credentialed school psychologists as defined by these or other (e.g., state certification boards) recognized standards. In specific instances, however, services by credentialed psychologist in other specialty areas (e.g., clinical, industrial/organizational, neuropsychology) might be used to supplement school psychological services and should be coordinated with school psychological services.

7.7 Psychologists providing contractual school psychological services will require regular evaluation of the quality of services provided as well as the continued need for contracted services.

7.8 A credentialed school psychologist who has completed a school psychology training program that meets the criteria specified in the NASP *Standards for Training and Field Placement Programs in School Psychology* and two full-time years (one of which may be internship) of satisfactory, properly supervised experience is considered qualified for personally supervised, independent practice with peer review, regardless of work setting. (NOTE: "Independent practice" as used in this paragraph refers to autonomous functioning within the employing school or agency. Contrast this with the licensure rules of various states for "private practice.")

7.9 A credentialed school psychologist or an organized group of credentialed school psychologists may engage in independent practice outside of a school agency or unit pursuant to existing rules regarding the independent practice of psychology within a given state. Units will support public policy that will provide for the independent practice of school psychology.

Appendix D

SUGGESTED COMPETENCIES FOR PROVIDING SCHOOL PSYCHOLOGICAL SERVICES TO CULTURALLY DIVERSE CLIENTELE[1]

COMPETENCIES[2] AND RESOURCES[3]

1. Awareness of how one's own cultural heritage, gender, class, ethnic-racial identity, sexual orientation, disability, and age cohort help shape personal values and beliefs, including assumptions, and biases related to identified groups (Hansen et al., 2000; also Lopez & Rogers, 2001; Rogers et al., 1999).
   Resources: Corey, Corey, & Callanan, 1998; Lynch & Hanson, 1998; Ortiz & Flanagan, 2002.
2. Knowledge of how school psychological theory, research questions and methods, and professional practices are culturally and historically embedded (Hansen et al., 2000; also Lopez & Rogers, 2001; Rogers et al., 1999).
   Resources: Gould, 1996; Levine & Levine, 1996; Nieto, 2000; Tharp, 1991.
3. Knowledge of the history of oppression, prejudice, and discrimination in the United States and its manifestation in the schools. Knowledge of the sociopolitical influences (e.g., poverty, stereotyping, stigmatization, and marginalization) that may impact pupil development, learning, and identity achievement (Hansen et al., 2000; also Nieto, 2000; Rogers et al., 1999).
   Resources: Gould, 1996; Lynch & Hansen, 1998; Henning-Stout & James, 2000; Levine & Levine, 1996; Nieto 2000.
4. Familiarity with law that prohibits discrimination in the schools and makes schools responsible for taking reasonable steps to remedy

[1]"Diverse Clientele" means students, parents, teachers, and other recipients of services who differ from "dominant" U.S. groups on characteristics such as race, ethnicity, national origin, religion, sexual orientation, disability, language, or socioeconomic status.

[2]Competencies adapted from APA (1993); Hansen, Pepitone-Arreloa-Rockwell, and Greene (2000); and Rodgers et. al. (1999); among others.

[3]These resources were selected because of their relevance to the children and schools. Additional resources can be found in Hansen et al. (2000) and Rogers et al. (1999).

harassment and hate crimes. Knowledge and skills to help promote a school environment free from discrimination and harassment, and that is accepting and respectful of individual differences (Lopez & Rogers, 2001; Rogers et al., 1999).
Resources: U.S. Department of Education & Bias Crimes Task Force of the National Association of Attorneys General, 1999; also Nieto, 2000; Rogers et al., 1999.

5. Knowledge of the origins, family structure, child-rearing practices, values, beliefs, worldview, language, and interactional style of identified groups the practitioner encounters in his or her schools (Hansen et al., 2000; also Lopez & Rogers, 2001; Rogers et al., 1999).
Resources: Lynch & Hanson, 1998; Okun, Fried, & Okun, 1999.
6. Ability to balance knowledge of characteristics common among members of an ethnic or other identified group with the understanding that each individual is unique, and to recognize that individuals have complex identities influenced by multiple factors including race, ethnicity, class, gender, disability, sexual orientation, age cohort, and personal history (Hays, 2001; also Hanson et al., 1999).
Resources: Hays, 2001; Lynch & Hanson, 1998.
7. Ability to accurately self-assess one's multicultural competence, including knowledge of when circumstances (personal biases, lack of requisite knowledge, skills, or language fluency) may negatively influence professional practice and adapt accordingly (e.g., obtain needed information, consultation, or supervision, or referring the student to a better qualified professional) (Hansen et al., 1999; also APA, 1993; Lopez & Rogers, 2001; Rogers et al., 1999).
Resources: Rogers et al., 1999.
8. Ability to demonstrate understanding of and respect for cultural differences in interacting with diverse clientele, and ability to establish rapport with students, parents, and teachers from diverse backgrounds in culturally sensitive ways. Knowledge of how to work with interpreters if relevant to job setting (APA, 1993; Hansen et al., 1999; Lopez & Rogers, 2001; Rogers et al., 1999).
Resources: Lynch & Hanson, 1998; Okun, Fried, & Okun, 1999; Rogers et al., 1999.
9. Ability to assist diverse students, parents, and professionals to better understand the culture of the school and community so that they can make informed choices relevant to mental health services and schooling (Hays, 2001; also Lopez & Rogers, 2001; Rogers et al., 1999). Skill in explaining psychoeducational assessment and intervention to parents and pupils from diverse backgrounds so that they can participate meaningfully in the process (APA, 1993).
Resources: Rogers et al., 1999.
10. Ability to conduct a valid psychoeducational assessment with pupils typically encountered in work setting, including selecting tools appropriate to the pupil's characteristics and background and administering and interpreting

assessment information in a culturally sensitive manner (APA, 1993; Lopez & Rogers, 2001; Rogers et al., 1999).
Resources: American Educational Research Association et al., 1999; Sattler, 2001; Dana, 2000.

11. Knowledge of best practices in planning and modifying curriculum and instruction to meet the needs of culturally and linguistically diverse students in the practitioner's work setting. Ability to select, design, and implement nonbiased and effective treatment plans for diverse clientele with learning or behavior problems (Rogers et al., 1999; also APA 1993, Hansen et al., 1999).
Resources: Aponte & Johnson, 2000; Rogers et al., 1999; Tharpe, 1991.

12. Ability to effectively consult across multiculturally diverse consultant-consultee-client groups (Rogers, 2000).
Resources: Ingraham & Meyers, 2000.

REFERENCES

Abramovitch, R., Freedman, J. L., Henry, K., & Van Brunschot; M. (1995). Children's capacity to agree to psychological research: Knowledge of risks and benefits and voluntariness. *Ethics & Behavior, 5,* 25–48.

Adler, T. (1993, September). APA, two other groups to revise test standards. *APA Monitor*, pp. 24–25.

ADD/ADHD students may be eligible under OHI. (1999, June). *California Special Education Alert, 5(11).* Retrieved November 14, 2001, from the LEXIS Legal News database.

Alberto, P. A., & Troutman, A. C. (1982). *Applied behavior analysis for teachers.* Columbus, OH: Merrill.

Allington, R. L., & McGill-Franzen, A. (1992). Unintended effects of educational reform in New York. *Educational Policy, 6,* 397–414.

American Educational Research Association, American Psychological Association, & National Council on Measurement in Education. (1999). *Standards for educational and psychological testing (2nd ed.).* Washington, DC: American Educational Research Association.

American Psychiatric Association. (2000). *Diagnostic and statistical manual of mental disorders: Text revision (DSM-IV-TR)* (4th ed.). Washington, DC: Author.

American Psychological Association. (1981). Specialty guidelines for the delivery of services by school psychologists. *American Psychologist, 36,* 670–681.

American Psychological Association. (1982). *Ethical principles in the conduct of research with human participants.* Washington, DC: Author.

American Psychological Association. (1986). *Guidelines for computer-based tests and interpretations.* Washington, DC: Author.

American Psychological Association. (1993a). Guidelines for providers of psychological services to ethnic, linguistic, and culturally diverse populations. *American Psychologist, 48,* 45–48.

American Psychological Association. (1993b). Record keeping guidelines. *American Psychologist, 48,* 45–48.

American Psychological Association. (1996a). Report of the Ethics Committee, 1995. *American Psychologist, 51,* 1279–1286.

American Psychological Association. (1996b). Rules and procedures. *American Psychologist, 51,* 529–548.

American Psychological Association. (1996c). Statement on the disclosure of test data. *American Psychologist, 51,* 644–648.

American Psychological Association. (1999). Warning signs: A violence prevention guide for youth from MTV and APA. Retrieved October 10, 1999, from http://helping.apa.org/warningsigns/index.html.

American Psychological Association. (2001). Report of the Ethics Committee, 2000. *American Psychologist, 56,* 680–688.

American Psychological Association. (2002). *Ethical Principles of Psychologists and Code of Conduct.* Retrieved October 13, 2002, from http://www.apa.org/ethics.

American Psychological Association's Committee on Accreditation. (2002). *CoA self-study instructions for internship programs.* Retrieved January 5, 2002, from http:// www.apa.org.

American Psychological Association Division 44 Committee on Lesbian, Gay, and Bisexual Concerns. (2000). Guidelines for psychotherapy with lesbian, gay, and bisexual clients. *American Psychologist, 55,* 1440–1451.

American Psychological Association Committee on Legal Issues. (1996). Strategies for private practitioners coping with subpoenas or compelled testimony for client records or test data. *Professional Psychology: Research and Practice, 27,* 245–251.

Angold, A., Erkanli, A., Egger, H. L., & Costello, E. J. (2000). Stimulant treatment for children: A community perspective. *Journal of the American Academy of Child and Adolescent Psychiatry, 39,* 975–983.

Aponte, J. F., & Crouch, R. T. (2000). The changing ethnic profile of the United States in the twenty-first century. In J. F. Aponte & J. Wohl (Eds.), *Psychological intervention and cultural diversity* (*2nd ed.*) (pp. 1–17). Boston: Allyn and Bacon.

Aponte, J. F., & Johnson, L. R. (2000). The impact of culture on the intervention and treatment of ethnic populations. In J. F. Aponte & J. Wohl (Eds.), *Psychological intervention and cultural diversity* (*2nd ed.*) (pp. 18–39). Boston: Allyn and Bacon.

Atkinson, D. R. (1993). Who speaks for cross-cultural counseling research? *The Counseling Psychologist, 21,* 218–224.

Bahr, M. W., Brish, B., & Croteau, J. M. (2000). Addressing sexual orientation and professional ethics in the training of school psychologists in school and university setting. *School Psychology Review, 29,* 217–230.

Bailey, J. A. (1980, March). School counselors: Test your ethics. *The School Counselor,* 285–293.

Baldick, T. L. (1980). Ethical discrimination ability of intern psychologists: A function of training in ethics. *Professional Psychology, 11,* 276–282.

Ballantine, H. T. (1979). The crisis in ethics, anno domini 1979. *New England Journal of Medicine, 301,* 634–638.

Barkley, R. A., & Edwards, G. (1998). Diagnostic interview, behavior rating scales, and the medical examination. In R. A. Barkley (Ed.), *Attention-Deficit Hyperactivity Disorder: A handbook for diagnosis and treatment* (*2nd ed.*) (pp. 263–293). New York: Guilford Press.

Batsche, G. M., & Peterson, D. W. (1983). School psychology and projective assessment: A growing incompatibility. *School Psychology Review, 12,* 440–445.

Bauder, D. (1989, February 6). Misdiagnosed as mentally retarded, deaf man spent years in institutions. *Midland Daily News,* p. B–1.

Beauchamp, T. L., & Childress, J. F. (1983). *Principles of biomedical ethics* (*2nd ed.*). New York: Oxford University Press.

Behring, S. T., Cabello, B., Kushida, D., & Murguia, A. (2000). Cultural modifications to current school-based consultation approaches reported by culturally diverse beginning consultants. *School Psychology Review, 29,* 354–367.

Bennett, B. E., Bryant, B. K., VandenBos, G., & Greenwood, A. (1990). *Professional liability and risk management.* Washington, DC: American Psychological Association.

Berman, A. L., & Jobes, D. A. (1991). *Adolescent suicide assessment and intervention.* Washington, DC: American Psychological Association.

Bernard, J., & Jara, C. (1986). The failure of clinical psychology graduate students to apply understood ethical principles. *Professional Psychology: Research and Practice, 17,* 313–315.

Bernstein, B. E., & Hartsell, T. L. (1998). *The portable lawyer for mental health professionals.* New York, NY: John Wiley & Sons.

Bersoff, D. N. (1979). Regarding psychologists testily: The legal regulation of psychological assessment in the public schools. *Maryland Law Review, 39,* 27–120.

Bersoff, D. N. (1981). The brief for *amici curiae* in the matter of Forrest versus Ambach. *Academic Psychology Bulletin, 3,* 133–162.

Bersoff, D. N. (1982). Larry P. and PASE: Judicial report cards on the validity of individual intelligence tests. In T. Kratochwill (Ed.), *Advances in school psychology* (Vol. 2, pp. 61–95). Hillsdale, NJ: Erlbaum.

Bersoff, D. N. (1983). Children as participants in psychoeducational assessment. In G. B. Melton, G. P. Koocher, & M. J. Saks (Eds.), *Children's competence to consent* (pp. 149–177). New York: Plenum Press.

Bersoff, D. N. (1994). Explicit ambiguity: The 1992 ethics code as an oxymoron. *Professional Psychology: Research and Practice, 25,* 382–387.

Bersoff, D. N. (1999). *Ethical conflicts in psychology (2nd ed.).* Washington, DC: American Psychological Association.

Bersoff, D. N., & Hofer, P. T. (1990). The legal regulation of school psychology. In C. R. Reynolds & T. B. Gutkin (Eds.), *The handbook of school psychology (2nd ed.)* (pp. 937–961). New York: John Wiley & Sons.

Bersoff, D. N., & Koeppl, P. M. (1993). The relation between ethical codes and moral principles. *Ethics and Behavior, 3,* 345–357.

Bersoff, D. N., & Prasse, D. (1978). Applied psychology and judicial decision making: Corporal punishment as a case in point. *Professional Psychology, 9,* 400–411.

Bersoff, D. N., & Ysseldyke, J. E. (1977). Non-discriminatory assessment: The law, litigation, and implications for the assessment of learning disabled children. In S. Jacob (Ed.), *The law: Assessment and placement of special education students* (pp. 65–92). Lansing: Michigan Department of Education.

Betan, E. J., & Stanton, A. L. (1999). Fostering ethical willingness: Integrating emotional and contextual awareness with rational analysis. *Professional Psychology: Research and Practice, 30,* 295–301.

Black, H. C. (1983). *Black's law dictionary (Abridged 5th ed.).* St. Paul, MN: West Publishing Co.

Borreca, C. P., Goldman, T. B., Horton, J. L., Mehfoud, K., Rodick, B., Weatherly, J. J., Wenkart, R. D., & Wynn, D. W. (1999). *The 1999 IDEA regulations: A practical analysis.* Alexandria, VA: National School Boards Association.

Borum, R. (2000). Assessing violence risk among youth. *Journal of Clinical Psychology, 56,* 1263–1288.

Borum, R., Fein, R., Vossekuil, B., & Berglund, J. (1999). Threat assessment: Defining an approach for evaluating risk of targeted violence. *Behavioral Sciences and the Law, 17,* 323–337.

Bosk, C. L. (1979). *Forgive and remember: Managing medical failure.* Chicago: University of Chicago Press.

Bower, E. M. (1982). Defining emotional disturbance: Public policy and research. *Psychology in the Schools, 19,* 55–60.

Bowman, D. H. (2002, February 6). Survey's sexuality questions anger elementary parents. *Education Week,* p. 10.

Braden, J. P. (2002). Best practices for school psychologists in educational accountability: High stakes testing and educational reform. In A. Thomas & J. Grimes (Eds.), *Best practices in school psychology IV* (pp. 301–320). Bethesda, MD: National Association of School Psychologists.

Bradley, A. (1998, December 9). Student-survey dispute spawns more parent rights. *Education Week,* p. 3.

Bradley, A. (2001, November 14). Police absolved in suit over gay student's suicide. *Education Week,* p. 4.

Bradley, K. L., & DuPaul, G. J. (1997). Attention-deficit/hyperactivity disorder. In G. G. Baer, K. M. Minke, & A. Thomas (Eds.), *Children's needs: II* (pp. 109–117). Bethesda, MD: National Association of School Psychologists.

Bradley-Johnson, S., Johnson, M. C., & Jacob-Timm, S. (1995). Where will—and where should—changes in education leave school psychology? *Journal of School Psychology, 33,* 187–200.

Brock, S. E., Lazarus, P. J., & Jimerson, S. R. (2002). *Best practices in school crisis prevention and intervention.* Besthesda, MD: National Association of School Psychologists.

Brooks-Gunn, J., & Furstenburg, F. F. (1989). Adolescent sexual behavior. *American Psychologist, 44,* 249–257.

Brophy, J. E., & Good, T. L. (1974). *Teacher-student relationships.* New York: Holt, Rinehart and Winston.

Brown, D. T. (1979). Issues in accreditation certification, and licensure. In G. D. Phye & D. J. Reschly (Eds.), *School psychology: Perspectives and issues* (pp. 49–82). New York: Academic Press.

Brown, D., Pryzwansky, W. B., & Schulte, A. C. (1987). *Psychological consultation: Introduction to theory and practice.* Boston: Allyn & Bacon.

Brown, R. T., Reynolds, C. R., & Whitaker, J. S. (1999). Bias in mental testing since *Bias in Mental Testing. School Psychology Quarterly, 14,* 208–238.

Burgdorf, R. L. (1991). The *Americans with Disabilities Act:* Analysis and implications of a second-generation civil rights statute. *Harvard Civil Rights-Civil Liberties Law Review, 26,* 413–522.

Callahan, C. M. (1997). Giftedness. In G. G. Baer, K. M. Minke, & A. Thomas (Eds.), *Children's needs: II* (pp. 431–448). Bethesda, MD: National Association of School Psychologists.

Campbell, D. T., & Fiske, D. W. (1959). Convergent and discriminate validation by the multitrait-multimethod matrix. *Psychological Bulletin, 56,* 81–105.

Canadian Psychological Association. (2000). *Canadian code of ethics for psychologists, third edition.* Available at http://www.cpa.ca.

Canter, A. (1989, November). Is parent permission always necessary? *Communique,* p. 9.

Canter, A. (2001a, May). Test protocols, Part I: Right to review and copy. *Communique,* p. 30, 32.

Canter, A. (2001b, September). Test protocols, Part II: Storage and disposal. *Communique,* p. 16–19.

Canter, M. B., Bennett, B. E., Jones, S. E., & Nagy, T. F. (1994). *Ethics for psychologists.* Washington, DC: American Psychological Association.

Cavell, T. A., Ennett, S. T., & Meehan, B. T. (2001). Preventing alcohol and substance abuse. In J. N. Hughes, A. M. La Greca, & J. C. Conoley (Eds.), *Handbook of psychological services for children and adolescents* (pp. 133–159). New York: Oxford University Press.

Center for Disease Control. (2001a). *Center for disease control national center for injury prevention and control factsheet.* Retrieved November 15, 2001, from http://www.cdc.gov/ncipc/factsheets/suifacts.htm.

Center for Disease Control. (2001b). *Center for Disease Control and Prevention: Morbidity and mortality weekly report.* Retrieved November 15, 2001, from http://www.cdc.gov/mmwr/preview/mmwrhtml/mm4929a7.htm.

Chalfant, J. C. (1989). Learning disabilities: Policy issues and promising approaches. *American Psychologist, 44,* 392–398.

Chalfant, J., & Pysh, M. (1989). Teacher assistance teams: Five descriptive studies on 96 teams. *Remedial and Special Education, 10(6),* 49–58.

Chalk, R., Frankel, M. S., & Chafer, S. B. (1980). *AAAS professional ethics project.* Washington, DC: American Association for the Advancement of Science.

Chestnut, C. R. (2001, November 17). Jury awards $1 million to fired special ed teacher. *The Oregonian.* Retrieved November 18, 2001, from http://www.OregonLive.com.

Christenson, S. L. (1995). Best practices in supporting home-school collaboration. In A. Thomas & J. Grimes (Eds.), *Best practices in school psychology–III* (pp. 253–267). Washington, DC: National Association of School Psychologists.

Christenson, S. L., Hurley, C. M., Sheridan, S. M., & Fenstermacher, K. (1997). Parents' and school psychologists' perspective on parent involvement activities. *School Psychology Review, 26,* 111–130.

Clarizio, H. F. (1987). Differentiating emotionally impaired from socially maladjusted students. *Psychology in the Schools, 24,* 237–242.

Cobb County (GA) School District. (1992). OCR complaint investigation letter of findings. *Individuals with Disabilities Education Law Report, 19,* 29–32.

Cobia, D. C., & Boes, S. R. (2000). Professional disclosure statements and formal plans for supervision: Two strategies for minimizing the risk of ethical conflicts in post-master's supervision. *Journal of Counseling and Development, 78,* 293–296.

Coles, N. S. (1981). Bias in testing. *American Psychologist, 36,* 1067–1077.

Cone, T. E., & Wilson, L. R. (1981). Quantifying a severe discrepancy: A critical analysis. *Learning Disability Quarterly, 3,* 76–87.

Conoley, J. C., & Conoley, C. W. (1982). *School consultation: A guide to practice and training.* New York: Pergamon Press.

Conoley, J. C., & Sullivan, J. R. (2002). Best practices in the supervision of interns. In A. Thomas & J. Grimes (Eds.), *Best practices in school psychology IV* (pp. 131–144). Bethesda, MD: National Association of School Psychologists.

Congress, E. P. (2001). Ethical issues in work with culturally diverse children and their families. In N. B. Webb (Ed)., *Culturally diverse parent-child and family relationships* (pp. 29–53). New York, NY: Columbia University Press.

Cooper, S. (1984). Minors' participation in therapy decisions: A written therapist-child agreement. *Journal of Child Adolescent Psychotherapy, 1,* 93–96.

Corey, G., Corey, M. S., & Callanan, P. (1998). *Issues and ethics in the helping professions (5th ed.).* Pacific Grove, CA: Brooks/Cole.

Corrao, J., & Melton, G. B. (1988). Legal issues in school-based behavior therapy. In J. C. Witt, S. N. Elliot, & F. M. Gresham (Eds.), *Handbook of behavior therapy in education* (pp. 377–399). New York: Plenum Press.

Cottone, R. R., & Claus, R. E. (2000). Ethical decision-making models: A review of the literature. *Journal of Counseling & Development, 78,* 275–283.

Coughlin, E. K. (1988, November 30). Psychologist sentenced for giving false data to federal government. *Chronicle of Higher Education,* p. A5.

Council of Administrators of Special Education. (1999). *Section 504 and the ADA—Promoting student access.* (Available from Council of Administrators of Special Education's online catalog, http://www.casecec.org.)

Council for Children with Behavior Disorders Executive Committee. (1987). Position paper on definition and identification of students with behavior disorders. *Behavioral Disorders, 13,* 9–19.

Council for Exceptional Children. (2000). *Making assessment accommodations: A toolkit for educators.* Notebook and video available from: The Council for Exceptional Children, 1920 Association Drive, Reston, VA 20191–1589.

Curtis, M. J., Hunley, S., & Prus, J. (1998). *Credentialing requirements for school psychologists.* Bethesda, MD: National Association of School Psychologists.

Curtis, M. J., Hunley, S. A., Walker, K. J., & Baker, A. C. (1999). Demographic characteristics and professional practices in school psychology. *School Psychology Review, 28,* 104–116.

Curtis, M. J., & Stollar, S. A. (2002). Best practices in system-level change. In A. Thomas & J. Grimes (Eds.), *Best practices in school psychology IV* (pp. 223–234). Bethesda, MD: National Association of School Psychologists.

D'Augelli, A. R. (1998). Developmental implications of victimization of lesbian, gay, and bisexual youths. In G. M. Herek (Eds.), *Psychological perspectives on lesbian and gay issues. Vol. 4: Stigma and sexual orientation: Understanding prejudice against lesbians, gay men, and bisexuals* (pp. 187–210). Thousand Oaks, CA: Sage.

Dalton, J. H. (1984). Discussing ethical issues in practicum courses. *Teaching of Psychology, 11,* 186–188.

Dana, R. H. (2000). Psychological assessment in the diagnosis and treatment of ethnic group members. In J. F. Aponte & J. Wohl (Eds.), *Psychological intervention and cultural diversity* (2nd *ed.*) (pp. 59–74). Boston: Allyn and Bacon.

Davis, J. L., & Mickelson, D. J. (1994). School counselors: Are you aware of ethical and legal aspects of counseling? *The School Counselor, 42,* 5–13.

Davis, J. M., & Sandoval, J. (1982). Applied ethics for school-based consultants. *Professional Psychology, 13,* 543–551.

Dawson, M. M. (1987). Beyond ability grouping: A review of the effectiveness of ability grouping and its alternatives. *School Psychology Review, 17,* 559–569.

Dawson, M. M. (1995). Best practices in promoting alternatives to ability grouping. In A. Thomas & J. Grimes (Eds.), *Best practices in school psychology III* (pp. 347–357). Washington, DC: National Association of School Psychologists.

Dekraai, M., Sales, B., & Hall, S. (1998). Informed consent, confidentiality, and duty to report laws in the conduct of child therapy. In T. R. Kratochwill & R. J. Morris (Eds.), *The practice of child therapy (3rd ed.)* (pp. 540–559). Boston, MA: Allyn & Bacon.

DeMers, S. T. (1994). Legal and ethical issues in school psychologists' participation in psychopharmacological interventions with children. *School Psychology Quarterly, 9*, 41–52.

DeMers, S. T., & Bersoff, D. (1985). Legal issues in school psychological practice. In J. R. Bergan (Ed.), *School psychology in contemporary society: An introduction* (pp. 319–339). Columbus, OH: Merrill.

DeMers, S. T., & Bricklin, P. (1995). Legal, professional, and financial constraints on psychologists' delivery of health care services in school settings. *School Psychology Quarterly, 10*, 217–235.

Diener, E., & Crandall, R. (1978). *Ethics in social and behavioral research.* Chicago: University of Chicago Press.

Discipline under Section 504. (1996, November 22). *The Special Educator, 12*(1), 6–8.

DuPaul, G. J., Barkley, R. A., & Connor, D. F. (1998). Stimulants. In R. A. Barkley (Ed.), *Attention-Deficit Hyperactivity Disorder: A handbook for diagnosis and treatment* (2nd *ed.*) (pp. 510–551). New York: Guilford Press.

Dunst, C. J., & Trivette, C. M. (1987). Enabling and empowering families: Conceptual and intervention issues. *School Psychology Review, 16*, 443–456.

Dwyer, K., Osher, D., & Warger, C. (1998). *Early warning, timely response: A guide to safe schools*. Washington, DC: U.S. Department of Education. Retrieved October 10, 1999, from http://www.ed.gov/offices/OSERS/OSEP/ earlywrn.html.

Eades, R. W. (1986). The school counselor or psychologist and problems of defamation. *Journal of School Law, 15*, 117–120.

East Lansing (MI) Public Schools. (1992). OCR complaint investigation letter of findings. *Individuals with Disabilities Education Law Report, 19*, 40–43.

Eberlein, L. (1987). Introducing ethics to beginning psychologists: A problem-solving approach. *Professional Psychology: Research and Practice, 18*, 353–359.

Elias, C. L. (1999). The school psychologist as expert witness: Strategies and issues in the courtroom. *School Psychology Review, 28*, 44–59.

Elizalde-Utnick, G. (2002). Best practices in building partnership with families. In A. Thomas & J. Grimes (Eds.), *Best practices in school psychology IV* (pp. 413–429). Besthesda, MD: National Association of School Psychologists.

Esler, A. N., Godber, Y., & Christenson, S. L. (2002). Best practices in supporting home-school collaboration. In A. Thomas & J. Grimes (Eds.), *Best practices in school psychology IV* (pp. 389–411). Besthesda, MD: National Association of School Psychologists.

Evans, L. D. (1996). Calculating achievement composite scores for regression discrepancy models. *Learning Disability Quarterly*, *19*, 242–249.

Evans, W. J. (1997). Torts. In C. J. Russo (Ed.), *The yearbook of school law 1997* (pp. 183-212). Dayton, OH: Education Law Association.

Eversole, T. (1993, September). Lesbian, gay and bisexual youth in school. *Communique*, 9–10.

Fagan, T. K., & Wise, P. S. (2000). *School psychology: Past, present, and future (2nd ed.)*. New York: Longman.

Fairfield-Suisun Unified School District. (1989). OCR complaint investigation letter of findings. *Education for the Handicapped Law Report, 353* (Suppl. 242), 205–208.

Fanibanda, D. K. (1976). Ethical issues of mental health consultation. *Professional Psychology, 7*, 547–552.

FBI Academy. (2000). *The School Shooter: A Threat Assessment Perspective.* Retrieved November 3, 2002, from http://www.fbi.gov/.

Feinberg, T., & Jacob, S. (2002). Administrative considerations in preventing and responding to crisis: A risk management approach. In S. E. Brock, P. J. Lazarus, & S. R. Jimerson (Eds.), *Best practices in school crisis prevention and intervention* (pp. 95–108). Bethesda, MD: National Association of School Psychologists.

Ferraraccio, M. (1999). Metal detectors in the public schools: Fourth Amendment concerns. *Journal of Law & Education, 28,* 209–229.

Ferguson, L. R. (1978). The competence and freedom of children to make choices regarding participation in research: A statement. *Journal of Social Issues, 34,* 114–121.

Figueroa, R. A. (1990). Best practices in the assessment of bilingual children. In A. Thomas & J. Grimes (Eds.), *Best practices in school psychology-II* (pp. 93–106). Washington, DC: National Association of School Psychologists.

Fine, M. A., & Ulrich, L. P. (1988). Integrating psychology and philosophy in teaching a graduate course in ethics. *Professional Psychology: Research and Practice, 19,* 542–546.

Fischer, L., & Sorenson, G. P. (1996). *School law for counselors, psychologists, and social workers (3rd ed.).* White Plains, New York: Longman.

Fischetti, B. A., & Crespi, T. D. (1999). Clinical supervision for school psychologists: National practices, trends, and future implications. *School Psychology International, 20,* 278–288.

Fish, M. C. (2002). Best practices in collaborating with parents of children with disabilities. In A. Thomas & J. Grimes, *Best practices in school psychology IV* (pp. 363–376). Bethesda, MD: National Association of School Psychologists.

Fisher, C. B., & Fryberg, D. (1994). Participant partners: College students weigh the costs and benefits of deceptive research. *American Psychologist, 49,* 417–427.

Flanagan, D. P., Andrews, T. J., & Genshaft, J. L. (1997). The functional utility of intelligence tests with special education populations. In D. P. Flanagan, J. L. Genshaft, & P. L. Harrison (Eds.), *Contemporary intellectual assessment* (pp. 457–483). New York: Guilford Press.

Flaugher, R. L. (1978). The many definitions of test bias. *American Psychologist, 33,* 671–679.

Fleming, E. R., & Fleming, D. C. (1987). Involvement of minors in special educational decision-making. *Journal of Law & Education, 16,* 389–402.

Folkman, S. (2000). Privacy and confidentiality. In B. D. Sales & S. Folkman (Eds.), *Ethics in research with human participants* (pp. 49–57). Washington, DC: American Psychological Association.

Forman, S. G., & Pfeiffer, A. (1997). Substance use and abuse. In G.G. Bear, K.M. Minke, A. Thomas (Eds.), *Children's Needs II* (pp. 917–924). Bethesda, MD: National Association of School Psychologists.

Forman, S. G., & Randolph, M. K. (1987). Children and drug abuse. In A. Thomas & J. Grimes (Eds.), *Children's needs: Psychological perspectives* (pp. 182–189). Washington, DC: National Association of School Psychologists.

Frankel, M. S., & Siang, S. (1999). Ethical and legal aspects of human subjects research. Retrieved November 20, 2001, from http://www.aaas.org/spp/dspp/sfrl/projects/intres/main.htm.

Friedman, S. L., Helm, D. T., & Marrone, J. (1999). Caring, control, and clinicians' influence: Ethical dilemmas in developmental disabilities. *Ethics & Behavior, 9,* 349–364.

Frisby, C. L. (1999a). Culture and test session behavior: Part I. *School Psychology Quarterly, 14,* 263–280.

Frisby, C. L. (1999b). Culture and test session behavior: Part II. *School Psychology Quarterly, 14,* 281–303.

Gallagher, J. J. (1989). A new policy initiative: Infants and toddlers with handicapping conditions. *American Psychologist, 44,* 387–391.

Gallessich, J. (1982). *The profession and practice of consultation.* San Francisco: Jossey-Bass.

Gawthrop, J. C., & Uhlemann, M. R. (1992). Effects of the problem-solving approach in ethics training. *Professional Psychology: Research and Practice, 23,* 38–42.

Gil, E. F., & Bob, S. (1999). Culturally competent research: An ethical perspective. *Clinical Psychology Review, 19,* 45–55.

Gould, S. J. (1996). *The mismeasure of man.* New York: W.W. Norton & Company.

Gregory, R. J. (2000). *Psychological testing (3rd ed.).* Boston: Allyn and Bacon.

Grisso, T., & Vierling, L. (1978). Minor's consent to treatment: A developmental perspective. *Professional Psychology, 9,* 412–427.

Grunder, T. M. (1978). Two formulas for determining the readability of subject consent forms. *American Psychologist, 33,* 773–774.

Gutkin, T. B., & Curtis, M. J. (1999). School-based consultation theory and practice: The art and science of indirect service delivery. In C. R. Reynolds & T. B. Gutkin (Eds.), *Handbook of school psychology (3rd ed.),* (pp. 598–637). New York: John Wiley & Sons.

Haas, L. J., & Malouf, J. L. (1989). *Keeping up the good work: A practitioner's guide to mental health ethics.* Sarasota, FL: Professional Resource Exchange.

Haas, L. J., Malouf, J. L., & Mayerson, N. H. (1986). Ethical dilemmas in psychological practice: Results of a national survey. *Professional Psychology: Research and Practice, 17,* 316–321.

Hakola, S. R. (1992). Legal rights of students with attention deficit disorder. *School Psychology Quarterly, 7,* 285–297.

Hammill, D. D., Brown, L., & Bryant, B. R. (1989). *A consumer's guide to tests in print.* Austin, TX: Pro-Ed.

Handelsman, M. M. (1986a). Problems with ethics training by "osmosis." *Professional Psychology: Research and Practice, 17,* 371–372.

Handelsman, M. M. (1986b). Ethics training at the master's level: A national survey. *Professional Psychology: Research and Practice, 17,* 24–26.

Hansen, J. C., Himes, B. S., & Meier, S. (1990). *Consultation: Concepts and practices.* Englewood Cliffs, NJ: Prentice-Hall.

Hansen, N. D., & Goldberg, S. G. (1999). Navigating the nuances: A matrix of considerations for ethical-legal dilemmas. *Professional Psychology: Research and Practice, 30,* 495–503.

Hansen, N. D., Pepitone-Arreola-Rockwell, F., & Greene, A. F. (2000). Multicultural competence: Criteria and case examples. *Professional Psychology: Research and Practice, 31,* 652–660.

Hare, R. (1981). The philosophical basis of psychiatric ethics. In S. Bloch & P. Chodoff (Eds.), *Psychiatric ethics* (pp. 31–45). Oxford, England: Oxford University Press.

Harris, A., & Kapche, R. (1978). Behavior modification in schools: Ethical issues and suggested guidelines. *Journal of School Psychology, 16,* 25–33.

Harris, K. R. (1985). Definitional, parametric, and procedural considerations in timeout interventions and research. *Exceptional Children, 51,* 279–288.

Hartshorne, T. S. (2002). Mistaking courage for denial: Family resilience after the birth of a child with severe disabilities. *Journal of Individual Psychology, 58,* 263–278.

Harvey, V. S. (1997). Improving readability of psychological reports. *Professional Psychology: Research and Practice, 28,* 271–274.

Harvey, V. S., & Struzziero, J. (2000). *Effective supervision in school psychology.* Bethesda, MD: National Association of School Psychologists.

Havey, J. M. (1999). School psychologists' involvement in special education due process hearings. *Psychology in the Schools, 36,* 117–122.

Hays, P. A. (2001). *Addressing cultural complexities in practice.* Washington, DC: American Psychological Association.

Hehir, T. (1993, October 25). Response to letter of inquiry from McDonald. *Individuals with Disabilities Education Law Report, 20,* 1159–1160.

Helton, G. B., Ray, B. A., & Biderman, M. D. (2000). Responses of school psychologists and teachers to administrative pressures to practice unethically: A national survey. *Special Services in the Schools, 16,* 111–134.

Henderson, D. H. (1986). Constitutional implications involving the use of corporal punishment in the public schools. *Journal of Law & Education, 15*, 255–269.

Henker, B., & Whalen, C. K. (1989). Hyperactivity and attention deficits. *American Psychologist, 44*, 216–223.

Henning-Stout, M. (1996). ¿Que podemos hacer? Roles for school psychologists with Mexican and Latino migrant children and families. *School Psychology Review, 25*, 152–164.

Henning-Stout, M., & James, S. (Guest Eds.) (2000). Mini-series: Lesbian, gay, bisexual, transgender and questioning youth. *School Psychology Review, 29*, 155–234.

Henning-Stout, M., James, S., & Macintosh, S. (2000). Reducing harassment of lesbian, gay, bisexual, transgender, and questioning youth in schools. *School Psychology Review, 29*, 180–191.

Herlihy, B., & Sheeley, V. L. (1987). Privileged communication in selected helping professions: A comparison among statutes. *Journal of Counseling and Development, 65*, 479–483.

Heumann, J. E. (1993). Response to letter of inquiry from G. Warrington. *Individuals with Disabilities Education Law Report, 20*, 539–540.

Hindman, S. E. (1986). The law, the courts, and the education of behaviorally disordered students. *Behavior Disorders, 11*, 280–289.

Hoff, K. E., Doepke, K., & Landau, S. (2002). Best practices in the assessment of children with attention deficit/hyperactivity disorder: Linking assessment to intervention. In A. Thomas & J. Grimes, *Best practices in school psychology IV* (pp. 1129–1150). Bethesda, MD: National Association of School Psychologists.

Holmes, D. S. (1976). Debriefing after psychological experiments: II. Effectiveness of postexperimental desensitizing. *American Psychologist, 31*, 868–875.

Holmes, D. S., & Urie, R. C. (1975). Effects of preparing children for psychotherapy. *Journal of Consulting and Clinical Psychology, 43*, 311–318.

Hopkins, B. R., & Anderson, B. S. (1985). *The counselor and the law* (2nd *ed.*). Alexandria, VA: American Association for Counseling and Development.

Horton, C. B., & Cruise, T. K. (2001). *Child abuse and neglect: The school's response*. New York: Guilford Press.

Hostetler, A. J. (1988, June). Indictment: Congress send message on fraud. *APA Monitor*, p. 5.

Hubbard, D. D., & Adams, J. (2002). Best practices in facilitating meaningful family involvement in educational decision making. In A. Thomas & J. Grimes, *Best practices in school psychology IV* (pp. 377–387). Bethesda, MD: National Association of School Psychologists.

Hubsch, A. W. (1989). Education and self-government: The right to education under state constitutional law. *Journal of Law & Education, 18*, 93–133.

Hughes, J. N. (1986). Ethical issues in school consultation. *School Psychology Review, 15*, 489–499.

Hummel, D. L., Talbutt, L. C., & Alexander, M. D. (1985). *Law and ethics in counseling*. New York: Van Nostrand-Reinhold.

Humphreys, K. L. (2000). Influences on ethical decision making among practicing school psychologists (Doctoral Dissertation, Kent State University, 2000). *Dissertation Abstracts International Section A: Humanities & Social Sciences, 60(7–A)*, 2370.

Hyman, I. A. (1990). *Reading, writing, and the hickory stick.* Lexington, MA: Lexington Books.

Hyman, I. A., & Perone, D. C. (1998). The other side of school violence: Educator policies and practices that may contribute to student misbehavior. *Psychology in the Schools, 36*, 7–27.

Hyman, I. A., Barrish, B. M., & Kaplan, J. (1997). Corporal punishment. In G. G. Baer, K. M. Minke, & A. Thomas (Eds.), *Children's needs: II* (pp. 235–243). Bethesda, MD: National Association of School Psychologists.

In the Matter of a Child with Disabilities. (1992). Ruling of a Connecticut hearing officer. *Individuals with Disabilities Education Law Report, 19,* 198–203.

Ingraham, C. L., & Meyers, J. (Guest Eds.). (2000). Mini-series: Multicultural and cross-cultural consultation in schools. *School Psychology Review, 29,* 315–428.

Irvin, T. B. (1979, January 9). Response to letter of inquiry from W. A. Hafner. *Education for the Handicapped Law Report, 23* (Suppl.), 181–182.

Jacob, S., & Brantley, J. C. (1987a). Ethical and legal considerations for microcomputer use in special education. In D. L. Johnson, C. D. Maddux, & A. C. Candler (Eds.), *Computers in the special education classroom* (pp. 185–194). New York: Haworth Press.

Jacob, S., & Brantley, J. C. (1987b). Ethical-legal problems with computer use and suggestions for best practices: A national survey. *School Psychology Review, 16,* 69–77.

Jacob, S., & Brantley, J. C. (1989). Ethics and computer-assisted assessment: Three case studies. *Psychology in the Schools, 26,* 163–167.

Jacob, S., & Feinberg, T. (2002). Legal and ethical issues in crisis prevention and response. In S. E. Brock, P. J. Lazarus, & S. R. Jimerson (Eds.), *Best practices in school crisis prevention and intervention* (pp. 709–732). Bethesda, MD: National Association of School Psychologists.

Jacob-Timm, S. (1996). Ethical and legal issues associated with the use of aversives in the public schools: The SIBIS controversy. *School Psychology Review, 2,* 184–198.

Jacob-Timm, S. (1998, April). *Training school psychologists in ethics and law.* Invited presentation, 1998 Trainers of School Psychologists Annual Conference, Orlando, FL.

Jacob-Timm, S. (1999). Ethical dilemmas encountered by members of the National Association of School Psychologists. *Psychology in the Schools, 36,* 205–217.

Jacob-Timm, S., & Hartshorne, T. S. (1994). Section 504 and school psychology. *Psychology in the Schools, 31,* 26–39.

Jensen, P. S. (1998). Ethical and pragmatic issues in the use of psychotropic agents in young children. *Canadian Journal of Psychiatry, 43,* 585–588.

Jimerson, S. R. (2001). Meta-analysis of grade retention research: Implications for practice in the 21st century. *School Psychology Review, 30,* 420–437.

Jitendra, A. K., & Rohena-Diaz, E. (1996). Language assessment of students who are linguistically diverse: Why a discrete approach is not the answer. *School Psychology Review, 25,* 40–56.

Jobes, D. A., & Berman, A. L. (1993). Suicide and malpractice liability: Assessing and revising policies, procedures, and practice in outpatient settings. *Professional Psychology: Research and Practice, 24,* 91–99.

Johnson, T. P. (1993). Managing student records. *West's Education Law Quarterly, 2,* 260–276.

Kalichman, S. C. (1999). *Mandated reporting of suspected child abuse: Ethics, law, and policy* (2nd *ed.*). Washington, DC: American Psychological Association.

Kaser-Boyd, N., Adelman, H. S., & Taylor, L. (1985). Minors' ability to identify risks and benefits of therapy. *Professional Psychology: Research and Practice, 16,* 411–417.

Kaufman, A. S. (1994). *Intelligent testing with the WISC-III.* New York: Wiley.

Keith-Spiegel, P. (1983). Children and consent to participate in research. In G. B. Melton, G. P. Koocher, & M. J. Saks (Eds.), *Children's competence to consent* (pp. 179–211). New York: Plenum Press.

Kenowa Hills (MI) Public Schools. (1992/1993). OCR complaint investigation letter of findings. *Individuals with Disabilities Education Law Report, 19,* 525–526.

Kirp, D. (1973). Schools as sorters. *University of Pennsylvania Law Review, 121,* 705–797.

Kitchener, K. S. (1986). Teaching applied ethics in counselor education: An integration of psychological processes and philosophical analysis. *Journal of Counseling and Development, 64,* 306–310.

Knapp, S. (1980). A primer on malpractice for psychologists. *Professional Psychology, 11,* 606–612.

Knapp, S., & VandeCreek, L. (1982). Tarasoff: Five years later. *Professional Psychology, 13,* 511–516.

Knapp, S., & VandeCreek, L. (1985). Psychotherapy and privileged communications in child custody cases. *Professional Psychology: Research and Practice, 16,* 398–407.

Knapp, S., & VandeCreek, L. (1997). Ethical and legal aspects of clinical supervision. In C. E. Watkins (Ed.), *Handbook of psychotherapy supervision* (pp. 589–599). New York: John Wiley & Sons.

Knoff, H. M. (1983). Personality assessment in the schools: Issues and procedures for school psychologists. *School Psychology Review, 12,* 391–398.

Koocher, G. P. & Keith-Spiegel, P. (1998). *Ethics in psychology (2nd ed.).* New York: Oxford.

Kozol, J. (1991). *Savage inequalities.* New York: Harper Perennial.

Kubiszyn, T., Brown, R. T., & DeMers, S. T. (1997). Pediatric psychopharmacology. In G. G. Baer, K. M. Minke, & A. Thomas (Eds.), *Children's needs: II* (pp. 925–934). Bethesda, MD: National Association of School Psychologists.

Kublick, R. J., Bard, E. M., & Perry, J. D. (2000). Manifestation determinations. In C. F. Telzrow & M. Tankersley (Eds)., *IDEA amendments of 1997.* Bethesda, MD: National Association of School Psychologists.

Lake Washington (WA) School District No. 414. (1985, June 28). OCR complaint investigation letter of findings. *Individuals with Disabilities Education Law Report, 257* (Suppl. 150), 611–615.

Lamb, D. H., Cochran, D. J., & Jackson, V. R. (1991). Training and organizational issues associated with identifying and responding to intern impairment. *Professional Psychology: Research and Practice, 22,* 291–296.

LeVay, S. (1996). *Queer science.* Cambridge, MA: The MIT Press.

Levine, D. U., & Levine, R. F. (1996). *Society and education* (9th *ed.*). Boston: Allyn and Bacon.

Lichtenstein, R. (1981). Comparative validity of two preschool screening tests: Correlational and classificational approaches. *Journal of Learning Disabilities, 14,* 68–72.

Lim, J. (1993, May 19). OCR policy letter to regional offices. *Special Education Report,* p. 5.

Lohrmann, S., & Zirkel, P. A. (1995, November 10). Helping you make the call. *The Special Educator, 11,* 1, 6.

Lopez, E. C. (1997). The cognitive assessment of limited English proficient and bilingual children. In D. P. Flanagan, J. L. Genshaft, & P. L. Harrison (Eds.), *Contemporary intellectual assessment* (pp. 503–516). New York: Guilford Press.

Lopez, E. C. (2002). Best practices in working with school interpreters to deliver psychological services to children and families. In A. Thomas & J. Grimes, *Best practices in school psychology IV* (pp. 1419–1432). Bethesda, MD: National Association of School Psychologists.

Lopez, E. C., & Gopaul-McNicol, S. (1997). English as a second language. In G. G. Baer, K. M. Minke, & A. Thomas (Eds.), *Children's needs: II* (pp. 523–531). Bethesda, MD: National Association of School Psychologists.

Lopez, E. C., & Rogers, M. R. (2001). Conceptualizing cross-cultural school psychology competencies. *School Psychology Quarterly, 16,* 270–302.

Lynch, E. W., & Hanson, M. J. (1998). *Developing cross-cultural competence* (2nd *ed.*). Baltimore, MD: Brookes.

Marshall, E. (2000). Duke study faults overuse of stimulants for children. *Science, 289,* 721.

Martin, R. (1979). *Educating handicapped children: The legal mandate.* Champaign, IL: Research Press.

Martin, R. (1992). *Continuing challenges in special education law* (looseleaf notebook). Urbana, IL: Carle Media.

Martin, R. P. (1985, April). Ethics column—Parents' rights to copies of test protocols: A draft position statement of the Division 16 Ethics Committee. *The School Psychologist,* p. 9.

Martins, B. K., Witt, J. C., Daly, E. J., & Vollmer, T. R. (1999). Behavior analysis: Theory and practice in educational settings. In C. R. Reynolds & T. B. Gutkin (Eds.), *The handbook of school psychology (3rd ed.)* (pp. 350–382). New York: John Wiley & Sons.

Matarazzo, J. D. (1986). Computerized psychological test interpretations. *American Psychologist, 41,* 14–24.

McConaughy, S. H., & Skiba, R. J. (1993). Comorbidity of externalizing and internalizing problems. *School Psychology Review, 22,* 421–436.

McDermott, P. A., & Watkins, M. W. (1985). *M-MAC Microcomputer systems manual.* San Antonio, TX: The Psychological Corporation.

McGivern, J. E., & McKevitt, B. C. (2002). Best practices in working with students using assistive technology. In A. Thomas & J. Grimes (Eds.), *Best practices in school psychology IV* (pp. 1537–1553). Bethesda, MD: National Association of School Psychologists

McGue, M. (2000). Authorship and intellectual property. In B. D. Sales & S. Folkman (Eds.), *Ethics in research with human participants* (pp. 75–95). Washington, DC: American Psychological Association.

McIntosh, D. E., & Phelps, L. (2000). Supervision in school psychology: Where will the future take us? *Psychology in the Schools, 37,* 33–38.

McMinn, M. R., Buchanan, T., Ellens, B. M., & Ryan, M. K. (1999). Technology, professional practice, and ethics: Survey findings and implications. *Professional Psychology: Research and Practice, 30,* 165–172.

Meara, N. M., Schmidt, L. D., & Day, J. D. (1996). Principles and virtues: A foundation for ethical decisions, policies, and character. *Counseling Psychology, 24,* 4–77.

Meddin, B. J., & Rosen, A. L. (1986). Child abuse and neglect: Prevention and reporting. *Young Children, 41,* 26–30.

Medway, F. J., & Rose, J. S. (1986). Grade retention. In T. R. Kratochwill (Ed.), *Advances in school psychology* (Vol. 5, pp. 141–175). Hillsdale, NJ: Erlbaum.

Melton, G. B., Koocher, G. P., & Saks, M. J. (Eds.). (1983). *Children's competence to consent.* New York: Plenum Press.

Messick, S. (1965). Personality measurement and the ethics of assessment. *American Psychologist, 20,* 136–142.

Messick, S. (1980). Test validity and the ethics of assessment. *American Psychologist, 35,* 1012–1027.

Messick, S. (1984). Assessment in context: Appraising student performance in relation to instructional quality. *Educational Researcher, 13,* 3–8.

Messick, S. (1995). Validity of psychological assessment. *American Psychologist, 50,* 741–749.

Messina, D. J. (1988). Corporal punishment v. classroom discipline: A case of mistaken identity. *Loyola Law Review, 34,* 35–110.

Meyers, A. B., & Landau, S. (2002). Best practices in school-based sexuality education and pregnancy prevention. In A. Thomas & J. Grimes (Eds.), *Best practices in school psychology IV* (pp. 337–351). Bethesda, MD: National Association of School Psychologists

Mowder, B. (1983). Assessment and intervention in school psychological services. In G. W. Hynd (Ed.), *The school psychologist* (pp. 145–167). Syracuse, NY: Syracuse University Press.

Muehleman, T., Pickens, B. K., & Robinson, F. (1985). Informing clients about the limits to confidentiality, risks, and their rights: Is self-disclosure inhibited? *Professional Psychology: Research and Practice, 16,* 385–397.

Mulvey, E. P., & Cauffman, E. (2001). The inherent limits of predicting school violence. *American Psychologist, 56,* 797–802.

Nagle, R. J. (1987). Ethics training in school psychology. *Professional School Psychology, 2,* 163–171.

Nagy, T. F. (2000). *Ethics in plain English*. Washington, DC: American Psychological Association.

National Association of School Psychologists. (1997). *Professional conduct manual (3rd ed.)*. Bethesda, MD: Author.

National Association of School Psychologists. (1999). Position statement on gay, lesbian, and bisexual youth. Retrieved November 24, 2001, from http://www.nasponline.org/information/position-paper.html.

National Association of School Psychologists. (2000a). *Professional conduct manual.* Bethesda, MD: Author.

National Association of School Psychologists. (2000b). *Standards for training and field placement programs in school psychology. Standards for the credentialing of school psychologists*. Retrieved January 5, 2002, from http://www.nasponline.

National Association of School Psychologists. (2001). Retrieved November 10, 2001, from http://www.nasponline.org/certification./statencsp.html.

National Center for Education Statistics. (2001). *Violence and Discipline Problems in U.S. Public Schools: 1996–97.* Retrieved November 5, 2001, from http:// nces.ed.gov/pubs98/violence/98030003.html.

National Commission for the Protection of Human Subjects of Biomedical and Behavioral Science Research. (1979). The Belmont report: Ethical principles and guidelines for the protection of human subjects of biomedical and behavioral research. *The Federal Register,* pp. 12065–12073.

National Institute of Allergy and Infectious Diseases. (2001). *National Institute of Allergy and Infectious Diseases-fact sheet.* Retrieved November 15, 2001, from http:// www.niaid.nih.gov/factsheets/stdstats.htm.

National Institutes of Health. (1991). National Institutes of Health consensus development conference statement. In *NIH consensus development conference on the treatment of destructive behaviors in persons with developmental disabilities* (NIH Publication No. 91-2410, pp. 1–29). Washington, DC: U.S. Government Printing Office.

National Institute of Mental Health. (2001). *National Institute of mental health-suicide facts.* Retrieved November 15, 2001, from http://www.nimh.nih.gov/research/suifact.htm.

National Institute on Drug Abuse. (2001). *National Institute on Drug Abuse.* Retrieved November 15, 2001, from http://www.nida.nih.gov/Infofax/ HSYouthtrends.html.

National School Safety Center. (1999). *Checklist for characteristics of violent youth.* Retrieved October 9, 1999, from http://www.nssc1.org/.

Newman, J. L. (1993). Ethical issues in consultation. *Journal of Counseling and Development, 72,* 148–156.

Nieto, S. (2000) *Affirming diversity: The sociopolitical context of multicultural education (2nd ed.).* NY: Longman.

Okun, B., Fried, J., & Okun, M. L. (1999). *Understanding diversity*. Pacific Grove, CA: Brooks/Cole.

Ortiz, S. O. (2002). Best practices in nondiscriminatory assessment. In A. Thomas & J. Grimes (Eds.), *Best practices in school psychology IV* (pp. 1321–1336). Bethesda, MD: National Association of School Psychologists.

Ortiz, S. O., & Flanagan, D. P. (2002). Best practices in working with culturally diverse children and families. In A. Thomas & J. Grimes (Eds.), *Best practices in school psychology IV* (pp. 337–351). Bethesda, MD: National Association of School Psychologists.

Page, E. B. (1980). Tests and decisions for the handicapped: A guide to evaluation under the new laws. *The Journal of Special Education, 14,* 423–483.

Paredes Scribner, A. (2002). Best assessment and intervention practices with second language learners. In A. Thomas & J. Grimes (Eds.), *Best practices in school psychology IV* (pp. 337–351). Bethesda, MD: National Association of School Psychologists.

Pelco, L. E., Jacobson, L., Ries, R. R., & Melka, S. (2000). Perspectives and practices in family-school partnerships: A national survey of school psychologists. *School Psychology Review, 29,* 235–250.

Pfohl, W., & Pfohl, V. (2002). Best practices in technology. In A. Thomas & J. Grimes (Eds.), *Best practices in school psychology IV* (pp. 195–207). Bethesda, MD: National Association of School Psychologists

Physicians' desk reference (*5th ed.*). (2001). Oradell, NJ: Medical Economics.

Pitcher, G., & Poland, S. (1992). Crisis intervention in the schools. New York: Guilford.

Plante, T. G. (1995). Training child clinical predoctoral interns and postdoctoral fellows in ethics and professional issues: An experiential model. *Professional Psychology: Research and Practice, 26,* 616–619.

Plante, T. G. (1999). Ten strategies for psychology trainees and practicing psychologists interested in avoiding ethical and legal perils. *Psychotherapy, 36,* 398–403.

Poland, S. (1989). *Suicide intervention in the schools.* New York: Guilford.

Poland, S., & Lieberman, R. (2002). Best practices in suicide intervention. In A. Thomas & J. Grimes (Eds.), *Best practices in school psychology IV* (pp. 1151–1165). Bethesda, MD: National Association of School Psychologists.

Poland, S., & McCormick, J. S. (1999). *Coping with crisis: Lessons learned.* Longmont, CO: Sopris West.

Pope, K. S., Tabachnick, B. G., & Keith-Spiegel, P. (1987). The beliefs and behaviors of psychologists as therapists. *American Psychologist, 42,* 993–1006.

Prilleltensky, I. (1991). The social ethics of school psychology: A priority for the 1990's. *School Psychology Quarterly, 6,* 200–222.

Prilleltensky, I. (1997). Values, assumptions, and practices: Assessing the moral implications of psychological discourse and action. *American Psychologist, 52,* 517–535.

Prus, J., & Mittelmeier, K. (1995). Appendix VIII: Summary of licensure requirements for independent practice in psychology and school psychology. In A. Thomas & J. Grimes (Eds.), *Best practices in school psychology: III* (pp. 1249–1256). Washington, DC: National Association of School Psychologists.

Pryzwansky, W. B. (1999). Accreditation and credentialing systems in school psychology. In C. R. Reynolds & T. B. Gutkin (Eds.), *The handbook of school psychology* (*3rd ed.*) (pp. 1145–1158). New York: John Wiley & Sons.

Pulliam, J. L. (1999). The attorney's role in responding to violence: A case study of Jonesboro, Arkansas. *School Law in Review 1999* (pp. 1–18). Alexandria, VA: National School Board Association.

Purcell, C. W. (1984). Limiting the use of corporal punishment in American schools: A call for more specific legal guidelines. *Journal of Law & Education, 13,* 183–195.

Rafoth, M. A. (2002). Best practices in preventing academic failure and promoting alternatives to retention. In A. Thomas & J. Grimes (Eds.), *Best practices in school psychology IV* (pp. 789–802). Bethesda, MD: National Association of School Psychologists.

Rapp, J., Carrington, F., & Nicholson, G. (1992). *School crime and violence: Victims' rights* (1992 rev.). Malibu, CA: Pepperdine.

Reddy, M., Borum, R., Berglund, J., Vossekuil, B., Fein, R., & Modzeleski, W. (2001). Evaluating risk for targeted violence in schools: Comparing risk assessment, threat assessment, and other approaches. *Psychology in the Schools, 38,* 157–172.

Remley, T. P., Herlihy, B., & Herlihy, S. (1997). The U.S. Supreme Court decision in Jaffee v. Remond: Implications for counselors. *Journal of Counseling and Development, 75,* 213–218.

Repp, A. C., & Singh, N. N. (Eds.). (1990). *Perspectives on the use of nonaversive and aversive interventions with persons with developmental disabilities.* Pacific Grove, CA: Brooks/Cole.

Reschly, D. J. (1979). Nonbiased assessment. In G. D. Phye & D. J. Reschly (Eds.), *School psychology: Perspectives and issues* (pp. 215–253). New York: Academic Press.

Reschly, D. J. (1997). Diagnostic and treatment utility of intelligence tests. In D. P. Flanagan, J. L. Genshaft, & P. L. Harrison (Eds.), *Contemporary intellectual assessment* (pp. 437–456). New York: Guilford Press.

Reschly, D. J. (2000). Assessment and eligibility determination in the Individuals with Disabilities Education Act of 1997. In C. F. Telzrow & M. Tankersley (Eds.), *IDEA Amendments of 1997* (pp. 65–104). Bethesda, MD: National Association of School Psychologists.

Reschly, D. J., & Bersoff, D. N. (1999). Law and school psychology. In C. R. Reynolds & T. B. Gutkin (Eds.), *Handbook of school psychology* (*3rd ed.*) (pp. 1077–1112). New York: John Wiley & Sons.

Reschly, D. J., & Wilson, M. S. (1995). School psychology practitioners and faculty: 1986 to 1991–1992 trends in demographics, roles, satisfaction, and system reform. *School Psychology Review, 24,* 2–80.

Rest, J. R. (1984). Research on moral development: Implications for training counseling psychologists. *Counseling Psychologist, 12,* 19–29.

Reutter, E. E. (1994). *The law of public education* (*4th ed.*). Westbury, New York: Foundation Press.

Reynolds, C. R., Lowe, P.A., Saenz, A. L. (1999). The problem of bias in psychological assessment. In C. R. Reynolds & T. B. Gutkin (Eds.), *Handbook of school psychology* (*2nd ed.*) (pp. 549–595). New York: John Wiley & Sons.

Rialto (CA) Unified School District. (1989). OCR complaint investigation letter of findings. *Education for the Handicapped Law Report,* 353 (Suppl. 241), 201–204.

Rizza, M. G., & McIntosh, D. E. (Eds.) (2001). New perspectives in gifted education [Special issue]. *Psychology in the Schools, 38(5).*

Rogers, M. R. (2000). Examining the cultural context of consultation. *School Psychology Review, 29,* 414–418.

Rogers, M. R., Ingraham, C. L., Bursztyn, A., Cajigas-Segredo, N., Esquivel, G., Hess, R., Nahari, S. G., & Lopez, E. (1999). Providing psychological services to racially, ethnically, culturally, and linguistically diverse individuals in the schools: Recommendations for practice. *School Psychology International, 20,* 243–264

Rosenberg, S. L. (1995). Best practices in maintaining an independent practice. In A. Thomas & J. Grimes (Eds.), *Best practices in school psychology: III* (pp. 145–152). Washington, DC: National Association of School Psychologists.

Ross, R. P., & Harrison, P. L. (1997). Ability grouping. In G. G. Baer, K. M. Minke, & A. Thomas (Eds.), *Children's needs: II* (pp. 457–465). Bethesda, MD: National Association of School Psychologists.

Ross, W. D. (1930). *The right and the good.* Oxford, England: Claredon Press.

Ross-Reynolds, G., & Hardy, B. S. (1985). Crisis counseling for disparate adolescent sexual dilemmas: Pregnancy and homosexuality. *School Psychology Review, 14,* 300–312.

Rushton, C. H., Will, J. C., & Murray, M. G. (1994). To honor and obey-DNR orders and the school. *Pediatric Nursing, 10,* 581–585.

Russell-Sage Foundation. (1970). *Guidelines for the collection, maintenance, and dissemination of pupil records.* Hartford, CT: Connecticut Printers.

Ryan, D., & Martin, A. (2000). Lesbian, gay, bisexual, and transgender parents in the school systems. *School Psychology Review, 29,* 207–216.

Sales, B. D., & Folkman, S. (2000). *Ethics in research with human participants.* Washington, DC: American Psychological Association.

Sales, B. D., Krauss, D. A., Sacken, D. M., & Overcast, T. D. (1999). The legal rights of students. In C. R. Reynolds & T. B. Gutkin (Eds.), *Handbook of school psychology* (*3rd ed.*) (pp. 1113–1145). New York: John Wiley & Sons.

Sattler, J. M. (1988). *Assessment of children (3rd ed.)*. San Diego, CA: Sattler.

Sattler, J.M. (2001). *Assessment of children: Cognitive applications (4th ed.)*. San Diego, CA: Sattler.

Sattler, J.M. (2002). *Assessment of children: Behavioral and clinical applications (4th ed.)*. San Diego, CA: Sattler.

Schill, K. (1993, Fall). Violence among students: Schools' liability under Section 1983. *School Law Bulletin,* 1–11.

Schimmel, D., & Fischer, L. (1977). *The rights of parents in the education of their children.* Columbia, MD: National Committee for Citizens in Education.

School psychologists begin 'student profiling' to combat violence. (1999, September 7). *Midland Daily News,* p. A–11.

Shah, S. A. (1969). Privileged communications, confidentiality, and privacy: Privileged communications. *Professional Psychology, 1,* 159–164.

Sheridan, S. M., Cowan, R. J., & Eagle, J. W. (2000). Partnering with parents in educational programming for students with special needs. In C. F. Telzrow & M. Tankersley (Eds.), *IDEA: Amendments of 1997* (pp. 307–349). Bethesda, MD: National Association of School Psychologists.

Sherry, P. (1991). Ethical issues in the conduct of supervision. *Counseling Psychologist, 19,* 566–584.

Shinn, M. R. (2002). Best practices in using curriculum-based measurement in problem-solving. In A. Thomas & J. Grimes (Eds.), *Best practices in school psychology IV* (pp. 671–697). Bethesda, MD: National Association of School Psychologists.

Short, R. J., & Shapiro, S. K. (1993). Conduct disorders: A framework for understanding and intervention in schools and communities. *School Psychology Review, 22,* 362–375.

Shuman, D. W., & Foote, W. (1999). *Jaffee v. Redmond's* impact: Life after the Supreme Court's recognition of a psychotherapist-patient privilege. *Professional Psychology: Research and Practice, 30,* 479–487.

Sieber, J. E. (2000). Planning research; Basic ethical decision-making. In B. D. Sales & S. Folkman (Eds.), *Ethics in research with human participants* (pp. 13–26). Washington, DC: American Psychological Association.

Siegel, M. (1979). Privacy, ethics, and confidentiality. *Professional Psychology, 10,* 249–258.

Simmonds, R. J., & Chanock, S. (1993). Medical issues related to caring for human immunodeficiency virus-infected children in and out of the home. *Pediatric Infectious Diseases Journal, 12,* 845–852.

Simon, R. I. (1999). The suicide prevention contract: Clinical, legal, and risk management issues. *Journal of the American Academy of Psychiatry & the Law, 27,* 445–450.

Sinclair, C. (1998). Nine unique features of the *Canadian Code of Ethics for Psychologists. Canadian Psychology, 39,* 167–176.

Slenkovich, J. E. (1986, November). The specific learning disability—A review of the legal requirements. *The Schools' Advocate,* pp. 41–42, 44–47.

Slenkovich, J. E. (1987, June). Chemical dependency doesn't fit within "other health impaired." *The Schools' Advocate,* p. 103.

Slenkovich, J. E. (1987, December). Counseling not same as psychological services. *The Schools' Advocate,* p. 143.

Slenkovich, J. E. (1988, February). The seriously emotionally disturbed definition. *The Schools' Advocate,* pp. 153–164.

Slenkovich, J. E. (1988a, March). Student records act revisited. *The Schools' Advocate,* pp. 165–170.

Slenkovich, J. E. (1988b, March). Students succeeding in regular education do not qualify as learning disabled. *The Schools' Advocate,* p. 166.

Slenkovich, J. E. (1988c, March). When is a service a related service? *The Schools' Advocate,* p. 168.

Smith, T. S., McGuire, J. M., Abbott, D. W., & Blau, B. I. (1991). Clinical ethical decision making: An investigation of the rationales used to justify doing less than one believes one should. *Professional Psychology: Research and Practice, 22,* 235–239.

Society for Research in Child Development. (1990, Winter). SRCD ethical standards for research with children. *SRCD Newsletter,* pp. 5–7.

Society for Research in Child Development. (1991, Fall). Report from the Committee for Ethical Conduct in Child Development Research. *SRCD Newsletter,* p. 6.

Solomon, R. S. (1984). *Ethics: A brief introduction.* New York: McGraw-Hill.

Stephens, R. D. (1994). Planning for safer and better schools: School violence prevention and intervention strategies. *School Psychology Review, 23,* 204–215.

Stoiber, K. C. (1997). Adolescent pregnancy and parenting. In G. G. Baer, K. M. Minke, & A. Thomas (Eds.), *Children's needs: II* (pp. 653–665). Bethesda, MD: National Association of School Psychologists.

Task force releases new privacy guide for students with disabilities. (March 8, 2001) *Section 504 Compliance Advisor, 5 (1).* LRP Publications.

Taft, R. (1965). Comments of Senator Robert Taft. *U.S. Code Congressional and Administrative News,* p. 1450.

Taylor, L., & Adelman, H. S. (1989). Reframing the confidentiality dilemma to work in children's best interests. *Professional Psychology: Research and Practice, 20,* 79–83.

Taylor, L., Adelman, H. S., & Kaser-Boyd, N. (1985). Minors' attitude and competence toward participation in psychoeducational decisions. *Professional Psychology: Research and Practice, 16,* 226–235.

Tharinger, D., & Stafford, M. (1995). Best practices in individual counseling of elementary-age students. In A. Thomas & J. Grimes (Eds.), *Best practices in school psychology: III* (pp. 893–907). Washington, DC: National Association of School Psychologists.

Tharp, R. G. (1991). Cultural diversity and treatment of children. *Journal of Consulting and Clinical Psychology, 59,* 799–812.

Thompson, R. A. (1990). Vulnerability in research: A developmental perspective on research risk. *Child Development, 61,* 1–16.

Tilly, D. W., Knoster, T. P., & Ikeda, M. J. (2000). Functional behavioral assessment. In C. F. Telzrow & M. Tankersley (Eds.), *IDEA amendments of 1997* (pp. 151–197). Besthesda, MD: National Association of School Psychologists.

Tryon, G. S. (2000). Ethical transgressions of school psychology graduate students: A critical incidents survey. *Ethics & Behavior, 10,* 271–279.

Turnbull, H. R., & Turnbull, A. P. (2000). *Free appropriate public education* (*6th ed.*). Denver, CO: Love.

Turnbull, A. P., & Turnbull, H. R. (2001). *Families, professionals, and exceptionality: A special partnership collaborating for empowerment* (*4th ed.*). Upper Saddle River, NJ: Merrill.

Turner, H. S., & Watson, T. S. (1999). Consultant's guide for the use of time-out in the preschool and elementary classroom. *Psychology in the Schools, 36,* 135–148.

Tymchuk, A. J. (1981). Ethical decision-making and psychological treatment. *Journal of Psychiatric Treatment and Evaluation, 3,* 507–513.

Tymchuk, A. J. (1985). Ethical decision-making and psychology students' attitudes toward training in ethics. *Professional Practice of Psychology, 6,* 219–232.

Tymchuk, A. J. (1986). Guidelines for ethical decision making. *Canadian Psychology, 27,* 36–43.

Tymchuk, A. J., Drapkin, R., Major-Kingsley, S., Ackerman, A. B., Coffman, E. W., & Baum, M. S. (1982). Ethical decision making and psychologists' attitudes toward training in ethics. *Professional Psychology, 13,* 412–421.

U.S. Department of Education. (1991). Joint policy memorandum. *Individuals with Disabilities Education Law Report, 18,* 116–119.

U.S. Department of Education & Bias Crimes Task Force of the National Association of Attorneys General. (1999). *Protecting students from harassment and hate crime.* Available: http://www.ed.gov/offices/OCR/.

U.S. Department of Health and Human Services. (1991, 1992). HHS policy clarification. *Individuals with Disabilities Education Law Report, 18,* 558–565.

U.S. Department of Health and Human Services. (2001). *Childstats.gov.* Retrieved November 15, 2001, from http://www.acf.dhhs.gov/programs/cb/publications/cm99/index.htm.

Vanderwood, M. L., & Powers, K. M. (2002). Best practices in standards-based district-wide assessment. In A. Thomas & J. Grimes (Eds.), *Best practices in school psychology IV* (pp. 255–263). Bethesda, MD: National Association of School Psychologists.

Van Houten, R., Axelrod, S., Bailey, J. S., Favell, J. E., Foxx, R. N., Iwata, B. A., & Lovaas, O. I. (1988). The right to effective behavioral treatment. *The Behavior Analyst, 11,* 111–114.

Vasquez, M. T. (1992). Psychologist as clinical supervisor: Promoting ethical practice. *Professional Psychology: Research and Practice, 23,* 196–202.

Vossekuil, B., Reddy, M., Fein, R., Borum, R., & Modzeleski, W. (2000). *U.S.S.S. Safe School Initiative: An interim report on the prevention of targeted violence in the schools.* Washington, DC: U.S. Secret Service, National Threat Assessment Center. Retrieved December 5, 2000, from http://www.treas.gov/ usss.

Waldo, S. L., & Malley, P. (1992). *Tarasoff* and its progeny: Implications for the school counselor. *The School Counselor, 40,* 46–54.

Ward, S. B. (2001). Intern supervision in school psychology. *School Psychology International, 22,* 269–284.

Watson, H., & Levine, M. (1989). Psychotherapy and mandated reporting of child abuse. *American Journal of Orthopsychiatry, 59,* 246–256.

Webb, N. B. (2001). Strains and challenges of culturally diverse practice. In N. B. Webb (Ed)., *Culturally diverse parent-child and family relationships* (pp. 337–350). New York: Columbia University Press.

Wechsler, D. (2002). *Wechsler Preschool and Primary Scale of Intelligence-III.* San Antonio: The Psychological Corporation.

Wechsler, D. (1991). *Wechsler Intelligence Scale for Children-Third Edition.* San Antonio: The Psychological Corporation.

Weirda, B. (1987, November). Related services—The medical exclusion. *The Schools' Advocate,* pp. 137–139.

Weithorn, L. A. (1983). Involving children in decisions affecting their own welfare: Guidelines for professionals. In G. B. Melton, G. P. Koocher, & M. J. Saks (Eds.), *Children's competence to consent* (pp. 235–260). New York: Plenum Press.

Welfel, E. R. (1992). Psychologist as ethics educator: Successes, failures, and unanswered questions. *Professional Psychology: Research and Practice, 23,* 182–189.

Welfel, E. R., & Kitchener, K. S. (1992). Introduction to the special section: Ethics education—An agenda for the '90s. *Professional Psychology: Research and Practice, 23,* 179–181.

Welfel, E. R., & Lipsitz, N. E. (1984). Ethical behavior of professional psychologists: A critical analysis of the research. *The Counseling Psychologist, 12,* 31–41.

White, R. M. (2000). Unraveling the Tuskegee study of untreated syphilis. *Archives of Internal Medicine, 160,* 585–598.

Wigmore, J. H. (1961). *Evidence* (Vol. 3, Sec. 2285). Boston: Little, Brown.

Williams, B. B., Mennuti, R. B., & Burdsall, J. (February, 2002). Helping school psychology interns become better ethical decision makers. Paper presented at the National Association of School Psychologists Convention, Chicago, IL.

Williams-Gray, B. (2001). A framework for culturally responsive practice. In N. B. Webb (Ed)., *Culturally diverse parent-child and family relationships* (pp. 55–83). New York: Columbia University Press.

Winett, R. A., & Winkler, R. C. (1972). Current behavior modification in the classroom: Be still, be quiet, be docile. *Journal of Applied Behavior Analysis, 5*; 499–504.

Wodrich, D. L., Swerdlik, M. E., Chenneville, T., & Landau, S. (1999). HIV/AIDS among children and adolescents: Implications for the changing role of school psychologists. *School Psychology Review, 28,* 228–241.

Wonderly, D. (April, 1989). Introductory comments. *Ethical behavior: Is there adequate training and support?* Symposia presented at the National Association of School Psychologists Convention, Boston, MA.

Wood, R. C., & Chestnutt, M. D. (1995). Violence in U.S. schools: The problems and some responses. *West's Education Law Quarterly, 4,* 413–428.

Woodcock, R. W., McGrew, K. S., & Mather, N. (2001). *The Woodcock-Johnson III*. Itasca, IL: Riverside.

Woody, R. H. (1988). *Protecting your mental health practice.* San Francisco: Jossey-Bass.

Yell, M. L., Drasgow, E., & Ford, L. (2000). The Individuals with Disabilities Education Act Amendments of 1997: Implications for school-based teams. In C. E. Telzrow & M. Tankersley (Eds.), *IDEA Amendments of 1997* (pp. 1–27). Bethesda, MD: National Association of School Psychologists.

Ysseldyke, J. E., & Christenson, S. L. (1988). Linking assessment to intervention. In J. L. Graden, J. E. Zins, & M. J. Curtis (Eds.), *Alternative educational delivery systems* (pp. 91–109). Washington, DC: National Association of School Psychologists.

Zachary, R. A., & Pope, K. S. (1984). Legal and ethical issues in the clinical use of computerized testing. In M. D. Schwartz (Ed.), *Using computers in clinical practice* (pp. 151–164). New York: Haworth Press.

Zingaro, J. C. (1983). Confidentiality: To tell or not to tell. *Elementary School Guidance and Counseling, 17,* 261–267.

Zins, J. E., & Erchul, W. P. (2002). Best practices in school consultation. In A. Thomas & J. Grimes (Eds.), *Best practices in school psychology IV* (pp. 625–643). Besthesda, MD: National Association of School Psychologists.

Zins, J. E., & Forman, S. G. (1988). Primary prevention in the schools: What are we waiting for? *School Psychology Review, 17,* 539–541.

Zirkel, P. A., & Kincaid, J. M. (1993). *Section 504, the ADA, and the schools* (looseleaf). Horsham, PA: LRP.

Zirkel, P. A., & Reichner, H. F. (1986). Is the *In Loco Parentis* doctrine dead? *Journal of Law & Education, 15,* 271–283.

TABLE OF CASES

"A" Family, In the Matter of the, 602 P.2d 157 (Mont. 1979).

Aguilar v. Felton, 473 U.S. 402, 105 S. Ct. 3232, 87 L.Ed.2d 290 (1985), *rev'd sub nom.* Agostini v. Felton, No. 96–552 (U.S. June 23, 1997).

Alamo Heights Independent School District v. State Board of Education, 790 F.2d 1153 (5th Cir. 1986).

Altman v. Bedford Central School District, 45 F. Supp. 2d 368, 1999 U.S. Dist. LEXIS 7811 (S.D.N.Y. 1999).

Armijo v. Wagon Mound Public Schools, 159 F.3d 1253 (10th Cir. 1998).

A.W. v. Northwest R-1 School District, 813 F.2d 158 (8th Cir. 1987), *cert. den.*, 108 S. Ct. 144.

Baker v. Owen, 395 F. Supp 294 (D.C. M.D. N.C., 1975), *aff'd,* 423 U.S. 908.

Bellotti v. Baird, 443 U.S. 622 (1979).

Benskin v. Taft City School District, 14 Clearinghouse Review 529 (1980).

Board of Education of the Hendrick Hudson Central School District v. Rowley, 458 U.S. 176, 102 S. Ct. 3034 (1982).

Board of Education, Sacramento City Unified School District v. Holland, 786 F. Supp. 874 (E.D. Cal. 1992), *aff'd sub nom.* Sacramento City Unified School District, Board of Education v. Rachel H., 14 F.3d 1398 (9th Cir. 1994), *cert. denied sub nom.* Sacramento City Unified School District Board of Education v. Holland, 114 S. Ct. 2697 (1994).

Brown v. Board of Education, 347 U.S. 483 (1954).

Burnside v. Byars, 363 F.2d 744 (5th Cir. 1966).

California Association of School Psychologists v. Superintendent of Public Instruction, 21 IDELR 130 (N.D. Cal. 1994).

Cedar Rapids Community School District v. Garret F. by Charlene F., 24 IDELR 648 (N.D. Iowa 1996).

Christopher M. v. Corpus Christi Independent School District, 17 IDELR 990, 992 (5th Cir. 1991).

Clevenger v. Oak Ridge School Board, 744 F.2d 514 (6th Cir. 1984).

Cordrey v. Euckert, 917 F.2d 1460 (6th Cir. 1990).

Crawford v. Honig, 37 F.3d 485 (9th Cir. 1994).

Cypress-Fairbanks Independent School District v. Michael F., 118 F.3d 245 (5th Cir 1997).

Daniel R.R. v. Texas Board of Education, El Paso Independent School District, 874 F.2d 1036 (5th Cir. 1989).

Hall v. Vance County Board of Education, 774 F.2d 629 (4th Cir. 1985).

Harlow v. Fitzgerald, 457 U.S. 800, 102 S. Ct. 2727 (1982).

Hayes v. Unified School District No. 377, 669 F. Supp. 1519 (D.Kan. 1987).

Hensley v. Eckerhart, 461 U.S. 424, 103 S. Ct. 1933, 76 L. Ed. 2d 40, 1983 U.S. LEXIS 160 (1983).

H.L. Etc., Appellant v. Scott M. Matheson, 101 S. Ct. 1164 (1981).

Hobson v. Hansen, 269 F. Supp. 401, 514 (D.D.C. 1967), *aff'd. sub nom,* Smuck v. Hobson, 408 F.2d 175 (D.C. Cir. 1969).

Hodgson v. Minnesota, 648 F. Supp. 756, 853 F.2d 1452, 42 U.S. 917, 106 L.Ed.2d 587 (1989).

Honig v. Doe, 108 S. Ct. 592 (1988).

Ingraham v. Wright, 430 U.S. 651, 97 S. Ct. 1401 (1977).

Irving Independent School District v. Tatro, 468 U.S. 883, 104 S. Ct. 3371 (1984).

Jaffee v. Redmond, 51 F.3d 1346, 1358, 116 S. Ct. 334 (1996).

J.D. by J.D. v. Pawlet School District, 33 IDELR 34 (2nd Cir. 2000).

John K. and Mary K. v. Board of Education for School District #65, Cook County, 504 N.E.2d 797 (Ill. App. 1 Dist. 1987).

Johnson v. Independent School District No. 4 of Bixby, Tulsa County, Oklahoma, 921 F.2d 1022 (10th Cir. 1990).

Kelson v. The City of Springfield, 767 F.2d 651 (9th Cir. 1985).

Kerkam v. McKenzie, 931 F.2d 84 (D.C. Cir. 1991).

Landstrom v. Illinois Department of Children and Family Services, 892 F.2d 670 (7th Cir. 1990).

Larry P. v. Riles, 343 F. Supp. 1306 (D.C. N.D. Cal., 1972), *aff'd.,* 502 F.2d 963 (9th Cir. 1974), *further proceedings,* 495 F. Supp. 926 (D.C. N.D. Cal., 1979), *aff'd.,* 502 F.2d 693 (9th Cir. 1984).

Lau v. Nichols, 414 U.S. 563 (1974).

Lyons by Alexander v. Smith, 829 F. Supp. 414 (D. D.C. 1993).

Marshall v. American Psychological Association, No. 87–1316 (D. D.C., December 7, 1987).

Martinez v. The School Board of Hillsborough County, Florida, 675 F. Supp. 1574 (M.D. Fla. 1987).

Max M. v. Thompson, 566 F. Supp. 1330, 1388 (N.D. Ill. (1983) *(Max I),* 592 F. Supp. 1437, 1450 (N.D. Ill. 1984) *(Max II).*

McKenzie v. Jefferson, 566 F. Supp. 404 (D. D.C. 1983).

McNeal v. Tate County School District, 508 F.2d 1017 (5th Cir. 1975).

Merriken v. Cressman, 364 F. Supp. 913 (D.C. E.D. Pa. 1973).

Milligan, et al. v. City of Slidell, No. 98-31335, 2000 WL 1285260 (5th Cir., Sept. 27).

Mills v. Board of Education of District of Columbia, 348 F. Supp. 866 (1972); *contempt proceedings,* 551 Educ. of the Handicapped L. Rep. 643 (D. D.C. 1980).

Mirand v. Board of Education of the City of New York, 84 N.Y.2d 44, 637 N.E.2d 263, 1994 N.Y. LEXIS 1345. 614 N.Y.S.2d 372 (N.Y. 1994).

Morales v. Turman, 383 F. Supp. 53 (D.C. E.D. Tex. 1974).

Nabozny v. Podlesny, 92 F.3d 446, 1996 U.S. App. LEXIS 18866 (7th Cir. 1996).

New Jersey v. T.L.O., 469 U.S. 325 (1985).

New York State Association for Retarded Children v. Carey, 393 F. Supp. 715 (D.C. E.D. N.Y. 1975).

Ohio v. Akron Center for Reproductive Health, 493 U.S. 802, L.Ed.2d 9 (1989).

Parents Against Abuse in Schools v. Williamsport Area School District, 594 A.2d 796 (Pa. Commw. Ct. 1991).

Parham v. J.R., 422 U.S. 584 (1979).

Parents in Action in Special Education (P.A.S.E.) v. Hannon, 506 F. Supp. 831 (N.D. Ill. 1980).

Penna v. New York State Division for Youth, 419 F. Supp. 203 (D.C. S.D. N.Y. 1976).

Pennsylvania Association for Retarded Citizens (P.A.R.C.) v. Commonwealth of Pennsylvania, 334 F. Supp. 1257 (D.C. E.D. Pa. 1971), 343 F. Supp. 279 (D.C. E.D. Pa. 1972).

Pesce v. J. Sterling Morton High School, 830 F.2d 789 (7th Cir. 1987).

Peter W. v. San Francisco Unified School District, 60 Cal.App.3d 814 (1976).

Phillis P. v. Claremont Unified School District, 183 Cal.App.3d 1193 (1986).

Planned Parenthood of Central Missouri v. Danforth, 428 U.S. 52 (1976).

Planned Parenthood of Southeastern Pennsylvania v. Casey, 112 S. Ct. 2791 (1992).

Rettig v. Kent City School District, 788 F.2d 328 (6th Cir. 1986).

Reusch v. Fountain, 872 F. Supp. 1421 (D. Md. 1994).

Riley v. Ambach, 551 Educ. of the Handicapped L. Rep. 668 (E.D.N.Y. 1980), *rev'd* 668 F.2d 635 (2nd Cir. 1981), *further proceedings*, 508 F. Supp. 1222 (E.D. N.Y. 1982).

Roland M. v. Concord School Committee, 910 F.2d 983 (1st Cir. 1990).

San Antonio Independent School District v. Rodriguez, 411 U.S. 1, 93 S. Ct. 1278 (1973).

Sandlin v. Johnson, 643 F.2d 1027 (4th Cir. 1981).

School Board of Nassau County, Florida v. Arline, 107 S. Ct. 1123 (1987).

School Committee of the Town of Burlington, Massachusetts v. Department of Education of Massachusetts, 471 U.S. 359 (1985).

Simmons v. Hooks, 843 F. Supp. 1296 (E.D. Ark. 1994).

Spielberg v. Henrico County Public Schools, 853 F.2d 256 (4th Cir. 1988).

State v. Grover, 437 N.W.2d. 60 (Minn. 1989).

Sterling v. Borough of Minersville, 232 F.3d 190, 2000 U.S. App. LEXIS 27855 (3rd Cir. 2000).

Tarasoff v. Regents of California, 118 Cal.Rptr. 129, 529 P.2d 553 (Cal. 1974). (Tarasoff I) Tarasoff v. Regents of California, 131 Cal.Rptr. 14, 551 P.2d 334 (Cal. 1976). (Tarasoff II)

Thomas v. Atascadero Unified School District, 662 F. Supp. 376 (C.D. Cal. 1987).

Timothy W. v. Rochester, New Hampshire School District, 875 F.2d 954 (1st Cir. 1989).

Tinker v. Des Moines Independent Community School District, 393 U.S. 503, 89 S. Ct. 733 (1969).

Valerie J. v. Derry CO-OP School District, 771 F. Supp. 492 (D. N.H. 1991).

Wisconsin v. Constantineau, 400 U.S. 433 (1971).

Wolman v. Walter, 433 U.S. 229, 97 S. Ct. 2593 (1977).

Wyatt v. Stickney, 325 F. Supp. 781 (M.D. Ala. N.D. 1971), 334 F. Supp. 1341 (1971), 344 F. Supp. 373, 387 (M.D. Ala. N.D. 1972).

Wyke v. Polk County School Board, 137 F.3d 1292 (11th Cir. 1998), 898 F. Supp. 852 (D. Fla., M.D. Fla. 1995).

Zelman v. Simmons-Harris, 122 S. Ct. 2460, 153 L. Ed. 2d 604, 2002 U.S. LEXIS 4885, 70 U.S.L.W. 4683, 2002 Daily Journal DAR 7295, 15 Fla. L. Weekly Fed. S 490.

TABLE OF FEDERAL LEGISLATION[1]

Americans with Disabilities Act of 1990 or ADA (Pub. L. No. 101–336), 42 U.S.C. § 12101. Regulations regarding nondiscrimination in state and local government services appear at 28 C.F.R. Part 35 (1996).

Bilingual Education Act of 1968 was added as an amendment to the Elementary and Secondary Education Act of 1965. The No Child Left Behind Act of 2001 (Pub. L. No. 107–110) continued funding for the education of children with limited English proficiency.

Child Abuse Prevention, Adoption, and Family Services Act of 1988 (Pub. L. No. 100–294), 42 U.S.C. § 1501.

Civil Rights Act of 1871 or "Section 1983," 42 U.S.C. § 1983.

Civil Rights Act of 1964 (Pub. L. No. 88–352), 42 U.S.C. § 2000d.

Education Amendments of 1972 (Pub. L. No. 92–318), 20 U.S.C. § 1681.

Education for All Handicapped Children Act of 1975 (Pub. L. No. 94–142), renamed the Individuals with Disabilities Education Act in 1990, 20 U.S.C. Chapter 33.

Education for the Handicapped Act Amendments of 1986 (Pub. L. No. 99–457). Now Part C of the Individuals with Disabilities Education Act.

Elementary and Secondary Education Act of 1965 or ESEA (Pub. L. No. 89–750). The No Child Left Behind Act of 2001 (Pub. L. No. 107–110) includes the most recent amendments to ESEA. Available at http://www.ed.gov/ .

Family Educational Rights and Privacy Act of 1974 (a part of Pub. L. No. 93–380) is commonly called "FERPA" or "The Buckley Amendment," 20 U.S.C. § 1232g. Regulations implementing FERPA appear at 34 C.F.R. § Part 99.

Handicapped Children's Protection Act of 1986 (Pub. L. No. 99–372). Now part of the Individuals with Disabilities Education Act.

Individuals with Disabilities Education Act (Pub. L. No. 101–476), 20 U.S.C. Chapter 33. Amended by Pub. L. No. 105–17 in June, 1997. Regulations appear at 34 C.F.R. Part 300.

Jacob K. Javits Gifted and Talented Students Education Act of 1988 (Pub. L. No. 100–297). Amended by No Child Left Behind Act of 2001 (Pub. L. No. 107–110).

National Research Act of 1974 (Pub. L. No. 93–348), 42 U.S.C. § 289. Regulations appear at 45 C.F.R. Part 46.

[1]U.S.C. refers to the United States Code (published by the U.S. government); U.S.C.A. refers to the United States Code Annotated (published by West Publishing Company); C.F.R. refers to the Code of Federal Regulations (published by the U.S. government).

No Child Left Behind Act of 2001 (Pub. L. No. 107–110). Most recent set of amendments to the Elementary and Secondary Education Act of 1965. Available at http://www.ed.gov/.

The Protection of Pupil Rights Act (previously Hatch Amendment). A 1978 amendment to ESEA. Amended in 1994 by Pub. L. No. 103–227 and in 2001 by Pub. L. No. 107–110.

The Rehabilitation Act of 1973 (Pub. L. No. 93–112), 29 U.S.C. § 794. Regulations implementing Section 504 appear at 34 C.F.R. Part 104 (1996).

AUTHOR INDEX

SUBJECT INDEX